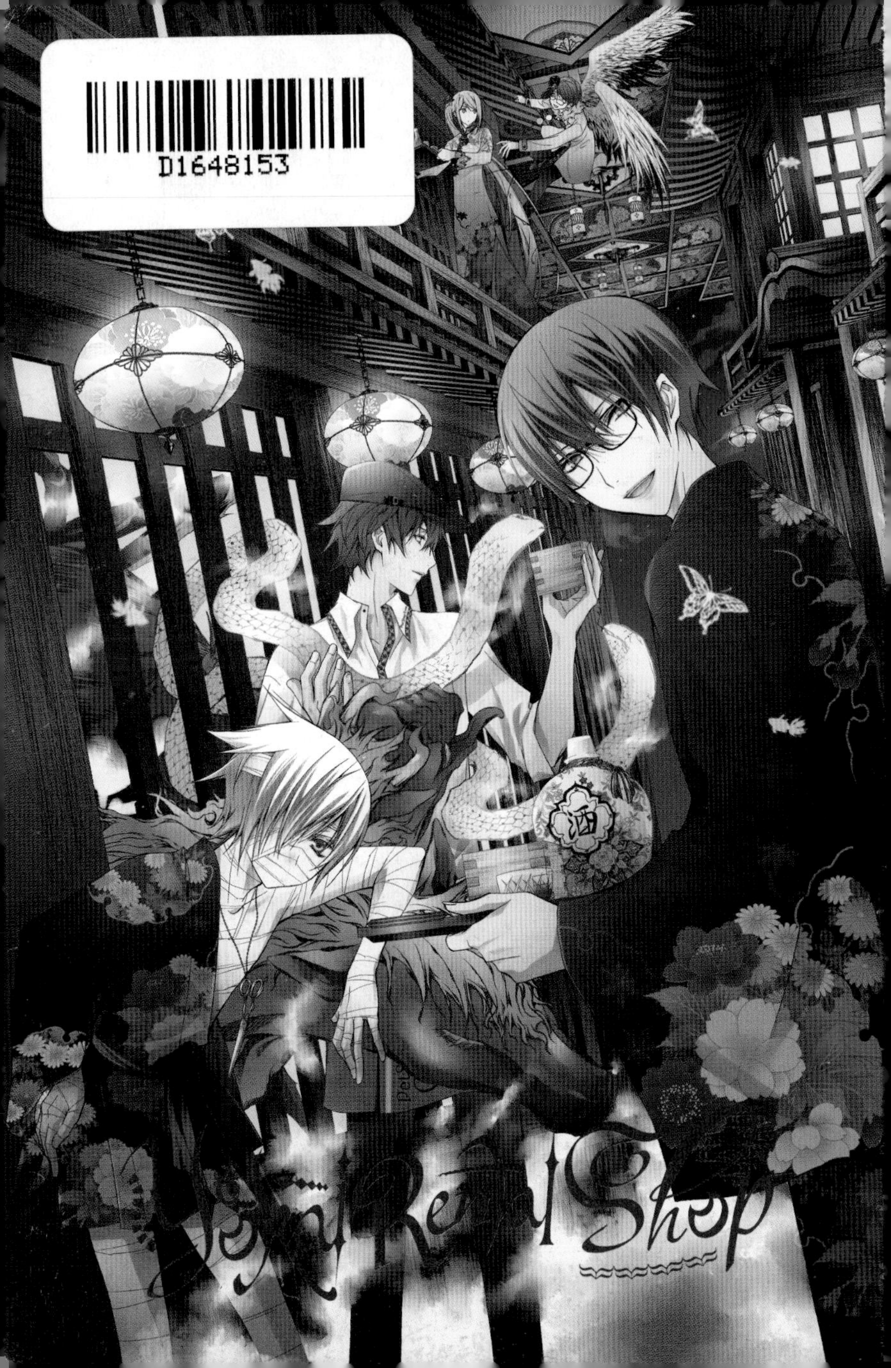
酒

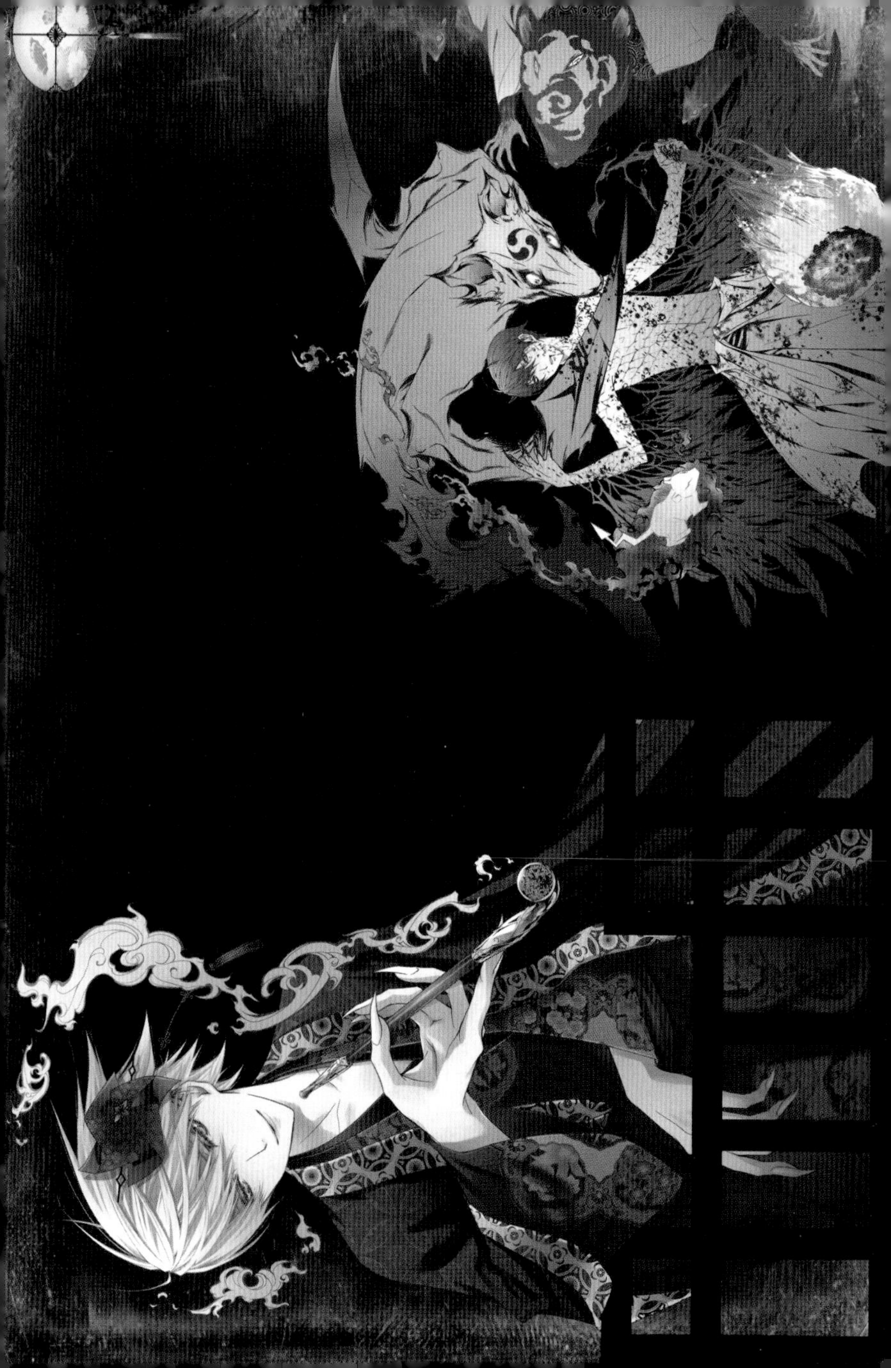

Rental 19: PROMISE

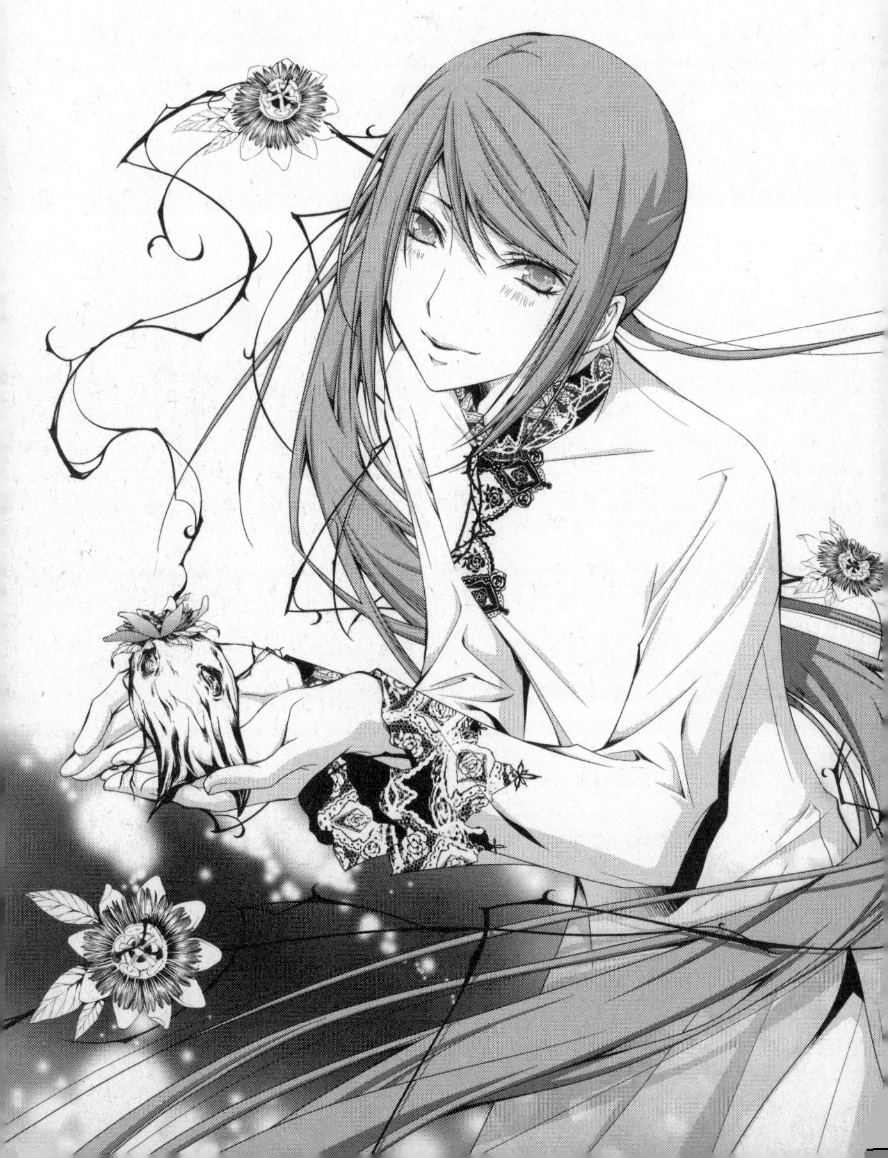

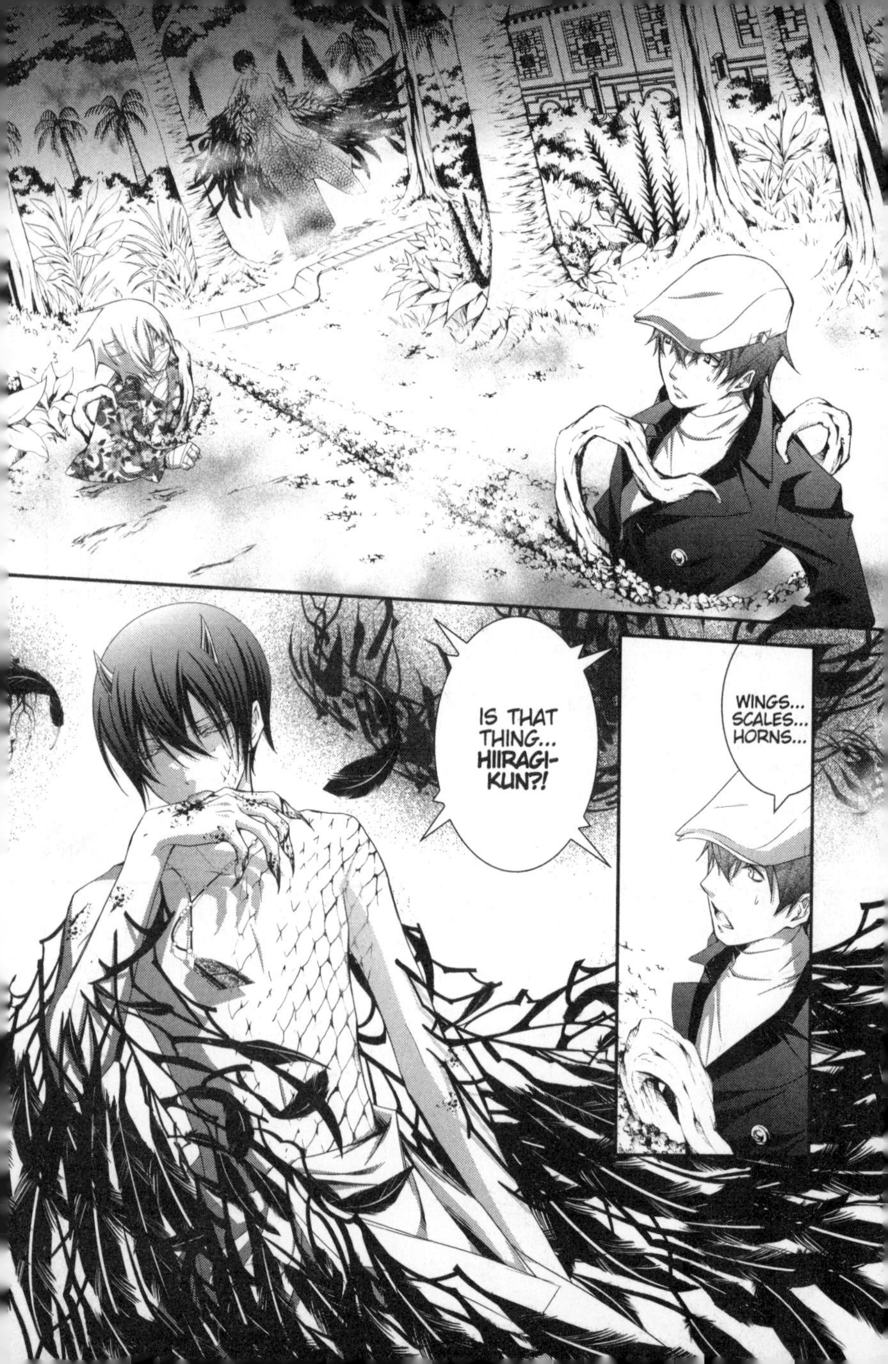
WINGS... SCALES... HORNS...
IS THAT THING... HIIRAGI-KUN?!

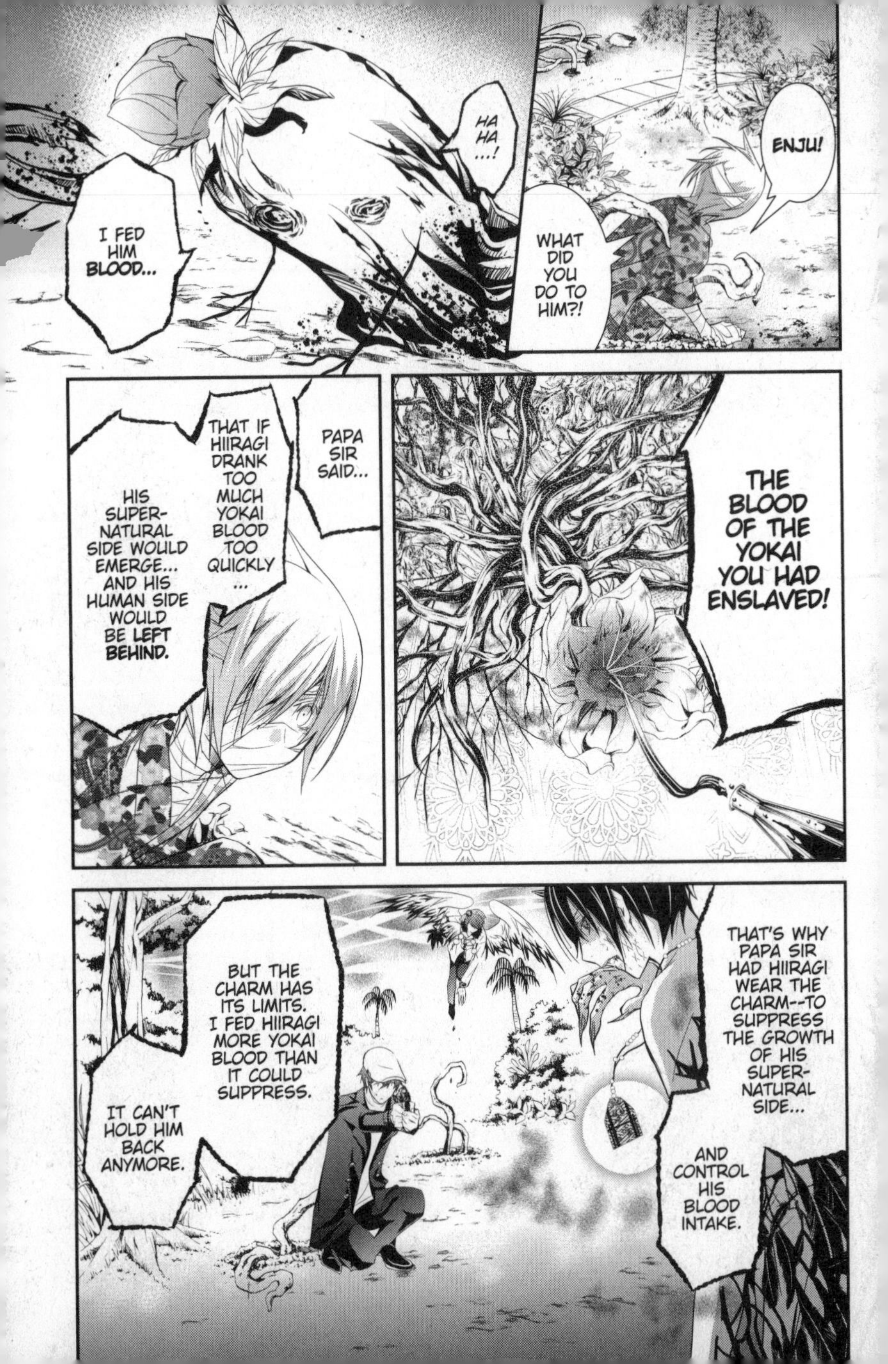
ENJU!
WHAT DID YOU DO TO HIM?!
HA HA ...!
I FED HIM BLOOD...
THE BLOOD OF THE YOKAI YOU HAD ENSLAVED!
PAPA SIR SAID...
THAT IF HIIRAGI DRANK TOO MUCH YOKAI BLOOD TOO QUICKLY ...
HIS SUPER-NATURAL SIDE WOULD EMERGE... AND HIS HUMAN SIDE WOULD BE LEFT BEHIND.
THAT'S WHY PAPA SIR HAD HIIRAGI WEAR THE CHARM--TO SUPPRESS THE GROWTH OF HIS SUPER-NATURAL SIDE...
AND CONTROL HIS BLOOD INTAKE.
BUT THE CHARM HAS ITS LIMITS. I FED HIIRAGI MORE YOKAI BLOOD THAN IT COULD SUPPRESS.
IT CAN'T HOLD HIM BACK ANYMORE.

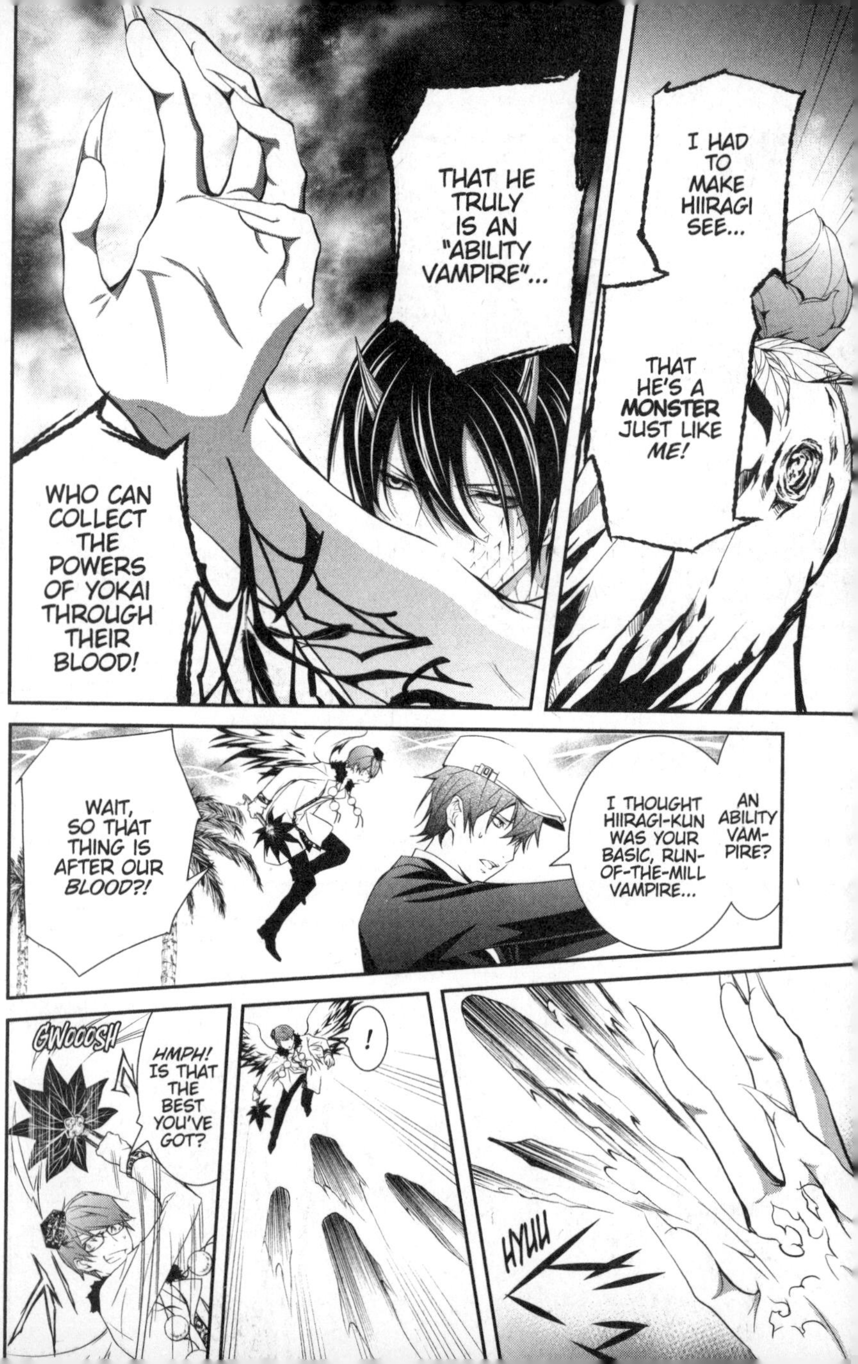
I HAD TO MAKE HIIRAGI SEE...
THAT HE TRULY IS AN "ABILITY VAMPIRE"...
WHO CAN COLLECT THE POWERS OF YOKAI THROUGH THEIR BLOOD!
THAT HE'S A MONSTER JUST LIKE *ME!*
AN ABILITY VAM-PIRE?
I THOUGHT HIIRAGI-KUN WAS YOUR BASIC, RUN-OF-THE-MILL VAMPIRE...
WAIT, SO THAT THING IS AFTER OUR *BLOOD?!*
HYUU
!
GWOOOSH
HMPH! IS THAT THE BEST YOU'VE GOT?

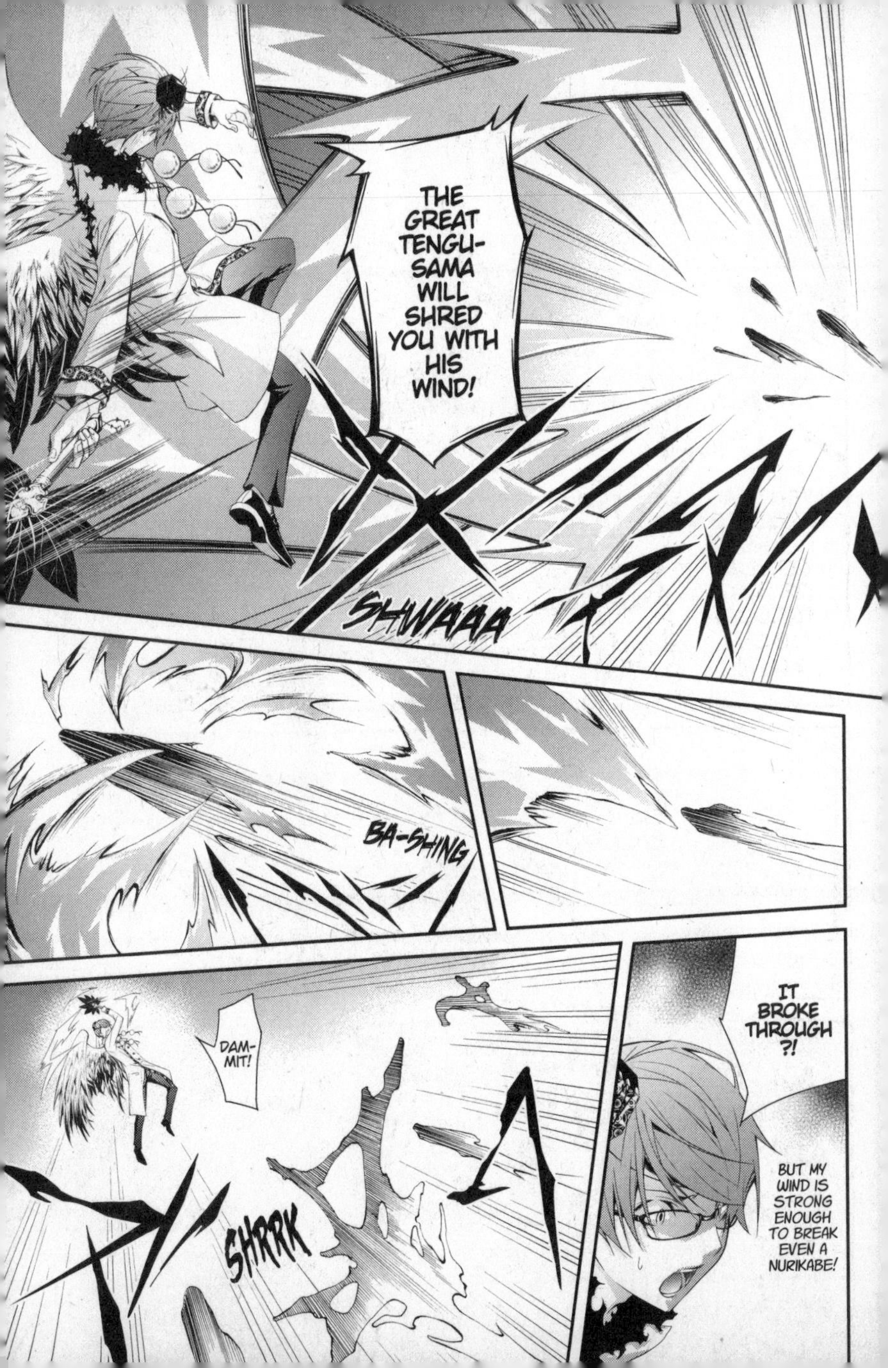
THE GREAT TENGU-SAMA WILL SHRED YOU WITH HIS WIND!
SHWAAA
BA-SHING
IT BROKE THROUGH?!
BUT MY WIND IS STRONG ENOUGH TO BREAK EVEN A NURIKABE!
DAM-MIT!
SHRRK

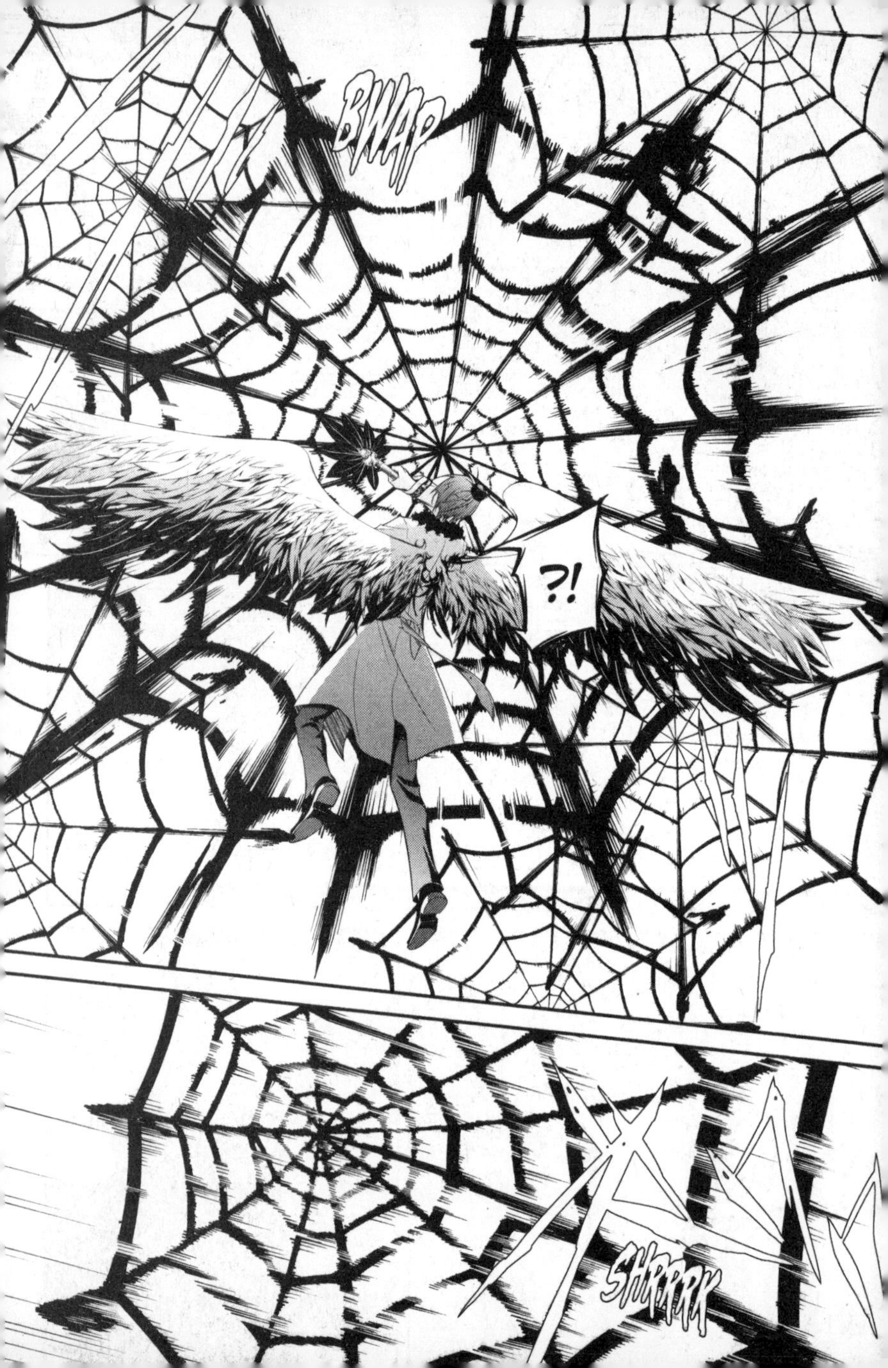
BWAP
?!
SHRRRK

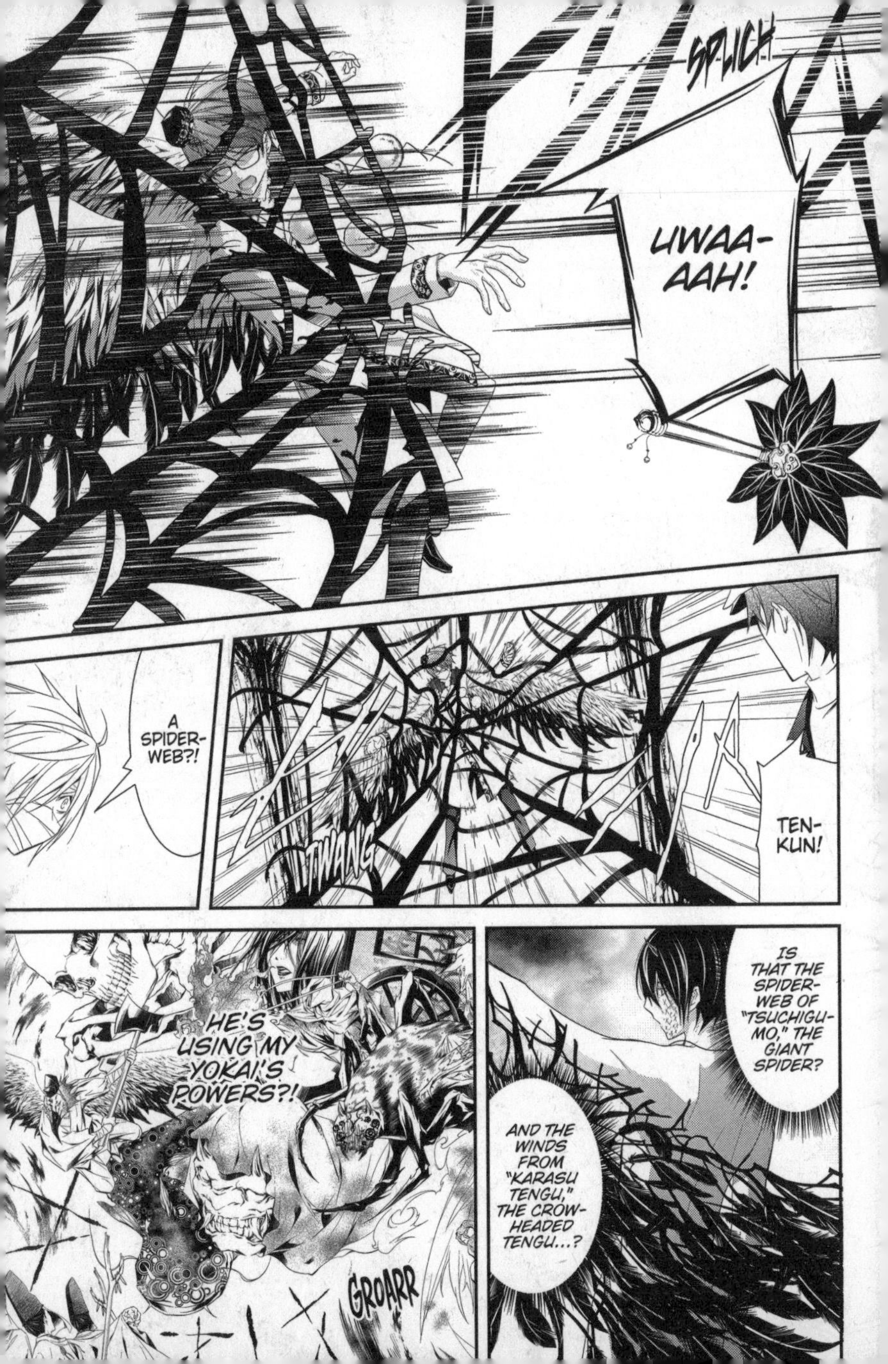
SPLICH
UWAAA-AAH!
TEN-KUN!
TWANG
A SPIDER-WEB?!
IS THAT THE SPIDER-WEB OF "TSUCHIGUMO," THE GIANT SPIDER?
AND THE WINDS FROM "KARASU TENGU," THE CROW-HEADED TENGU...?
HE'S USING MY YOKAI'S POWERS?!
GROARR

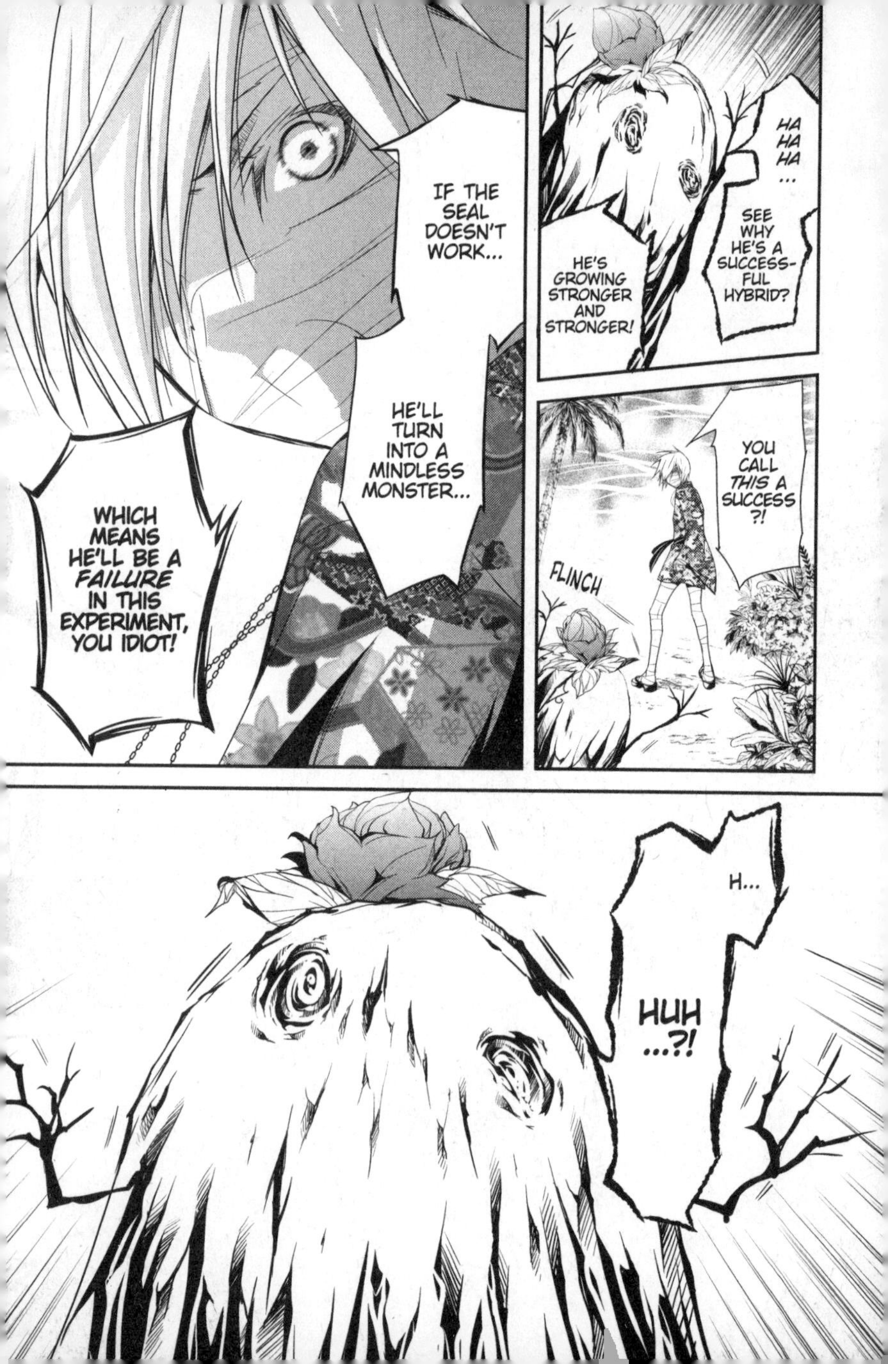
HA HA HA ...
SEE WHY HE'S A SUCCESSFUL HYBRID?
HE'S GROWING STRONGER AND STRONGER!
YOU CALL *THIS* A SUCCESS ?!
FLINCH
IF THE SEAL DOESN'T WORK...
HE'LL TURN INTO A MINDLESS MONSTER...
WHICH MEANS HE'LL BE A *FAILURE* IN THIS EXPERIMENT, YOU IDIOT!
H...
HUH ...?!

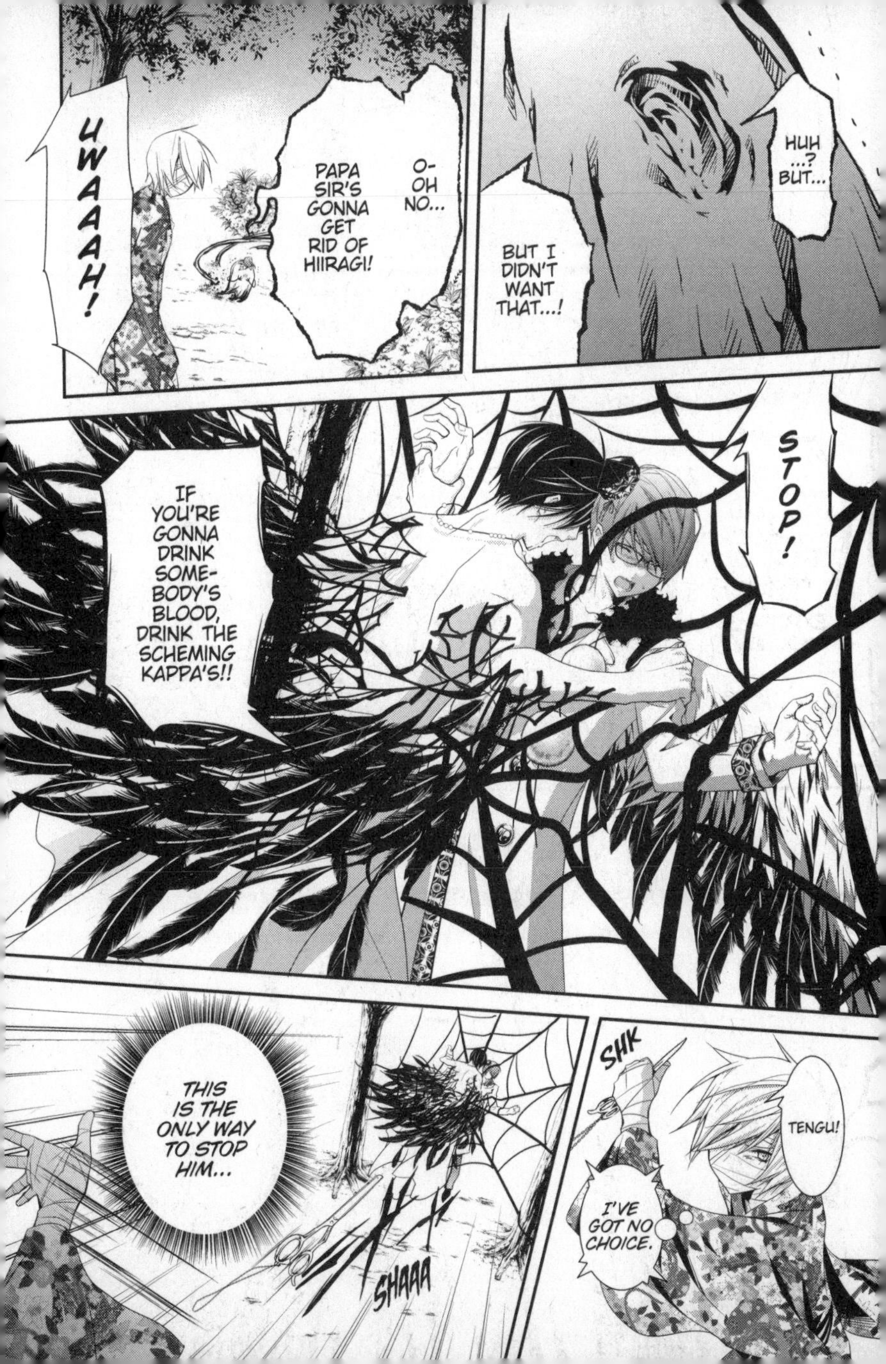
HUH ...? BUT...
BUT I DIDN'T WANT THAT...!
O-OH NO...
PAPA SIR'S GONNA GET RID OF HIIRAGI!
UWAAAH!
STOP!
IF YOU'RE GONNA DRINK SOMEBODY'S BLOOD, DRINK THE SCHEMING KAPPA'S!!
SHK
TENGU!
I'VE GOT NO CHOICE.
THIS IS THE ONLY WAY TO STOP HIM...
SHAAA

SHK

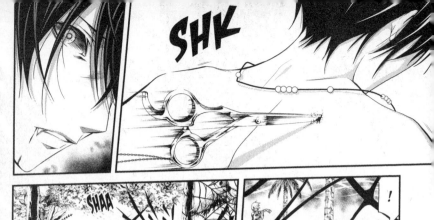

SHAA

BAN-
DAGES!
RUN!

!

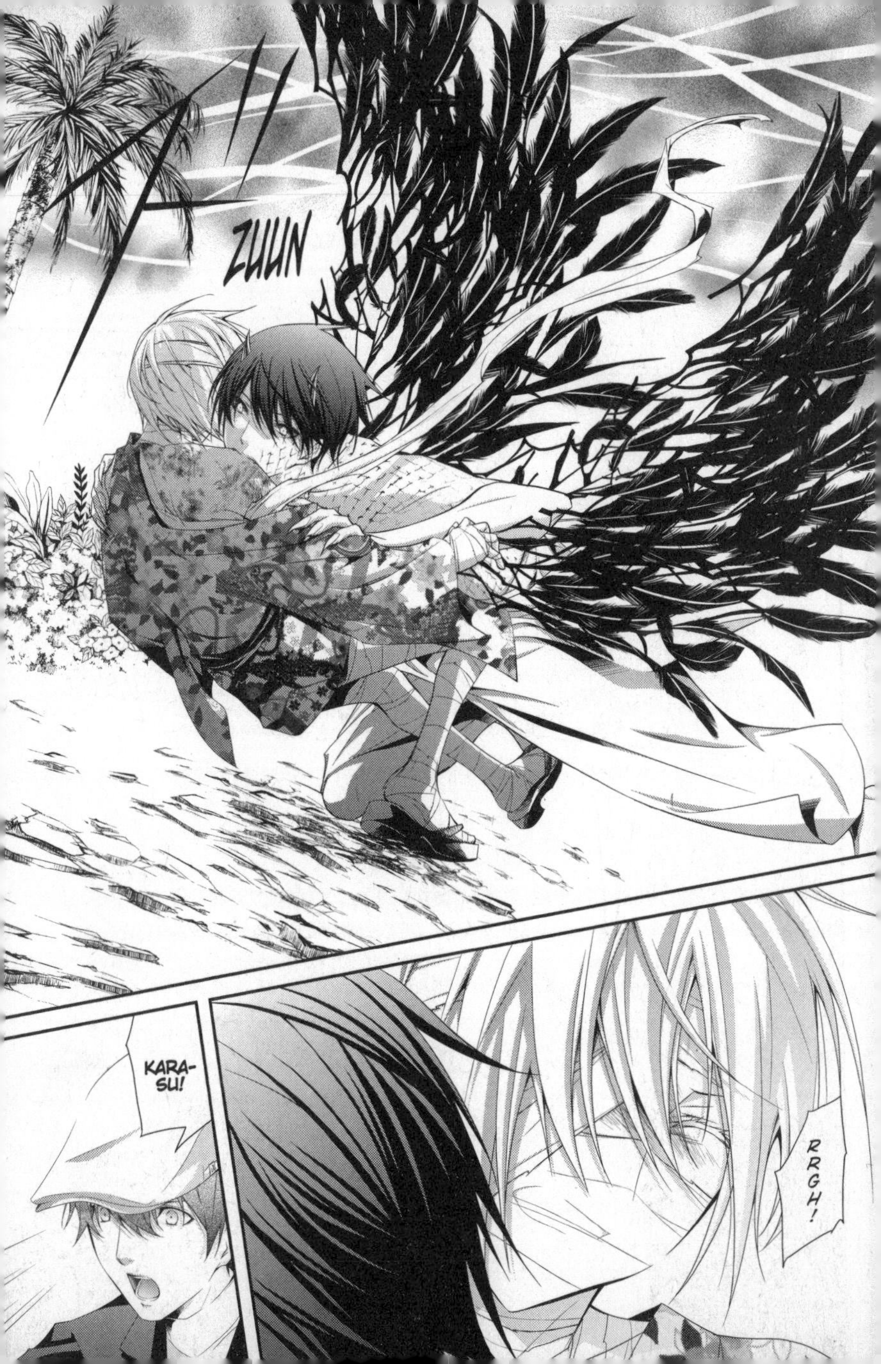
ZUUN
RRGH!
KARA-SU!

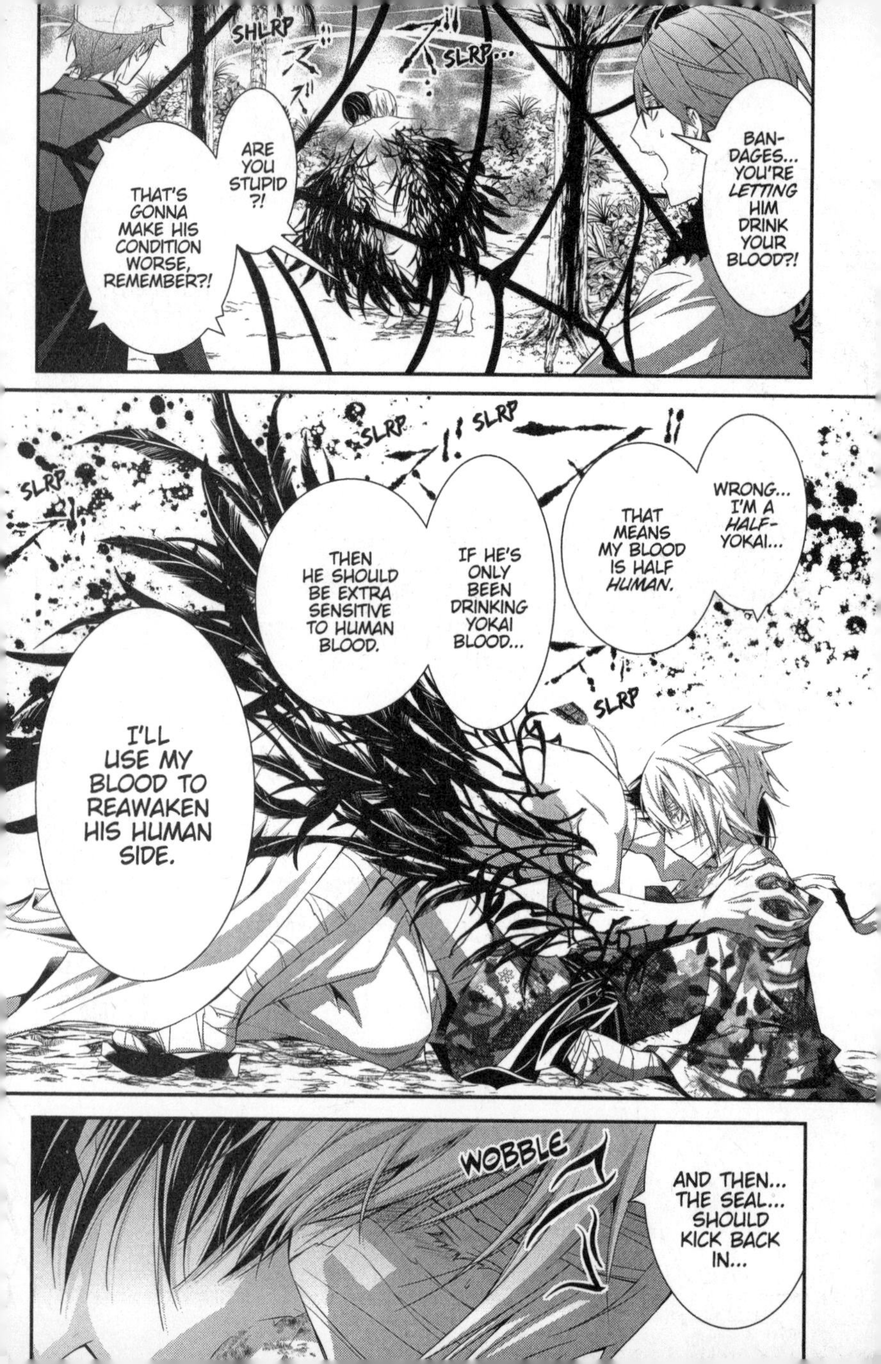
SLRP...
SHLRP
BAN-DAGES... YOU'RE *LETTING* HIM DRINK YOUR BLOOD?!
ARE YOU STUPID ?!
THAT'S GONNA MAKE HIS CONDITION WORSE, REMEMBER?!
SLRP
SLRP
WRONG... I'M A *HALF*-YOKAI...
THAT MEANS MY BLOOD IS HALF *HUMAN*.
IF HE'S ONLY BEEN DRINKING YOKAI BLOOD...
THEN HE SHOULD BE EXTRA SENSITIVE TO HUMAN BLOOD.
SLRP
SLRP
I'LL USE MY BLOOD TO REAWAKEN HIS HUMAN SIDE.
AND THEN... THE SEAL... SHOULD KICK BACK IN...
WOBBLE

BAN-
DAG-
ES...
YOU...

YOU'LL
COLLAPSE
AGAIN!

YOU
CAN'T!

SHLRRP...

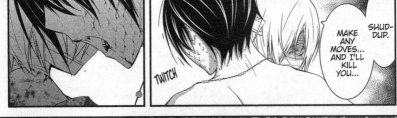

TWITCH

MAKE
ANY
MOVES...
AND I'LL
KILL
YOU...

SHUD-
DUP.

RR...

AHH
...

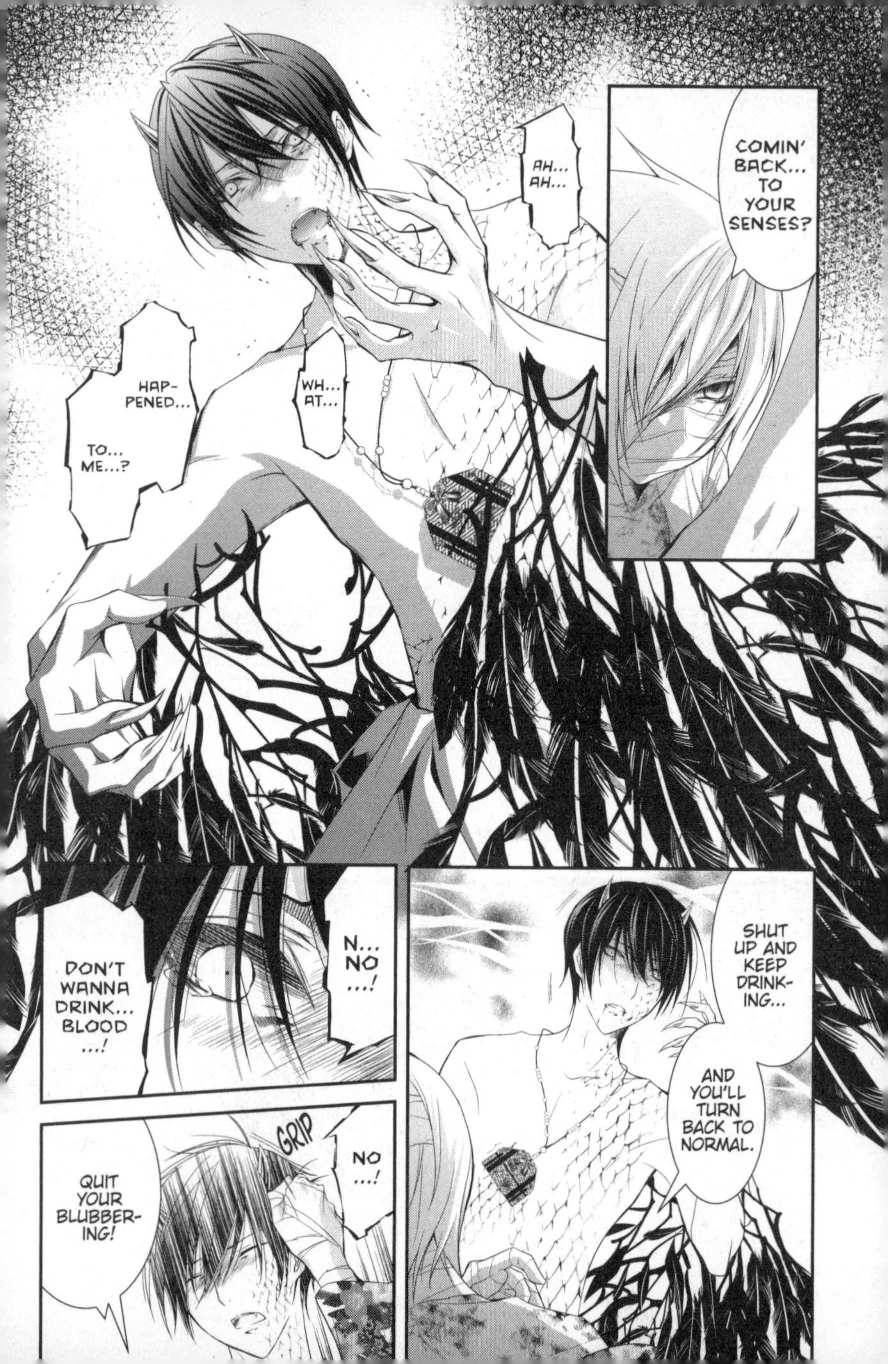
COMIN' BACK... TO YOUR SENSES?
AH... AH...
WH... AT...
HAP-PENED...
TO... ME...?
SHUT UP AND KEEP DRINK-ING...
AND YOU'LL TURN BACK TO NORMAL.
N... NO ...!
DON'T WANNA DRINK... BLOOD ...!
GRIP
NO ...!
QUIT YOUR BLUBBER-ING!

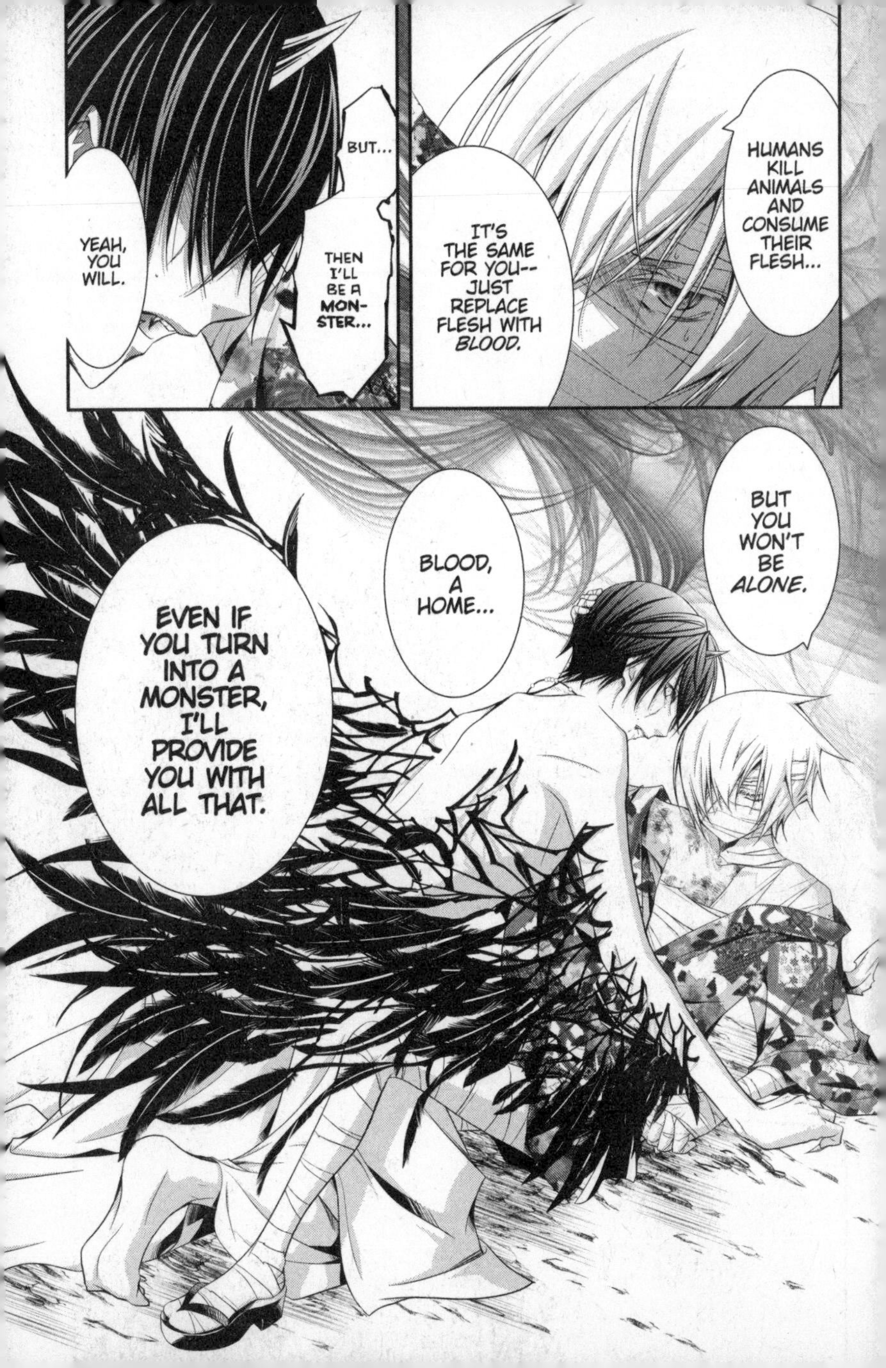
HUMANS KILL ANIMALS AND CONSUME THEIR FLESH...
IT'S THE SAME FOR YOU-- JUST REPLACE FLESH WITH *BLOOD.*
BUT...
THEN I'LL BE A **MONSTER...**
YEAH, YOU WILL.
BUT YOU WON'T BE *ALONE.*
BLOOD, A HOME...
EVEN IF YOU TURN INTO A MONSTER, I'LL PROVIDE YOU WITH ALL THAT.

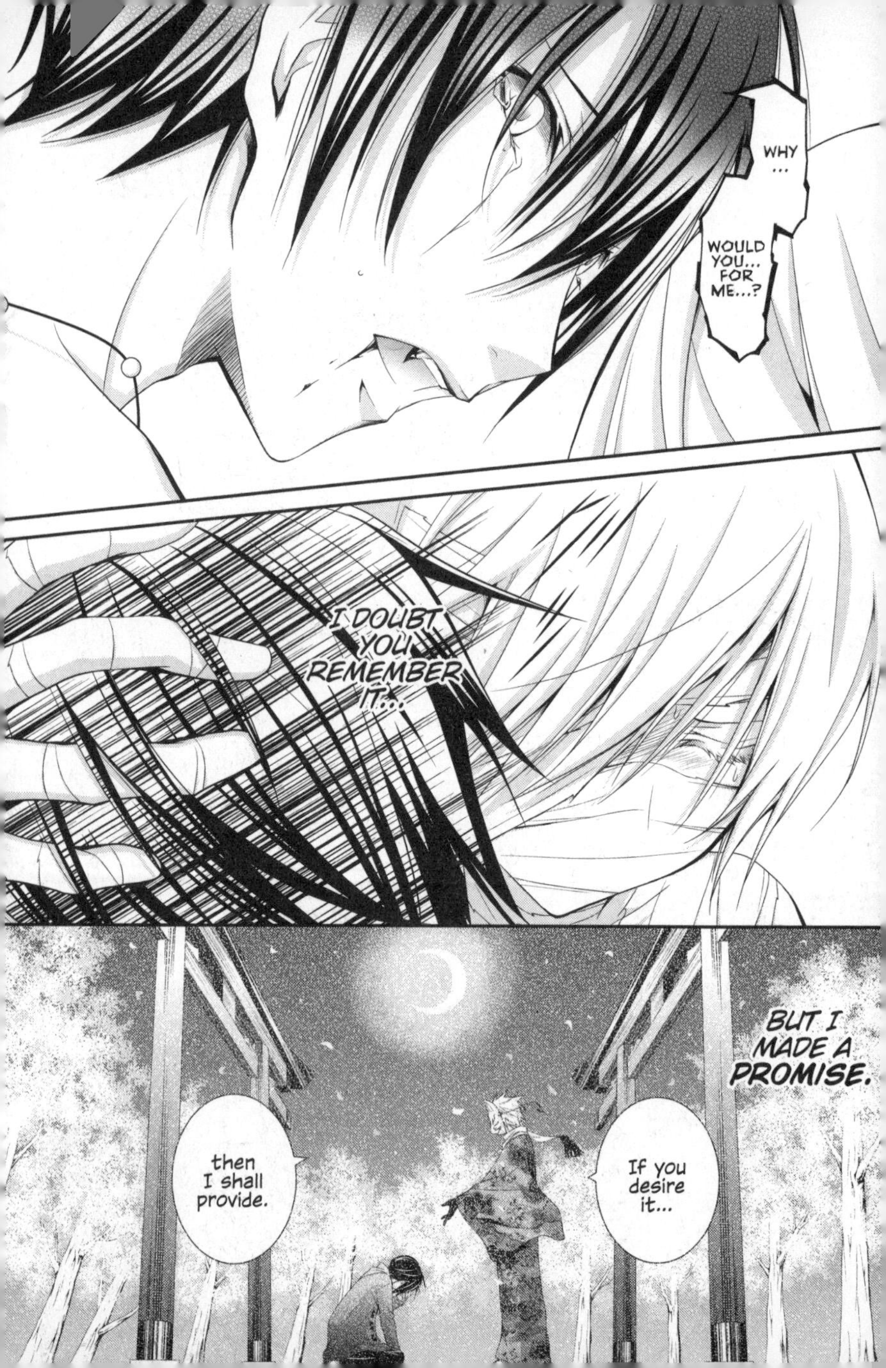
WHY...
WOULD YOU... FOR ME...?
I DOUBT YOU REMEMBER IT...
BUT I MADE A PROMISE.
If you desire it...
then I shall provide.

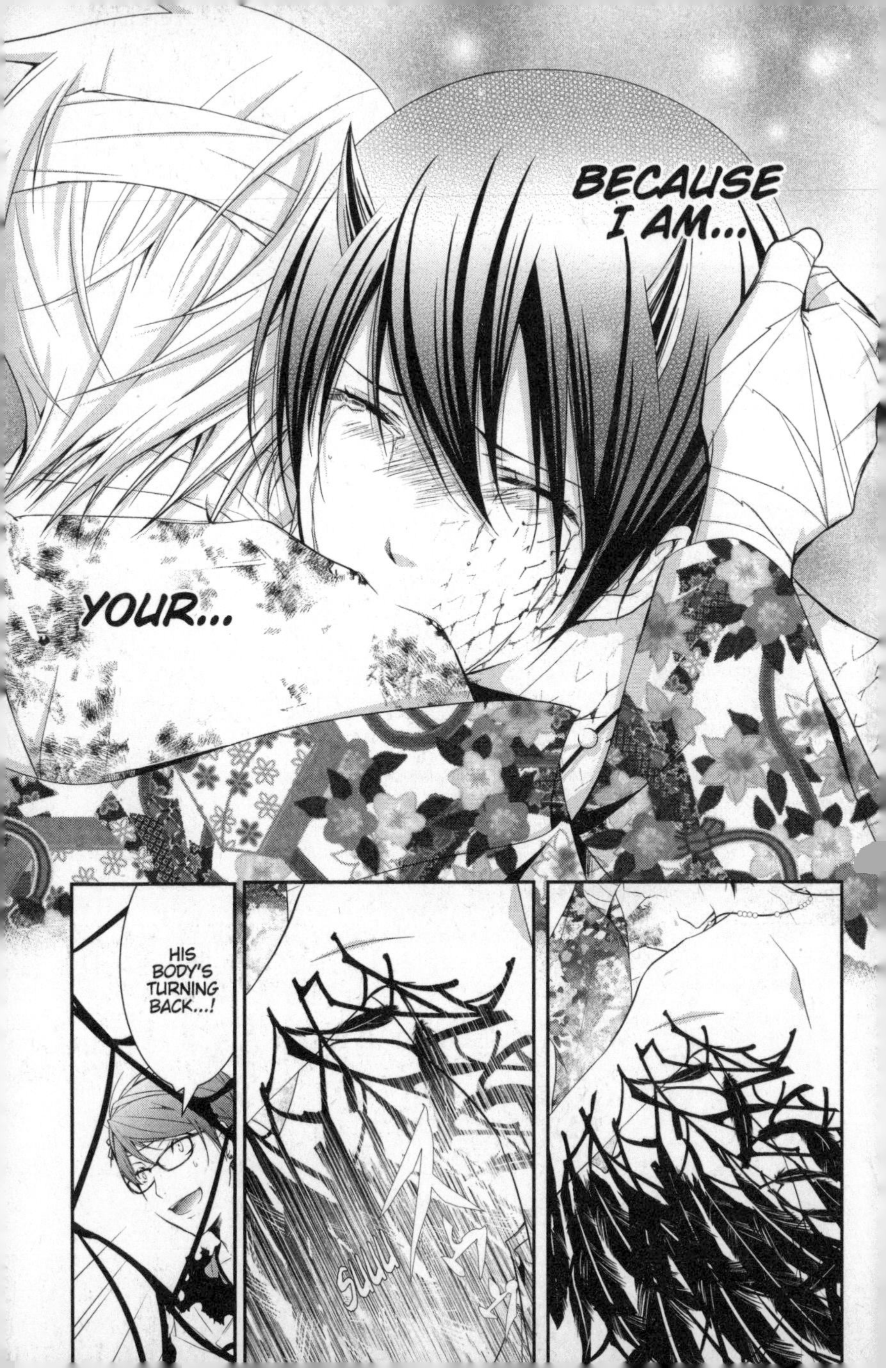
BECAUSE I AM...
YOUR...
HIS BODY'S TURNING BACK...!

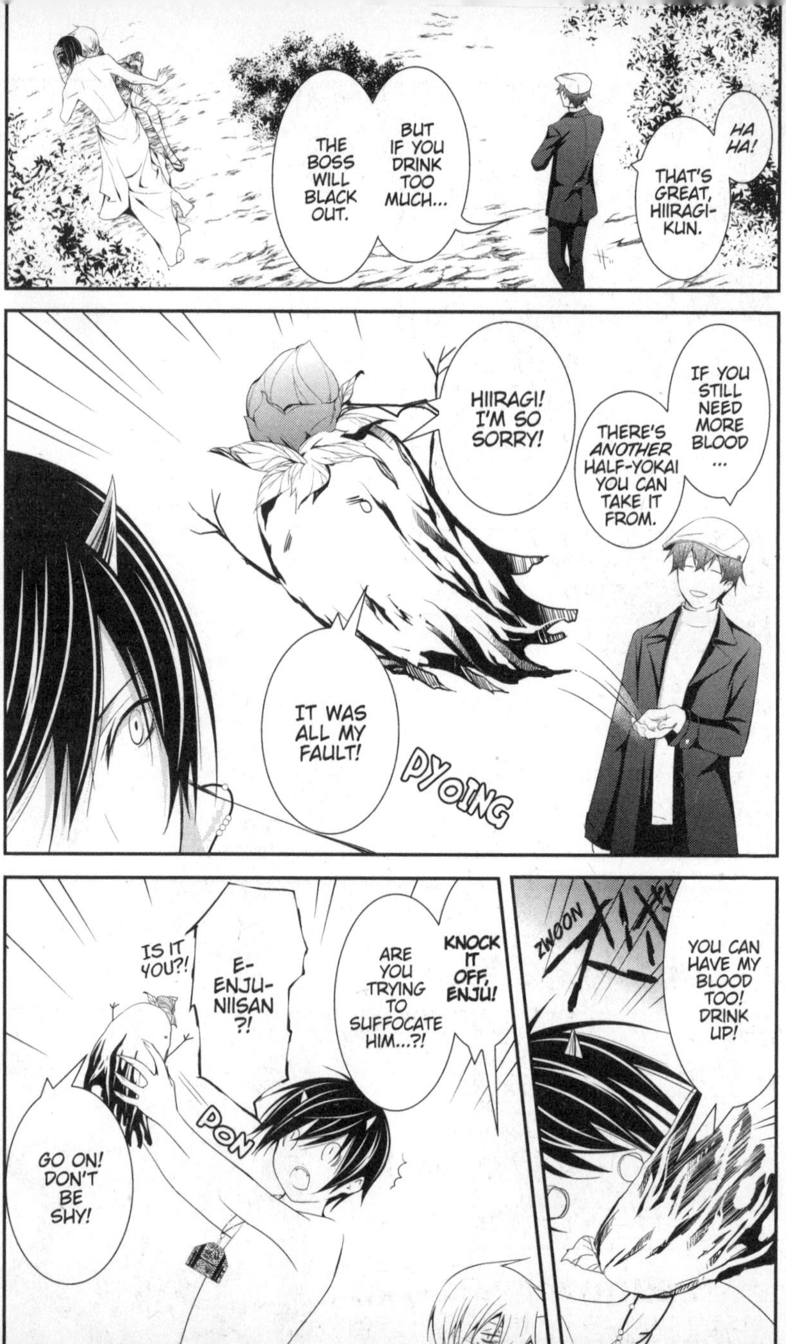
HA HA!
THAT'S GREAT, HIIRAGI-KUN.
BUT IF YOU DRINK TOO MUCH...
THE BOSS WILL BLACK OUT.
IF YOU STILL NEED MORE BLOOD ...
THERE'S ANOTHER HALF-YOKAI YOU CAN TAKE IT FROM.
HIIRAGI! I'M SO SORRY!
IT WAS ALL MY FAULT!
PYOING
ZWOON
YOU CAN HAVE MY BLOOD TOO! DRINK UP!
KNOCK IT OFF, ENJU!
ARE YOU TRYING TO SUFFOCATE HIM...?!
E-ENJU-NIISAN?!
IS IT YOU?!
PON
GO ON! DON'T BE SHY!

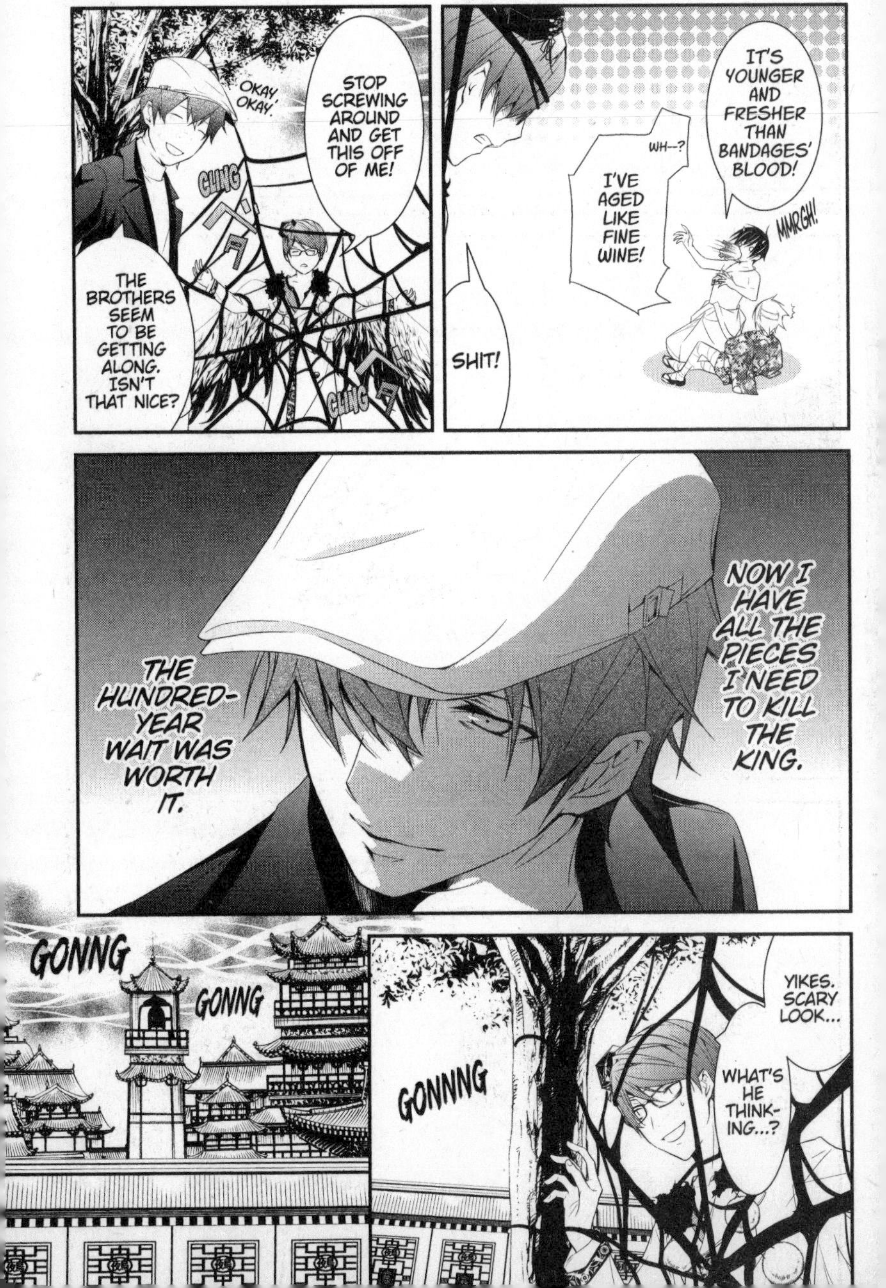
IT'S YOUNGER AND FRESHER THAN BANDAGES' BLOOD!
WH--?
I'VE AGED LIKE FINE WINE!
MMRGH!
SHIT!
STOP SCREWING AROUND AND GET THIS OFF OF ME!
OKAY, OKAY.
CLING
THE BROTHERS SEEM TO BE GETTING ALONG. ISN'T THAT NICE?
CLING
NOW I HAVE ALL THE PIECES I NEED TO KILL THE KING.
THE HUNDRED-YEAR WAIT WAS WORTH IT.
YIKES. SCARY LOOK...
WHAT'S HE THINKING...?
GONNNG
GONNG
GONNG

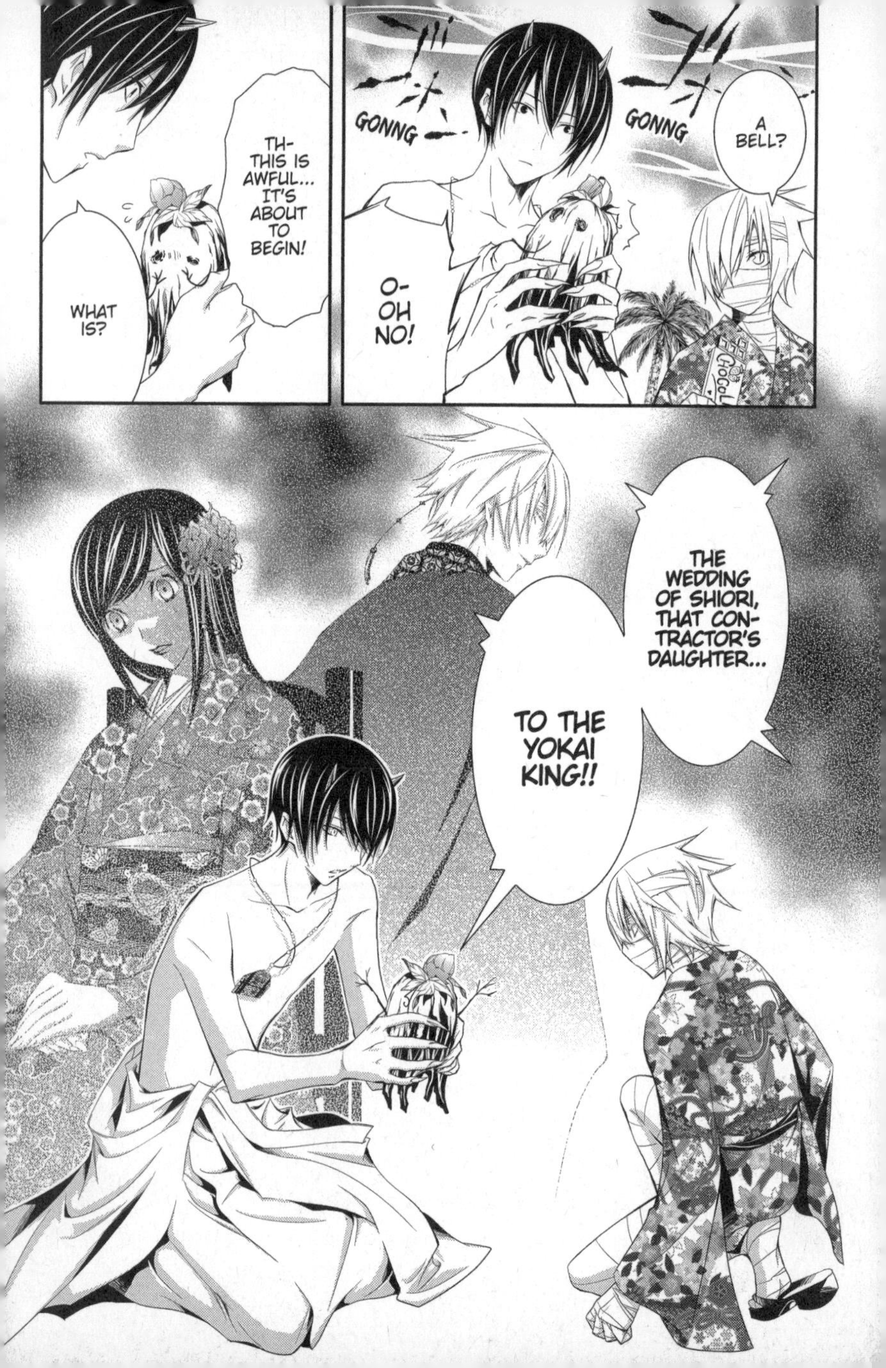
GONNG
GONNG
A BELL?
O-OH NO!
TH-THIS IS AWFUL... IT'S ABOUT TO BEGIN!
WHAT IS?
THE WEDDING OF SHIORI, THAT CONTRACTOR'S DAUGHTER...
TO THE YOKAI KING!!

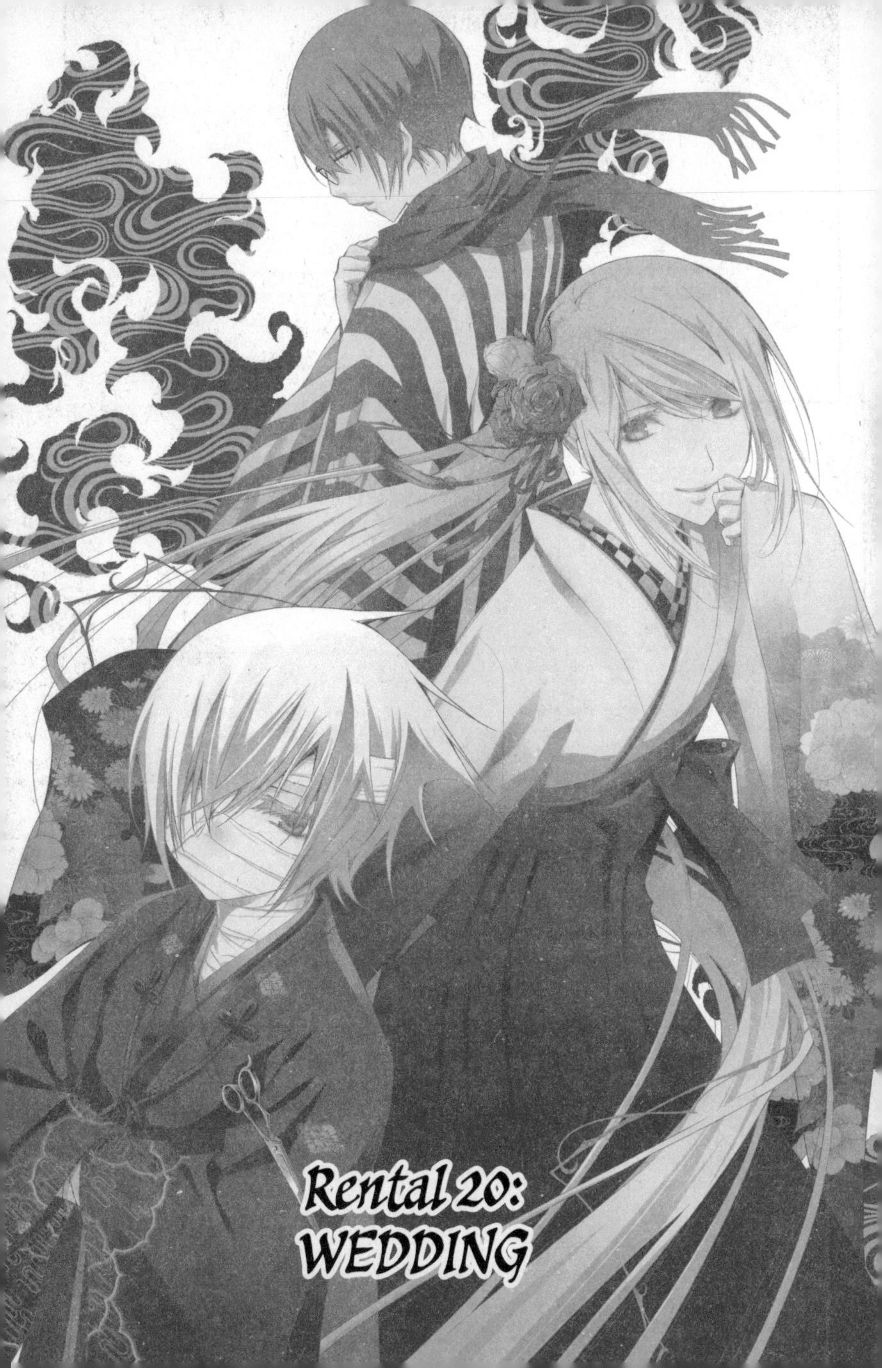
Rental 20:
WEDDING

Yokai Rental Shop

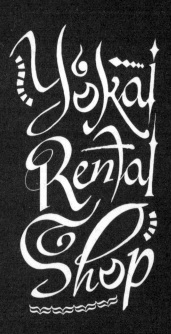

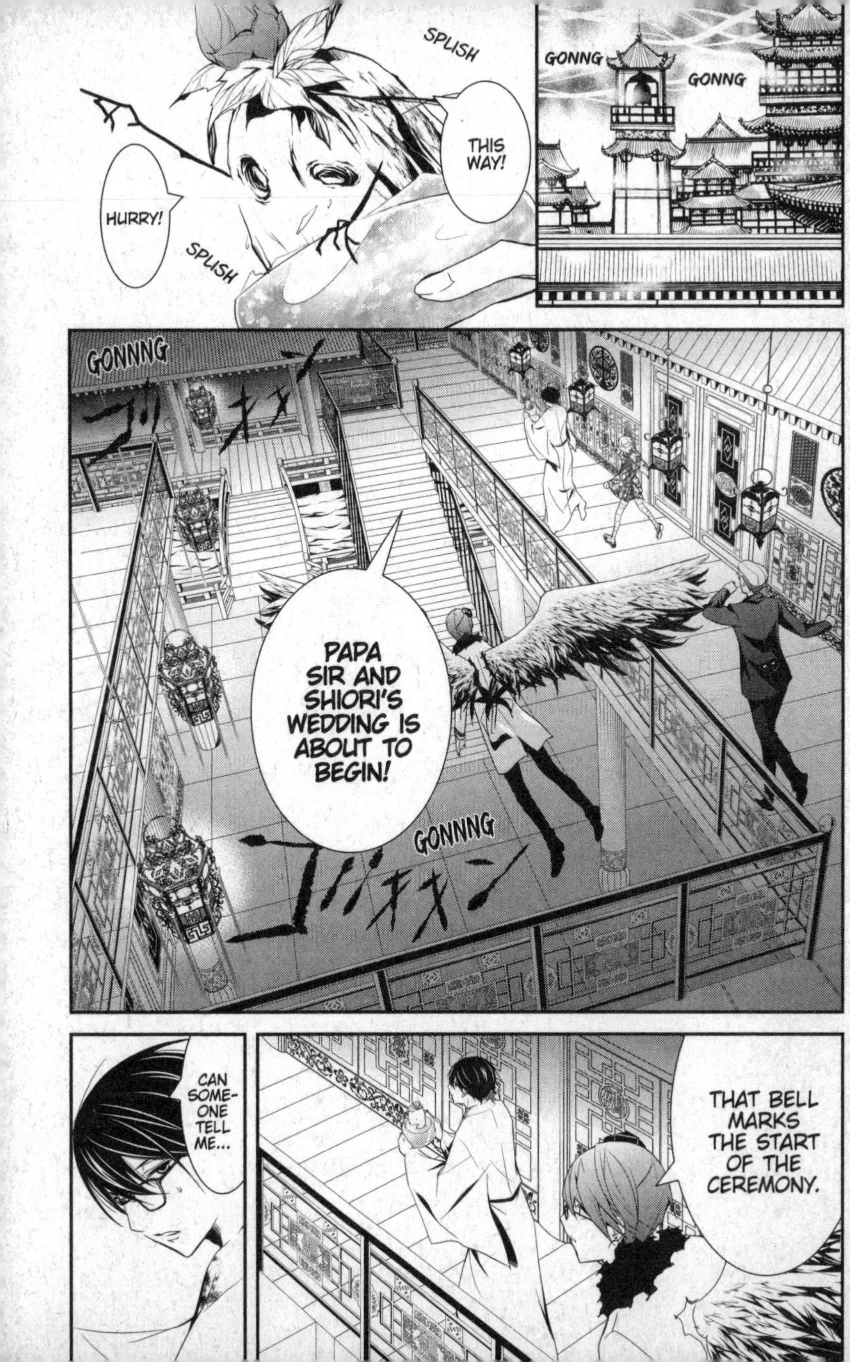
GONNG
GONNG
SPLISH
THIS WAY!
HURRY!
SPLISH
GONNNG
PAPA SIR AND SHIORI'S WEDDING IS ABOUT TO BEGIN!
GONNNG
THAT BELL MARKS THE START OF THE CEREMONY.
CAN SOME-ONE TELL ME...

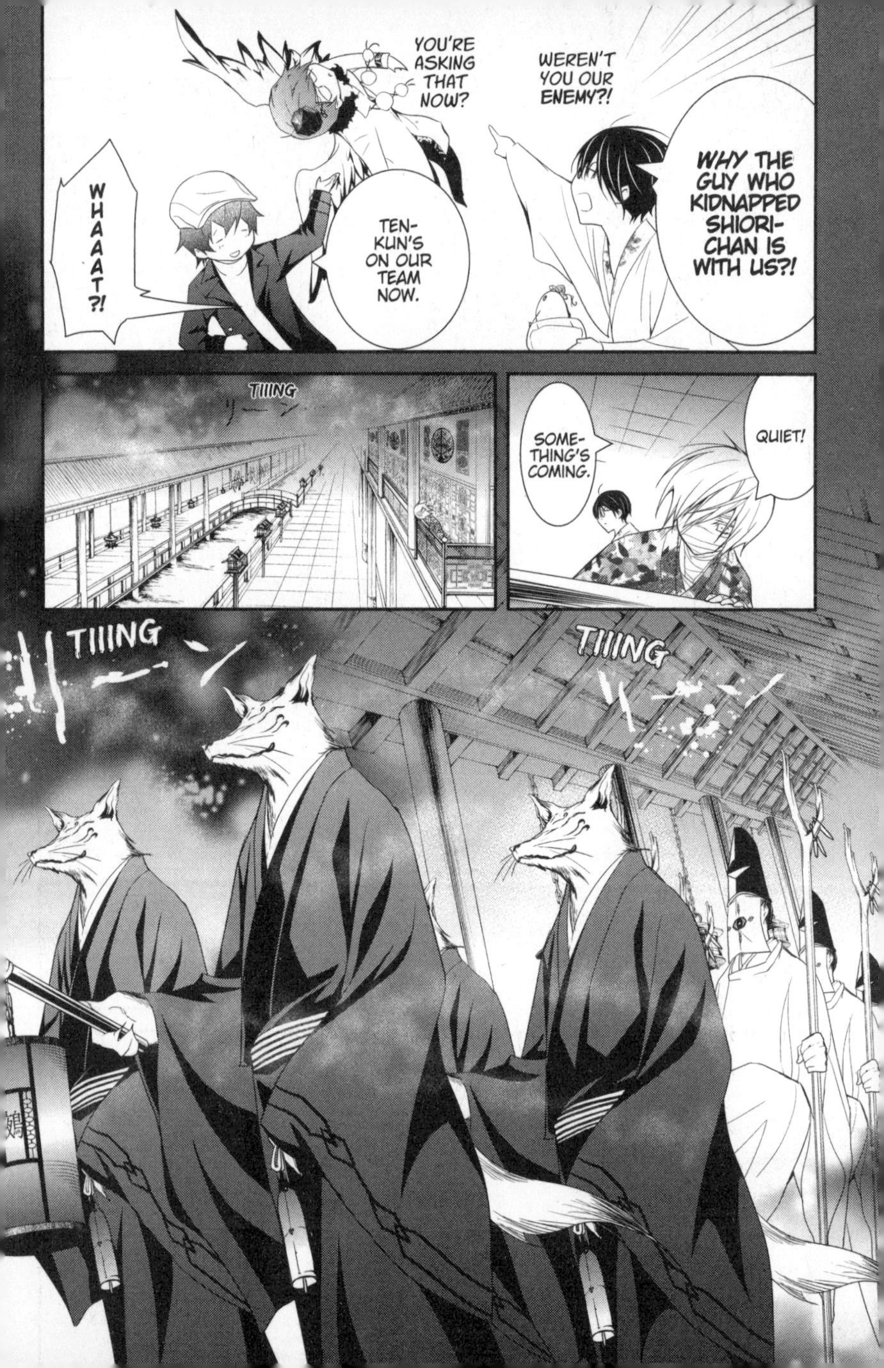
WHY THE GUY WHO KIDNAPPED SHIORI-CHAN IS WITH US?!
WEREN'T YOU OUR ENEMY?!
YOU'RE ASKING THAT NOW?
TEN-KUN'S ON OUR TEAM NOW.
WHAAAAT?!
QUIET!
SOME-THING'S COMING.
TIIING
TIIING
TIIING

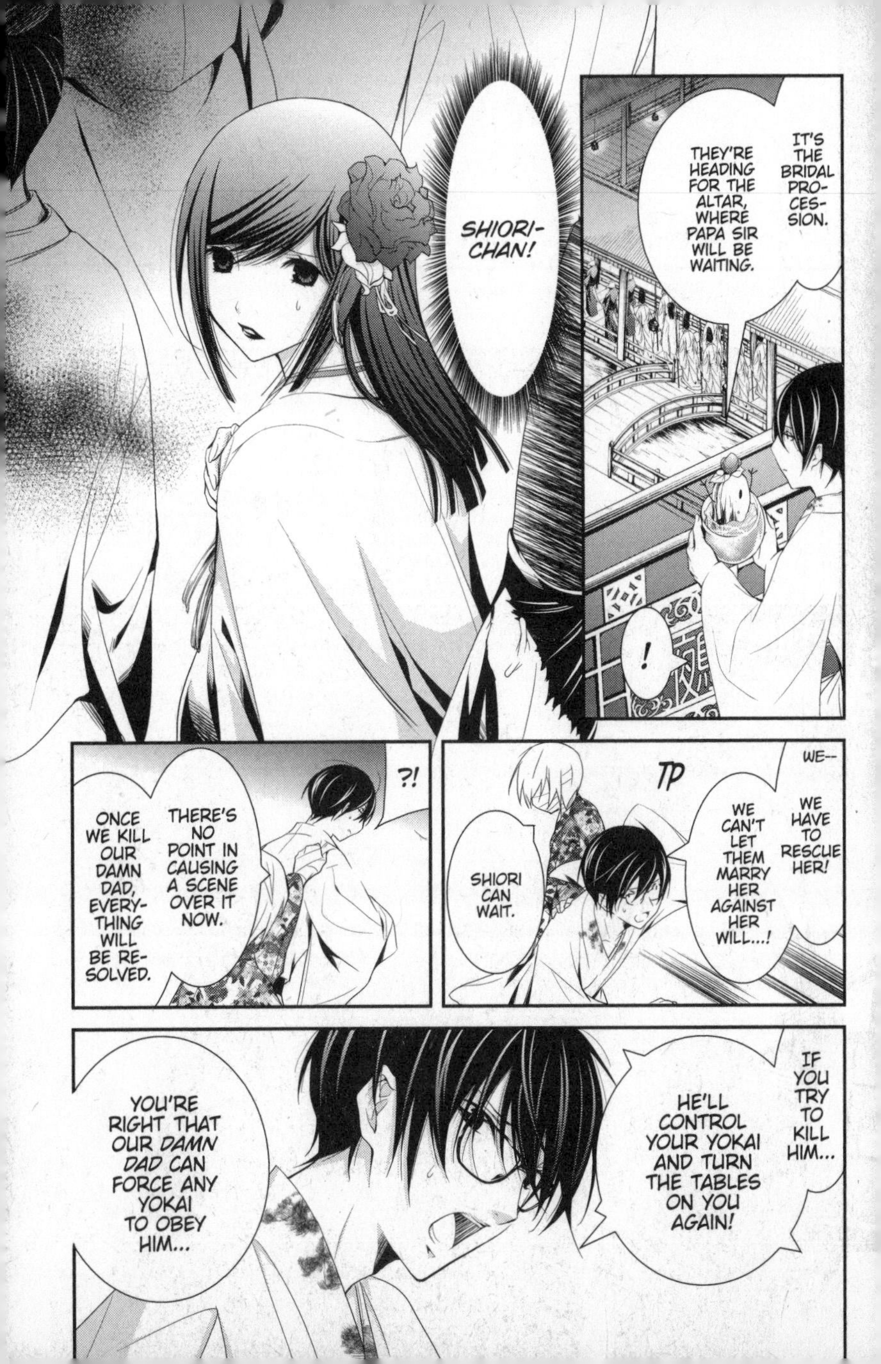
IT'S THE BRIDAL PRO-CES-SION.
THEY'RE HEADING FOR THE ALTAR, WHERE PAPA SIR WILL BE WAITING.
!
SHIORI-CHAN!
WE--
WE HAVE TO RESCUE HER!
TP
WE CAN'T LET THEM MARRY HER AGAINST HER WILL...!
SHIORI CAN WAIT.
?!
THERE'S NO POINT IN CAUSING A SCENE OVER IT NOW.
ONCE WE KILL OUR DAMN DAD, EVERY-THING WILL BE RE-SOLVED.
IF YOU TRY TO KILL HIM...
HE'LL CONTROL YOUR YOKAI AND TURN THE TABLES ON YOU AGAIN!
YOU'RE RIGHT THAT OUR *DAMN DAD* CAN FORCE ANY YOKAI TO OBEY HIM...

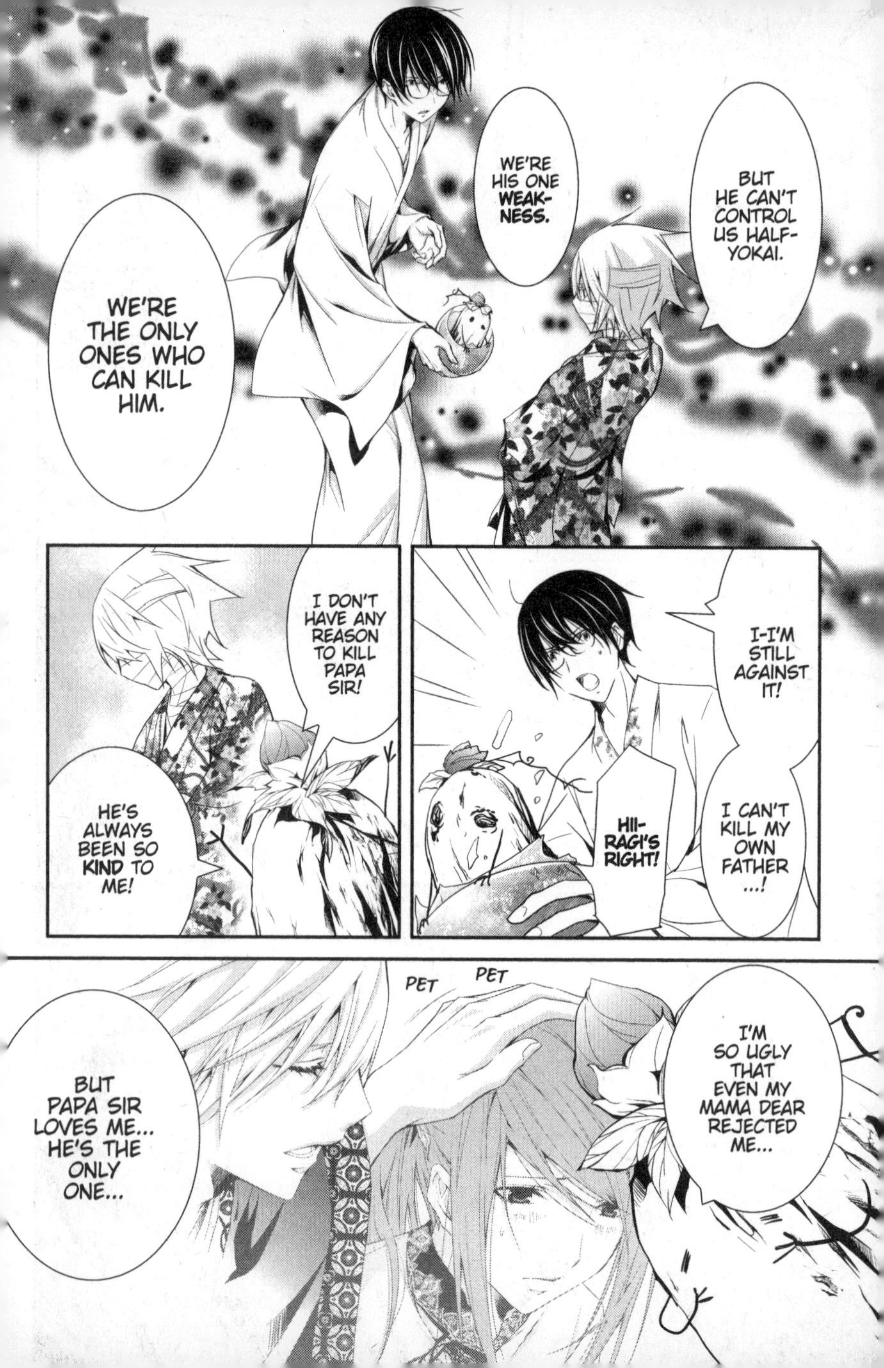
BUT HE CAN'T CONTROL US HALF-YOKAI.
WE'RE HIS ONE WEAK-NESS.
WE'RE THE ONLY ONES WHO CAN KILL HIM.
I-I'M STILL AGAINST IT!
I CAN'T KILL MY OWN FATHER ...!
HII-RAGI'S RIGHT!
I DON'T HAVE ANY REASON TO KILL PAPA SIR!
HE'S ALWAYS BEEN SO KIND TO ME!
PET PET
I'M SO UGLY THAT EVEN MY MAMA DEAR REJECTED ME...
BUT PAPA SIR LOVES ME... HE'S THE ONLY ONE...

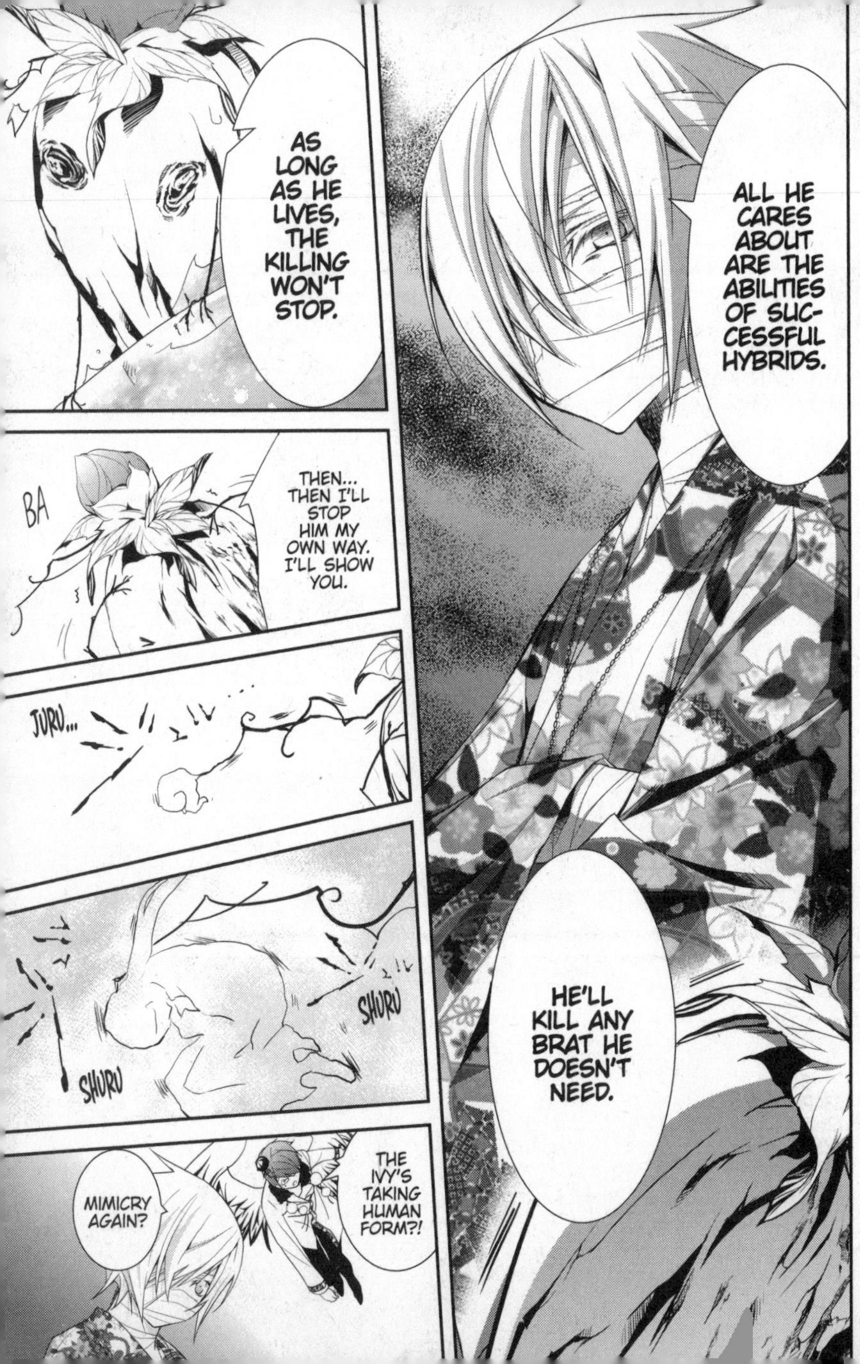
ALL HE CARES ABOUT ARE THE ABILITIES OF SUC-CESSFUL HYBRIDS.
HE'LL KILL ANY BRAT HE DOESN'T NEED.
AS LONG AS HE LIVES, THE KILLING WON'T STOP.
THEN... THEN I'LL STOP HIM MY OWN WAY. I'LL SHOW YOU.
BA
JURU...
SHURU
SHURU
THE IVY'S TAKING HUMAN FORM?!
MIMICRY AGAIN?

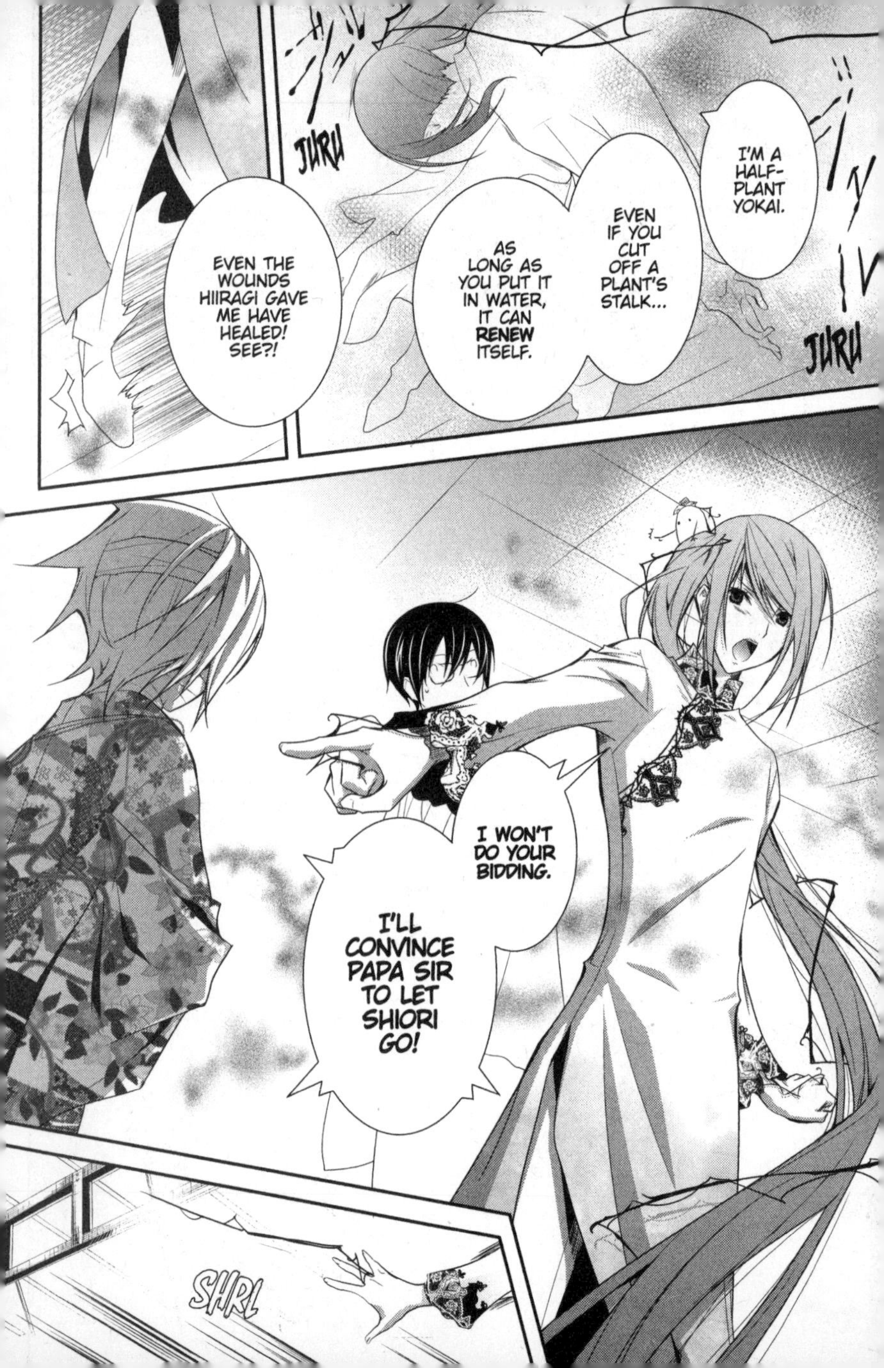
I'M A HALF-PLANT YOKAI.
EVEN IF YOU CUT OFF A PLANT'S STALK...
AS LONG AS YOU PUT IT IN WATER, IT CAN RENEW ITSELF.
JURU
JURU
EVEN THE WOUNDS HIIRAGI GAVE ME HAVE HEALED! SEE?!
I WON'T DO YOUR BIDDING.
I'LL CONVINCE PAPA SIR TO LET SHIORI GO!
SHRL

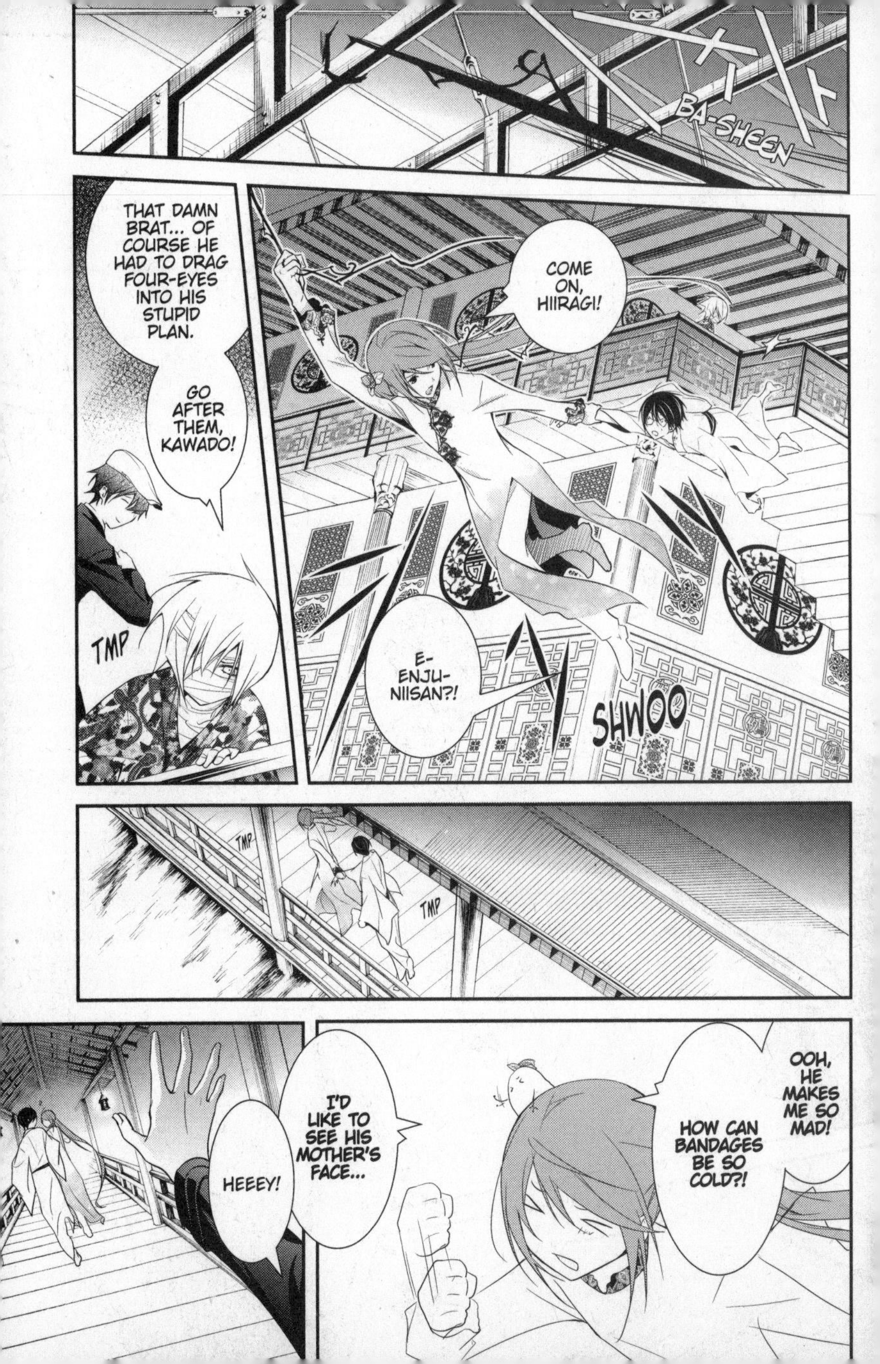
BA-SHEEN
COME ON, HIIRAGI!
E-ENJU-NIISAN?!
SHWOO
THAT DAMN BRAT... OF COURSE HE HAD TO DRAG FOUR-EYES INTO HIS STUPID PLAN.
GO AFTER THEM, KAWADO!
TMP
TMP
TMP
OOH, HE MAKES ME SO MAD!
HOW CAN BANDAGES BE SO COLD?!
I'D LIKE TO SEE HIS MOTHER'S FACE...
HEEEY!

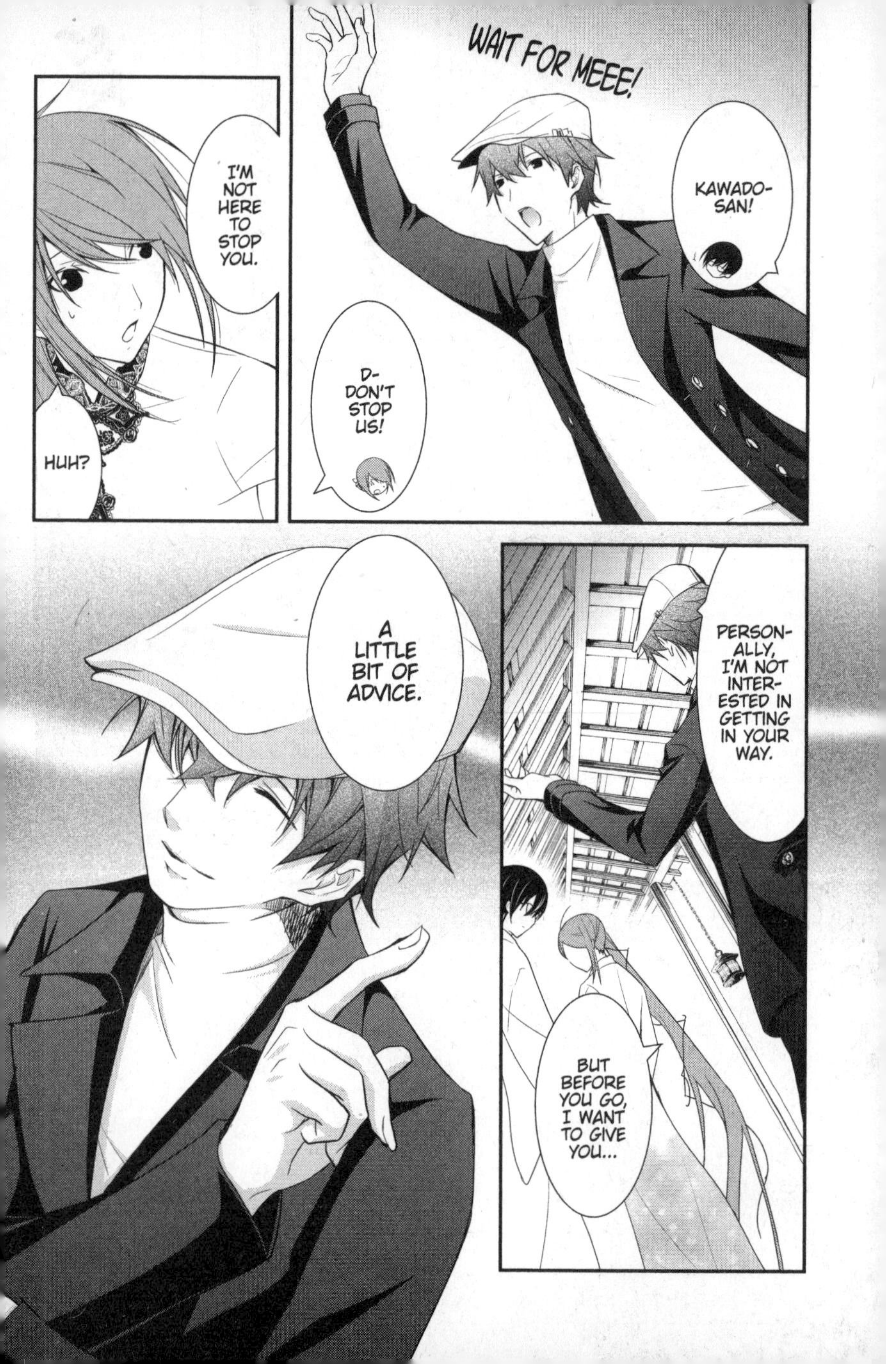
WAIT FOR MEEE!
KAWADO-SAN!
D-DON'T STOP US!
I'M NOT HERE TO STOP YOU.
HUH?
PERSONALLY, I'M NOT INTERESTED IN GETTING IN YOUR WAY.
BUT BEFORE YOU GO, I WANT TO GIVE YOU...
A LITTLE BIT OF ADVICE.

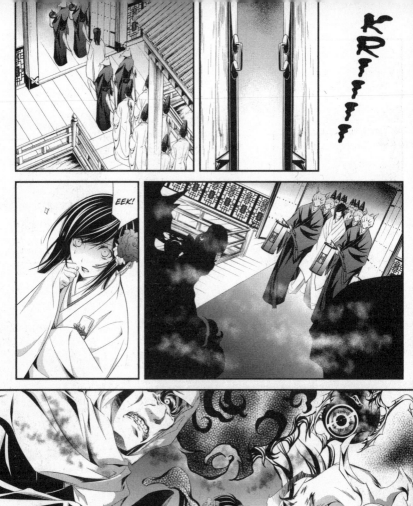

KRIIII

EEK!

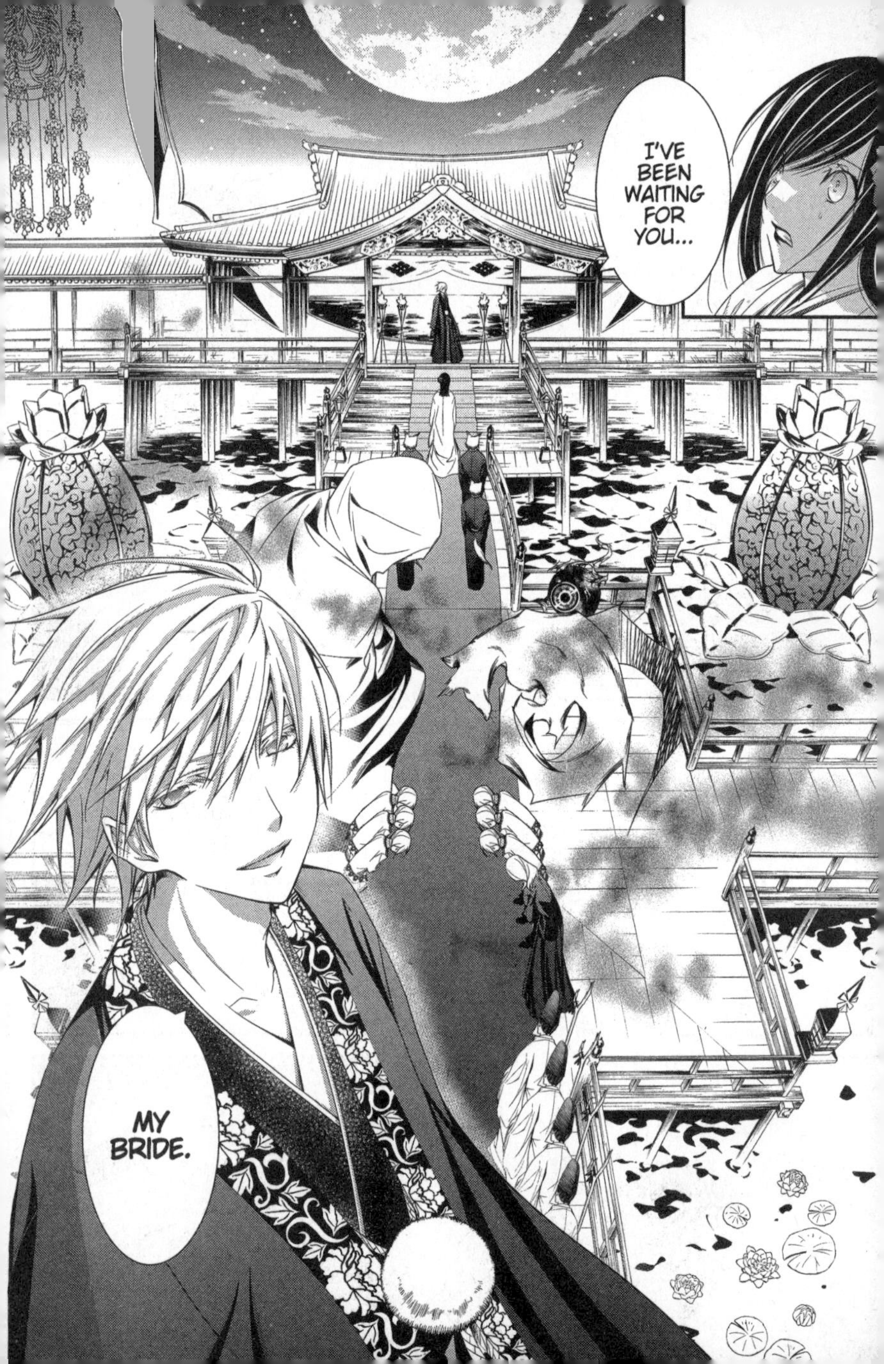
I'VE BEEN WAITING FOR YOU...
MY BRIDE.

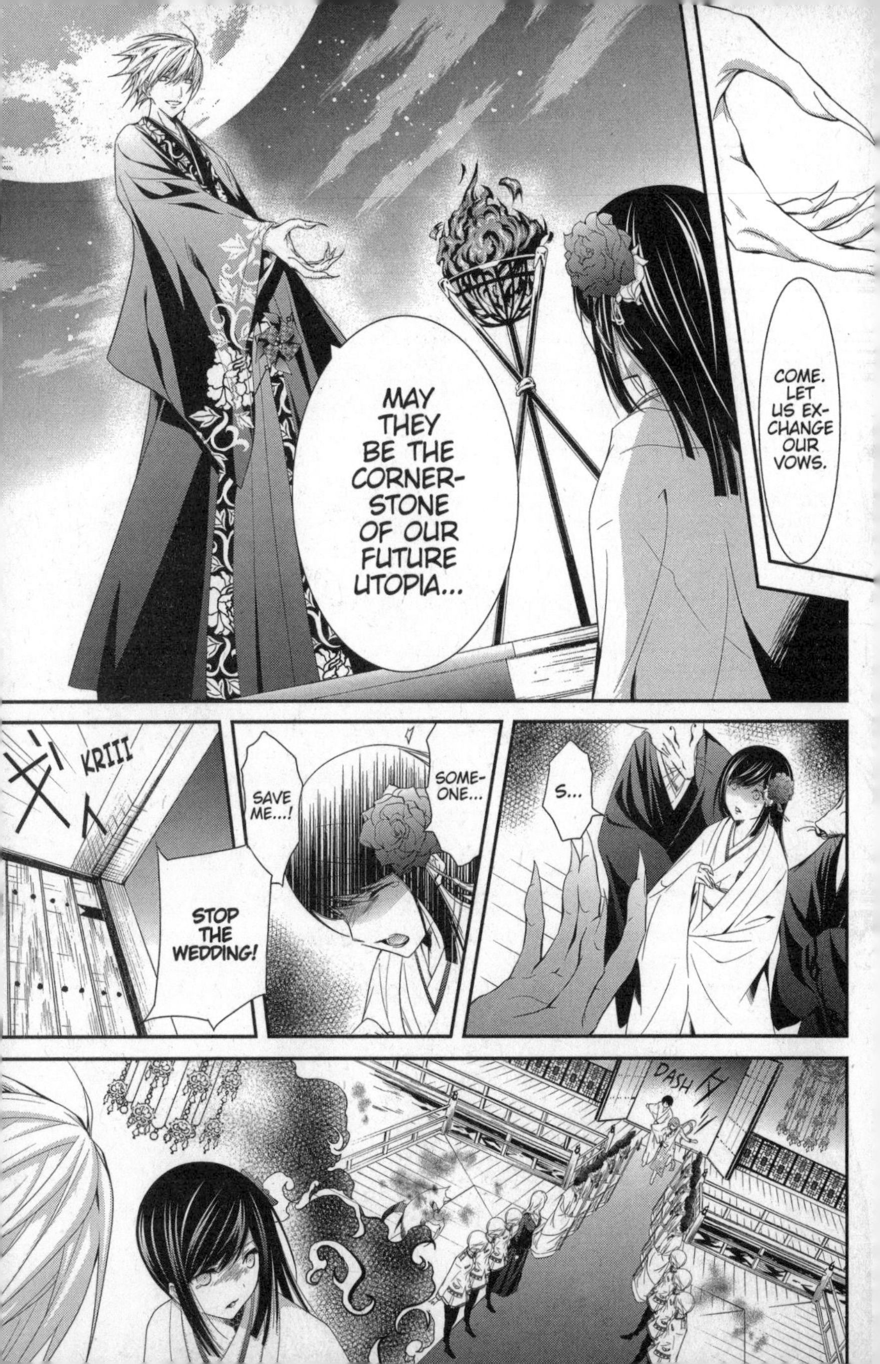
COME. LET US EX-CHANGE OUR VOWS.
MAY THEY BE THE CORNER-STONE OF OUR FUTURE UTOPIA...
S...
SOME-ONE...
SAVE ME...!
KRIII
STOP THE WEDDING!
DASH

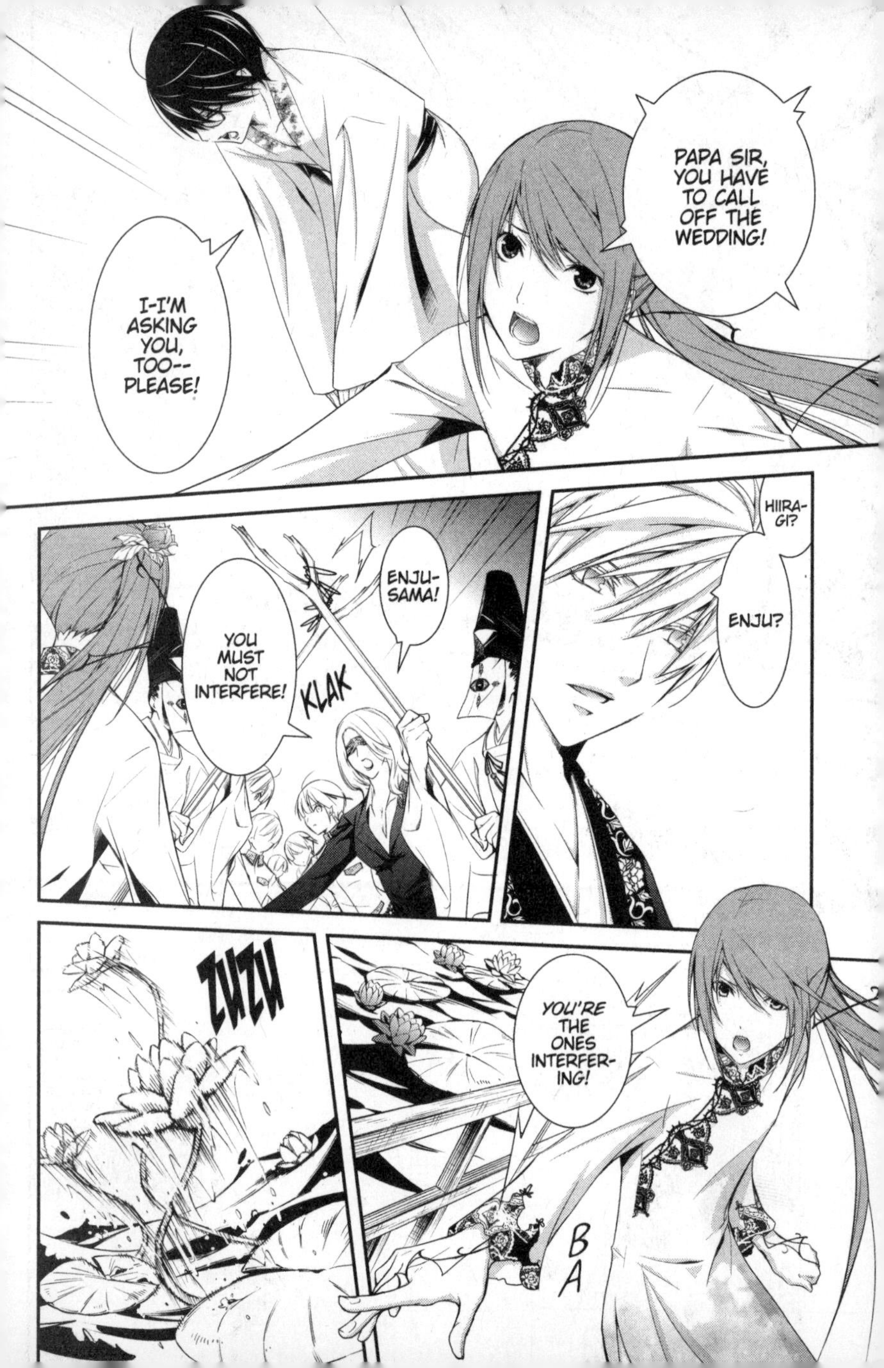
PAPA SIR, YOU HAVE TO CALL OFF THE WEDDING!
I-I'M ASKING YOU, TOO-- PLEASE!
HIIRA-GI?
ENJU?
ENJU-SAMA!
YOU MUST NOT INTERFERE!
KLAK
YOU'RE THE ONES INTERFER-ING!
BA
ZUZU

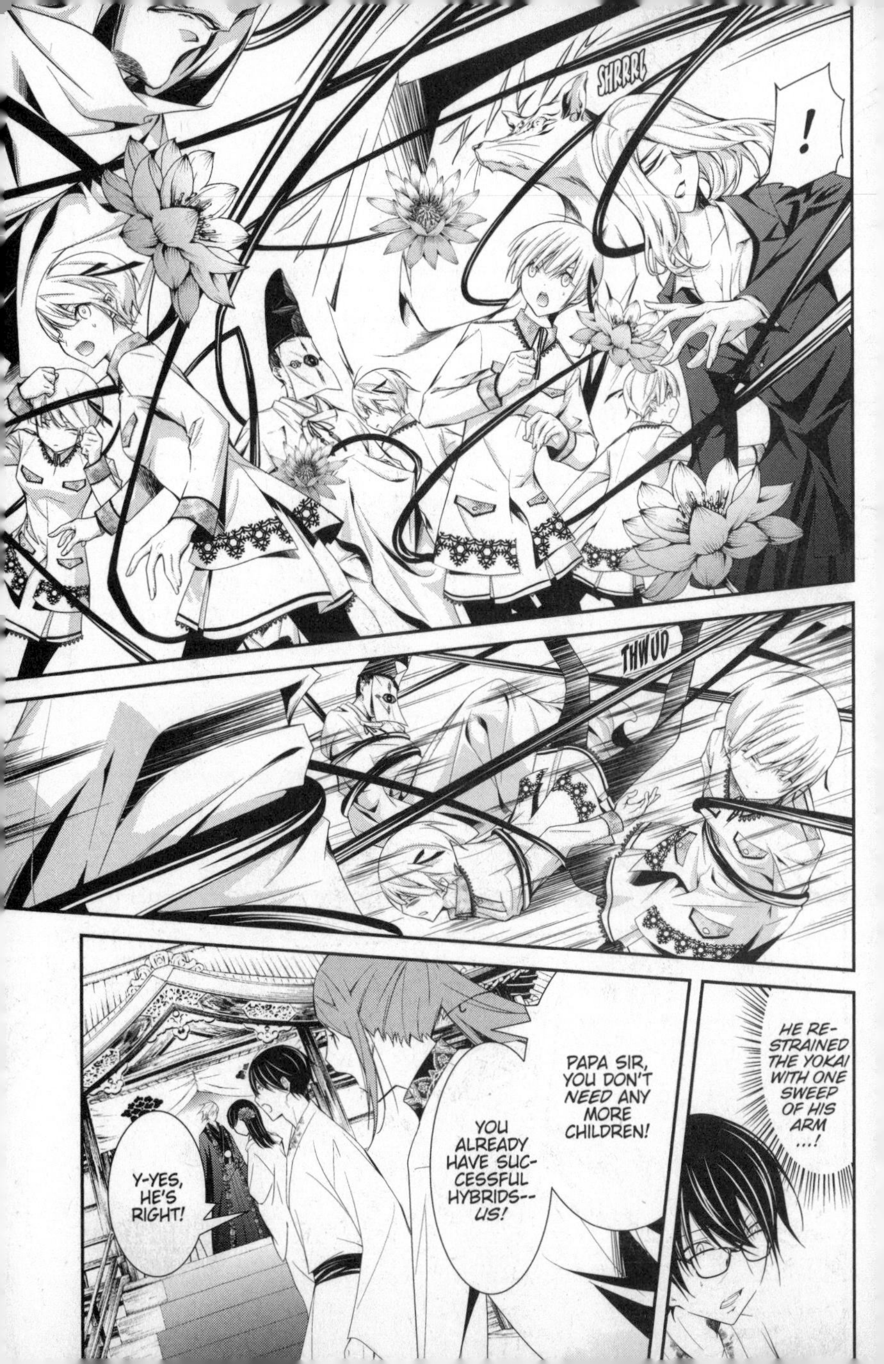
!
SHRRRL
THWUD
HE RE-STRAINED THE YOKAI WITH ONE SWEEP OF HIS ARM ...!
PAPA SIR, YOU DON'T NEED ANY MORE CHILDREN!
YOU ALREADY HAVE SUC-CESSFUL HYBRIDS-- US!
Y-YES, HE'S RIGHT!

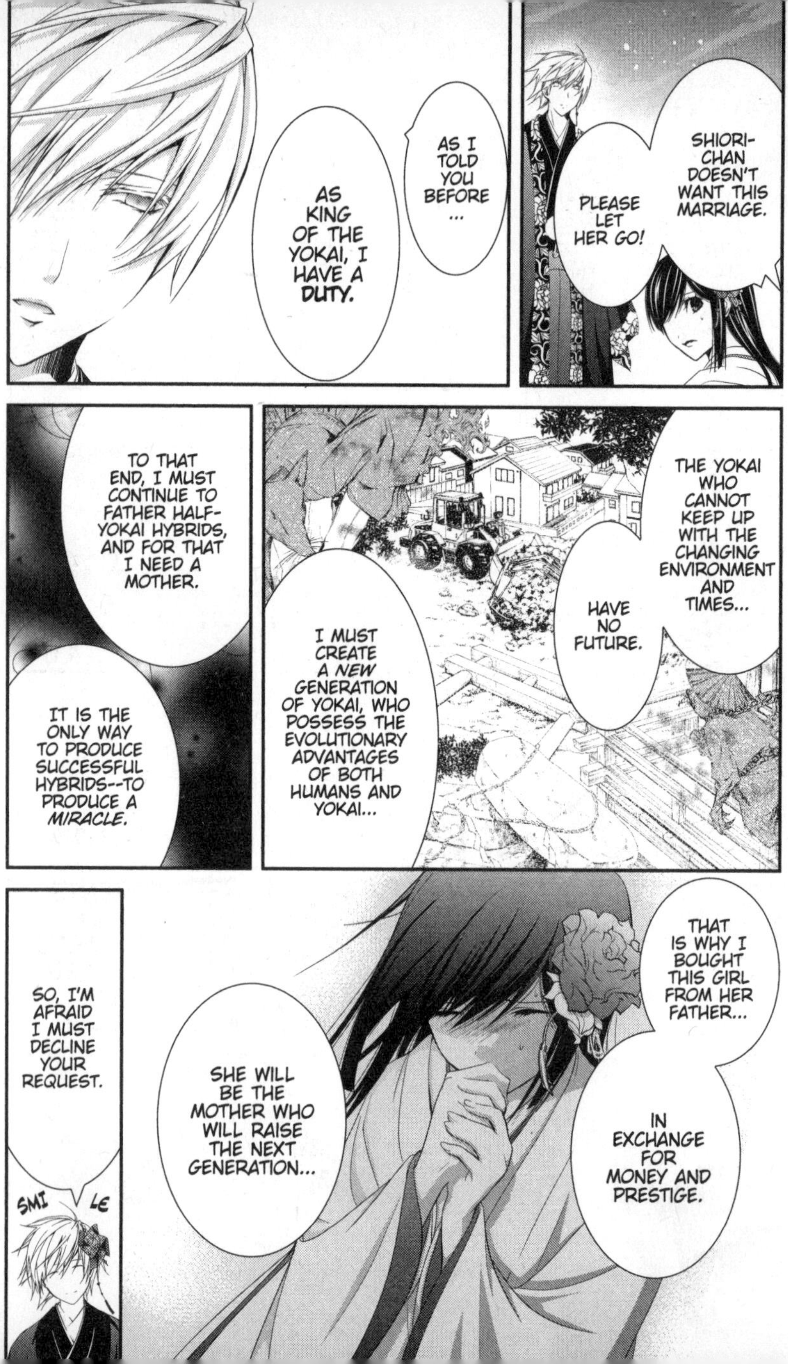
SHIORI-CHAN DOESN'T WANT THIS MARRIAGE.
PLEASE LET HER GO!
AS I TOLD YOU BEFORE...
AS KING OF THE YOKAI, I HAVE A DUTY.
THE YOKAI WHO CANNOT KEEP UP WITH THE CHANGING ENVIRONMENT AND TIMES...
HAVE NO FUTURE.
I MUST CREATE A NEW GENERATION OF YOKAI, WHO POSSESS THE EVOLUTIONARY ADVANTAGES OF BOTH HUMANS AND YOKAI...
TO THAT END, I MUST CONTINUE TO FATHER HALF-YOKAI HYBRIDS, AND FOR THAT I NEED A MOTHER.
IT IS THE ONLY WAY TO PRODUCE SUCCESSFUL HYBRIDS--TO PRODUCE A MIRACLE.
THAT IS WHY I BOUGHT THIS GIRL FROM HER FATHER...
IN EXCHANGE FOR MONEY AND PRESTIGE.
SHE WILL BE THE MOTHER WHO WILL RAISE THE NEXT GENERATION...
SO, I'M AFRAID I MUST DECLINE YOUR REQUEST.
SMI LE

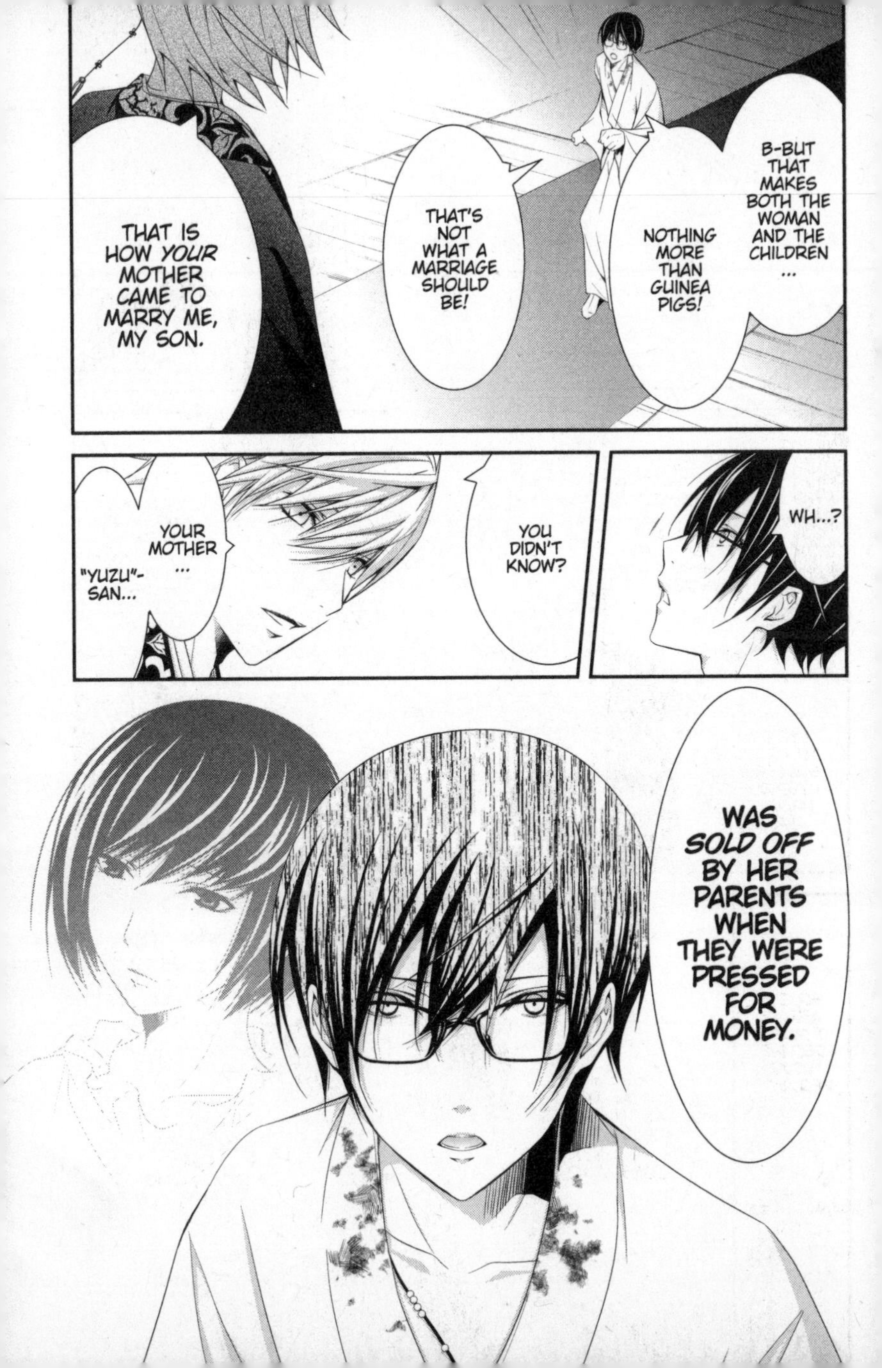
B-BUT THAT MAKES BOTH THE WOMAN AND THE CHILDREN ...
NOTHING MORE THAN GUINEA PIGS!
THAT'S NOT WHAT A MARRIAGE SHOULD BE!
THAT IS HOW *YOUR* MOTHER CAME TO MARRY ME, MY SON.
WH...?
YOU DIDN'T KNOW?
YOUR MOTHER ...
"YUZU"-SAN...
WAS *SOLD OFF* BY HER PARENTS WHEN THEY WERE PRESSED FOR MONEY.

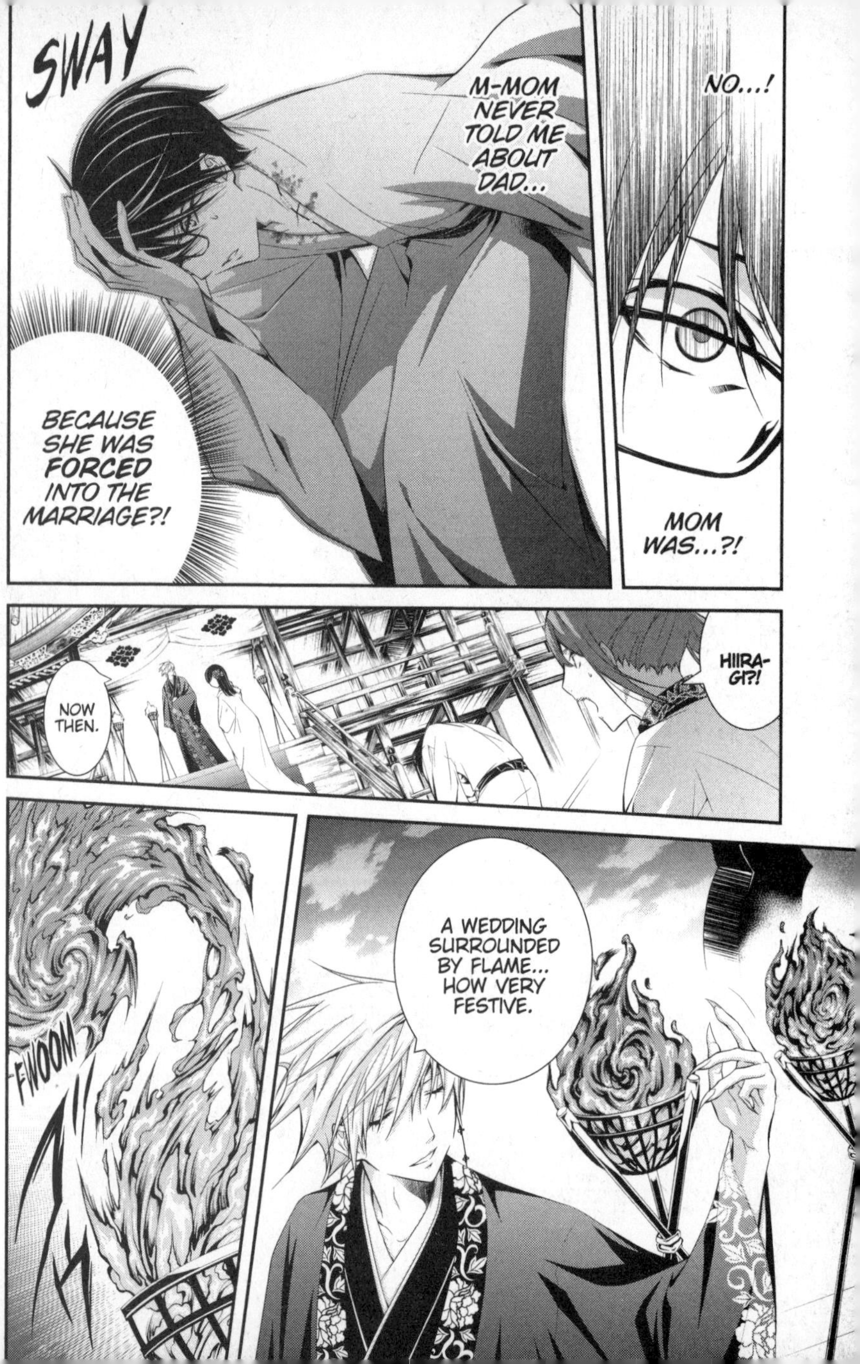
NO...!
MOM WAS...?!
SWAY
M-MOM NEVER TOLD ME ABOUT DAD...
BECAUSE SHE WAS FORCED INTO THE MARRIAGE?!
HIIRA-GI?!
NOW THEN.
A WEDDING SURROUNDED BY FLAME... HOW VERY FESTIVE.
FWOOM

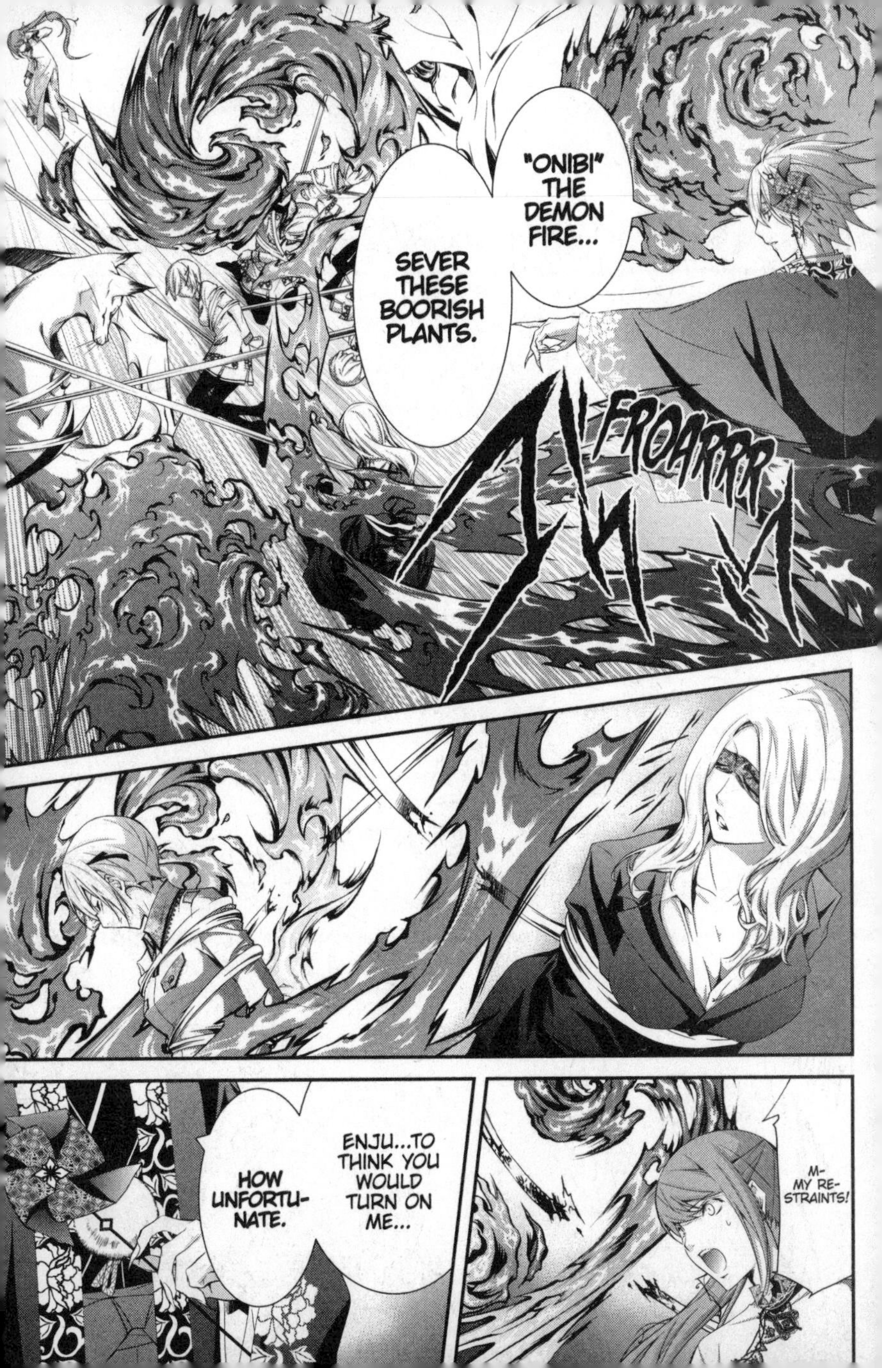
"ONIBI" THE DEMON FIRE...
SEVER THESE BOORISH PLANTS.
FROARRRR
M- MY RE-STRAINTS!
ENJU...TO THINK YOU WOULD TURN ON ME...
HOW UNFORTU-NATE.

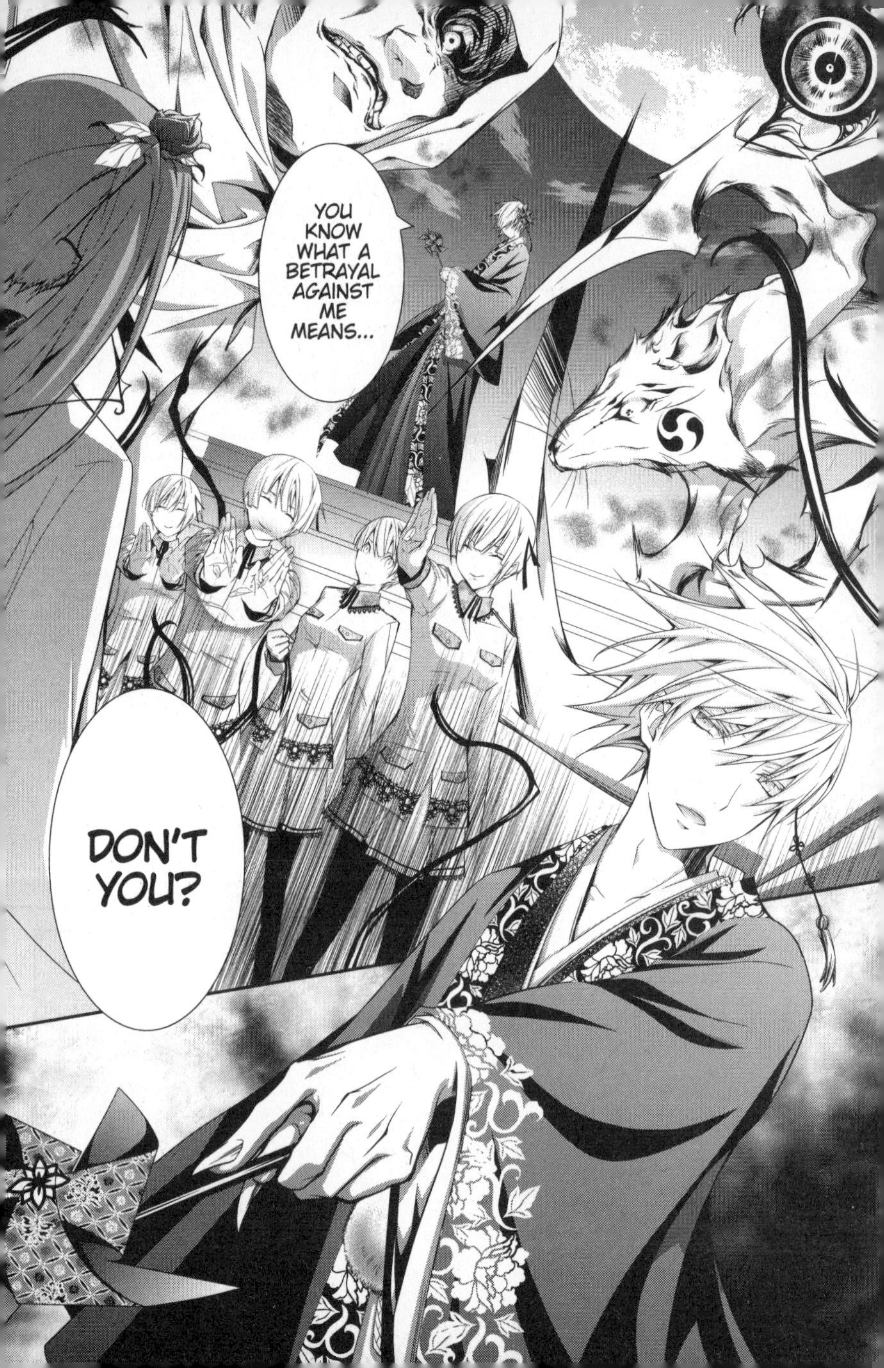
YOU KNOW WHAT A BETRAYAL AGAINST ME MEANS...
DON'T YOU?

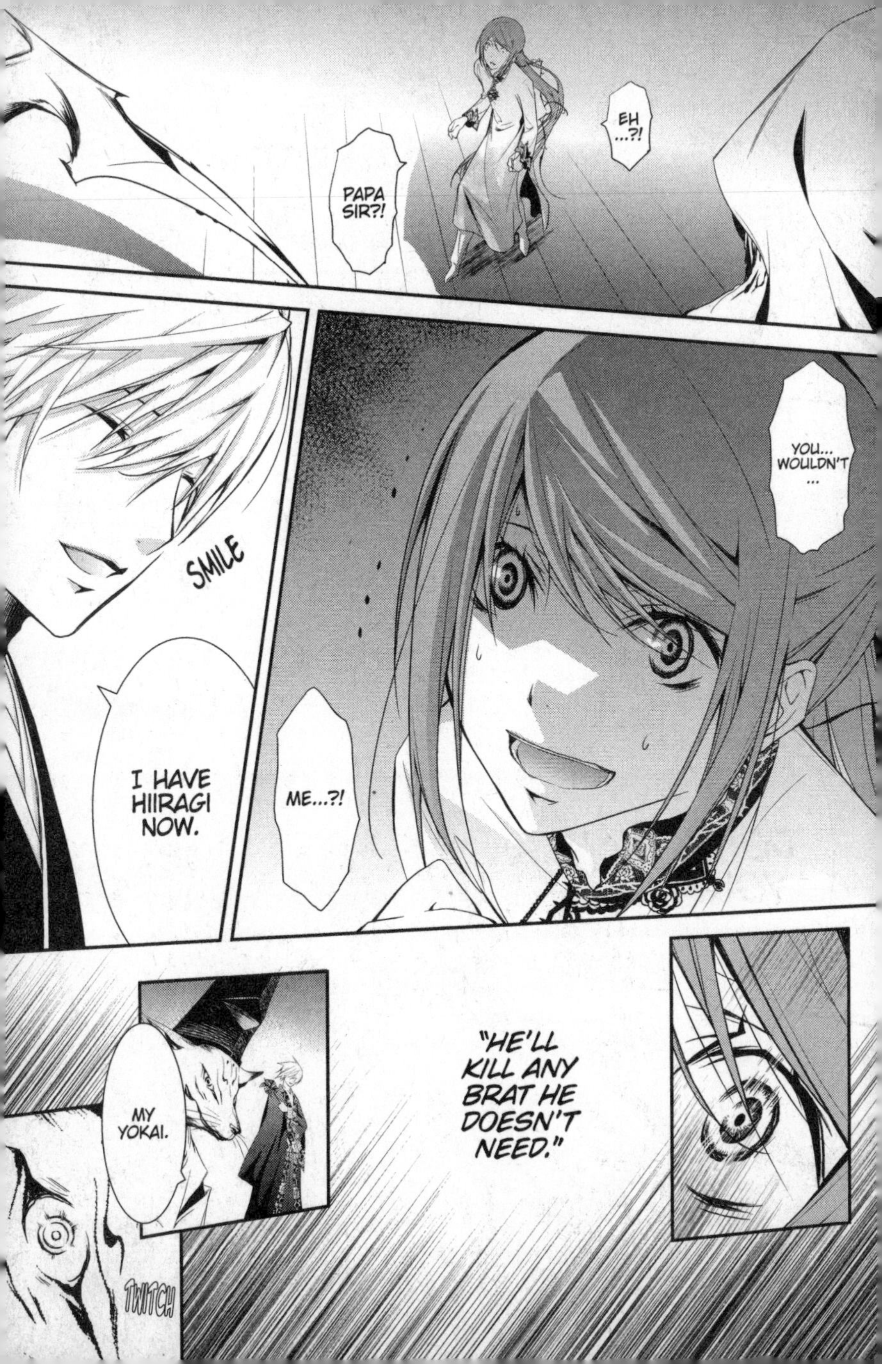
EH ...?!
PAPA SIR?!
YOU... WOULDN'T ...
ME...?!
SMILE
I HAVE HIIRAGI NOW.
"HE'LL KILL ANY BRAT HE DOESN'T NEED."
MY YOKAI.
TWITCH

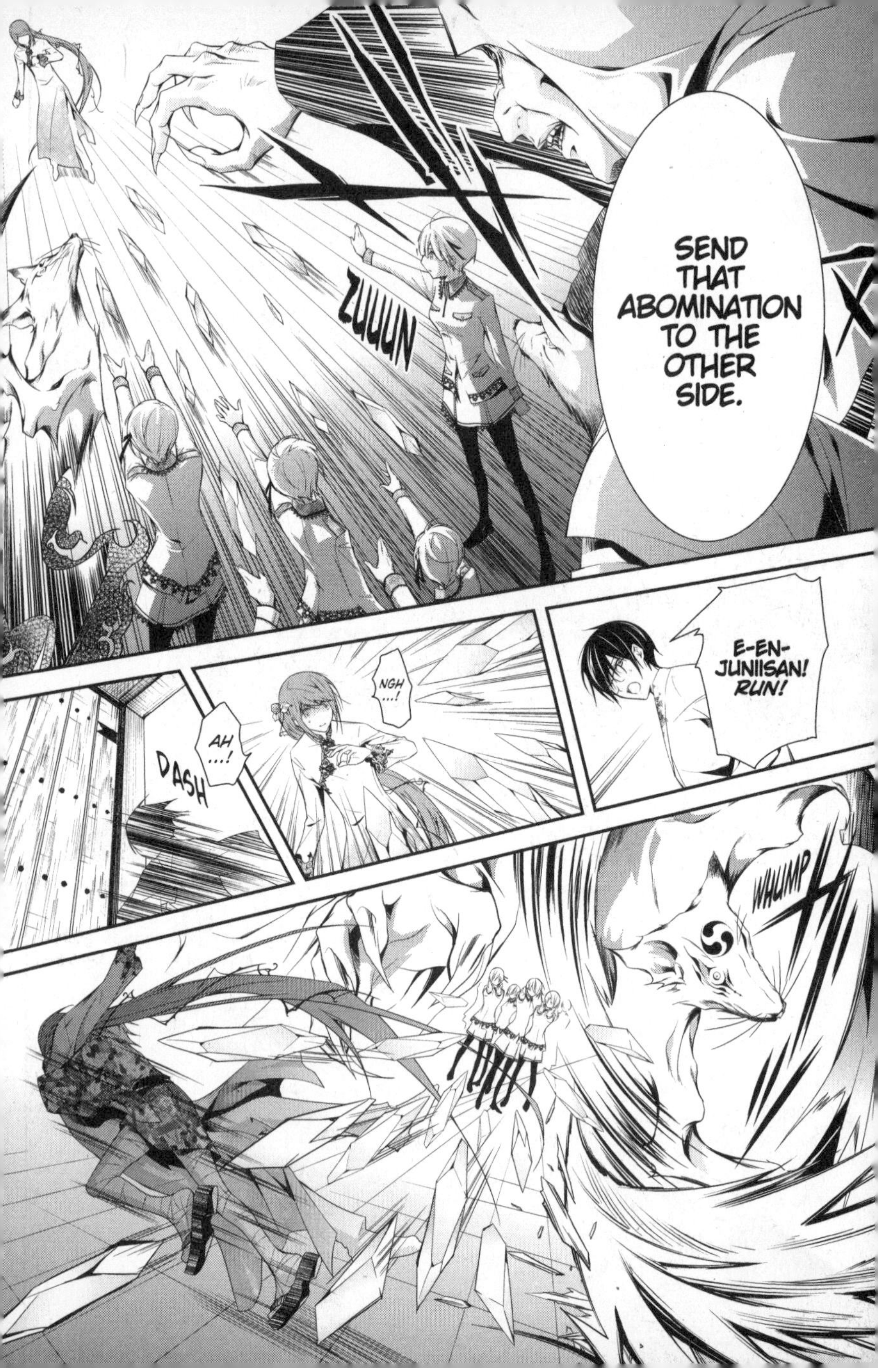
SEND THAT ABOMINATION TO THE OTHER SIDE.
ZUUUN
E-EN-JUNIISAN! RUN!
NGH ...!
AH ...!
DASH
WHUMP

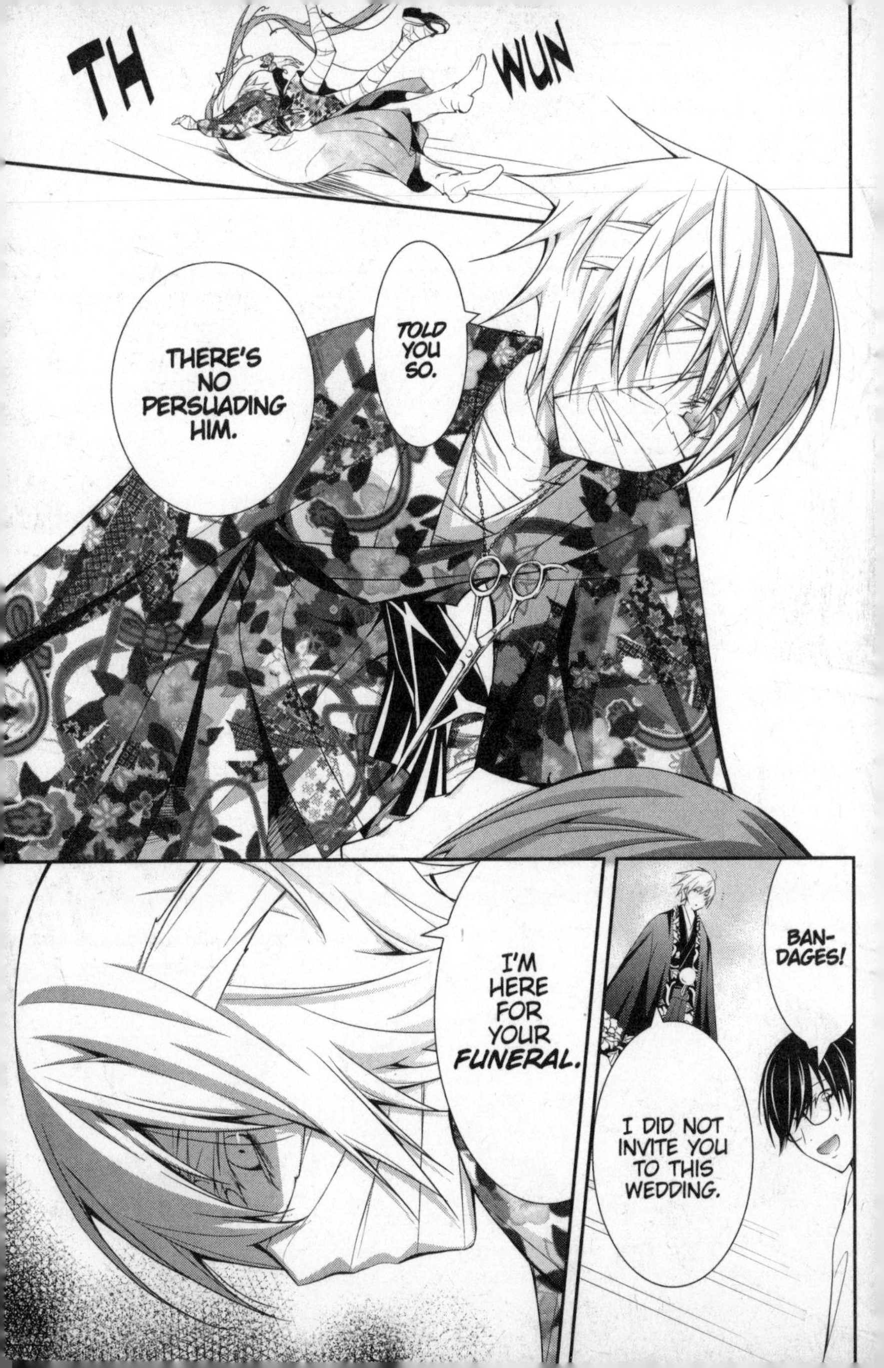
TH WUN
TOLD YOU SO.
THERE'S NO PERSUADING HIM.
BAN-DAGES!
I DID NOT INVITE YOU TO THIS WEDDING.
I'M HERE FOR YOUR *FUNERAL*.

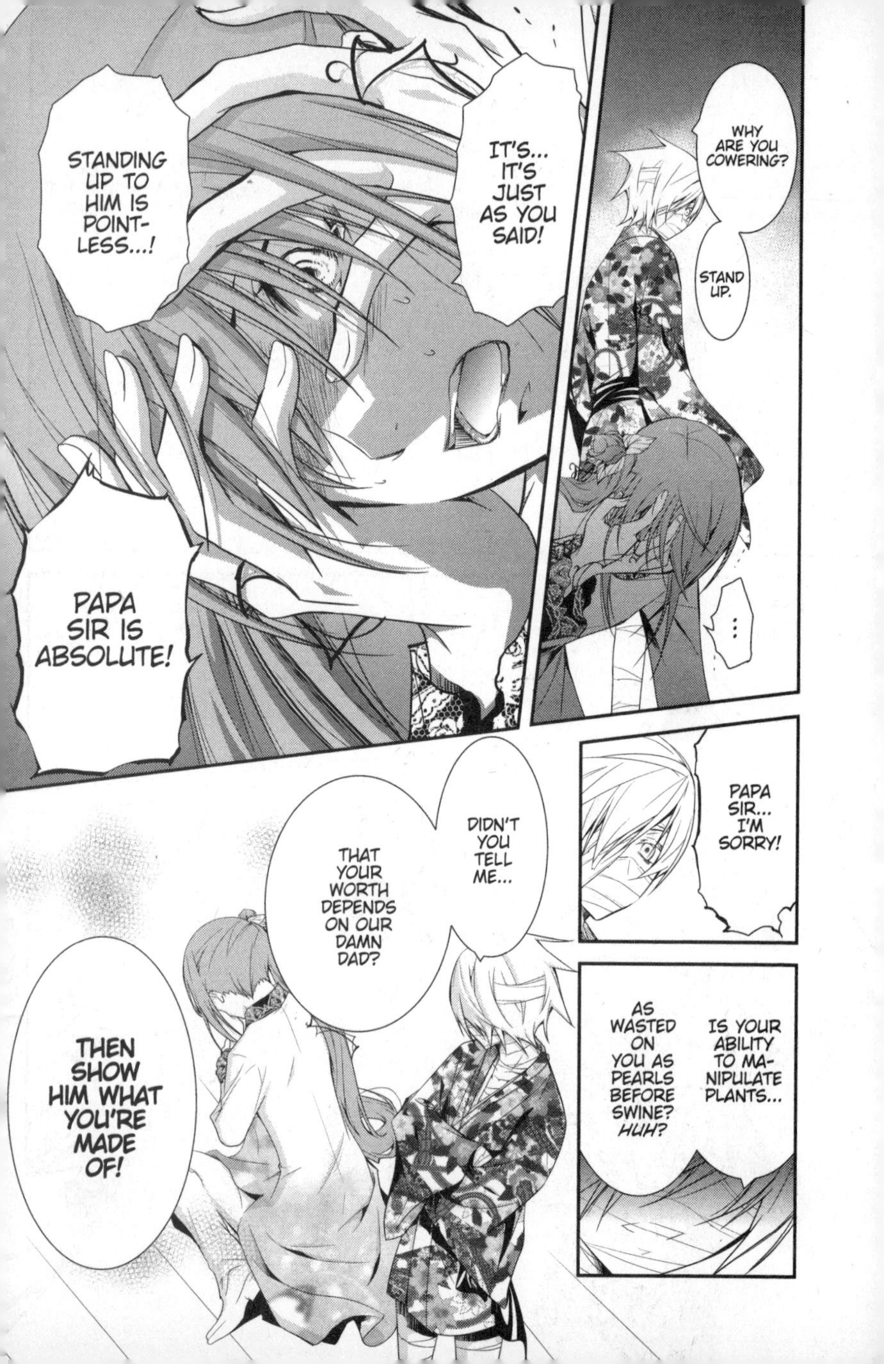
WHY ARE YOU COWERING?
STAND UP.
...
IT'S... IT'S JUST AS YOU SAID!
STANDING UP TO HIM IS POINTLESS...!
PAPA SIR IS ABSOLUTE!
PAPA SIR... I'M SORRY!
IS YOUR ABILITY TO MANIPULATE PLANTS...
AS WASTED ON YOU AS PEARLS BEFORE SWINE? *HUH?*
DIDN'T YOU TELL ME...
THAT YOUR WORTH DEPENDS ON OUR DAMN DAD?
THEN SHOW HIM WHAT YOU'RE MADE OF!

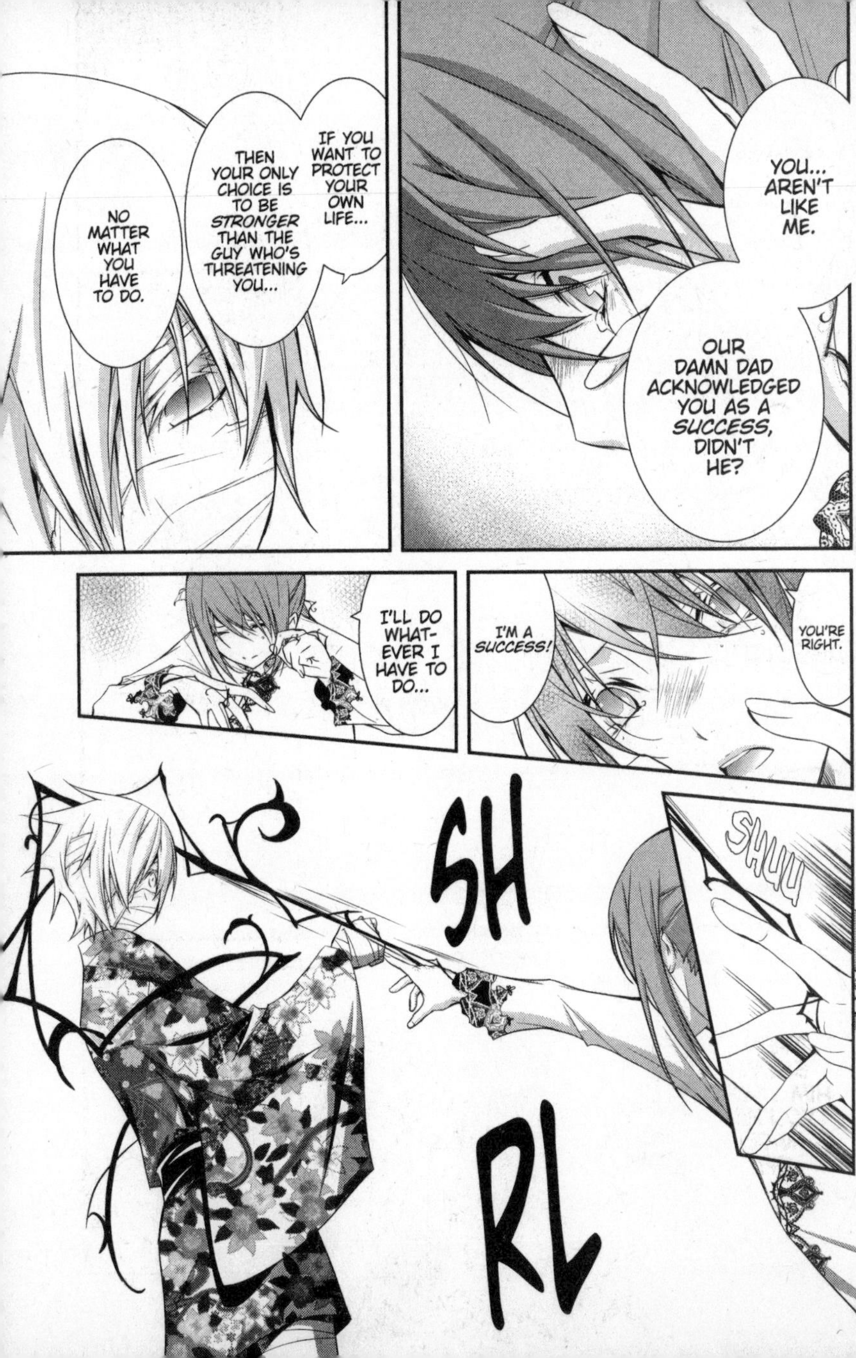
YOU... AREN'T LIKE ME.
OUR DAMN DAD ACKNOWLEDGED YOU AS A *SUCCESS*, DIDN'T HE?
IF YOU WANT TO PROTECT YOUR OWN LIFE...
THEN YOUR ONLY CHOICE IS TO BE *STRONGER* THAN THE GUY WHO'S THREATENING YOU...
NO MATTER WHAT YOU HAVE TO DO.
YOU'RE RIGHT.
I'M A *SUCCESS!*
I'LL DO WHAT-EVER I HAVE TO DO...
SHUU
SH
RL

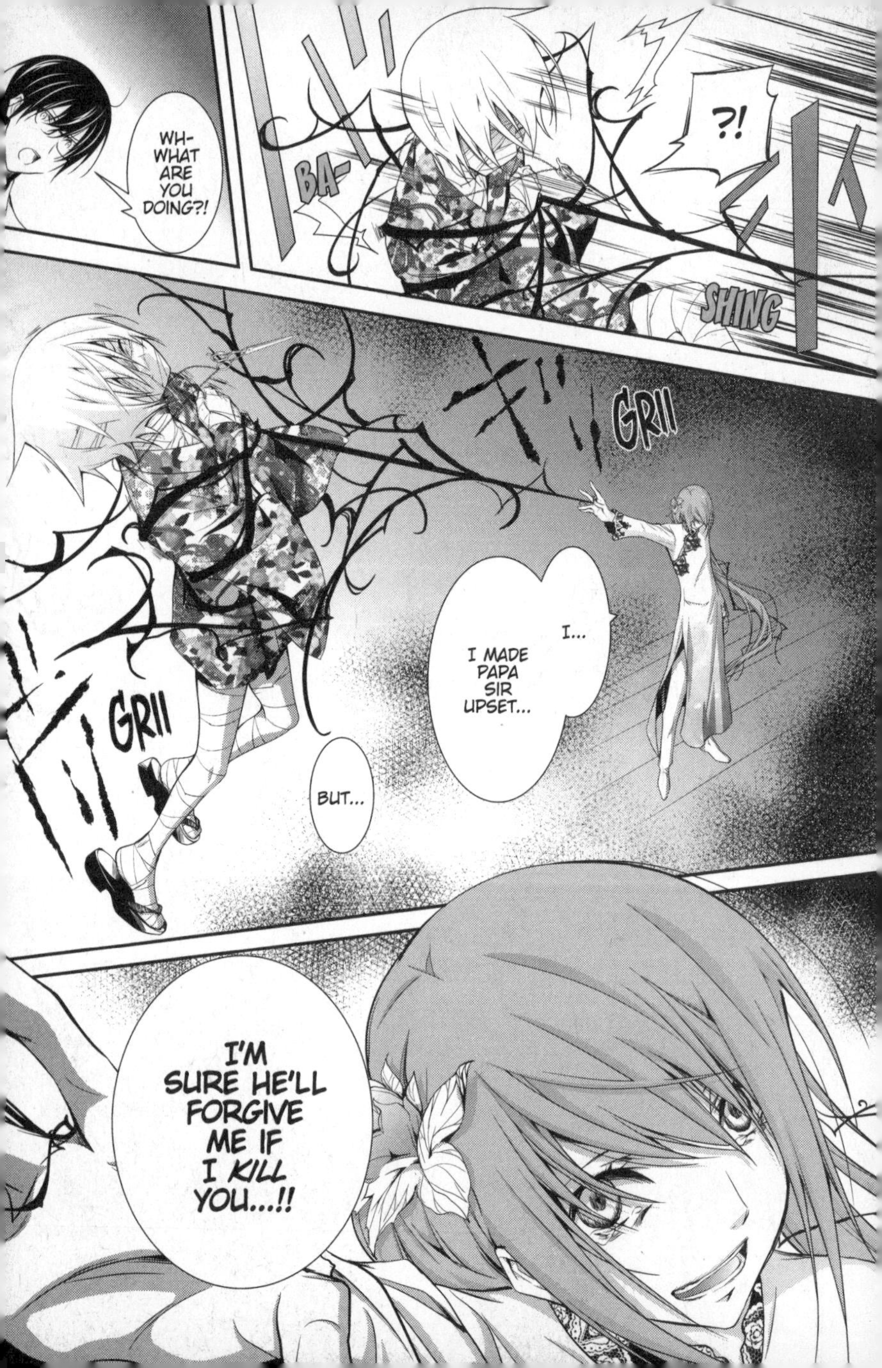
?!
BA-
SHING
WH-WHAT ARE YOU DOING?!
GRII
I...
I MADE PAPA SIR UPSET...
BUT...
GRII
I'M SURE HE'LL FORGIVE ME IF I *KILL* YOU...!!

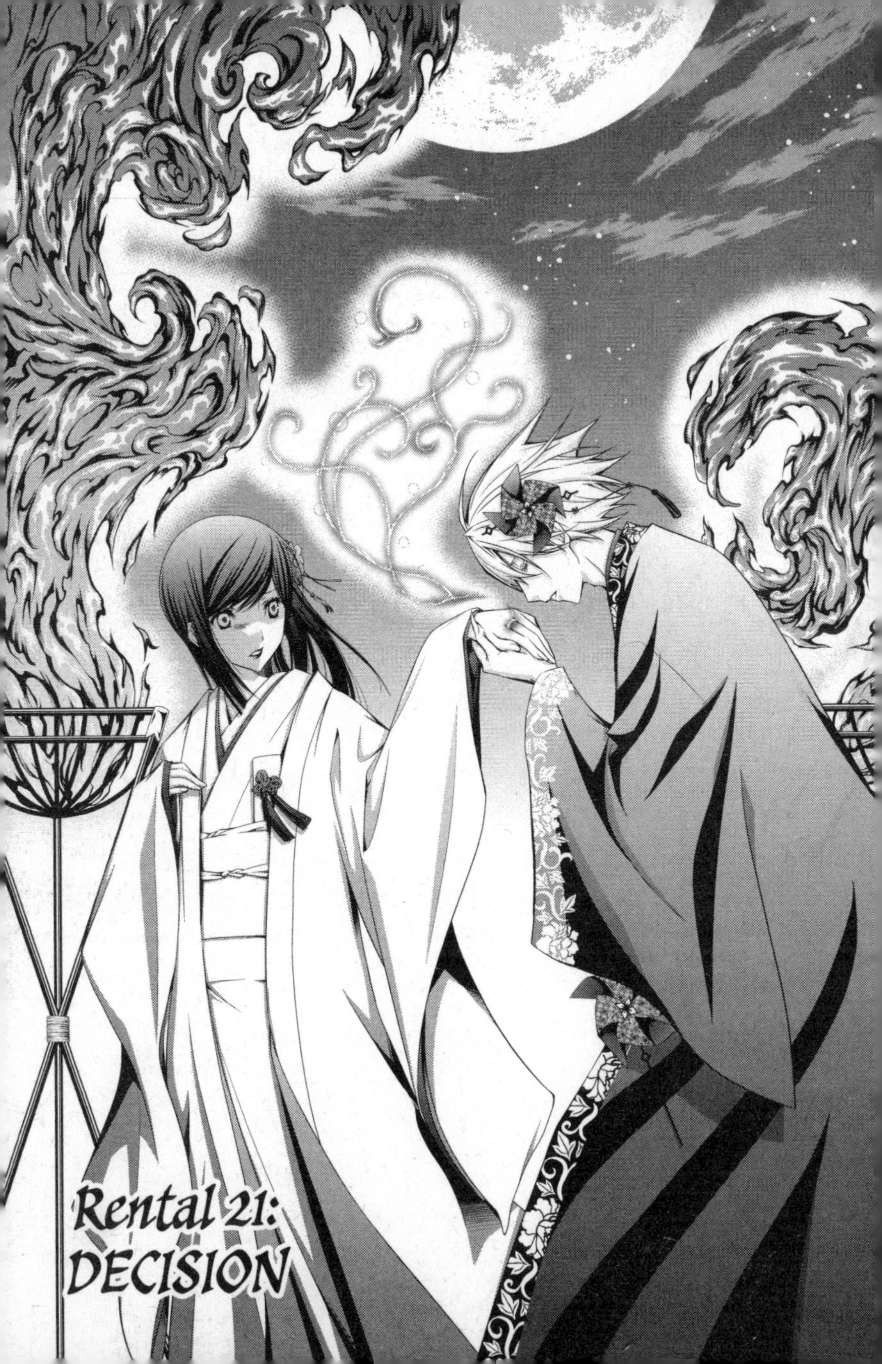
Rental 21:
DECISION

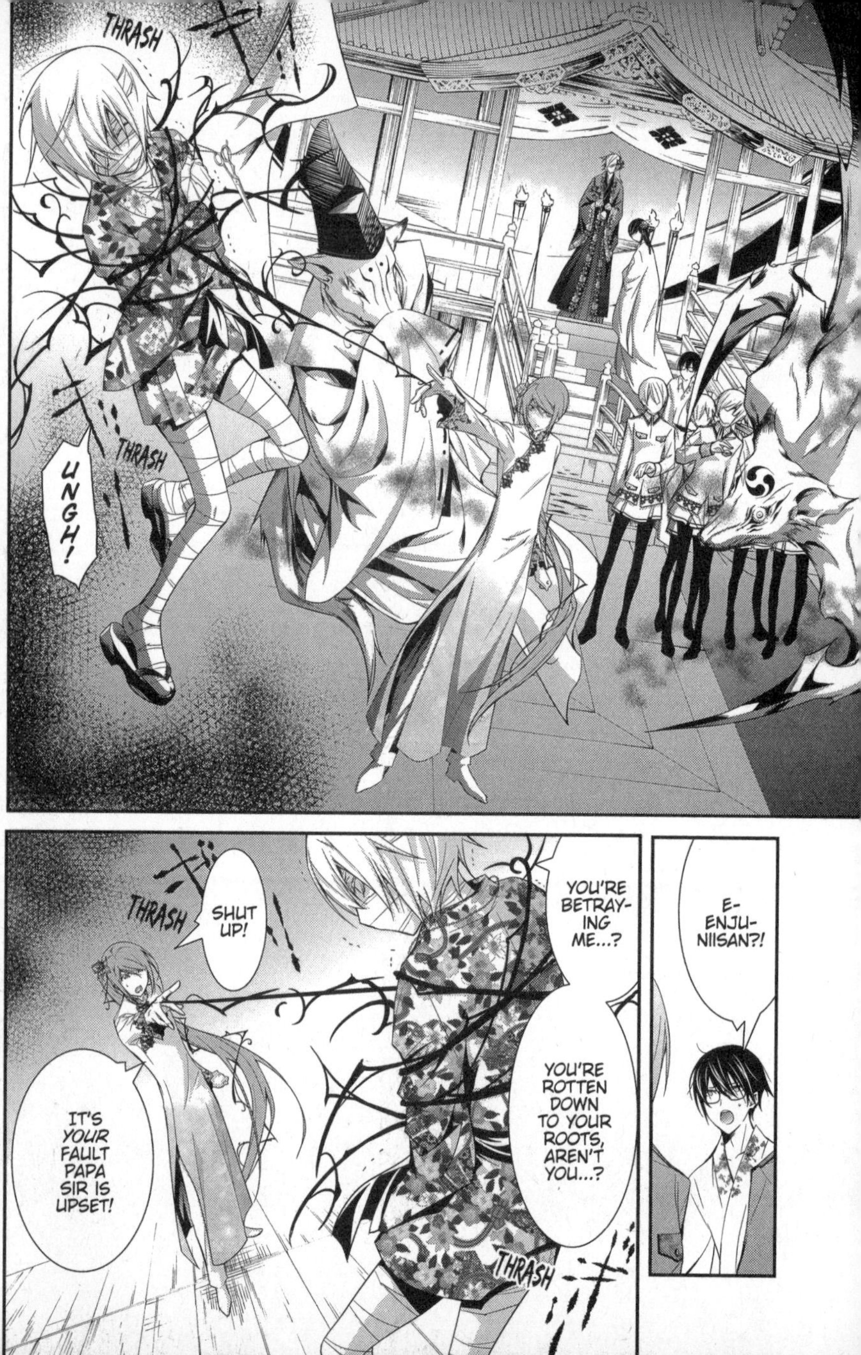
THRASH
UNGH!
THRASH
E-ENJU-NIISAN?!
YOU'RE BETRAY-ING ME...?
YOU'RE ROTTEN DOWN TO YOUR ROOTS, AREN'T YOU...?
THRASH
SHUT UP!
THRASH
IT'S *YOUR* FAULT PAPA SIR IS UPSET!
THRASH

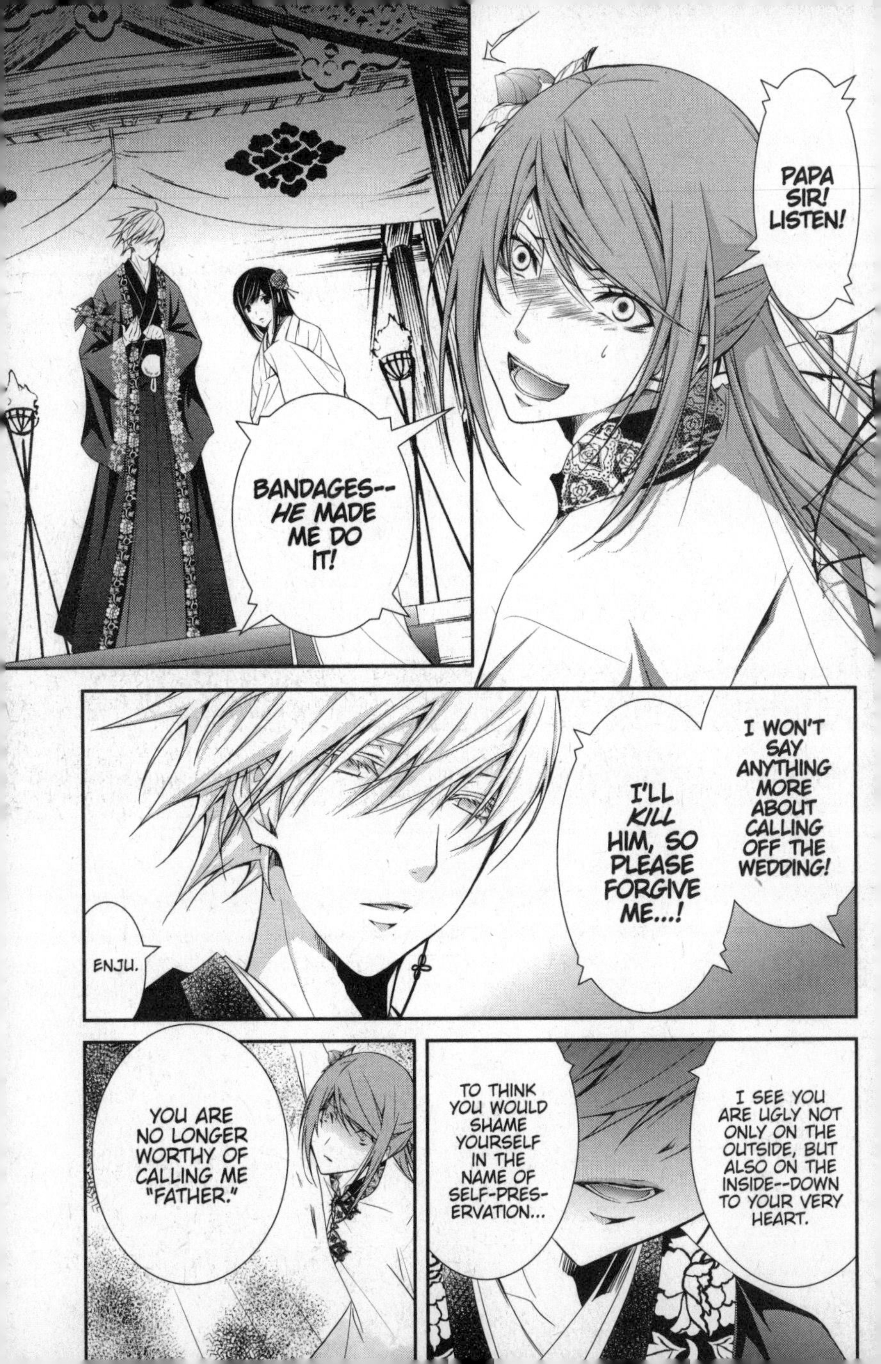
PAPA SIR! LISTEN!
BANDAGES-- HE MADE ME DO IT!
I WON'T SAY ANYTHING MORE ABOUT CALLING OFF THE WEDDING!
I'LL *KILL* HIM, SO PLEASE FORGIVE ME...!
ENJU.
I SEE YOU ARE UGLY NOT ONLY ON THE OUTSIDE, BUT ALSO ON THE INSIDE--DOWN TO YOUR VERY HEART.
TO THINK YOU WOULD SHAME YOURSELF IN THE NAME OF SELF-PRESERVATION...
YOU ARE NO LONGER WORTHY OF CALLING ME "FATHER."

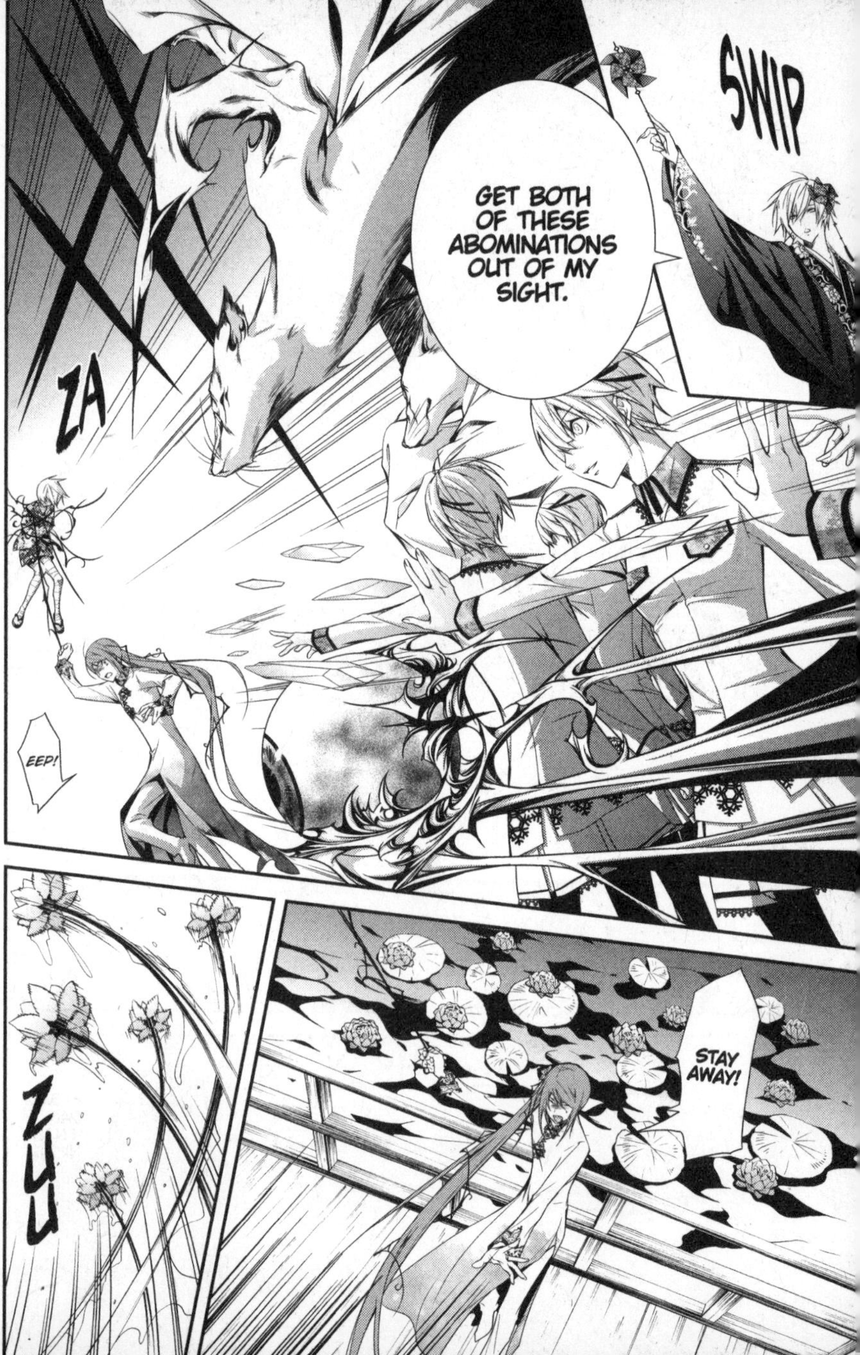
SWIP
GET BOTH OF THESE ABOMINATIONS OUT OF MY SIGHT.
ZA
EEP!
STAY AWAY!
ZUU

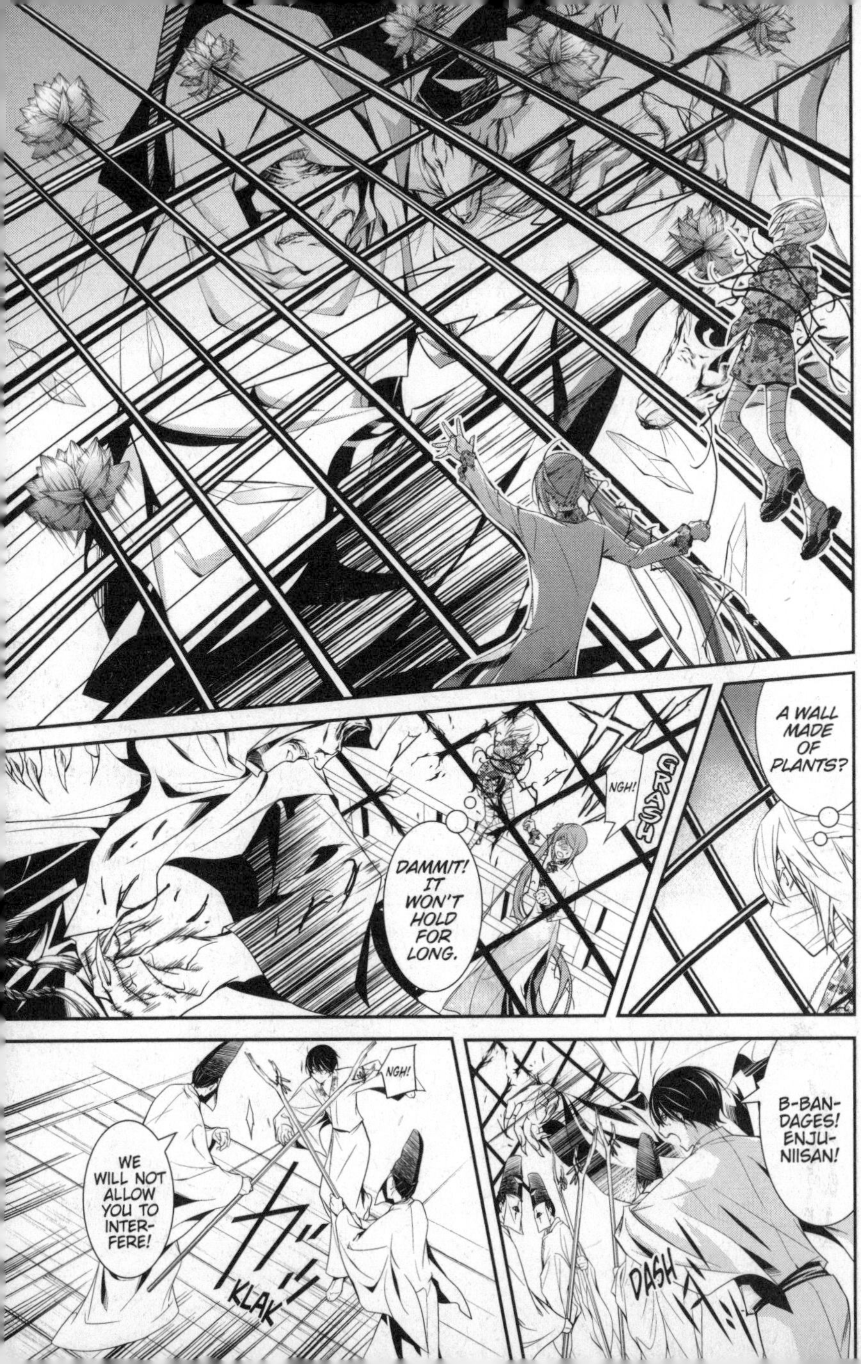
A WALL MADE OF PLANTS?
GRASH
NGH!
DAMMIT! IT WON'T HOLD FOR LONG.
B-BANDAGES! ENJU-NIISAN!
DASH
NGH!
WE WILL NOT ALLOW YOU TO INTERFERE!
KLAK

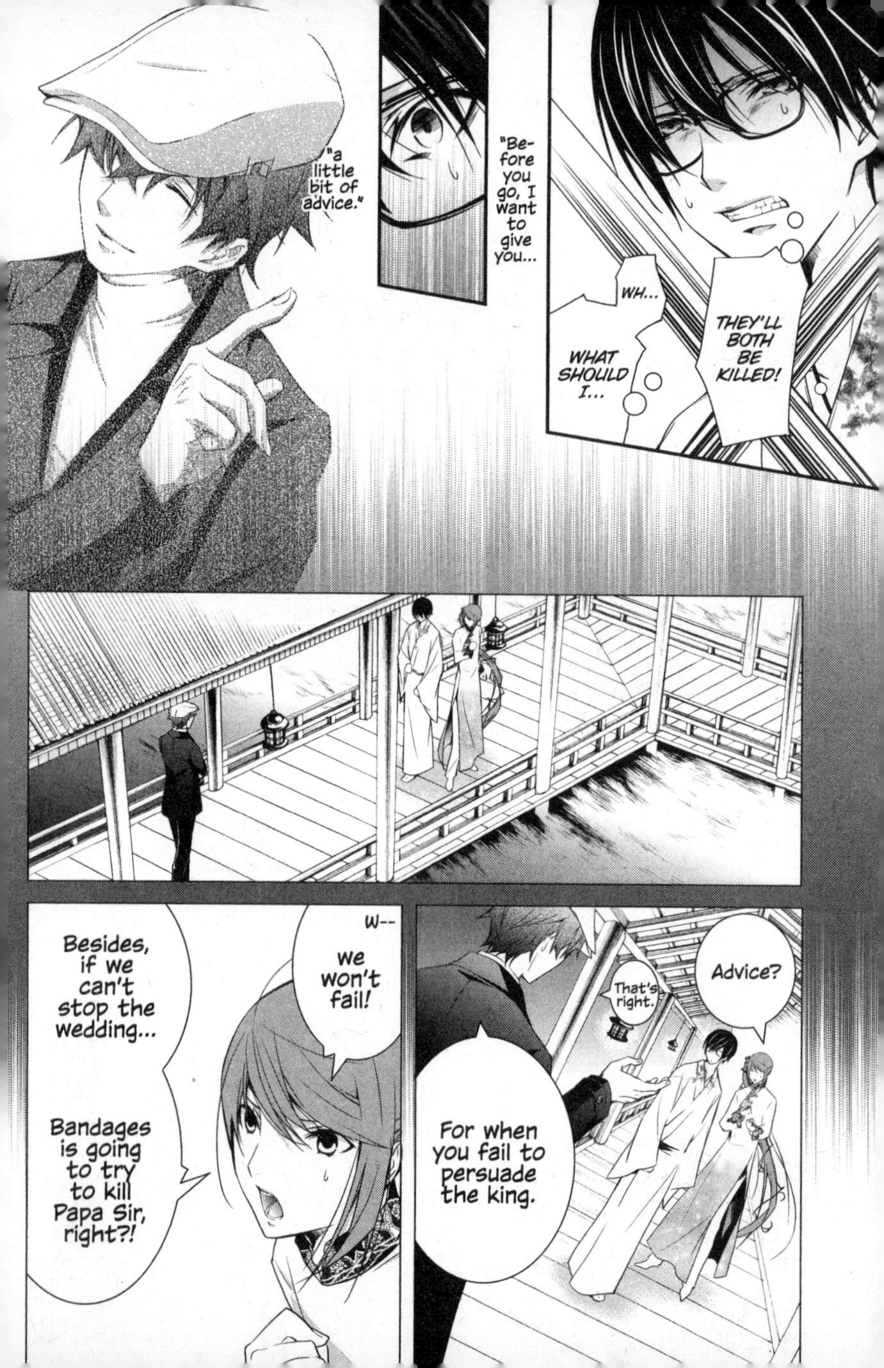
THEY'LL BOTH BE KILLED!
WH...
WHAT SHOULD I...
"Be-fore you go, I want to give you...
"a little bit of advice."
Advice?
That's right.
For when you fail to persuade the king.
W--
we won't fail!
Besides, if we can't stop the wedding...
Bandages is going to try to kill Papa Sir, right?!

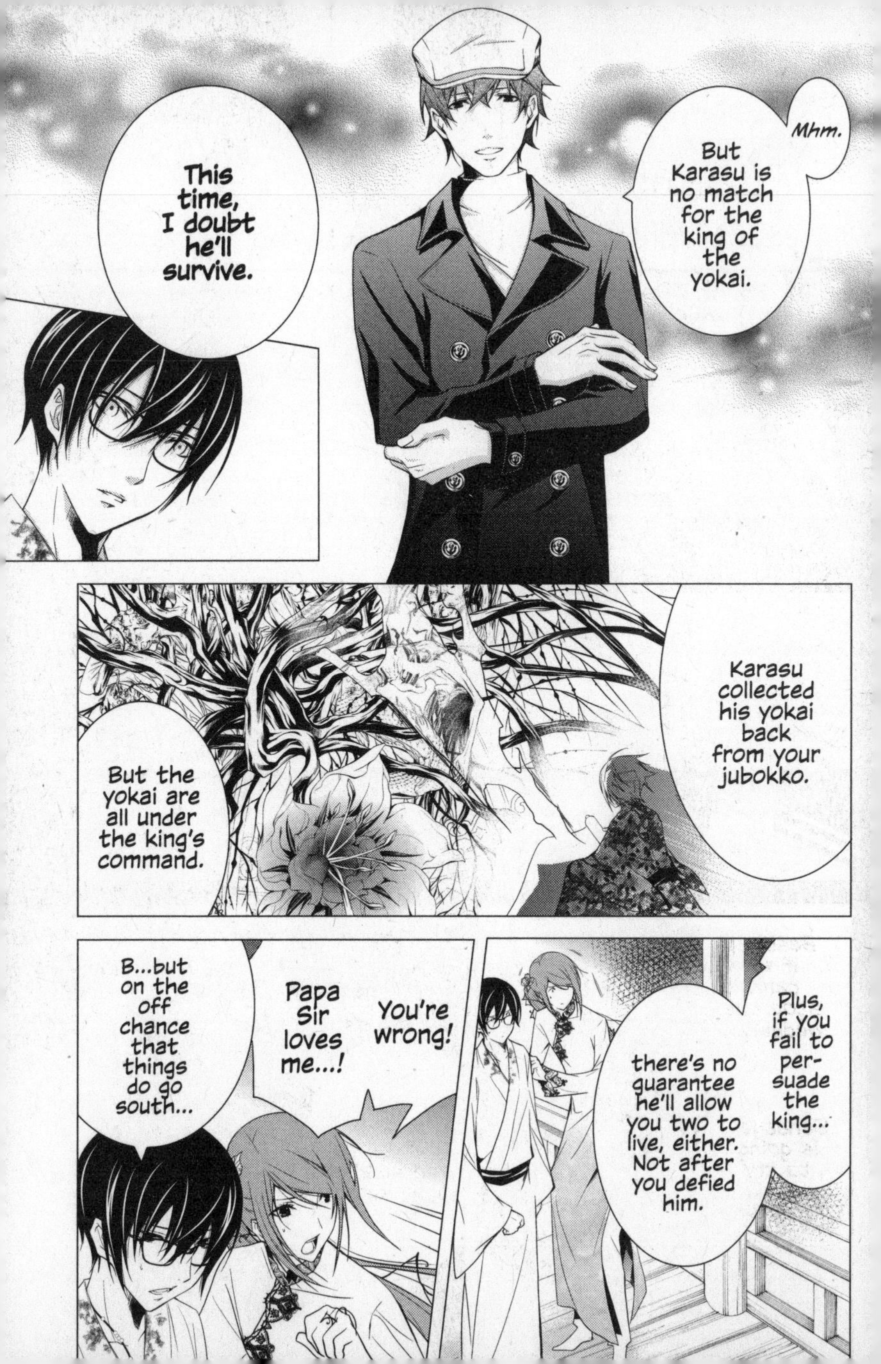
Mhm.
But Karasu is no match for the king of the yokai.
This time, I doubt he'll survive.
Karasu collected his yokai back from your jubokko.
But the yokai are all under the king's command.
Plus, if you fail to persuade the king...
there's no guarantee he'll allow you two to live, either. Not after you defied him.
You're wrong!
Papa Sir loves me...!
B...but on the off chance that things do go south...

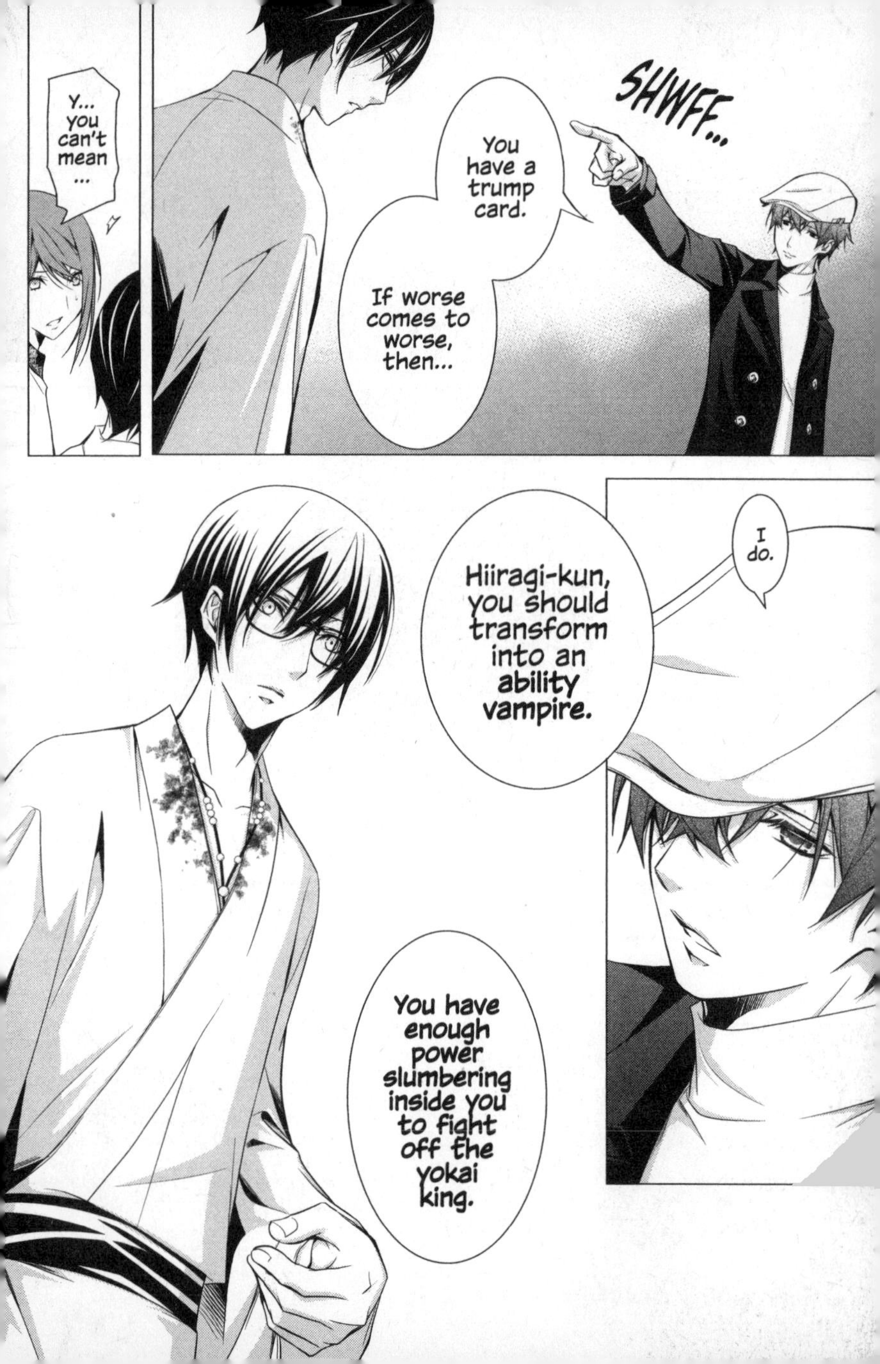

SHWFF...
You have a trump card.
If worse comes to worse, then...
Y... you can't mean...
I do.
Hiiragi-kun, you should transform into an ability vampire.
You have enough power slumbering inside you to fight off the yokai king.

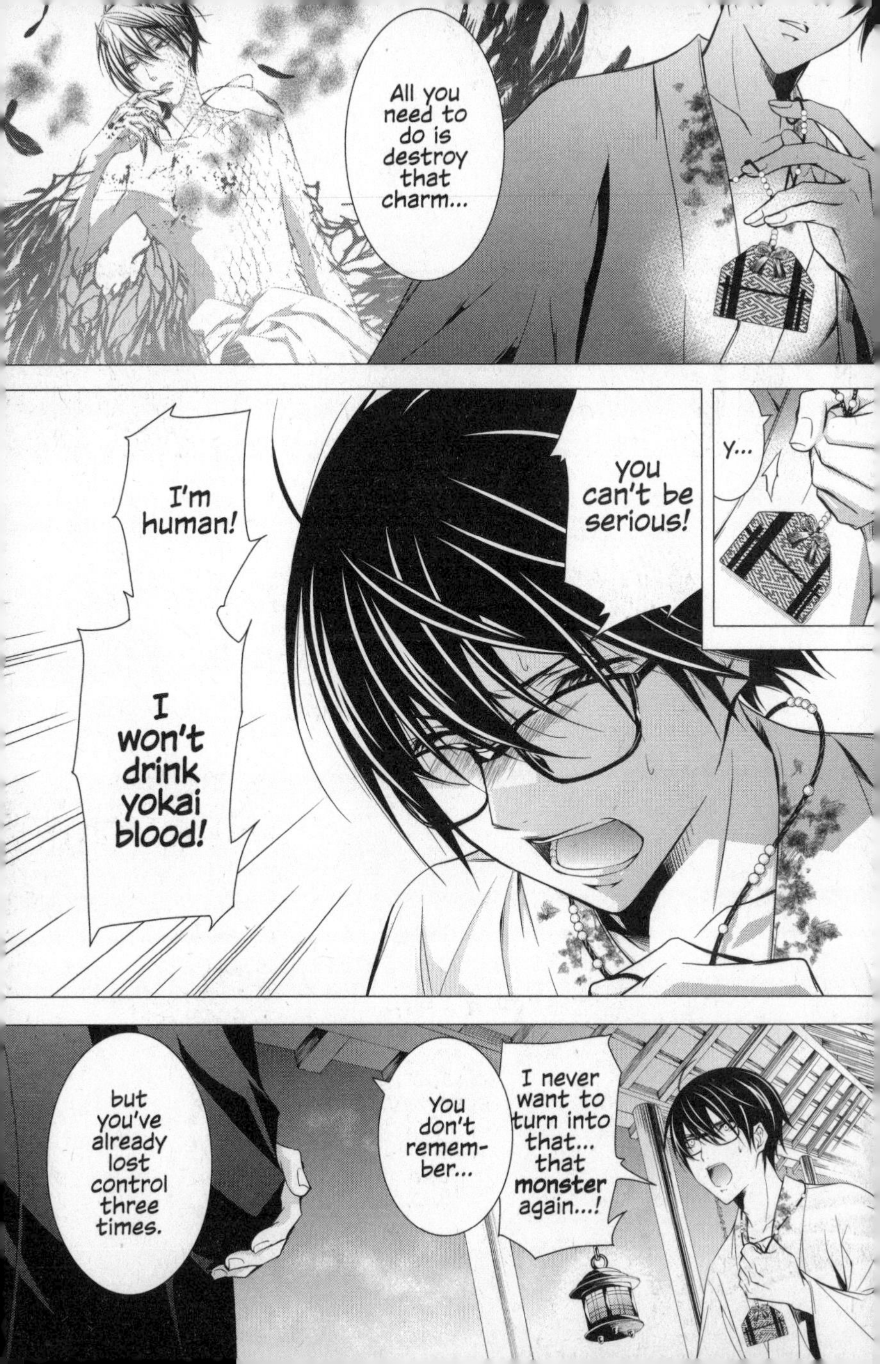
All you need to do is destroy that charm...
Y...
you can't be serious!
I'm human!
I won't drink yokai blood!
I never want to turn into that... that **monster** again...!
You don't remember...
but you've already lost control three times.

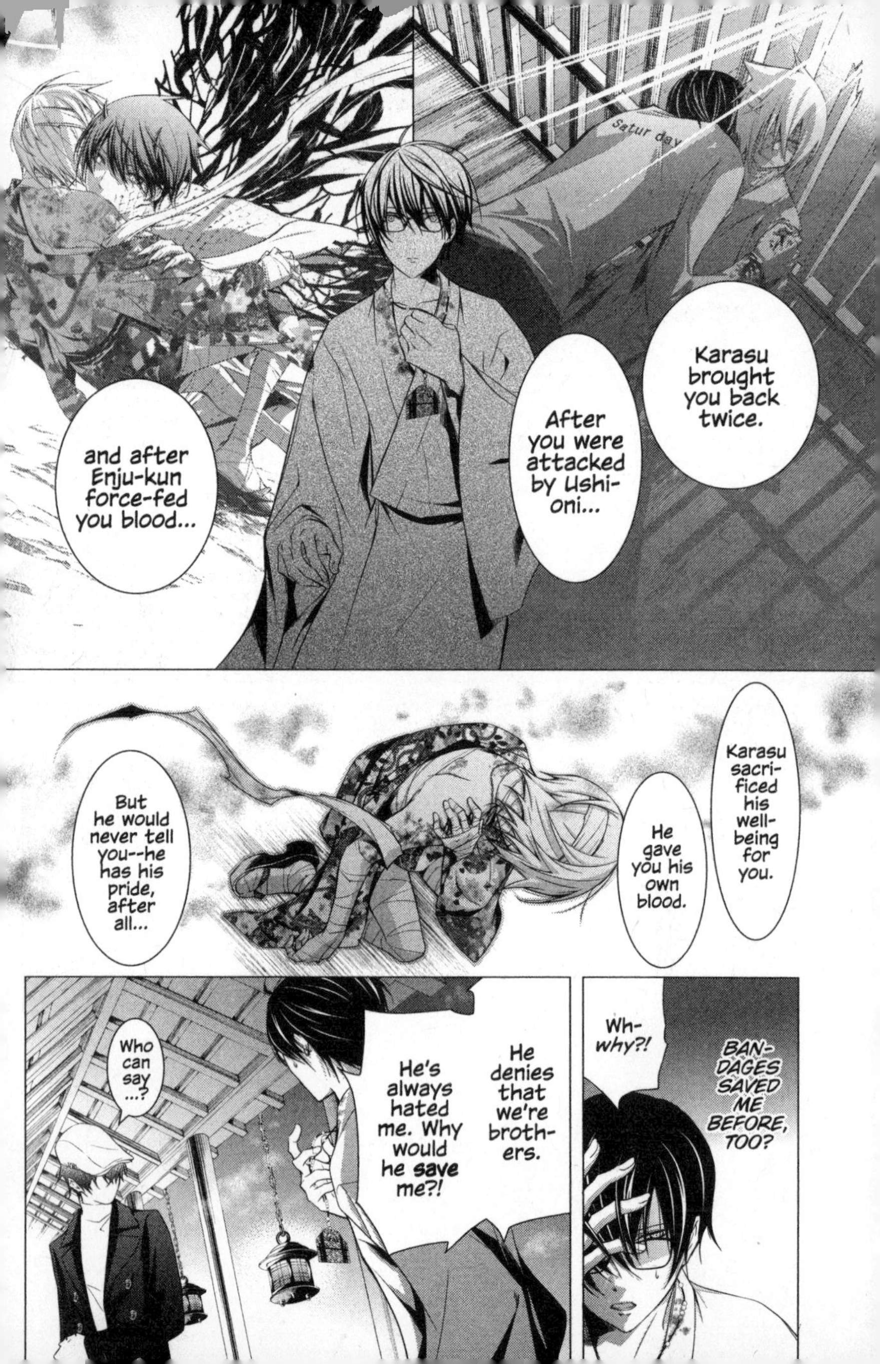
Satur day
Karasu brought you back twice.
After you were attacked by Ushi-oni...
and after Enju-kun force-fed you blood...
Karasu sacrificed his well-being for you.
He gave you his own blood.
But he would never tell you--he has his pride, after all...
Wh-why?!
BANDAGES SAVED ME BEFORE, TOO?
He denies that we're brothers.
He's always hated me. Why would he save me?!
Who can say ...?

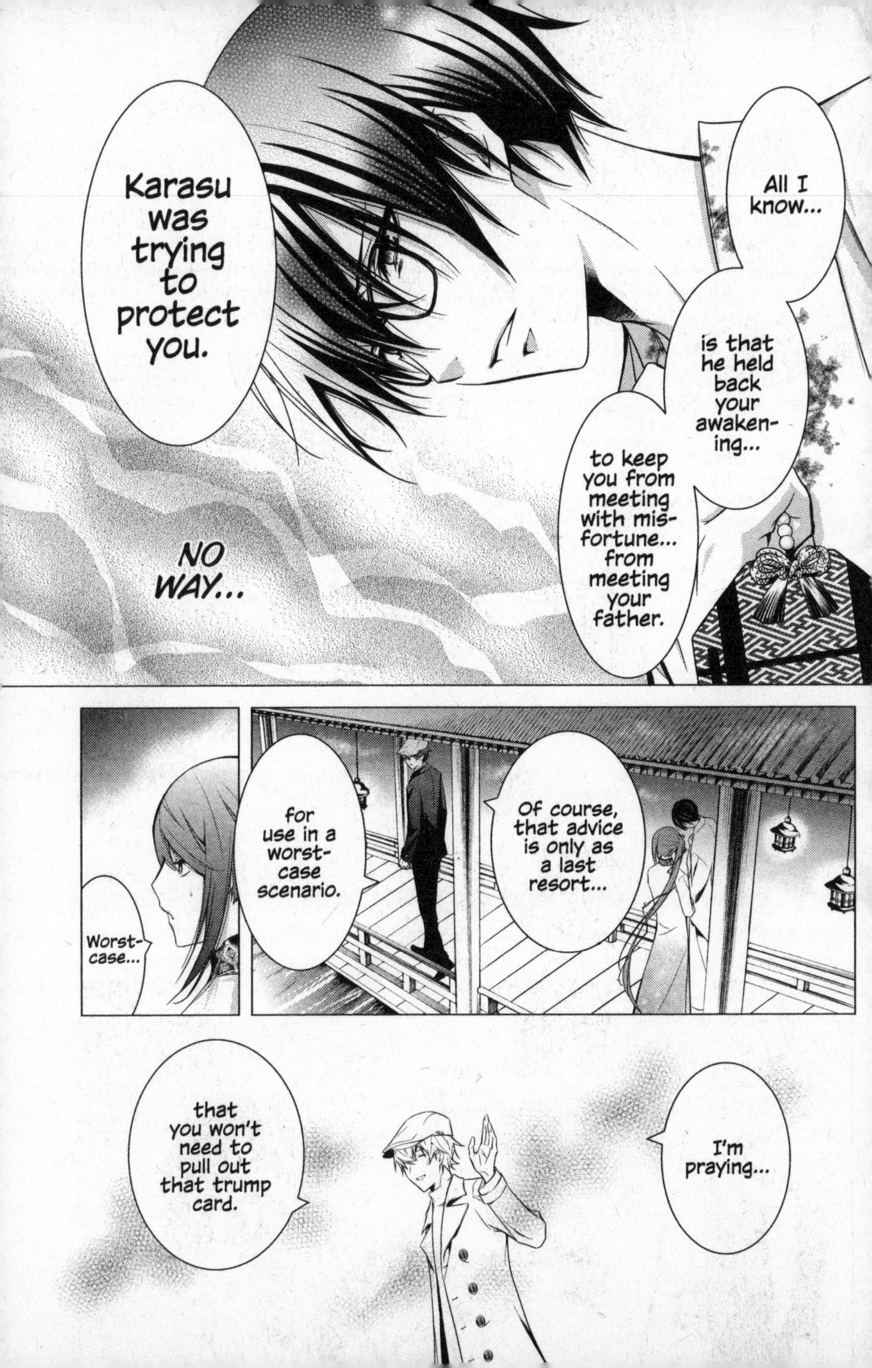
All I know...
is that he held back your awaken-ing...
to keep you from meeting with mis-fortune... from meeting your father.
Karasu was trying to protect you.
NO WAY...
Of course, that advice is only as a last resort...
for use in a worst-case scenario.
Worst-case...
I'm praying...
that you won't need to pull out that trump card.

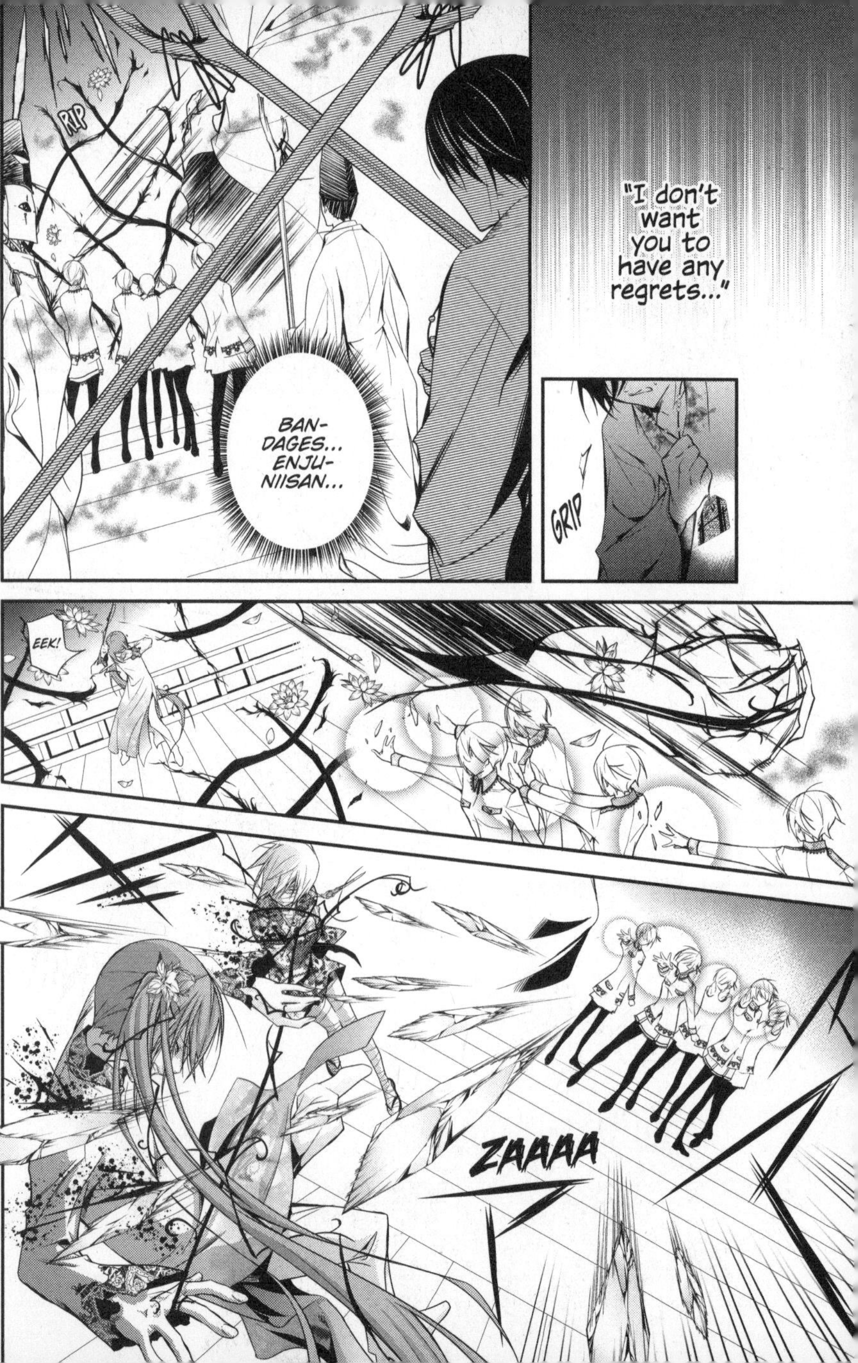
"I don't want you to have any regrets..."
GRIP
RIP
BAN-DAGES... ENJU-NIISAN...
EEK!
ZAAAA

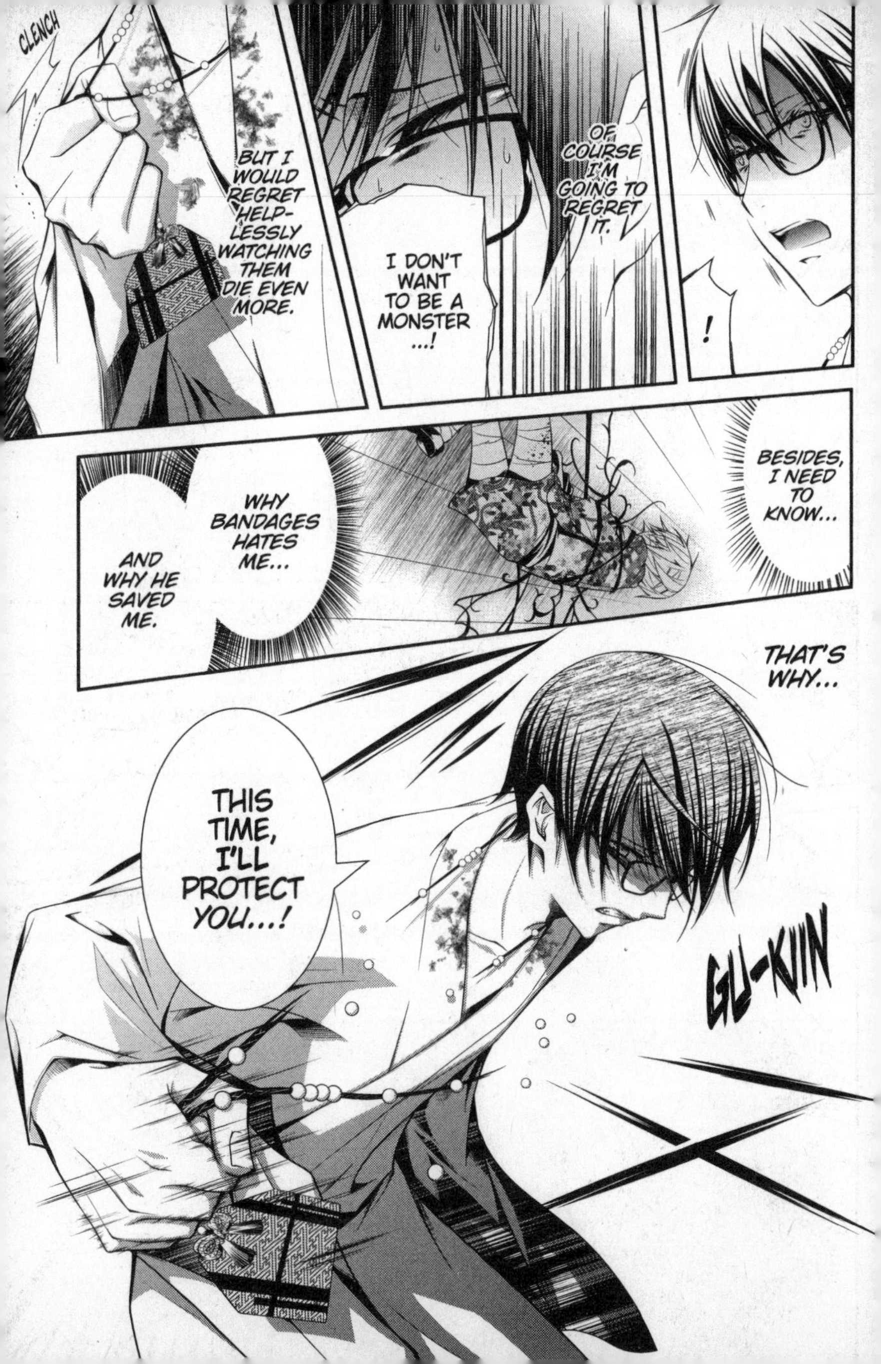
OF COURSE I'M GOING TO REGRET IT.
!
I DON'T WANT TO BE A MONSTER ...!
CLENCH
BUT I WOULD REGRET HELP-LESSLY WATCHING THEM DIE EVEN MORE.
BESIDES, I NEED TO KNOW...
WHY BANDAGES HATES ME...
AND WHY HE SAVED ME.
THAT'S WHY...
THIS TIME, I'LL PROTECT YOU...!
GU-KIIN

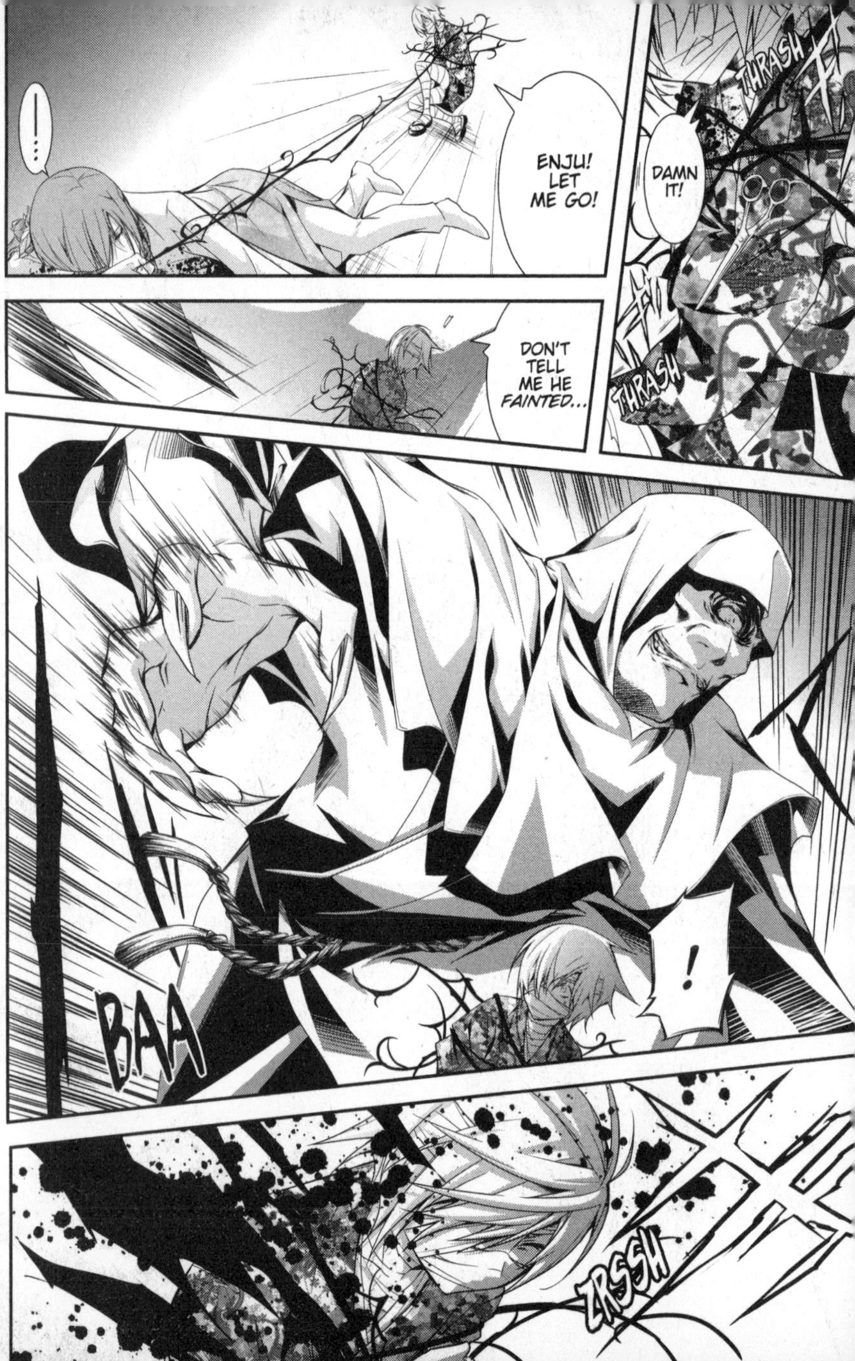
THRASH
DAMN IT!
THRASH
ENJU! LET ME GO!
!...
DON'T TELL ME HE FAINTED...
!
BAA
ZRSSH

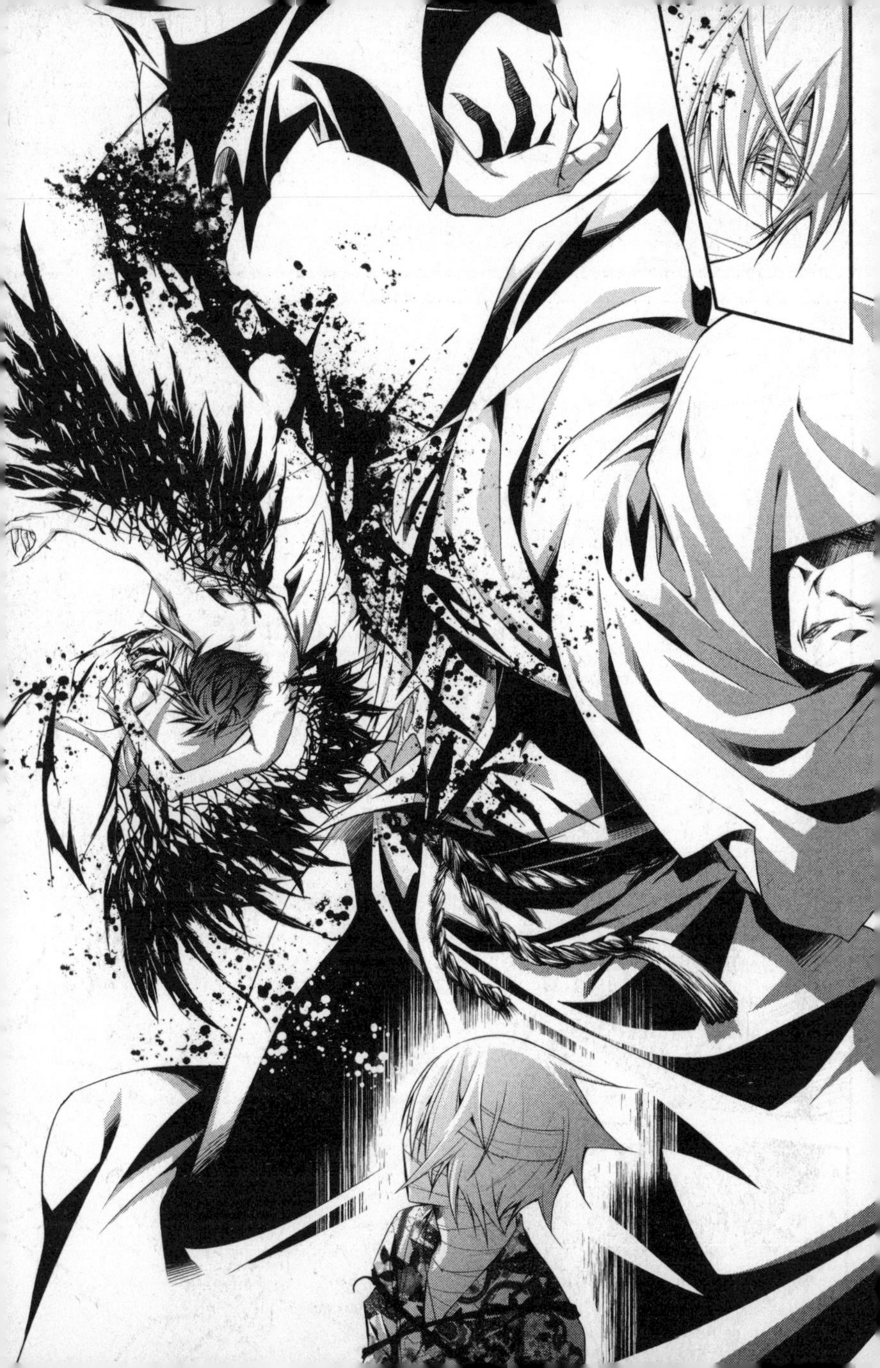

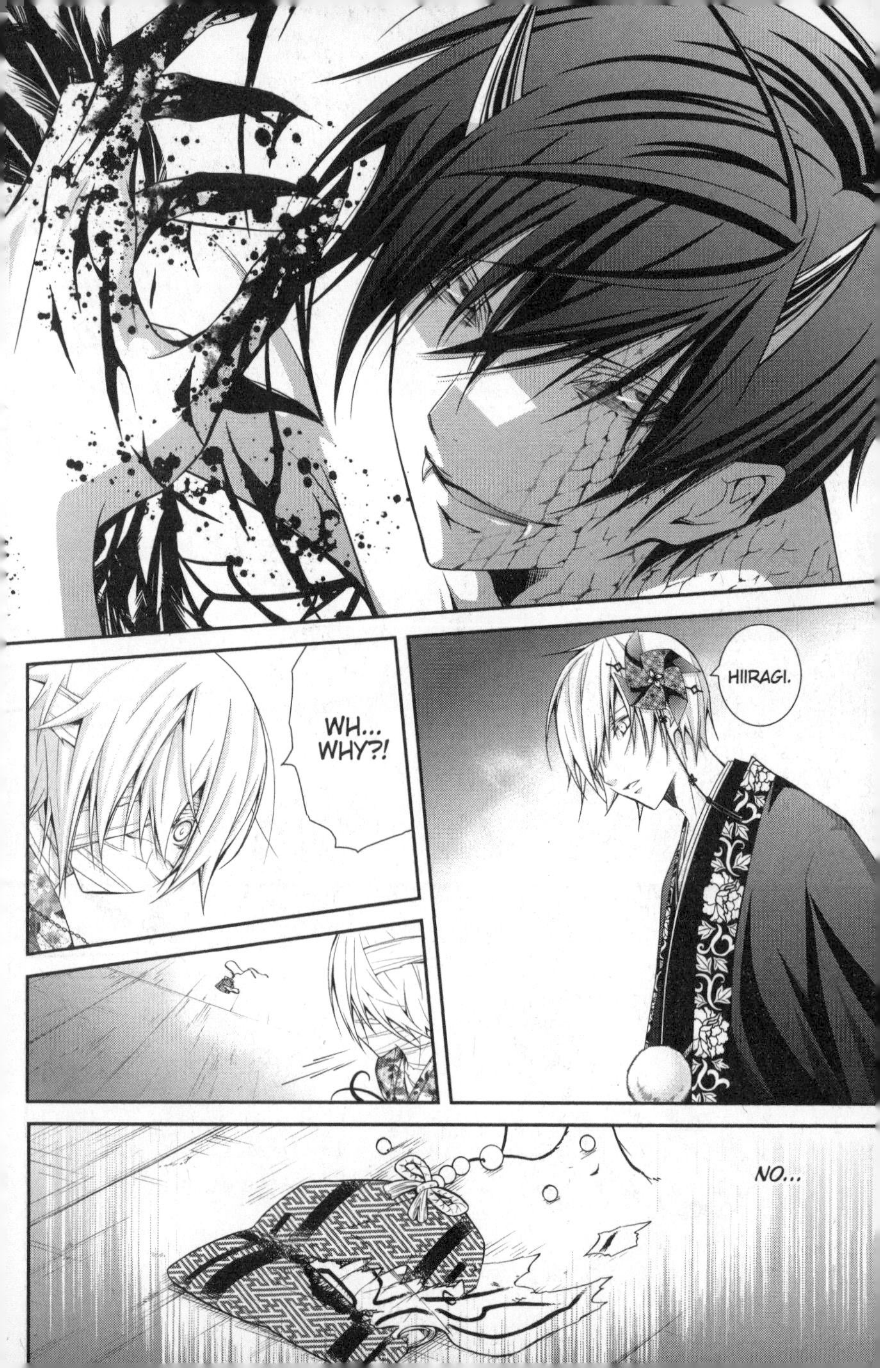
HIIRAGI.
WH... WHY?!
NO...

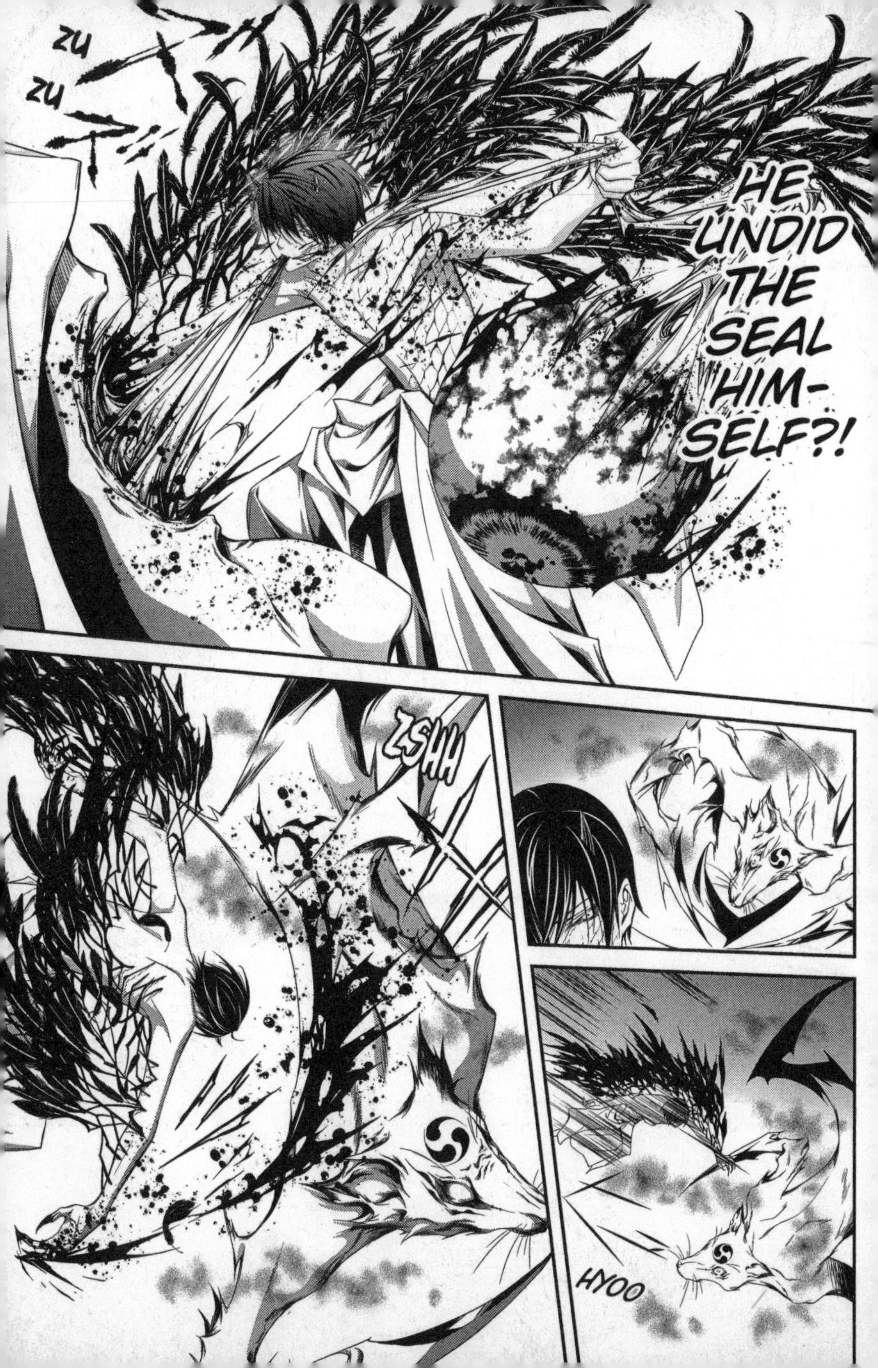
HE UNDID THE SEAL HIM-SELF?!
ZU
ZU
HYOO
ZSHH

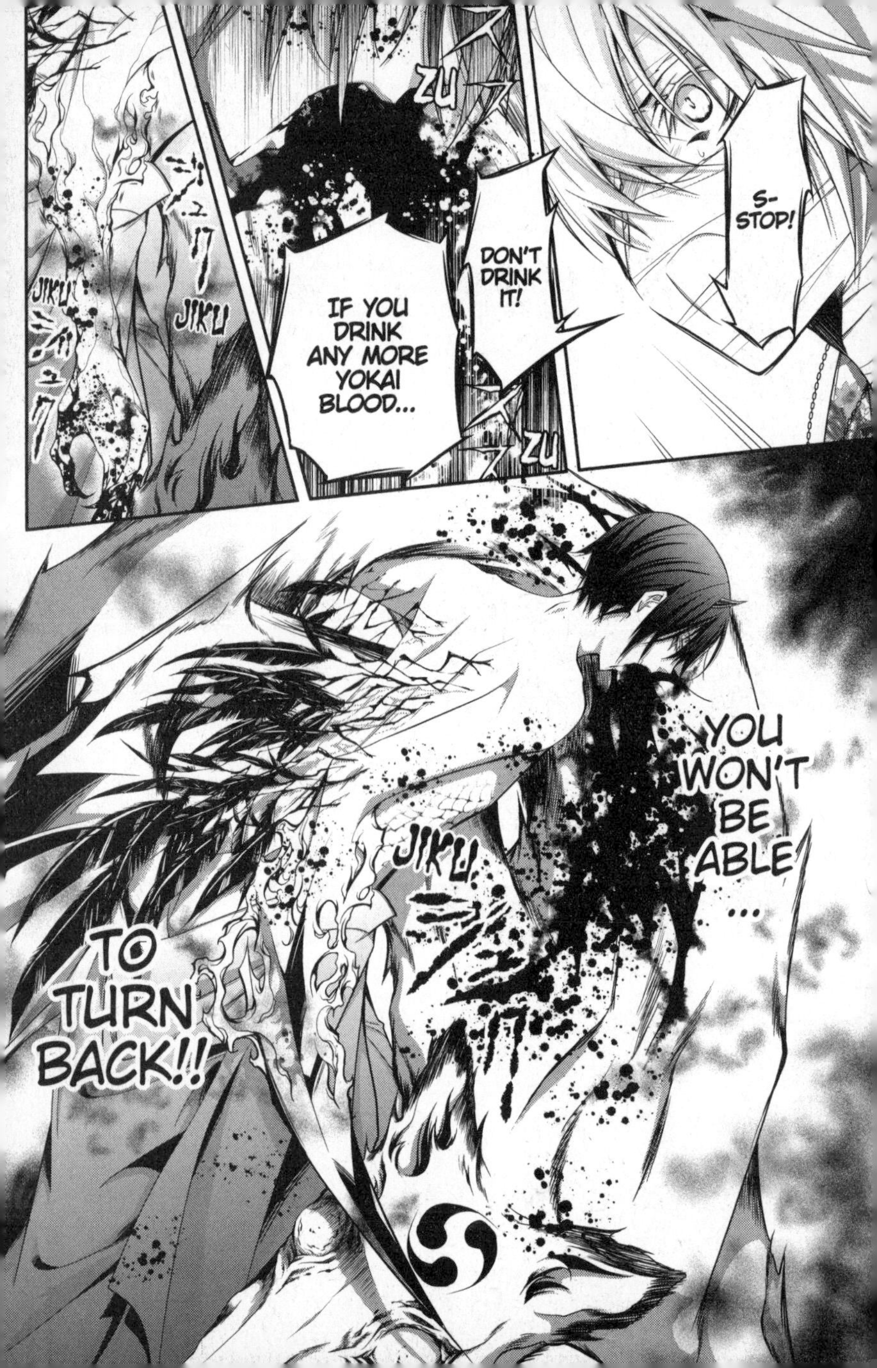
S-STOP!
DON'T DRINK IT!
IF YOU DRINK ANY MORE YOKAI BLOOD...
ZU
ZU
JIKU
JIKU
YOU WON'T BE ABLE...
JIKU
TO TURN BACK!!

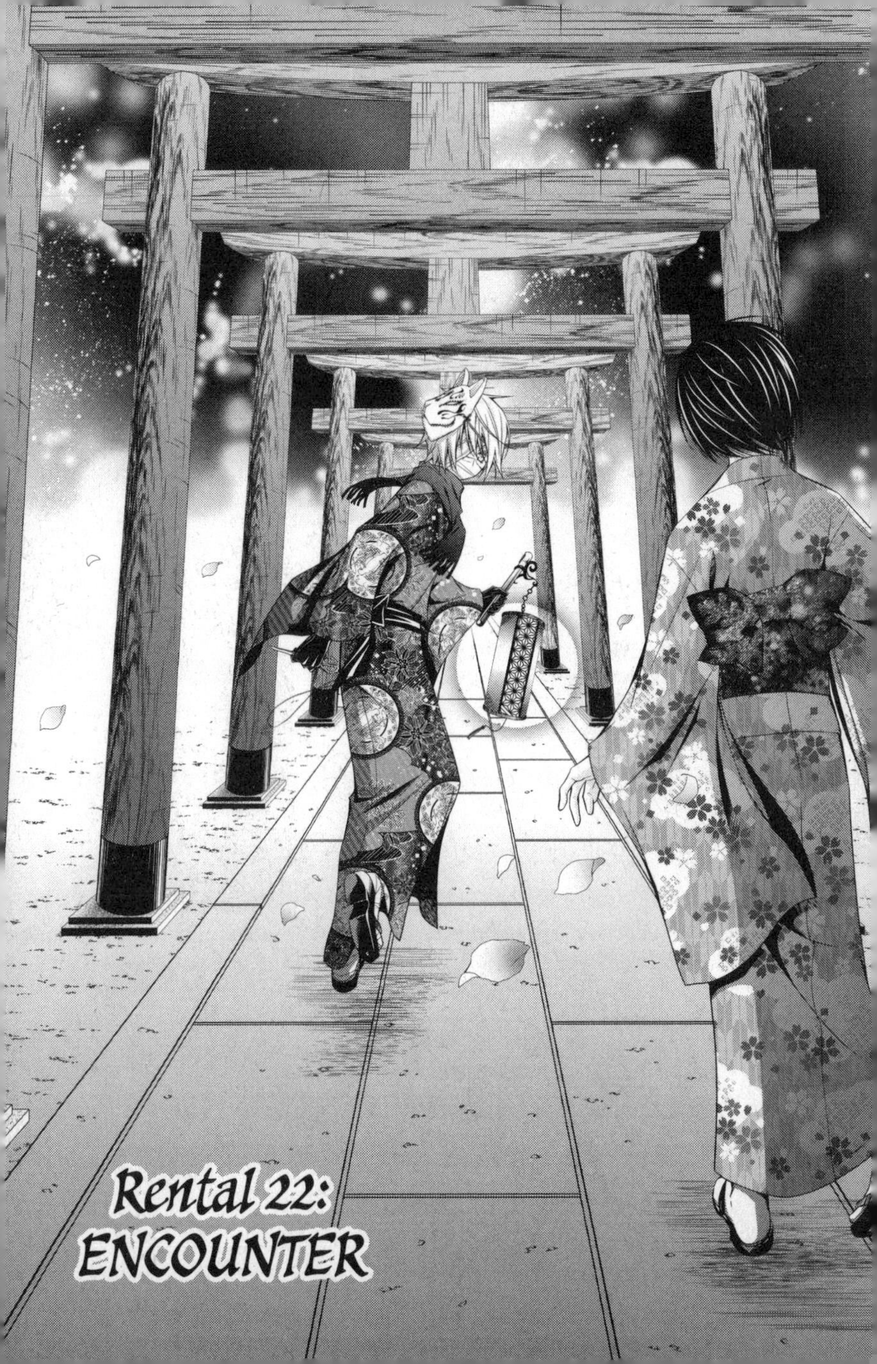
Rental 22:
ENCOUNTER

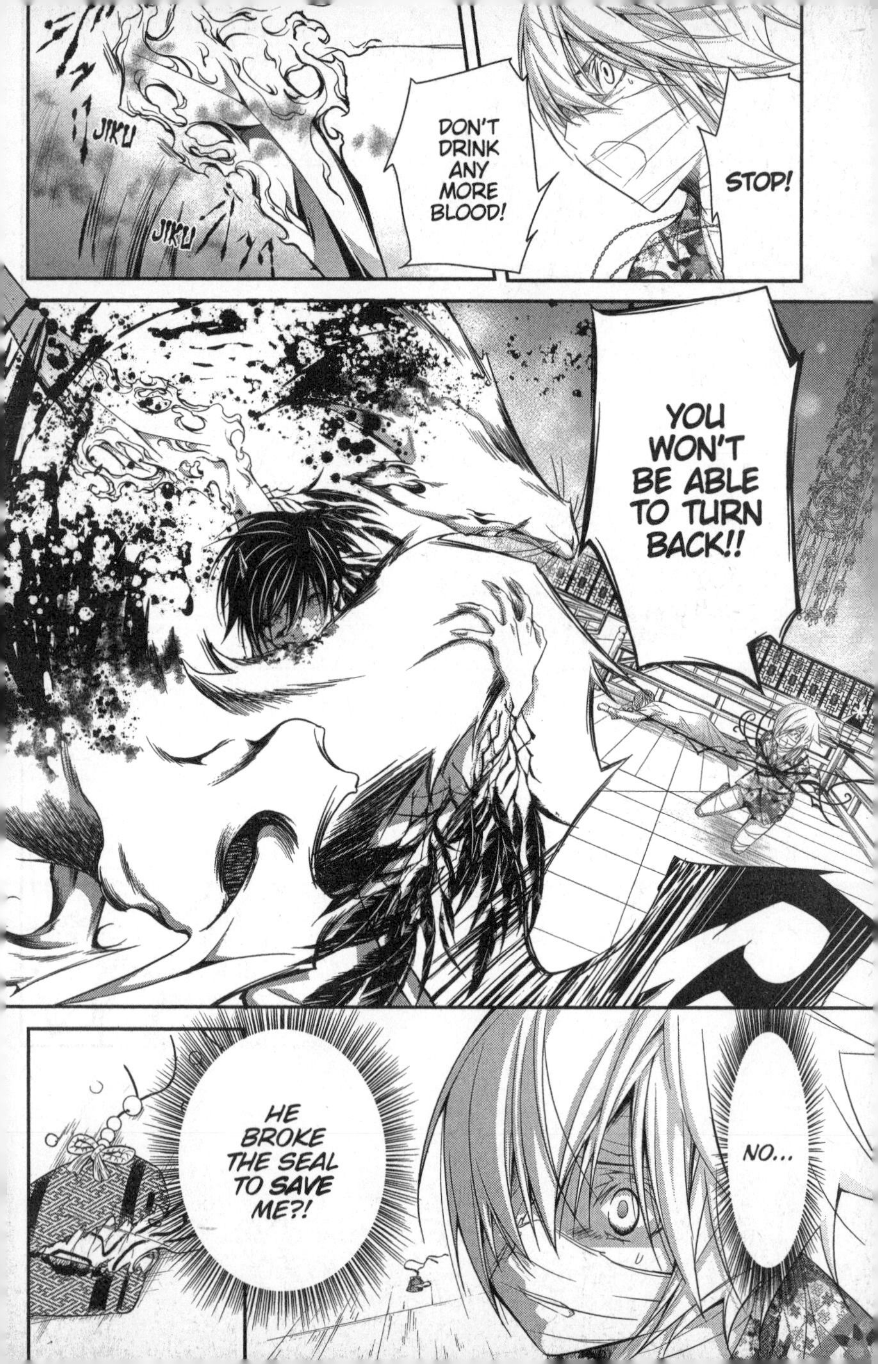
STOP!
DON'T DRINK ANY MORE BLOOD!
JIKU
JIKU
YOU WON'T BE ABLE TO TURN BACK!!
NO...
HE BROKE THE SEAL TO SAVE ME?!

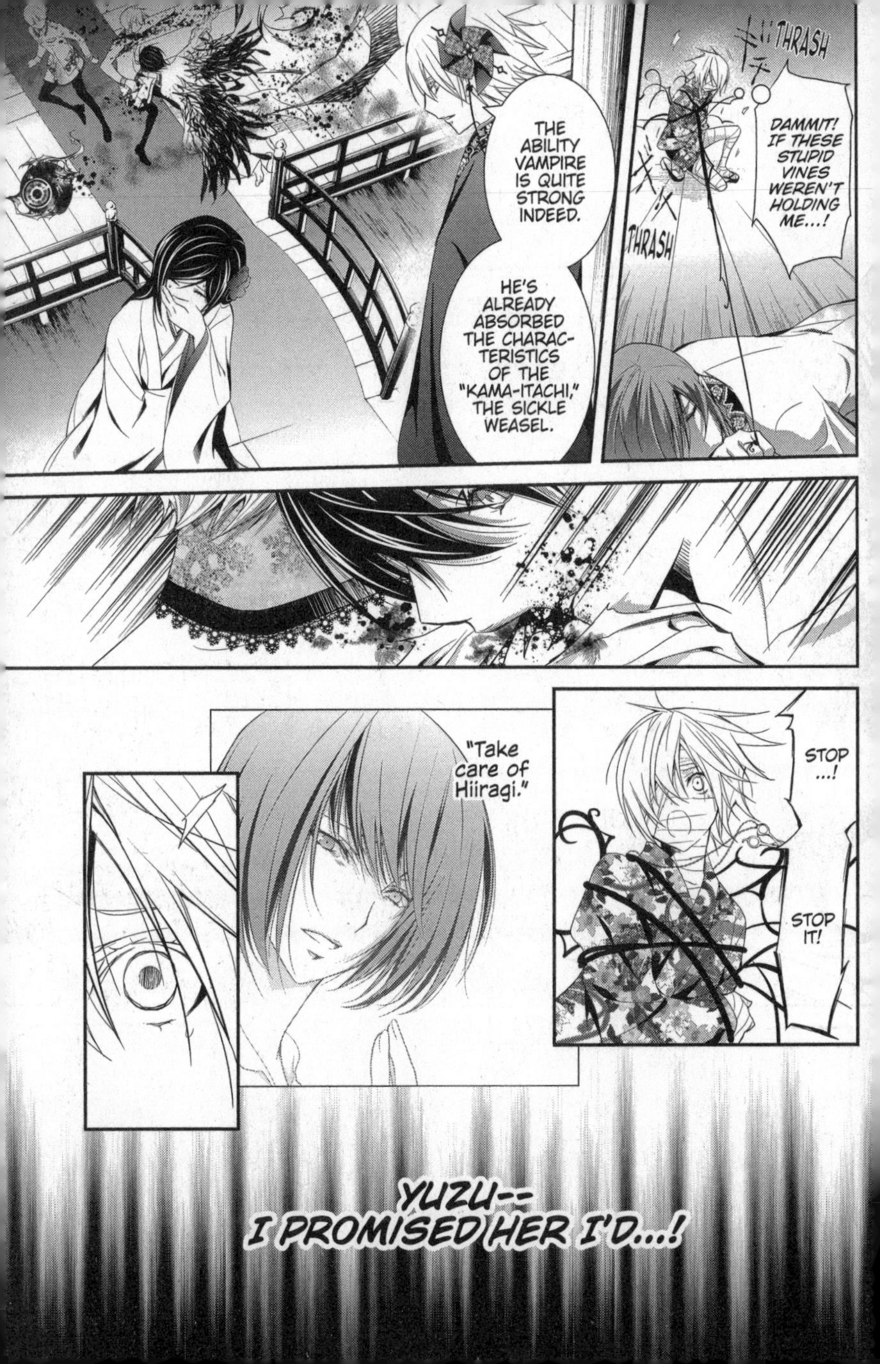
THRASH
DAMMIT! IF THESE STUPID VINES WEREN'T HOLDING ME...!
THRASH
THE ABILITY VAMPIRE IS QUITE STRONG INDEED.
HE'S ALREADY ABSORBED THE CHARACTERISTICS OF THE "KAMA-ITACHI," THE SICKLE WEASEL.
STOP ...!
STOP IT!
"Take care of Hiiragi."
YUZU--
I PROMISED HER I'D...!

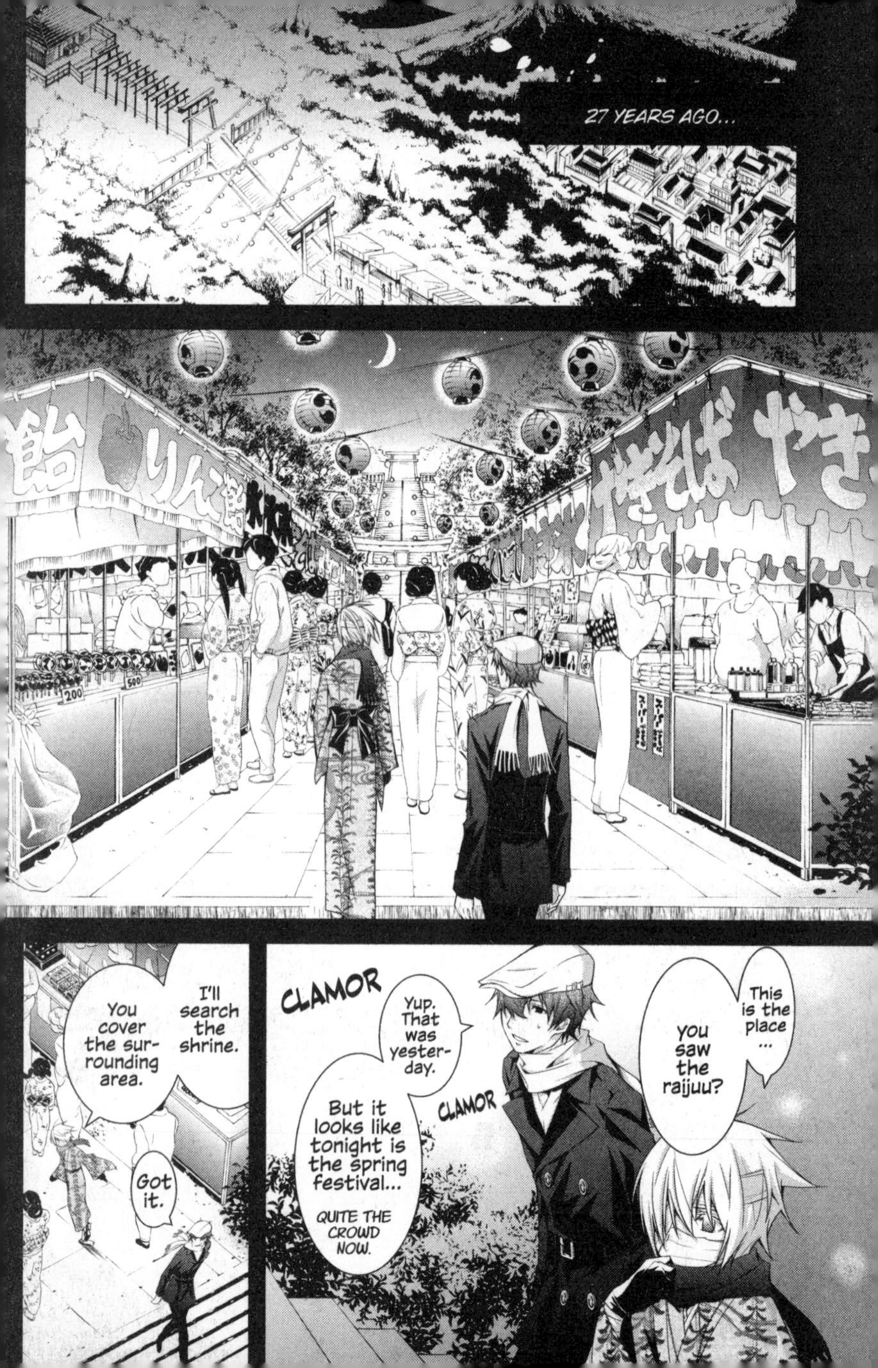
27 YEARS AGO...
This is the place ... you saw the raijuu?
Yup. That was yesterday.
CLAMOR
CLAMOR
But it looks like tonight is the spring festival...
QUITE THE CROWD NOW.
I'll search the shrine.
You cover the surrounding area.
Got it.

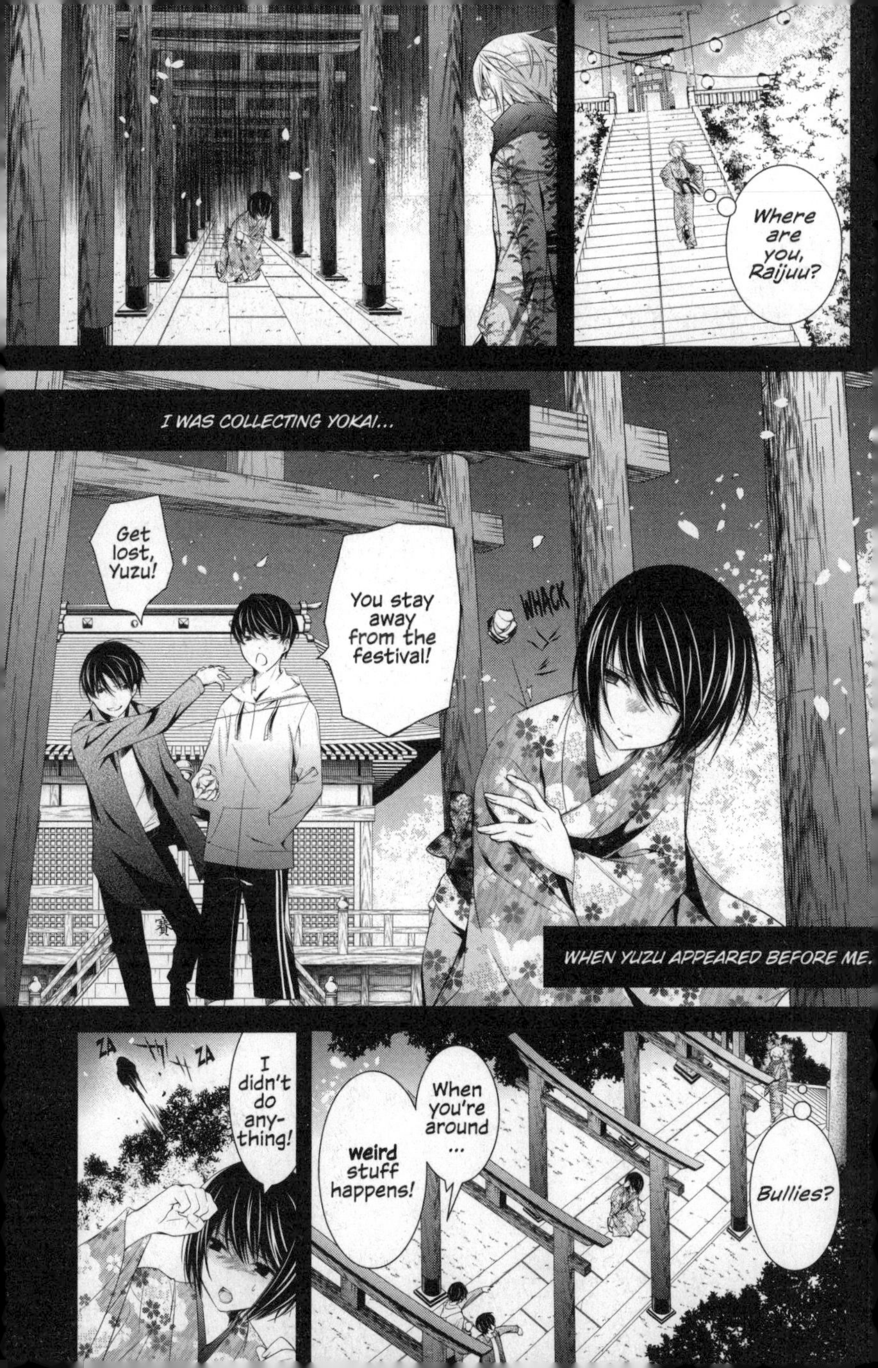

Where are you, Raijuu?
I WAS COLLECTING YOKAI...
Get lost, Yuzu!
You stay away from the festival!
WHACK
WHEN YUZU APPEARED BEFORE ME.
Bullies?
When you're around...
weird stuff happens!
I didn't do anything!
ZA
ZA

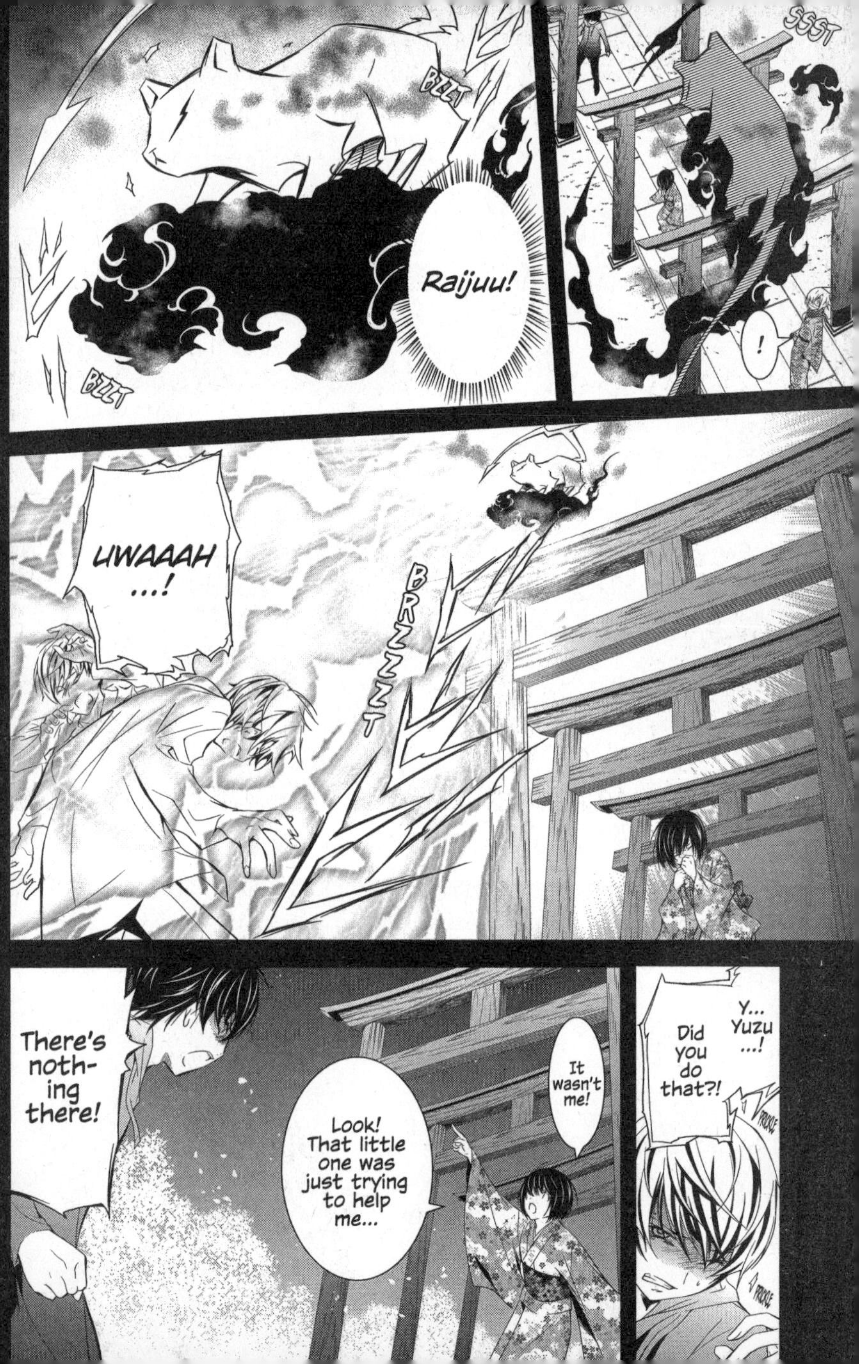
SSST
!
BZZT
Raijuu!
BZZT
UWAAAH ...!
BRZZZZT
Y... Yuzu ...!
Did you do that?!
PRICKLE
PRICKLE
It wasn't me!
Look! That little one was just trying to help me...
There's noth-ing there!

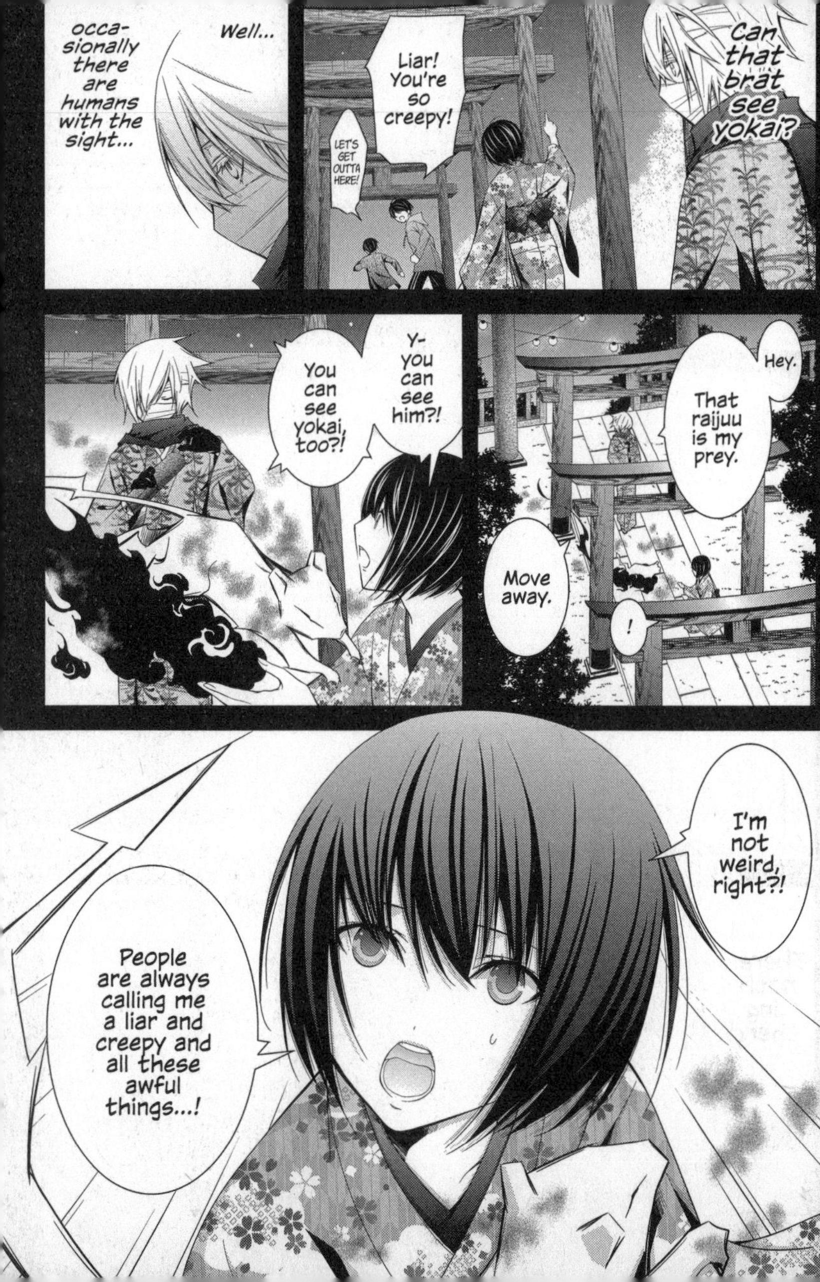
Can that brat see yokai?
Liar! You're so creepy!
LET'S GET OUTTA HERE!
Well...
occasionally there are humans with the sight...
Hey.
That raijuu is my prey.
Move away.
!
Y-you can see him?!
You can see yokai, too?!
I'm not weird, right?!
People are always calling me a liar and creepy and all these awful things...!

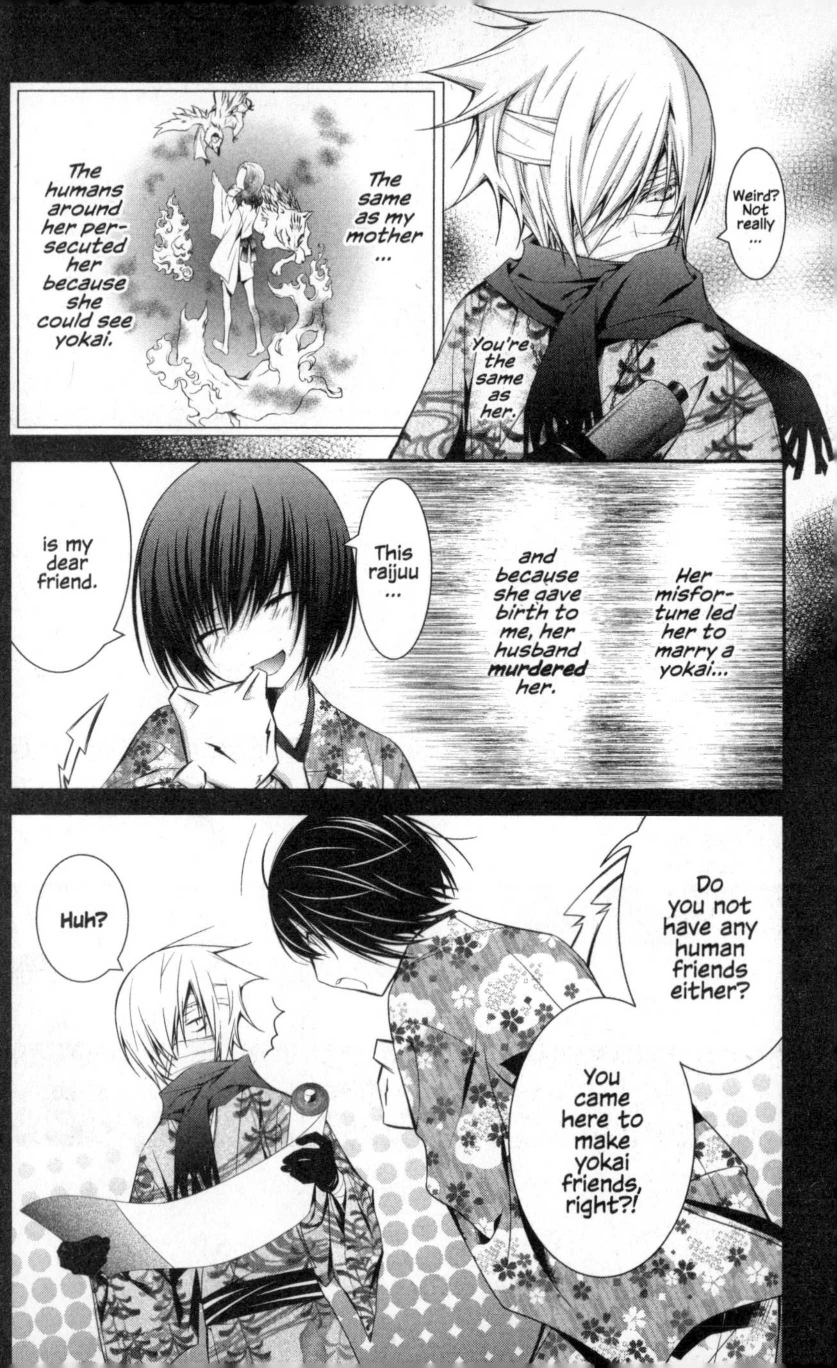
Weird? Not really ...
You're the same as her.
The same as my mother ...
The humans around her persecuted her because she could see yokai.
Her misfortune led her to marry a yokai...
and because she gave birth to me, her husband murdered her.
This raijuu ...
is my dear friend.
Do you not have any human friends either?
You came here to make yokai friends, right?!
Huh?

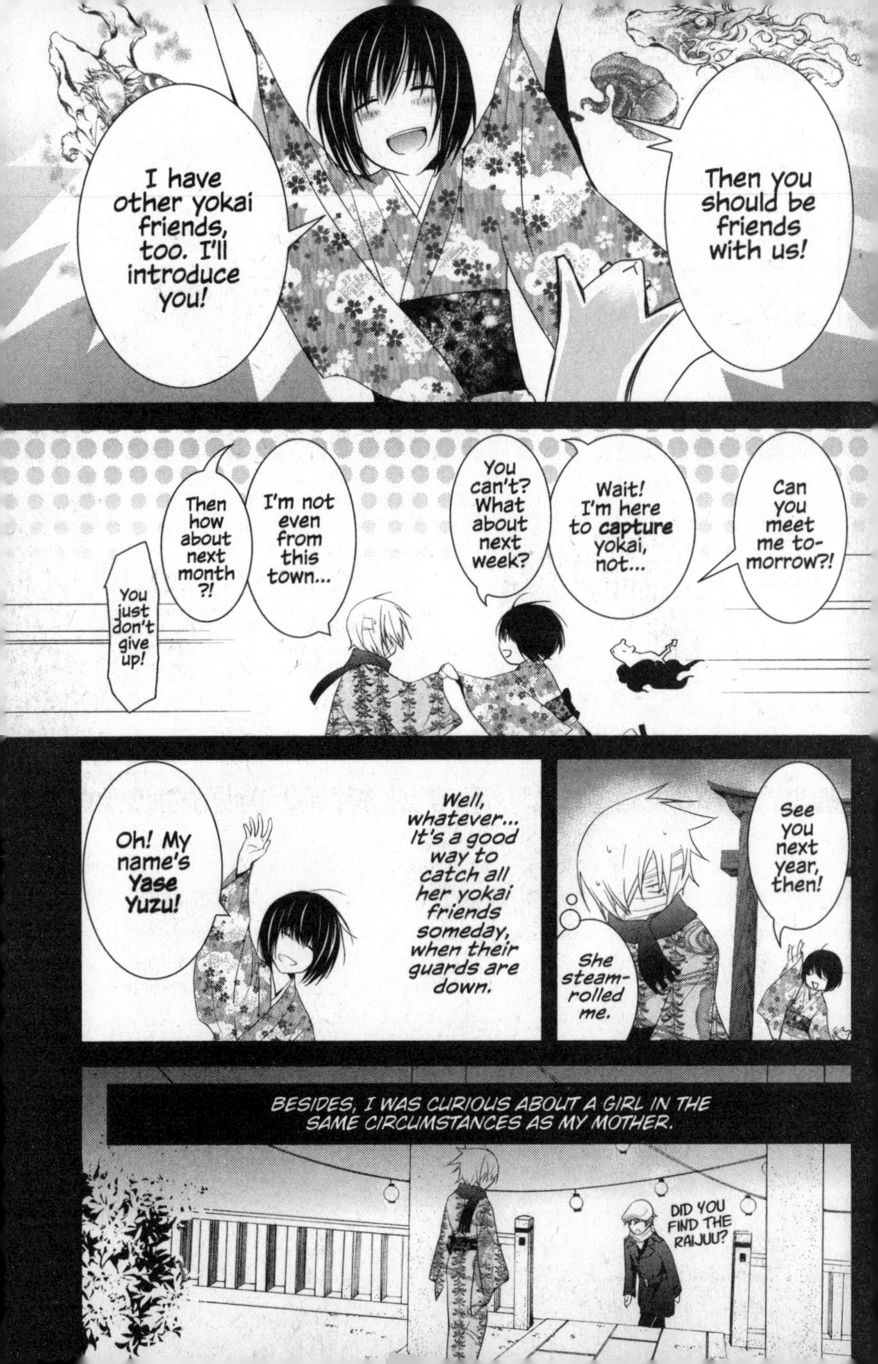
Then you should be friends with us!
I have other yokai friends, too. I'll introduce you!
Can you meet me to-morrow?!
Wait! I'm here to capture yokai, not...
You can't? What about next week?
I'm not even from this town...
Then how about next month?!
You just don't give up!
See you next year, then!
She steam-rolled me.
Well, whatever... It's a good way to catch all her yokai friends someday, when their guards are down.
Oh! My name's Yase Yuzu!
BESIDES, I WAS CURIOUS ABOUT A GIRL IN THE SAME CIRCUMSTANCES AS MY MOTHER.
DID YOU FIND THE RAIJUU?

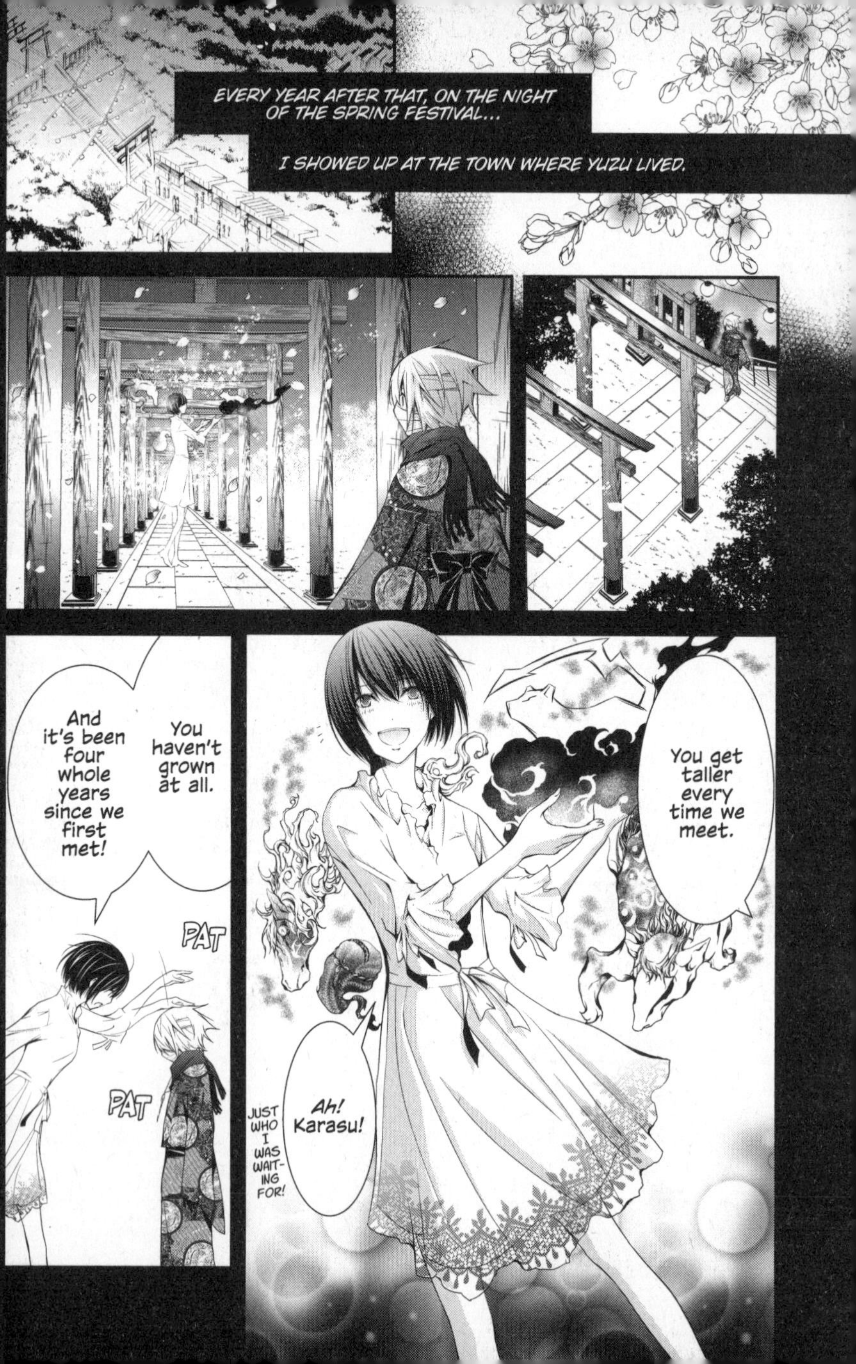
EVERY YEAR AFTER THAT, ON THE NIGHT OF THE SPRING FESTIVAL...
I SHOWED UP AT THE TOWN WHERE YUZU LIVED.
Ah! Karasu!
JUST WHO I WAS WAITING FOR!
You get taller every time we meet.
You haven't grown at all.
And it's been four whole years since we first met!
PAT
PAT

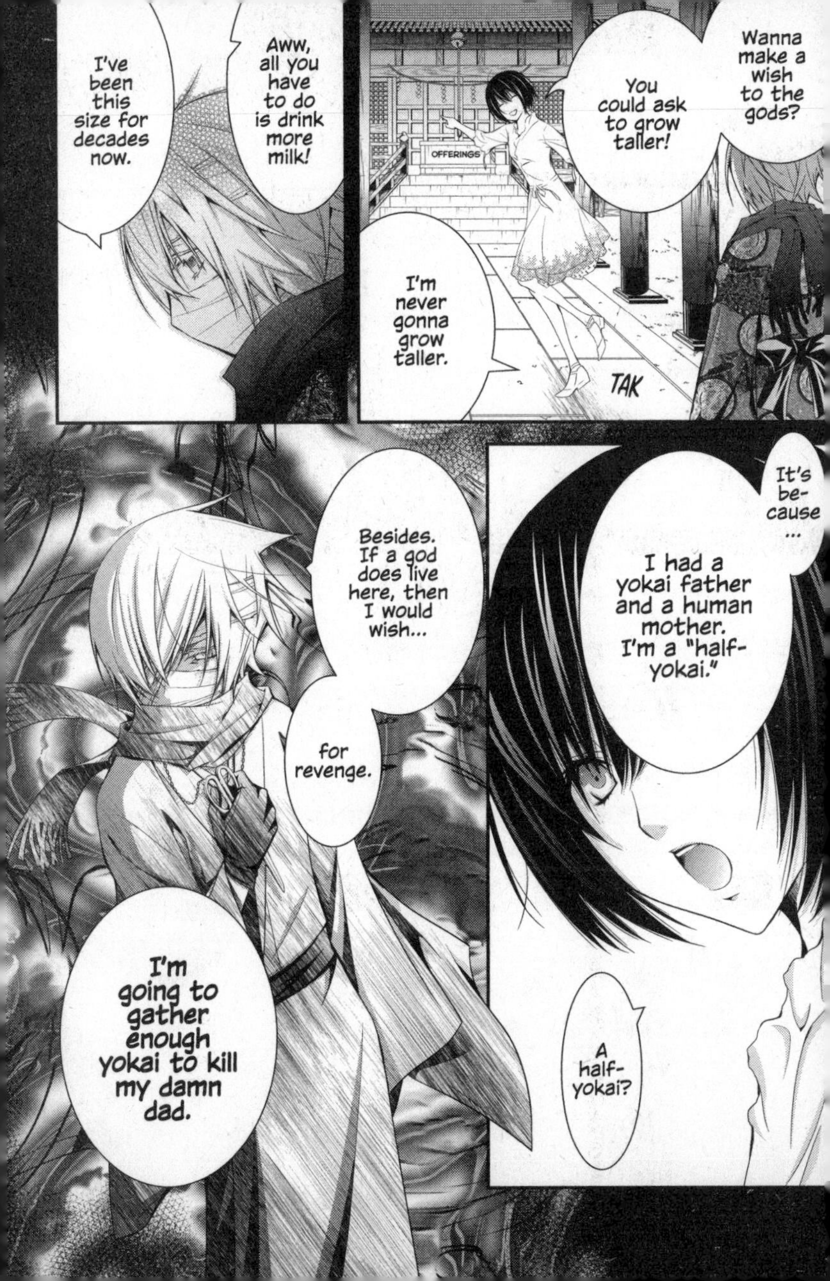
Wanna make a wish to the gods?
You could ask to grow taller!
OFFERINGS
I'm never gonna grow taller.
TAK
Aww, all you have to do is drink more milk!
I've been this size for decades now.
It's be-cause...
I had a yokai father and a human mother. I'm a "half-yokai."
A half-yokai?
Besides. If a god does live here, then I would wish...
for revenge.
I'm going to gather enough yokai to kill my damn dad.

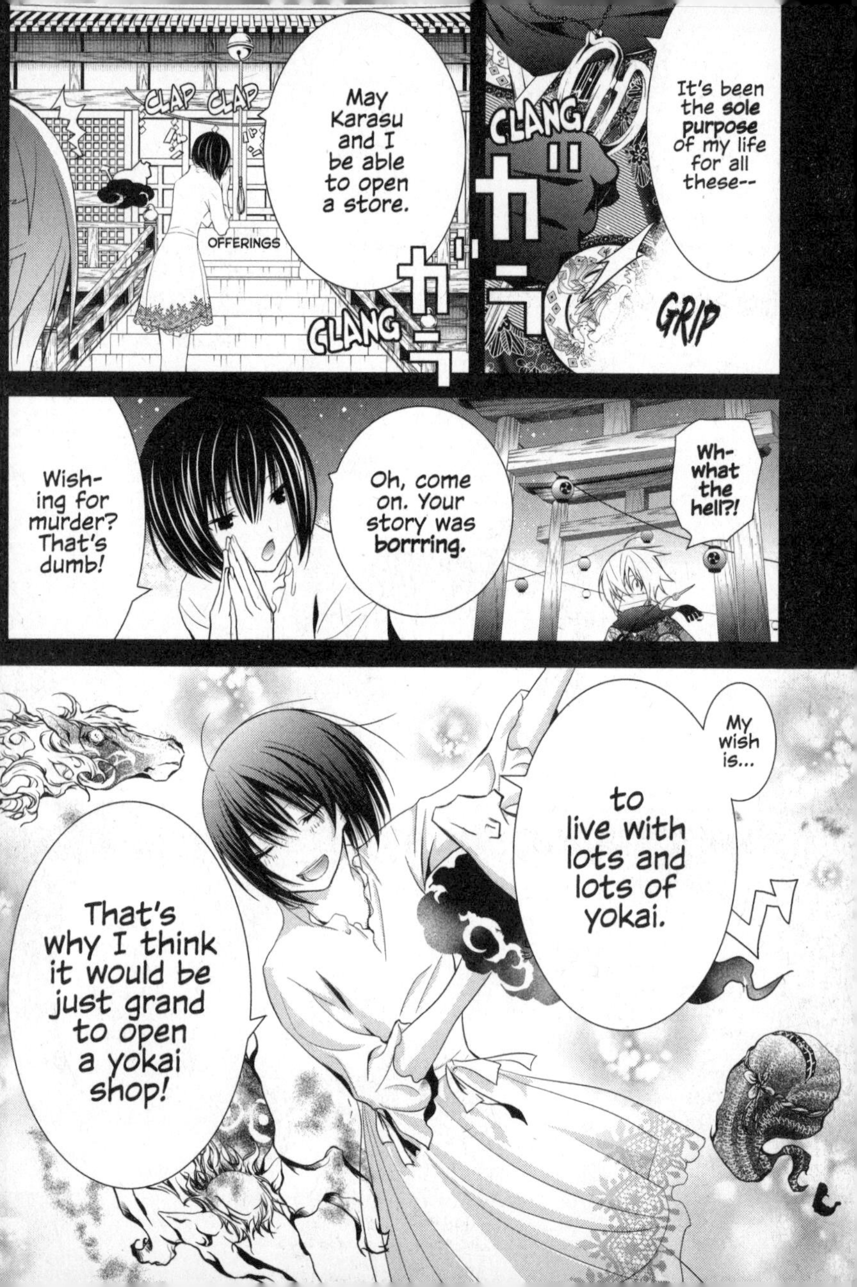
It's been the sole purpose of my life for all these--
CLANG
GRIP
May Karasu and I be able to open a store.
CLAP CLAP
OFFERINGS
CLANG
Wh- what the hell?!
Oh, come on. Your story was borrring.
Wishing for murder? That's dumb!
My wish is...
to live with lots and lots of yokai.
That's why I think it would be just grand to open a yokai shop!

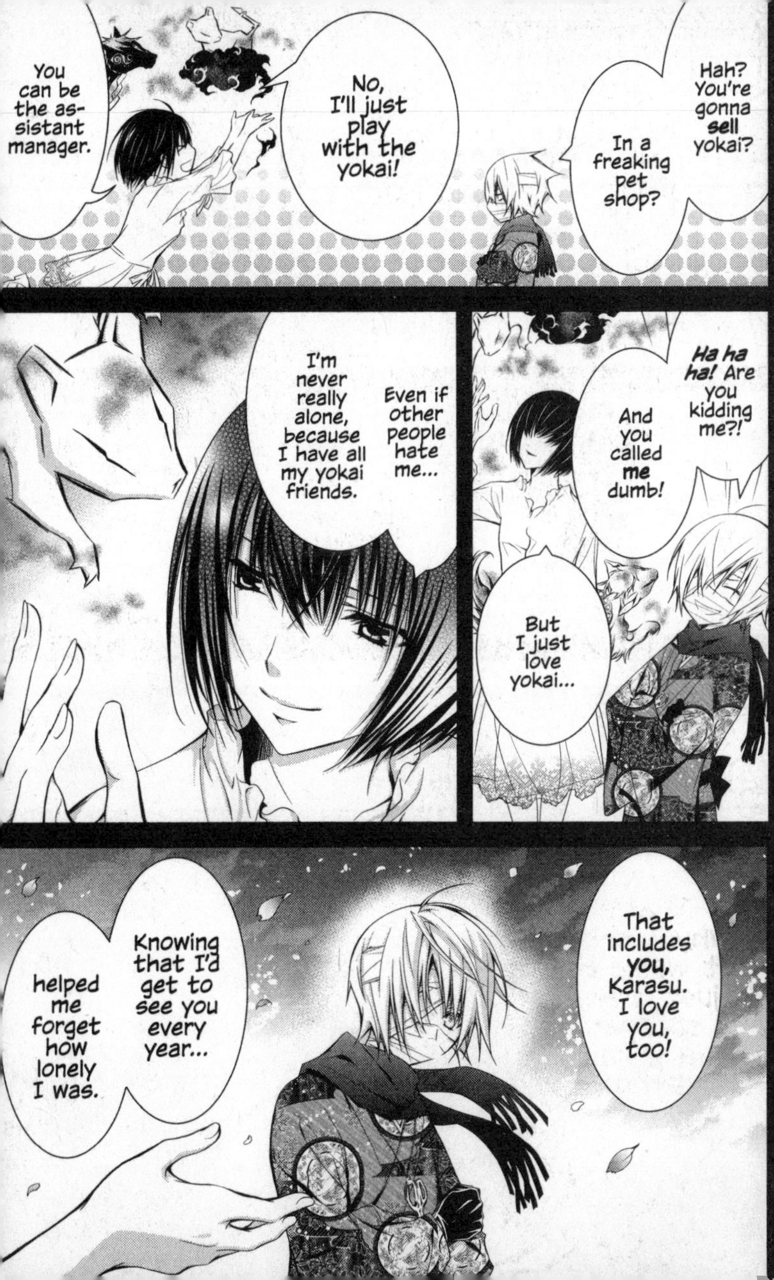
Hah? You're gonna **sell** yokai?
In a freaking pet shop?
No, I'll just play with the yokai!
You can be the as-sistant manager.
Ha ha ha! Are you kidding me?!
And you called **me** dumb!
But I just love yokai...
Even if other people hate me...
I'm never really alone, because I have all my yokai friends.
That includes **you,** Karasu. I love you, too!
Knowing that I'd get to see you every year...
helped me forget how lonely I was.

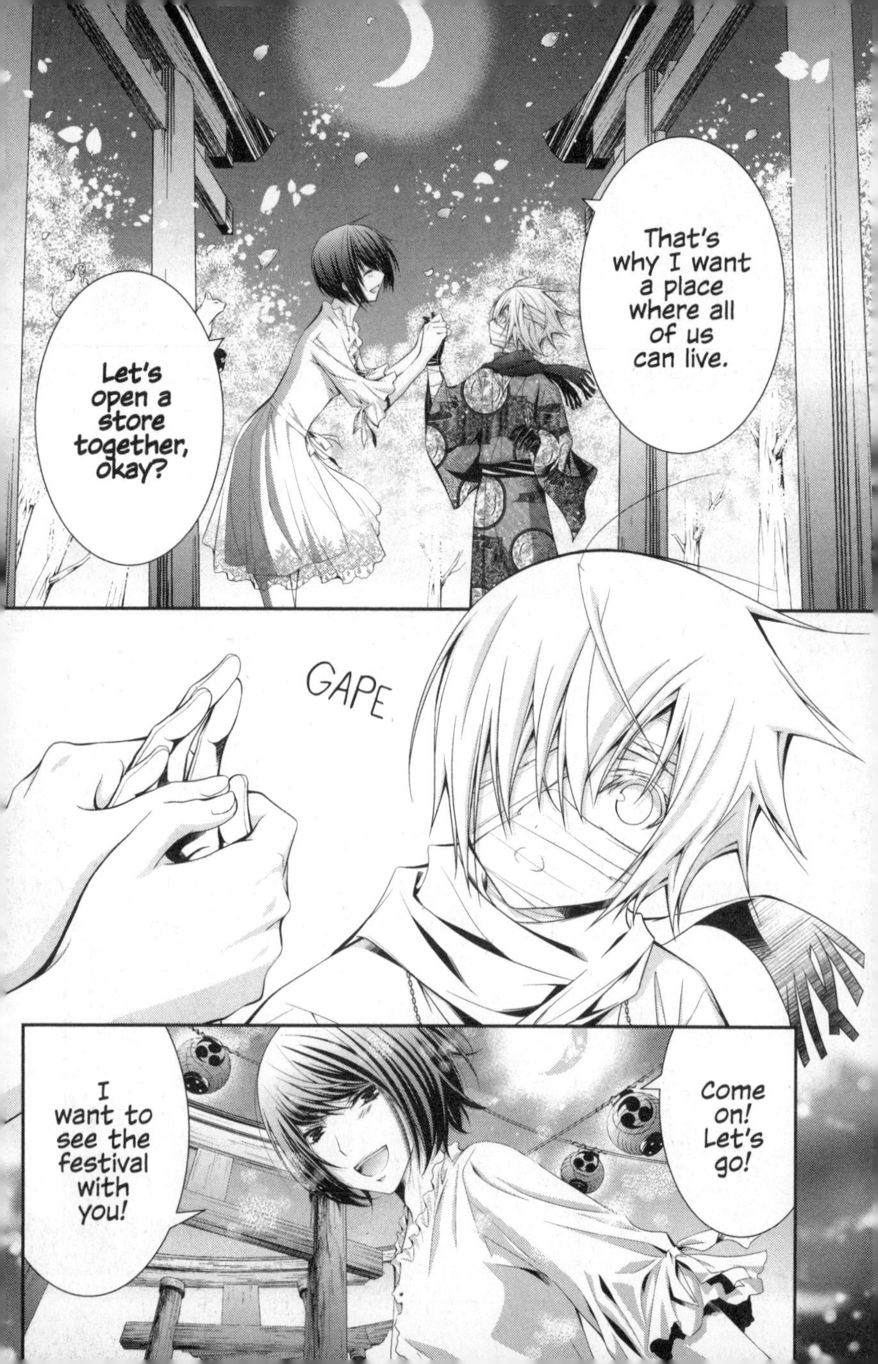
That's why I want a place where all of us can live.
Let's open a store together, okay?
GAPE
Come on! Let's go!
I want to see the festival with you!

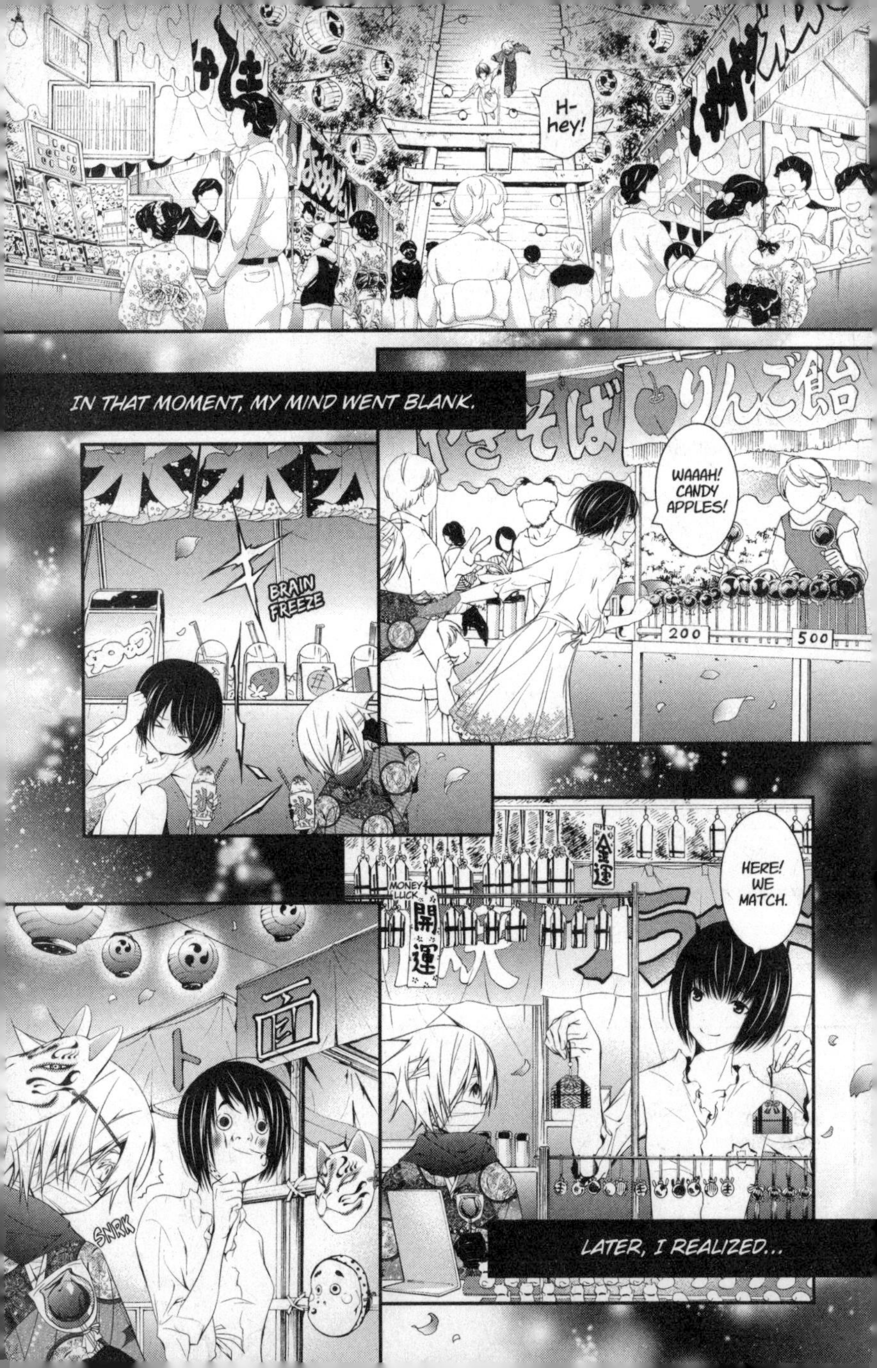
H-hey!
IN THAT MOMENT, MY MIND WENT BLANK.
りんご飴
WAAAH! CANDY APPLES!
200
500
BRAIN FREEZE
金運
HERE! WE MATCH.
MONEY LUCK
開運
LATER, I REALIZED...
SNRK

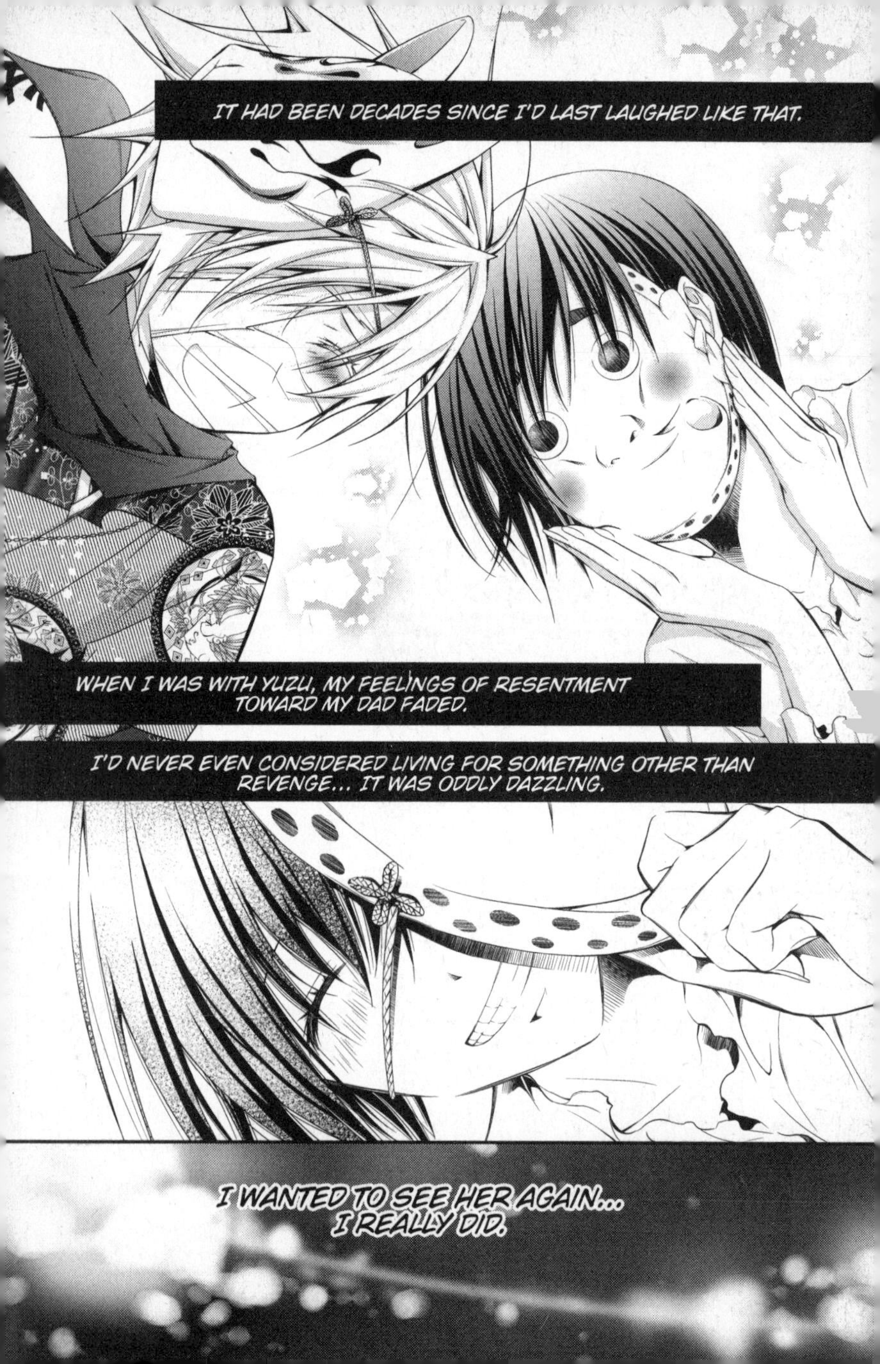
IT HAD BEEN DECADES SINCE I'D LAST LAUGHED LIKE THAT.
WHEN I WAS WITH YUZU, MY FEELINGS OF RESENTMENT TOWARD MY DAD FADED.
I'D NEVER EVEN CONSIDERED LIVING FOR SOMETHING OTHER THAN REVENGE... IT WAS ODDLY DAZZLING.
I WANTED TO SEE HER AGAIN... I REALLY DID.

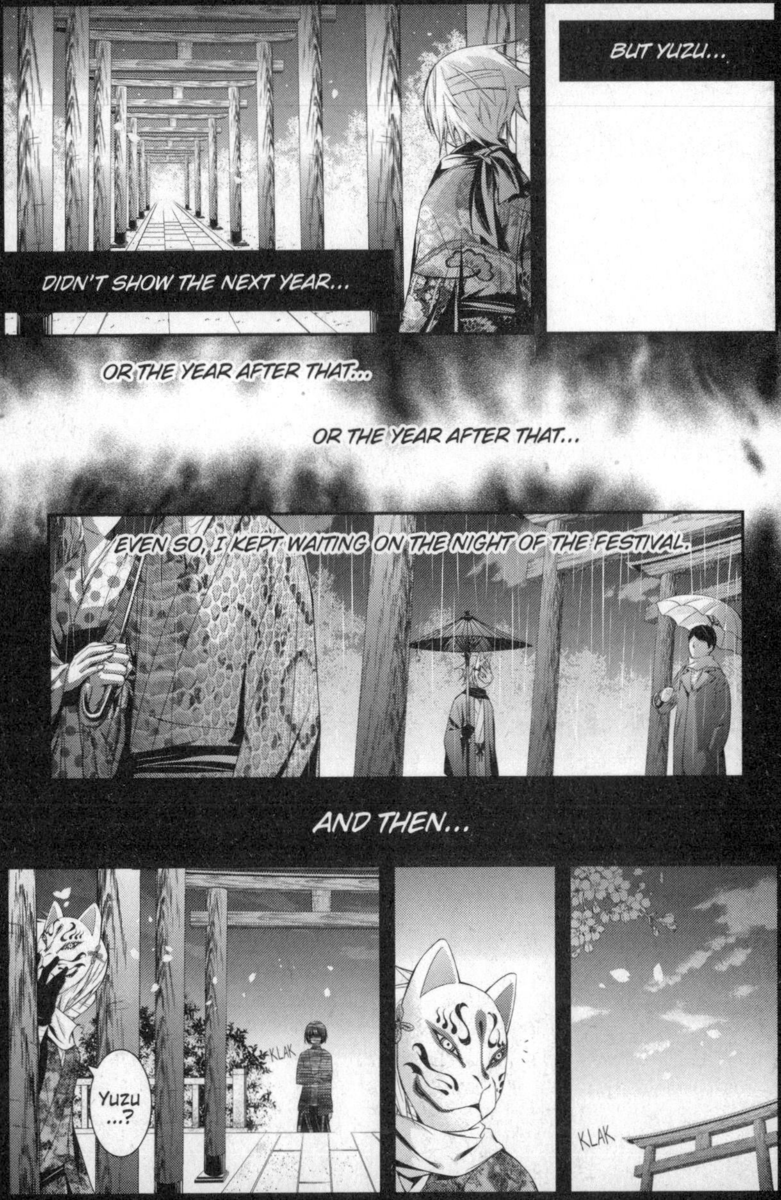
BUT YUZU...
DIDN'T SHOW THE NEXT YEAR...
OR THE YEAR AFTER THAT...
OR THE YEAR AFTER THAT...
EVEN SO, I KEPT WAITING ON THE NIGHT OF THE FESTIVAL.
AND THEN...
KLAK
KLAK
Yuzu ...?

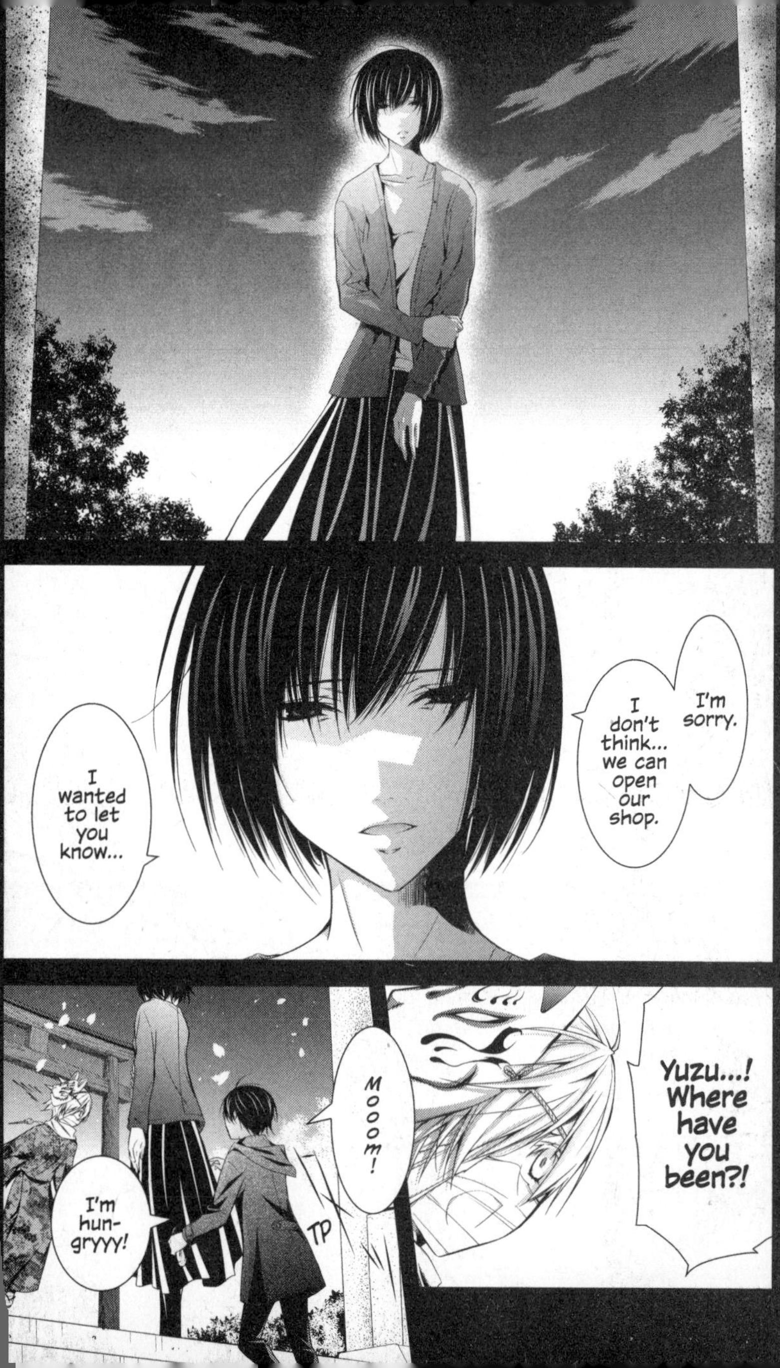

I'm sorry.
I don't think... we can open our shop.
I wanted to let you know...
Yuzu...! Where have you been?!
Mooom!
TP
I'm hun-gryyy!

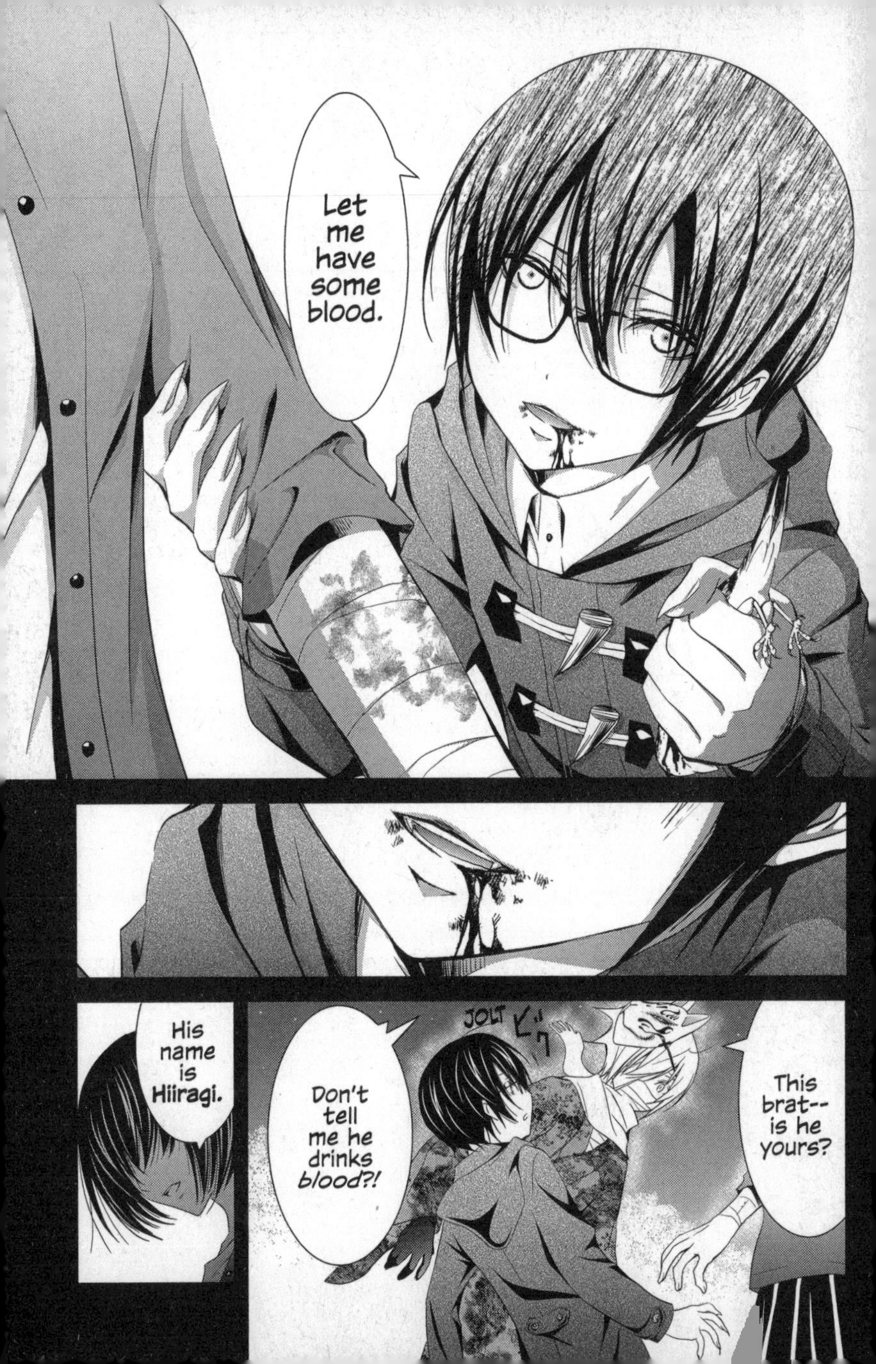
Let me have some blood.
This brat-- is he yours?
JOLT
Don't tell me he drinks *blood*?!
His name is Hiiragi.

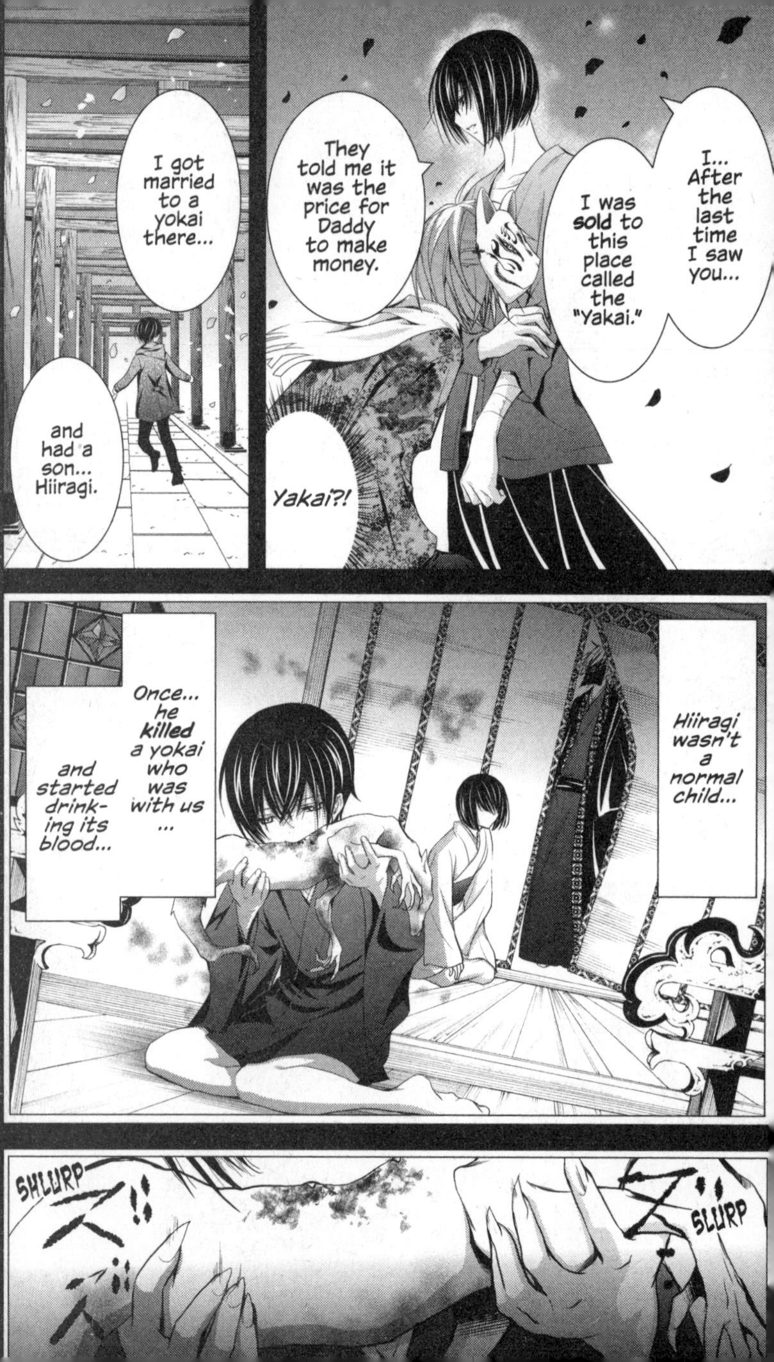
I... After the last time I saw you...
I was sold to this place called the "Yakai."
They told me it was the price for Daddy to make money.
Yakai?!
I got married to a yokai there...
and had a son... Hiiragi.
Hiiragi wasn't a normal child...
Once... he killed a yokai who was with us ...
and started drinking its blood...
SLURP
SHLURP

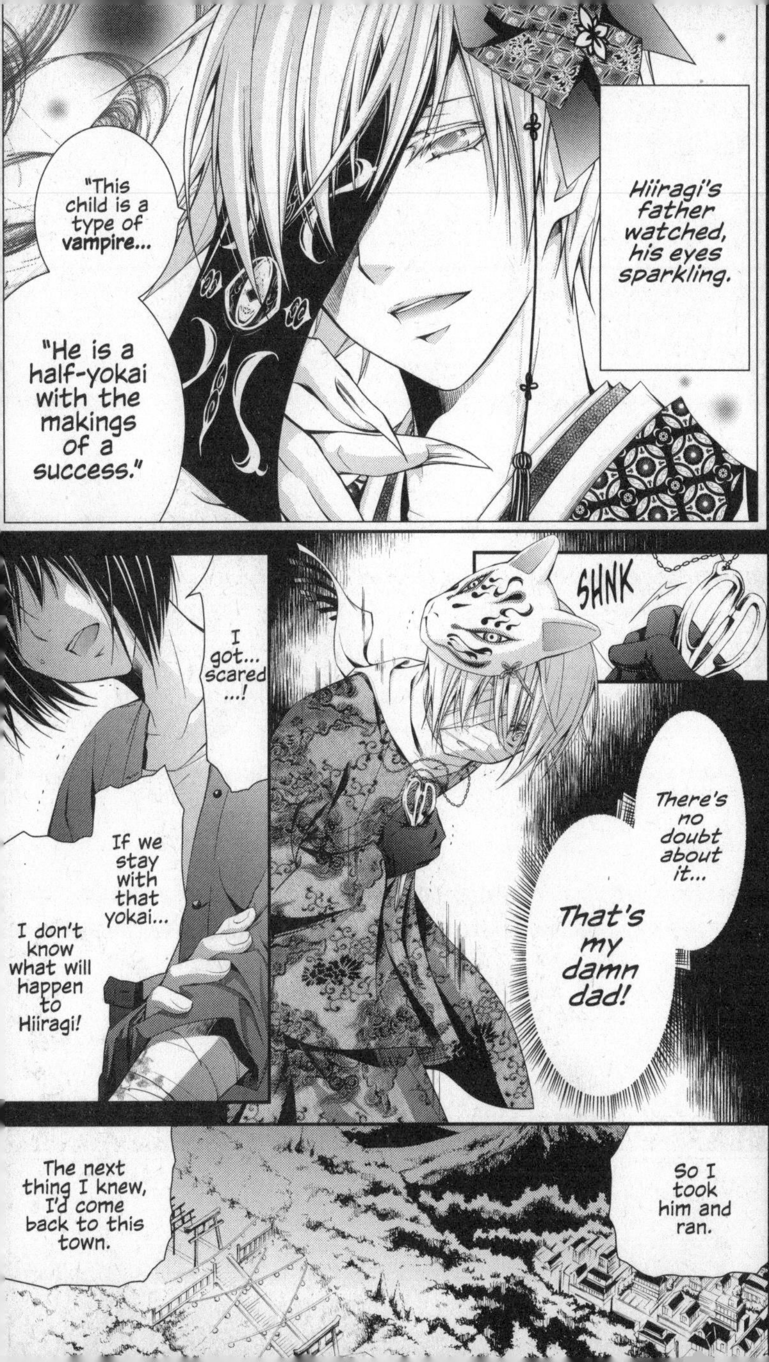
Hiiragi's father watched, his eyes sparkling.
"This child is a type of vampire...
"He is a half-yokai with the makings of a success."
SHNK
There's no doubt about it...
That's my damn dad!
I got... scared...!
If we stay with that yokai...
I don't know what will happen to Hiiragi!
So I took him and ran.
The next thing I knew, I'd come back to this town.

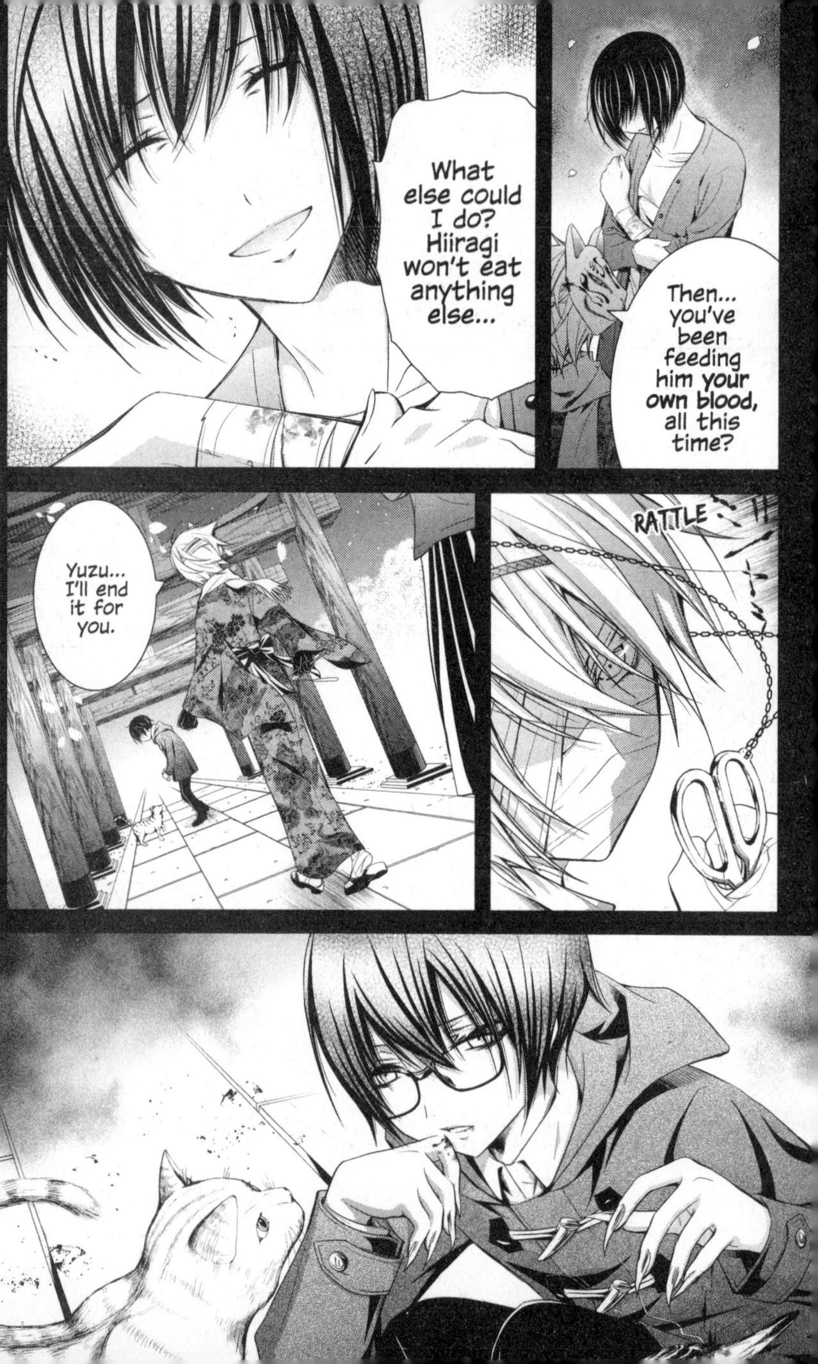
Then... you've been feeding him your own blood, all this time?
What else could I do? Hiiragi won't eat anything else...
RATTLE
Yuzu... I'll end it for you.

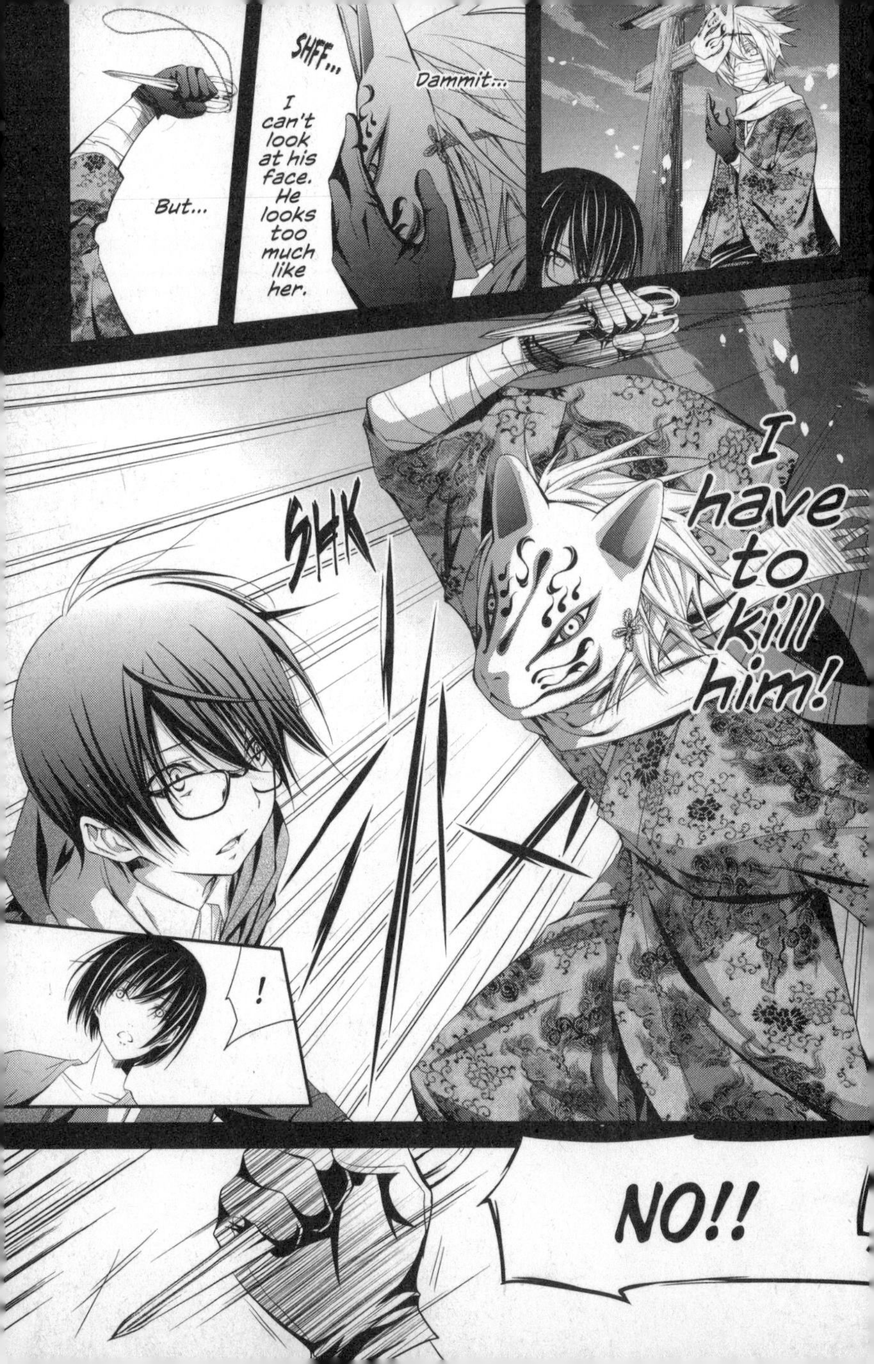
SHFF...
Dammit...
I can't look at his face. He looks too much like her.
But...
I have to kill him!
SHK
!
NO!!

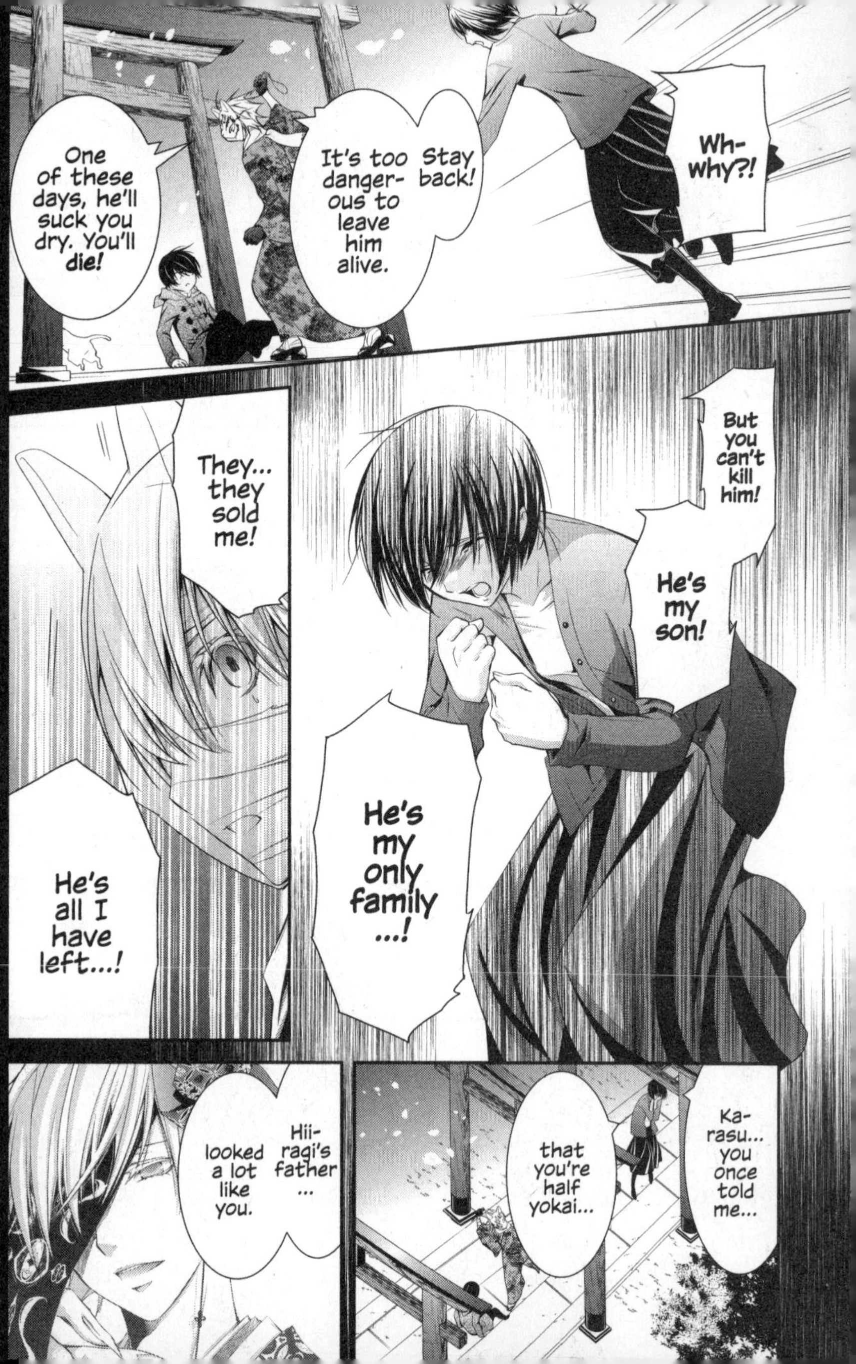
Wh-why?!
Stay back!
It's too danger-ous to leave him alive.
One of these days, he'll suck you dry. You'll die!
But you can't kill him!
He's my son!
He's my only family...!
They... they sold me!
He's all I have left...!
Ka-rasu... you once told me...
that you're half yokai...
Hii-ragi's father...
looked a lot like you.

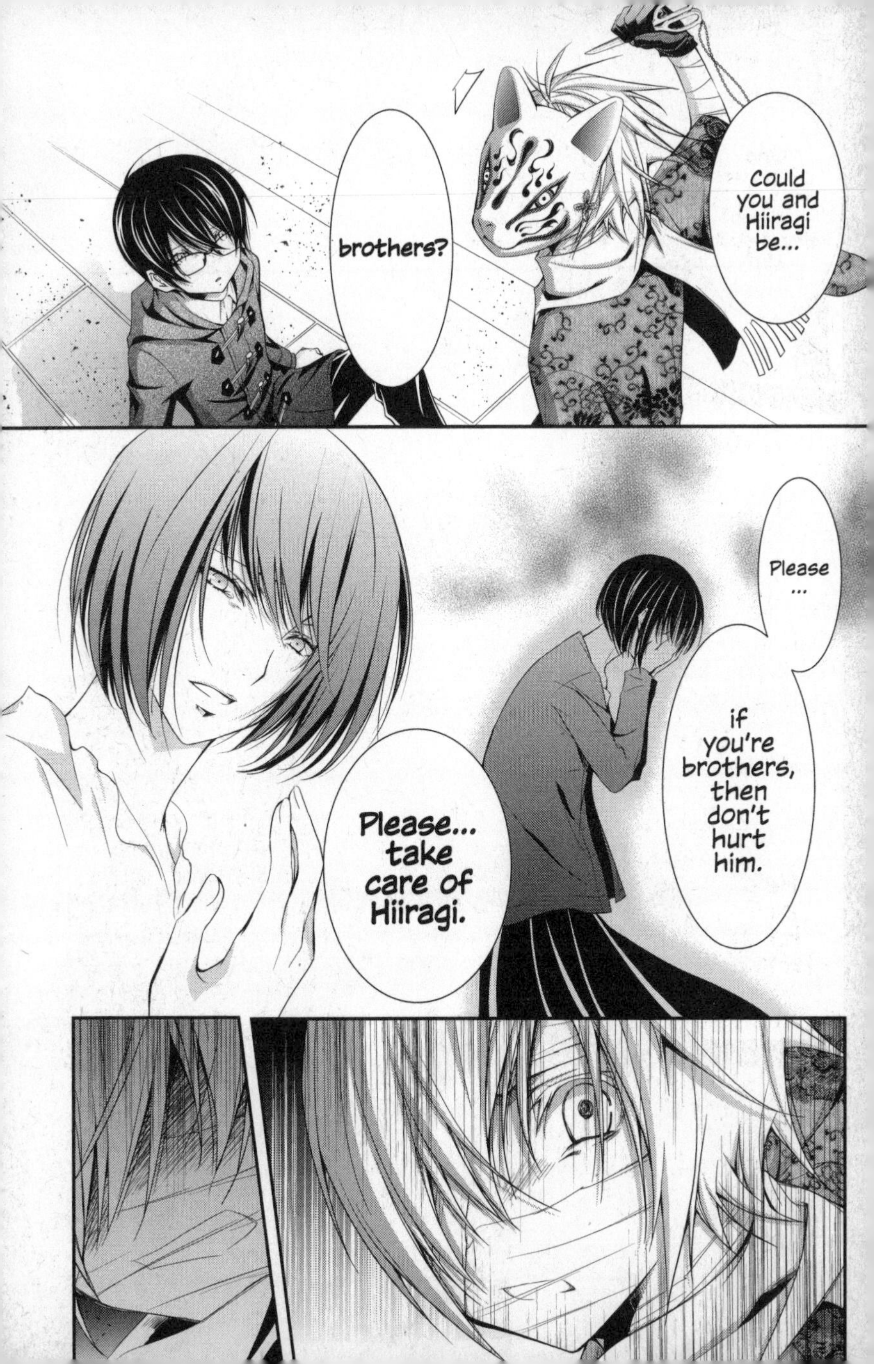
Could you and Hiiragi be...
brothers?
Please ...
if you're brothers, then don't hurt him.
Please... take care of Hiiragi.

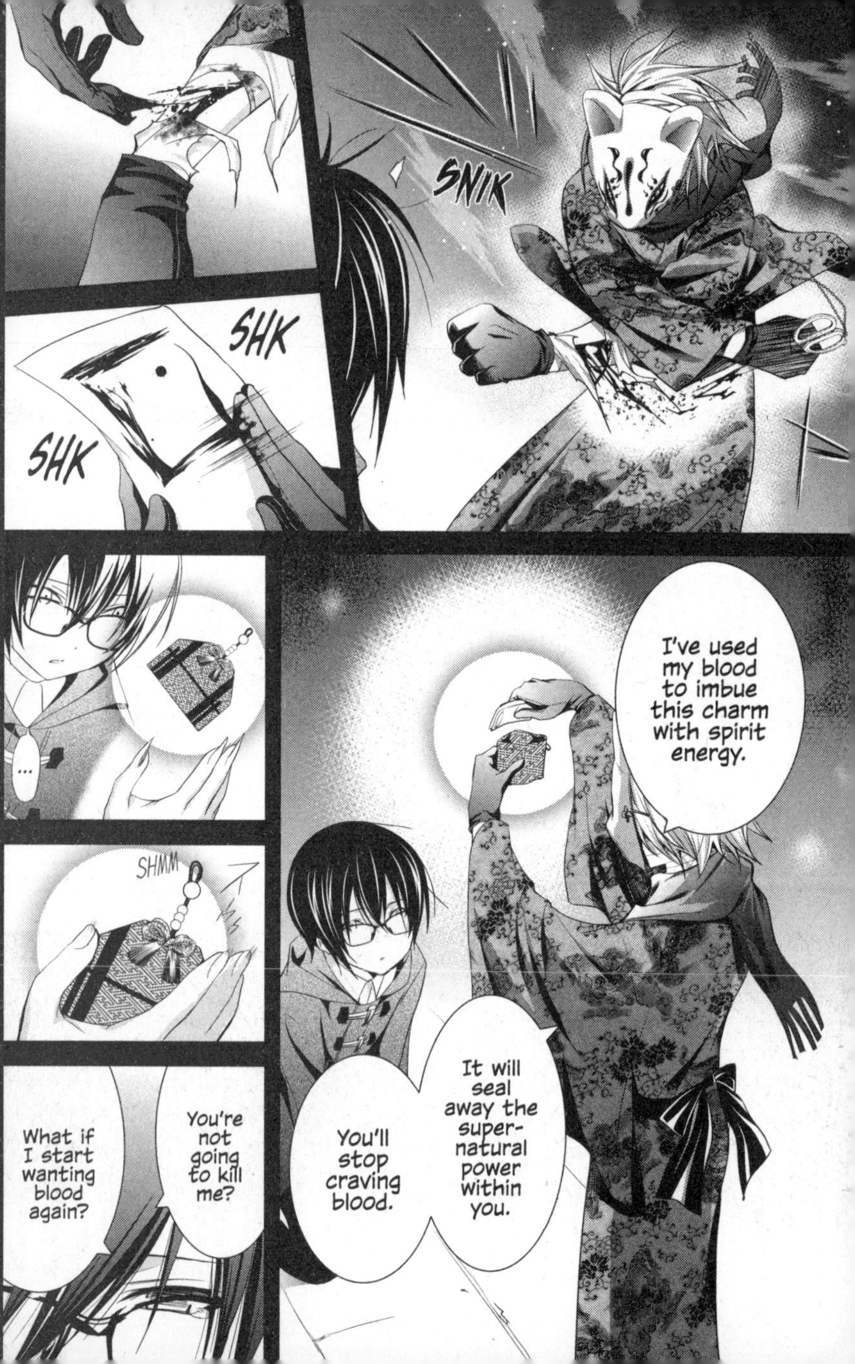
SNIK
SHK
SHK
I've used my blood to imbue this charm with spirit energy.
It will seal away the super-natural power within you.
You'll stop craving blood.
...
SHMM
You're not going to kill me?
What if I start wanting blood again?

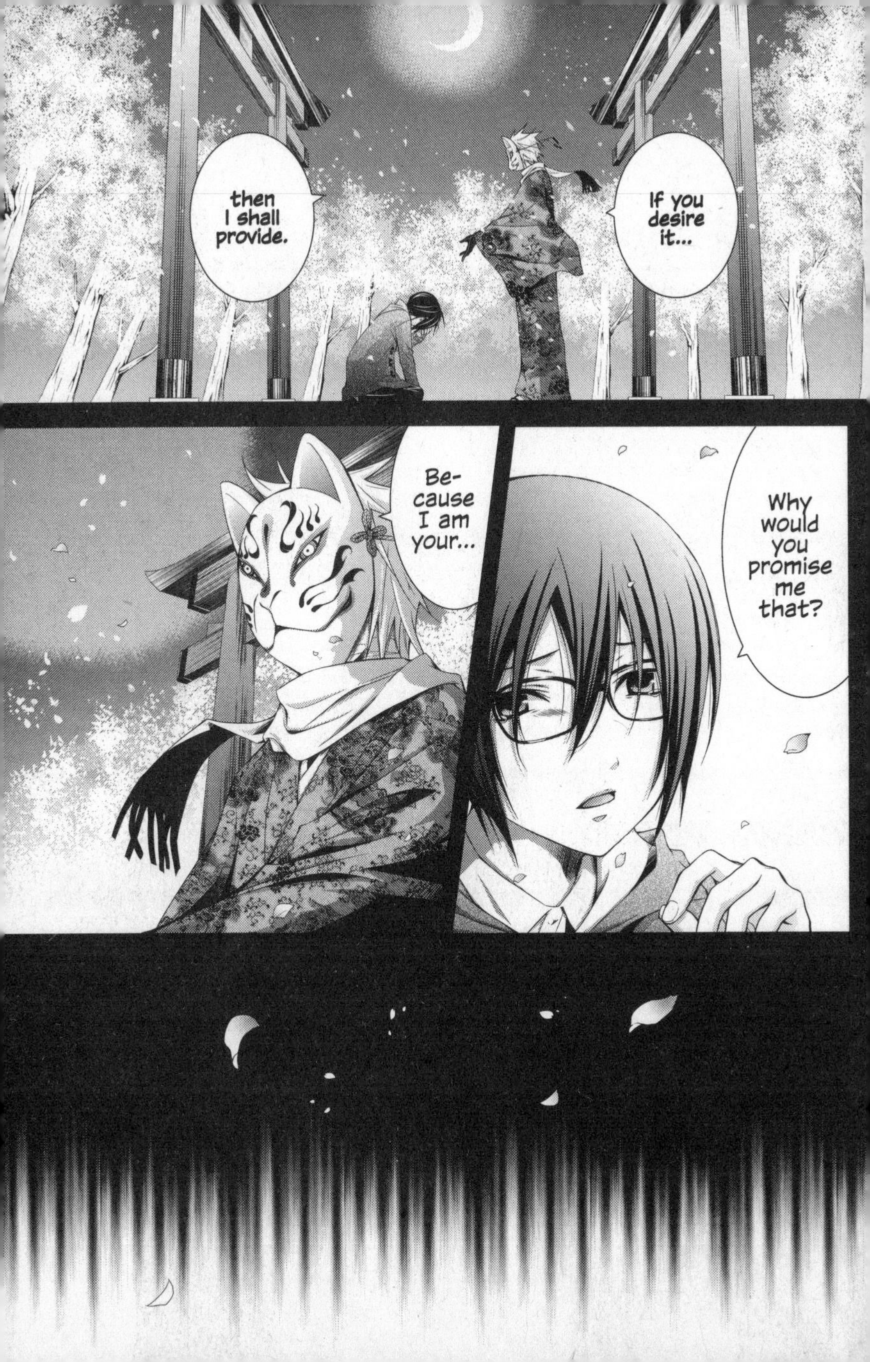
If you desire it...
then I shall provide.
Why would you promise me that?
Be-cause I am your...

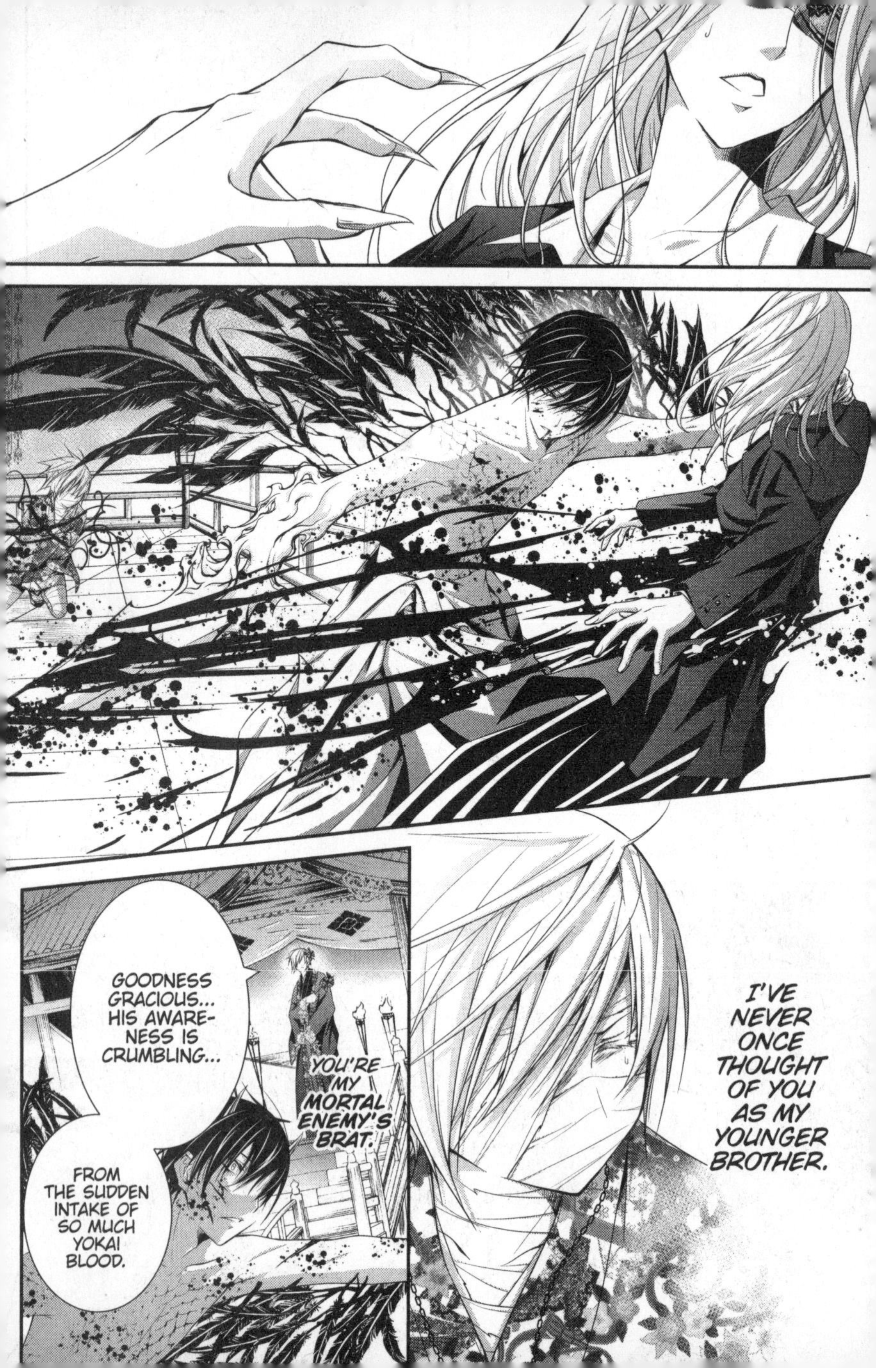
I'VE NEVER ONCE THOUGHT OF YOU AS MY YOUNGER BROTHER.
YOU'RE MY MORTAL ENEMY'S BRAT.
GOODNESS GRACIOUS... HIS AWARENESS IS CRUMBLING...
FROM THE SUDDEN INTAKE OF SO MUCH YOKAI BLOOD.

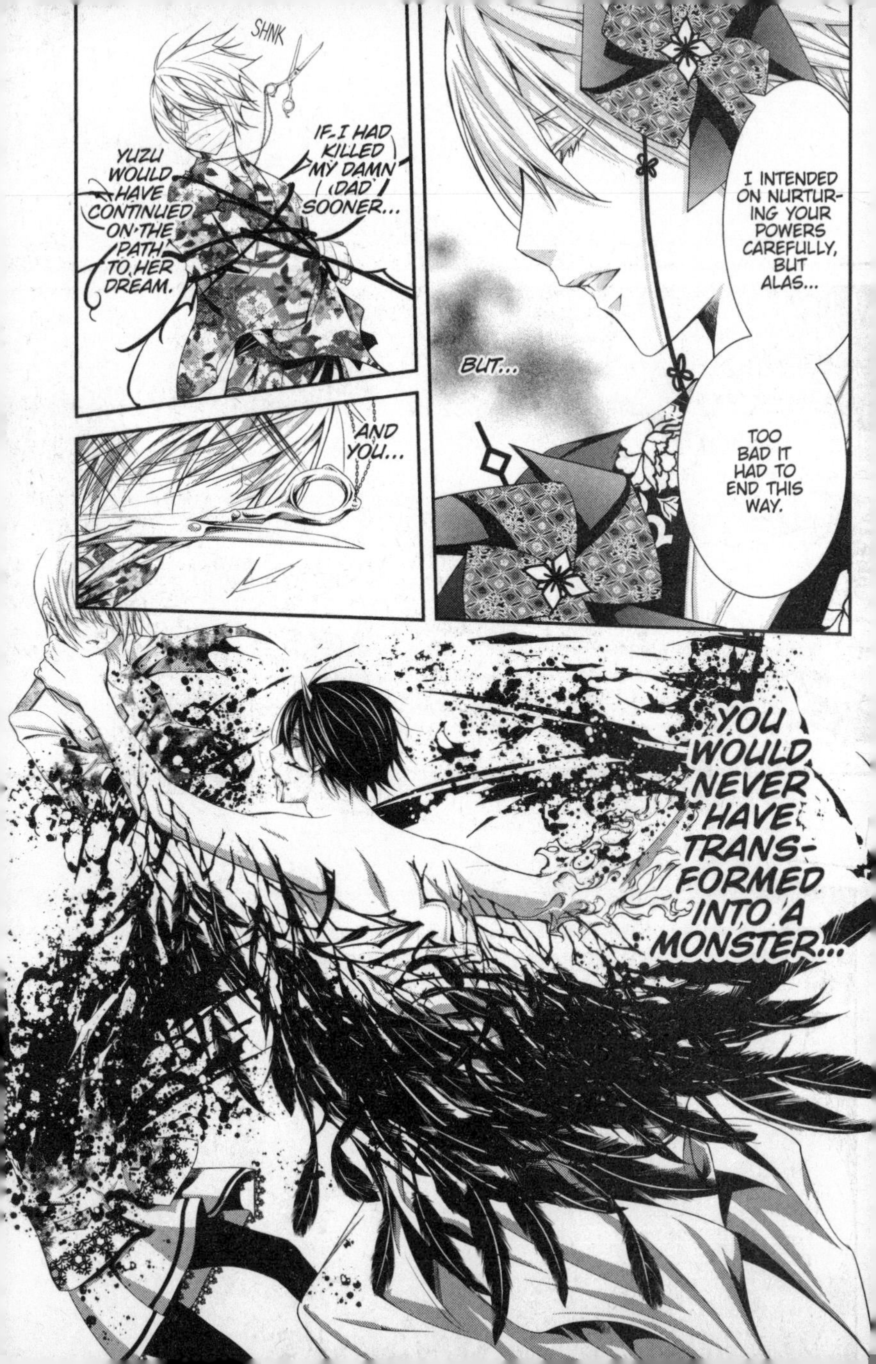
I INTENDED ON NURTURING YOUR POWERS CAREFULLY, BUT ALAS...
TOO BAD IT HAD TO END THIS WAY.
BUT...
SHNK
IF I HAD KILLED MY DAMN DAD SOONER...
YUZU WOULD HAVE CONTINUED ON THE PATH TO HER DREAM.
AND YOU...
YOU WOULD NEVER HAVE TRANSFORMED INTO A MONSTER...

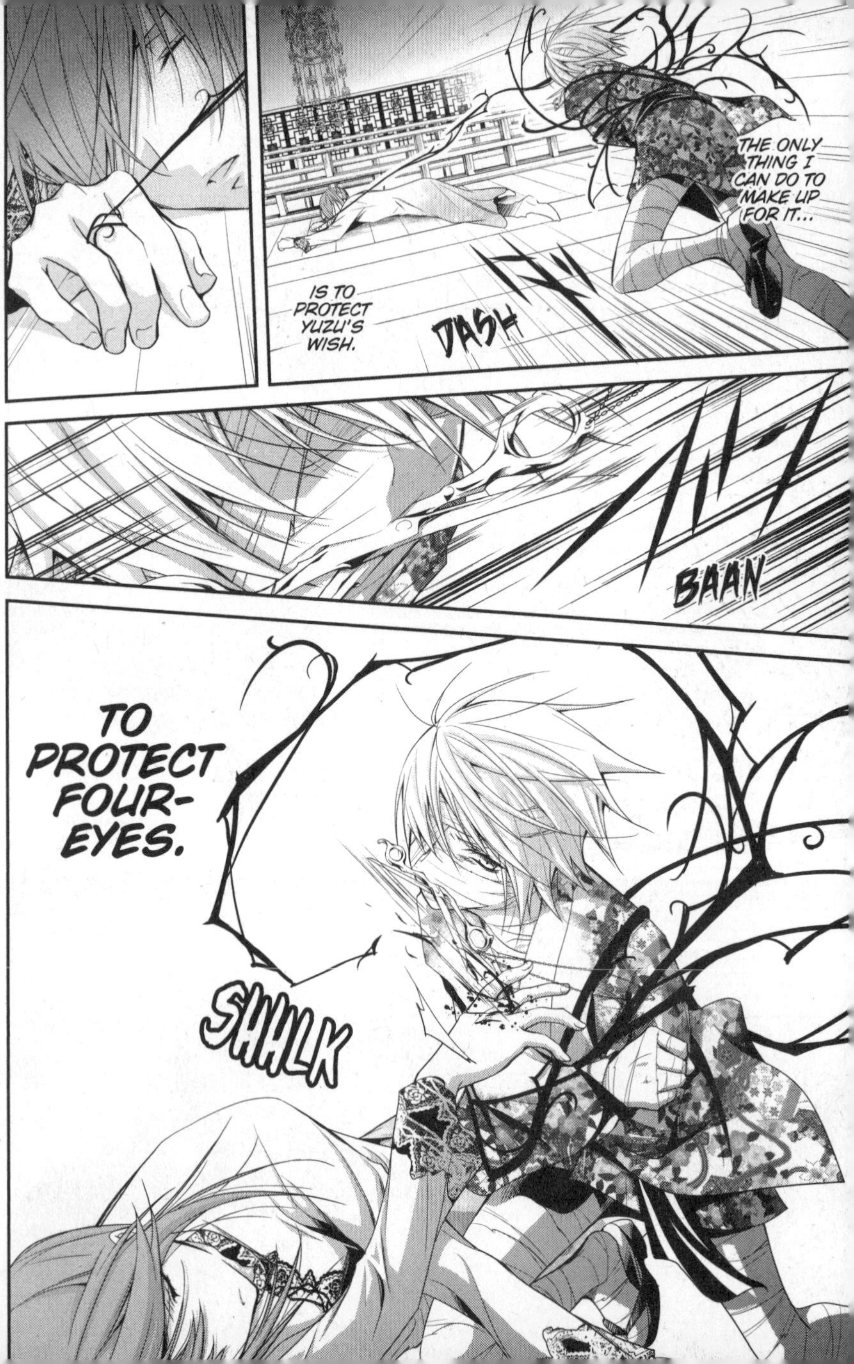
THE ONLY THING I CAN DO TO MAKE UP FOR IT...
IS TO PROTECT YUZU'S WISH.
DASH
BAAN
TO PROTECT FOUR-EYES.
SHHLK

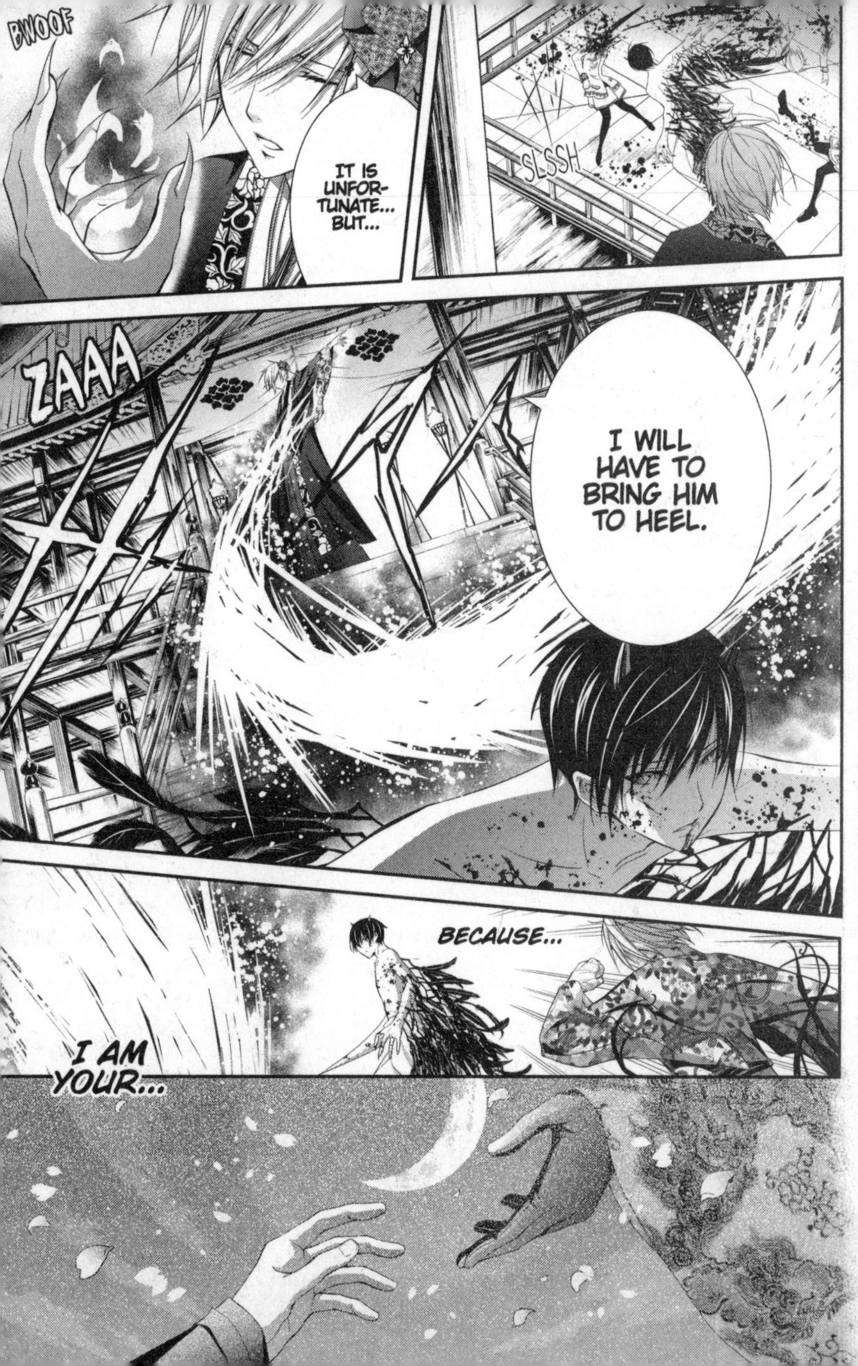
SLSSH
BWOOF
IT IS UNFORTUNATE... BUT...
ZAAA
I WILL HAVE TO BRING HIM TO HEEL.
BECAUSE...
I AM YOUR...

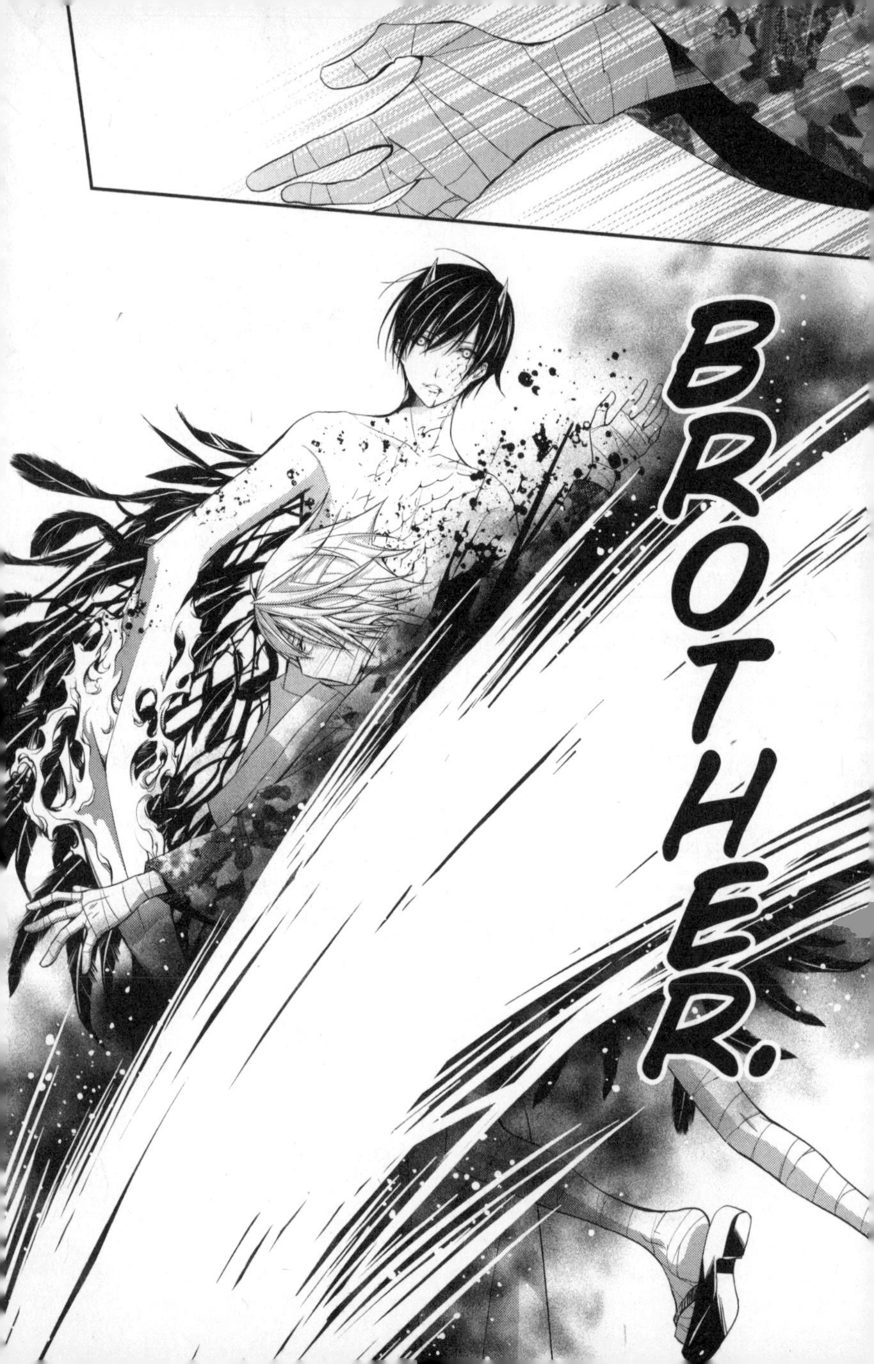
BROTHER.

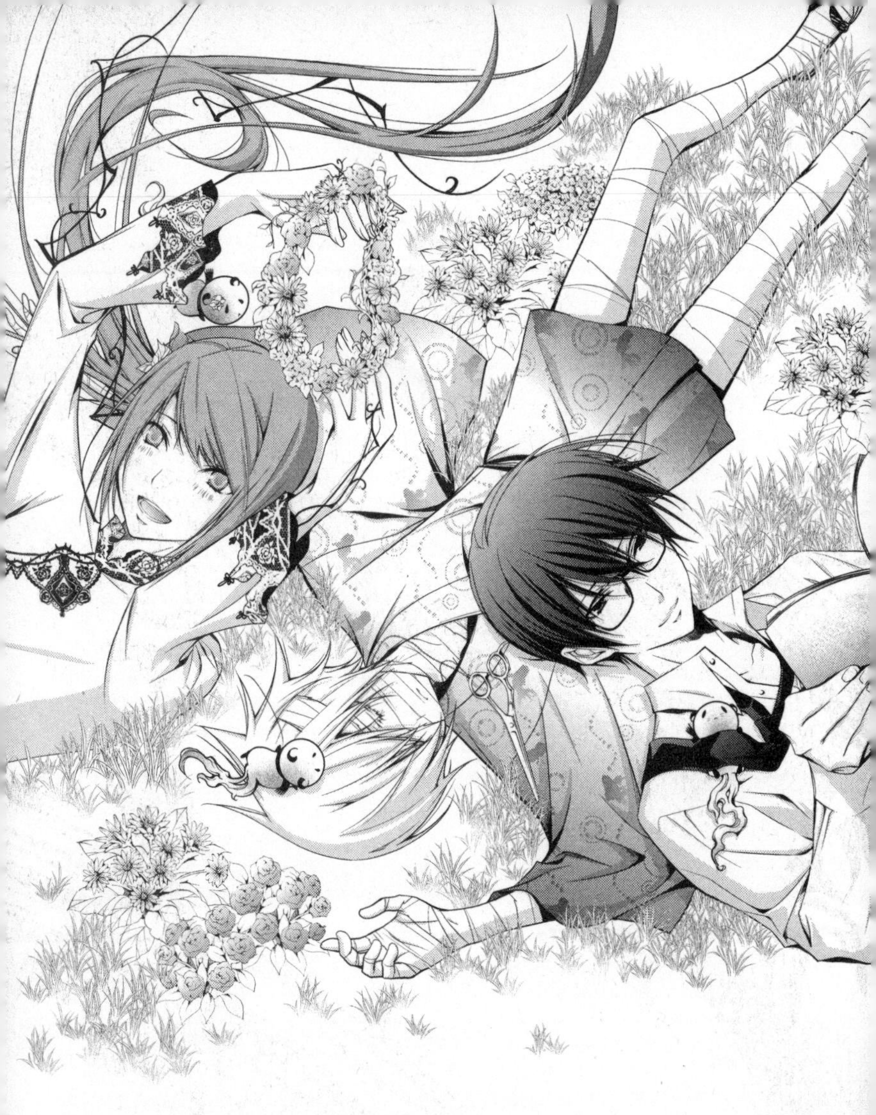

Rental 23: BROTHERS

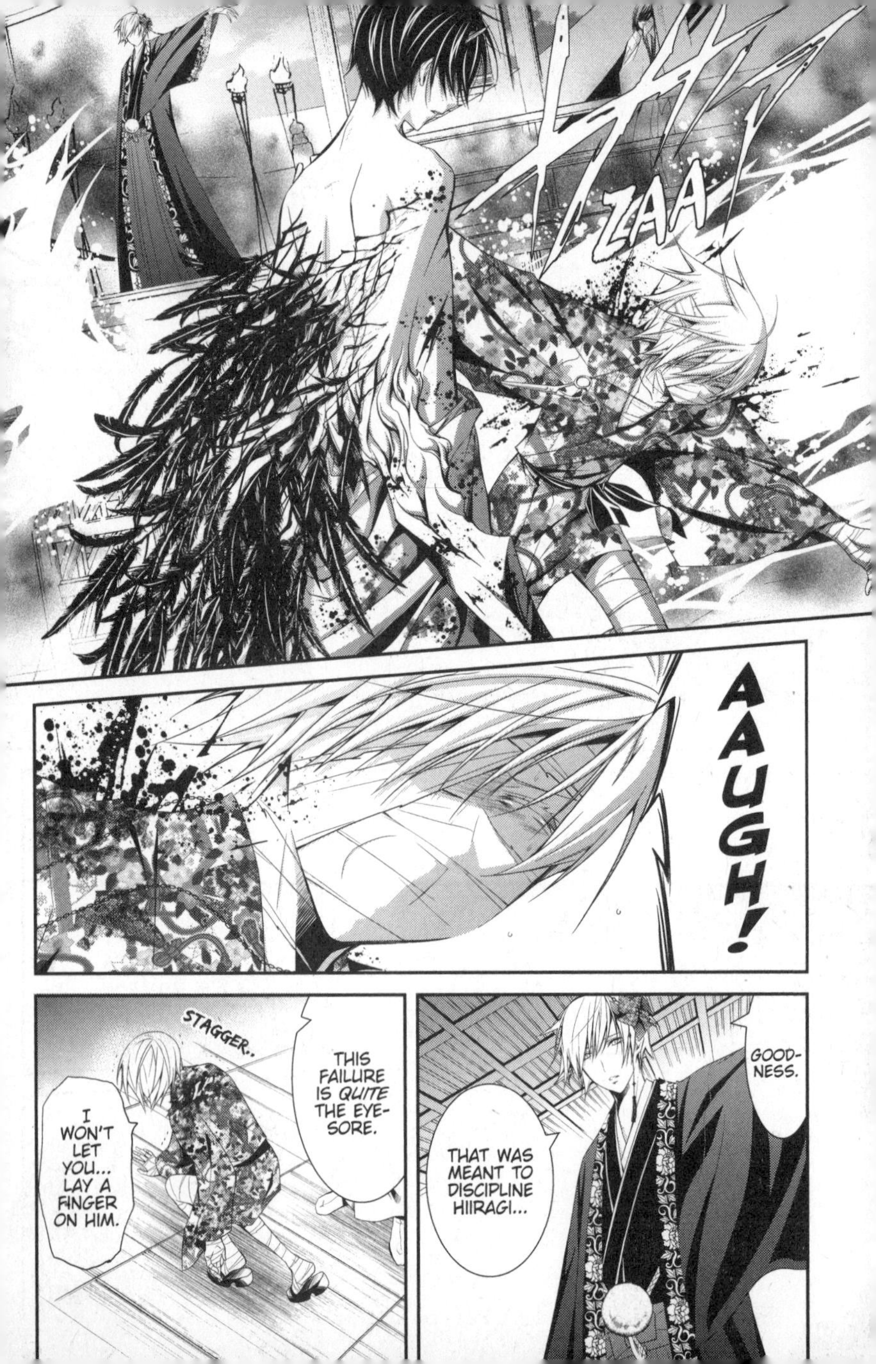
ZAA!
AAUGH!
GOOD-NESS.
THAT WAS MEANT TO DISCIPLINE HIIRAGI...
THIS FAILURE IS *QUITE* THE EYE-SORE.
STAGGER..
I WON'T LET YOU... LAY A FINGER ON HIM.

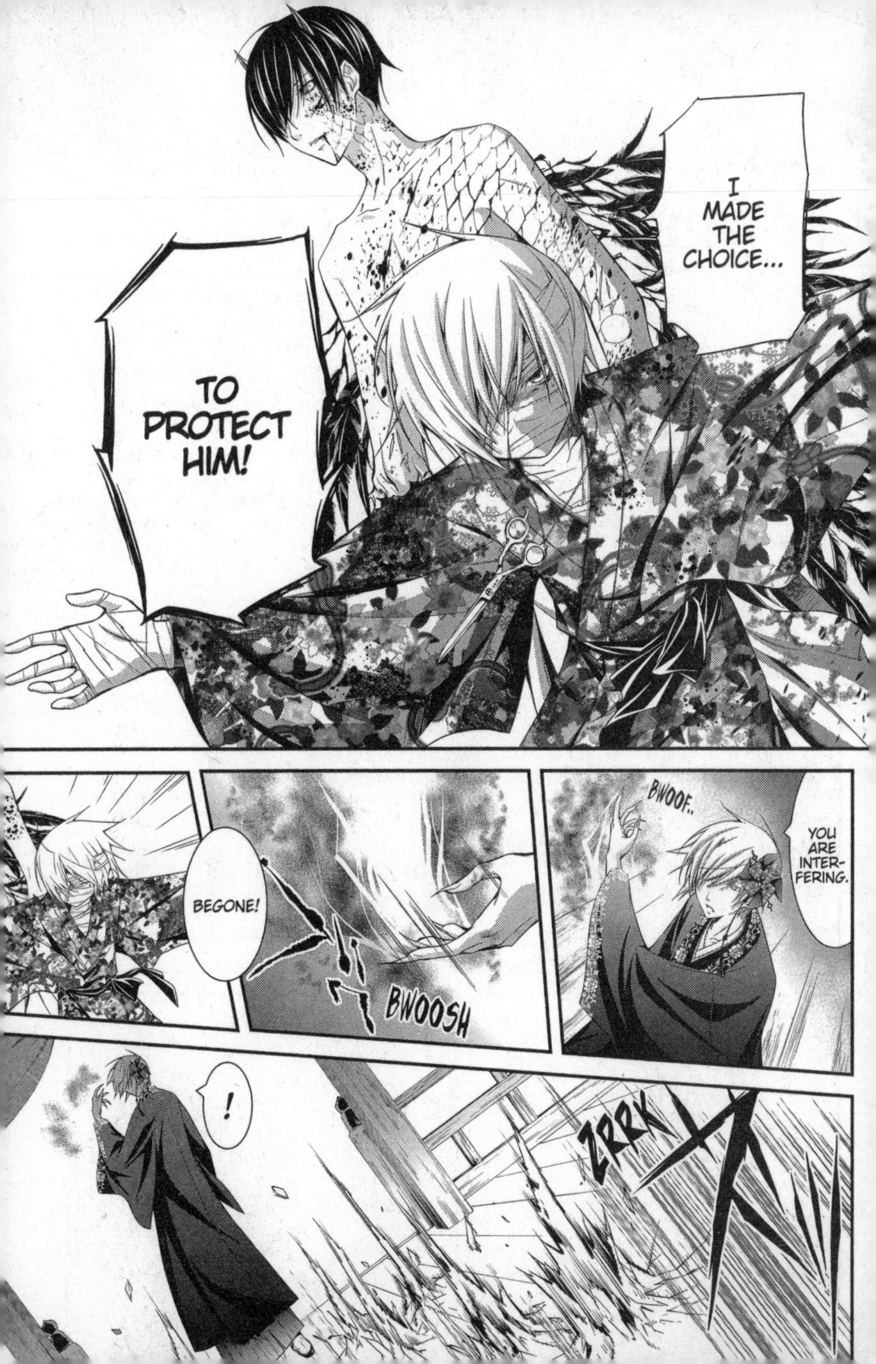
I MADE THE CHOICE...
TO PROTECT HIM!
YOU ARE INTER-FERING.
BWOOF..
BWOOSH
BEGONE!
ZRRK
!

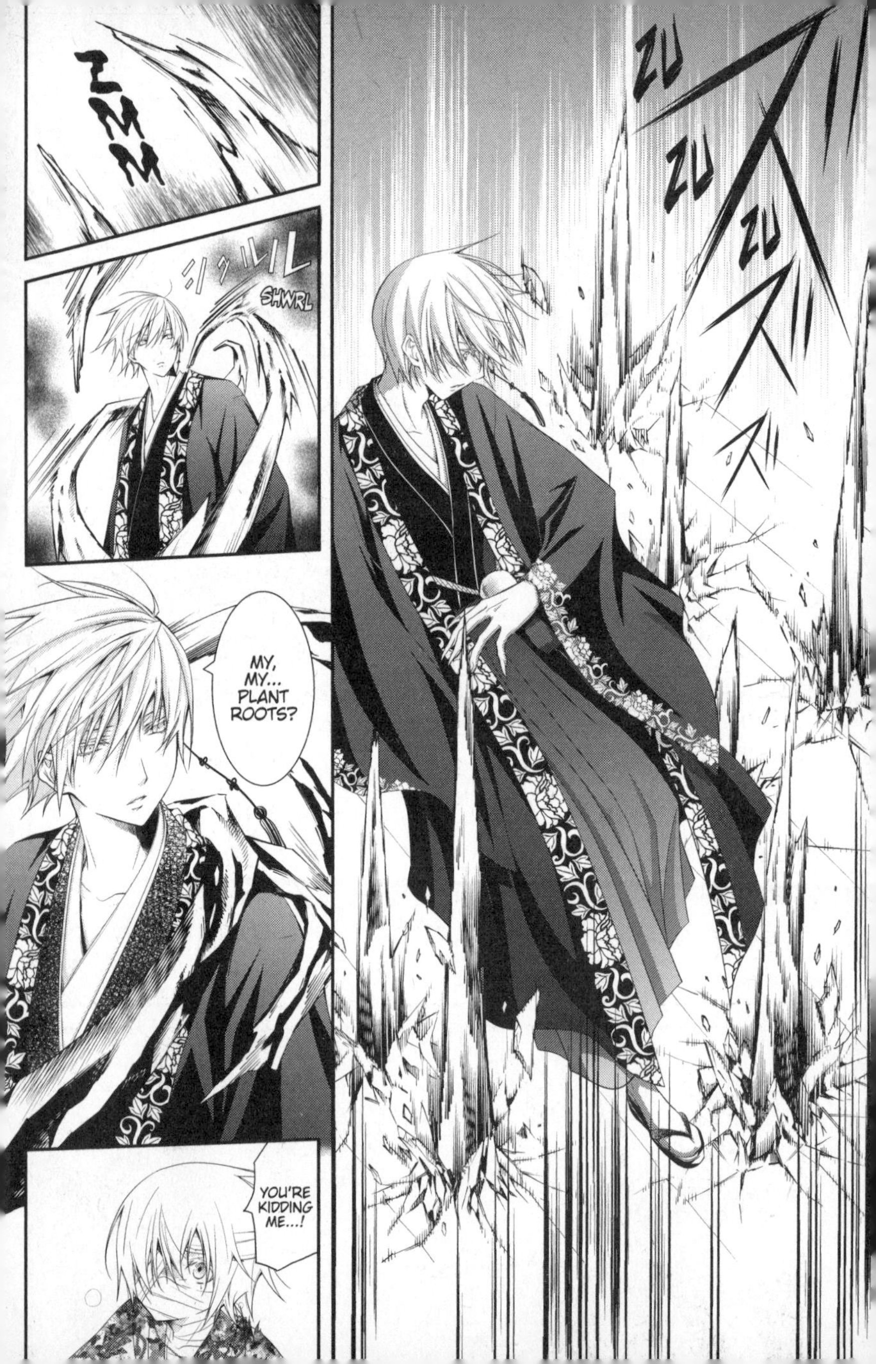
ZU
ZU
ZU
ZMM
SHWRL
MY, MY... PLANT ROOTS?
YOU'RE KIDDING ME...!

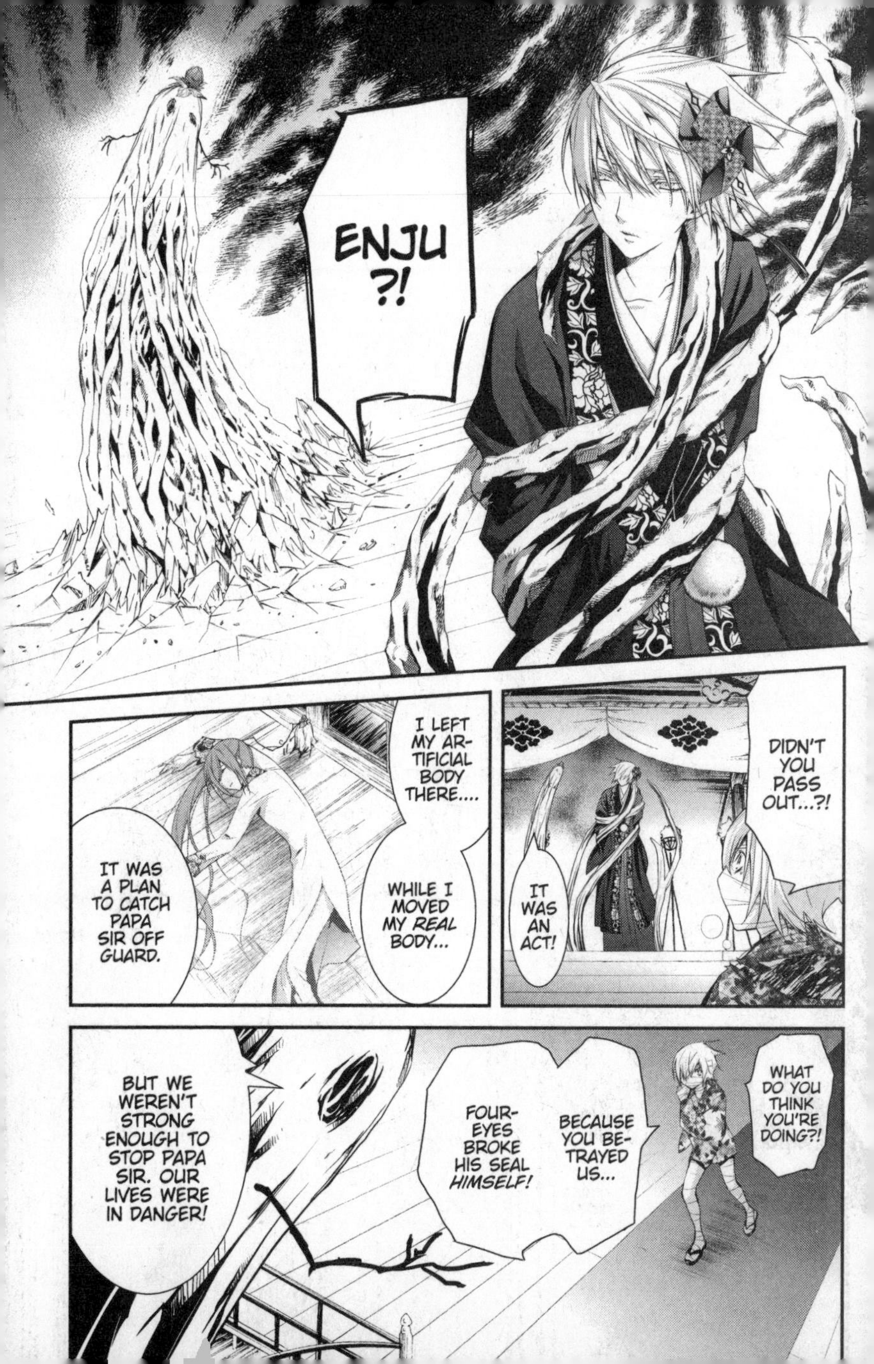
ENJU ?!
DIDN'T YOU PASS OUT...?!
IT WAS AN ACT!
I LEFT MY AR-TIFICIAL BODY THERE....
WHILE I MOVED MY *REAL* BODY...
IT WAS A PLAN TO CATCH PAPA SIR OFF GUARD.
WHAT DO YOU THINK YOU'RE DOING?!
BECAUSE YOU BE-TRAYED US...
FOUR-EYES BROKE HIS SEAL *HIMSELF*!
BUT WE WEREN'T STRONG ENOUGH TO STOP PAPA SIR. OUR LIVES WERE IN DANGER!

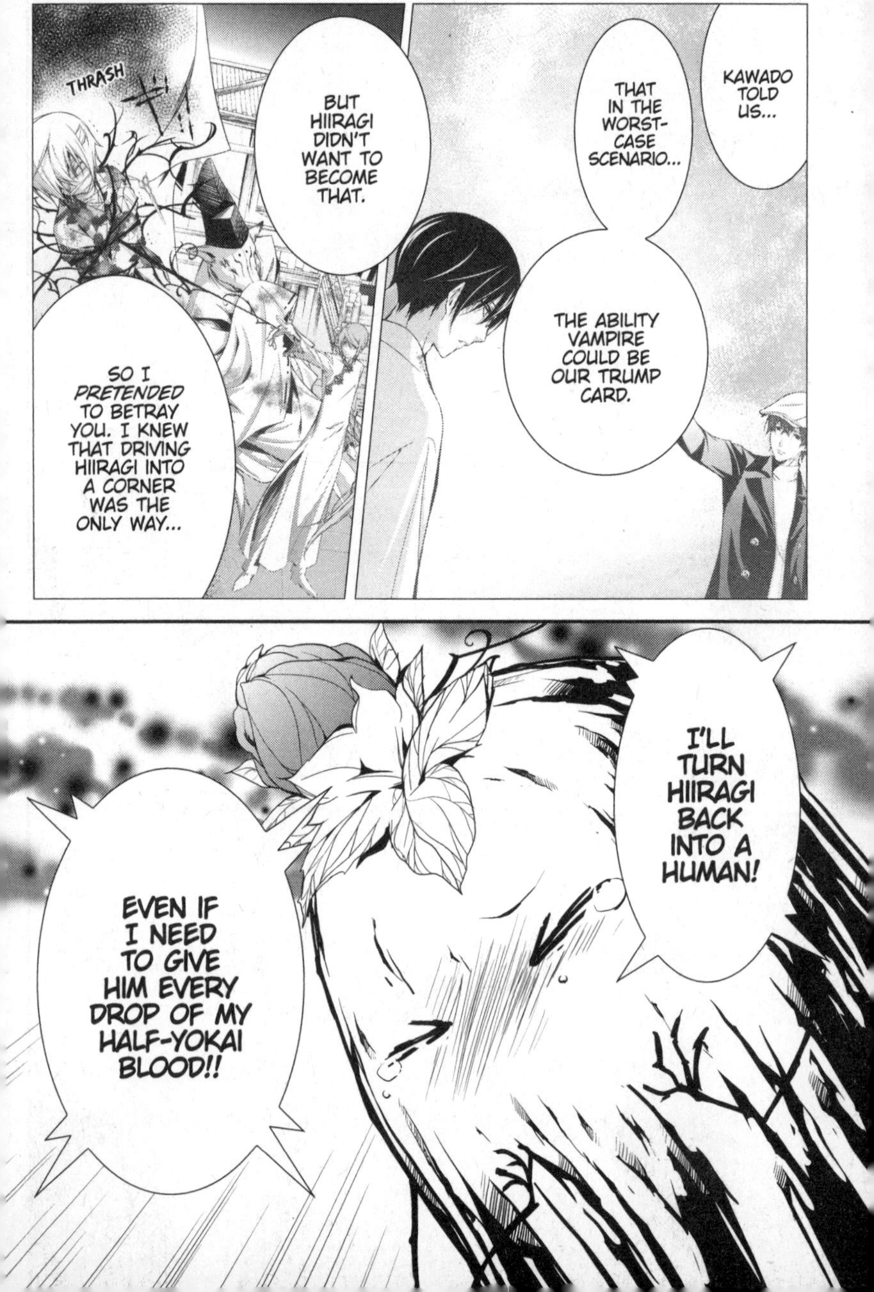
KAWADO TOLD US...
THAT IN THE WORST-CASE SCENARIO...
THE ABILITY VAMPIRE COULD BE OUR TRUMP CARD.
BUT HIIRAGI DIDN'T WANT TO BECOME THAT.
THRASH
SO I *PRETENDED* TO BETRAY YOU. I KNEW THAT DRIVING HIIRAGI INTO A CORNER WAS THE ONLY WAY...
I'LL TURN HIIRAGI BACK INTO A HUMAN!
EVEN IF I NEED TO GIVE HIM EVERY DROP OF MY HALF-YOKAI BLOOD!!

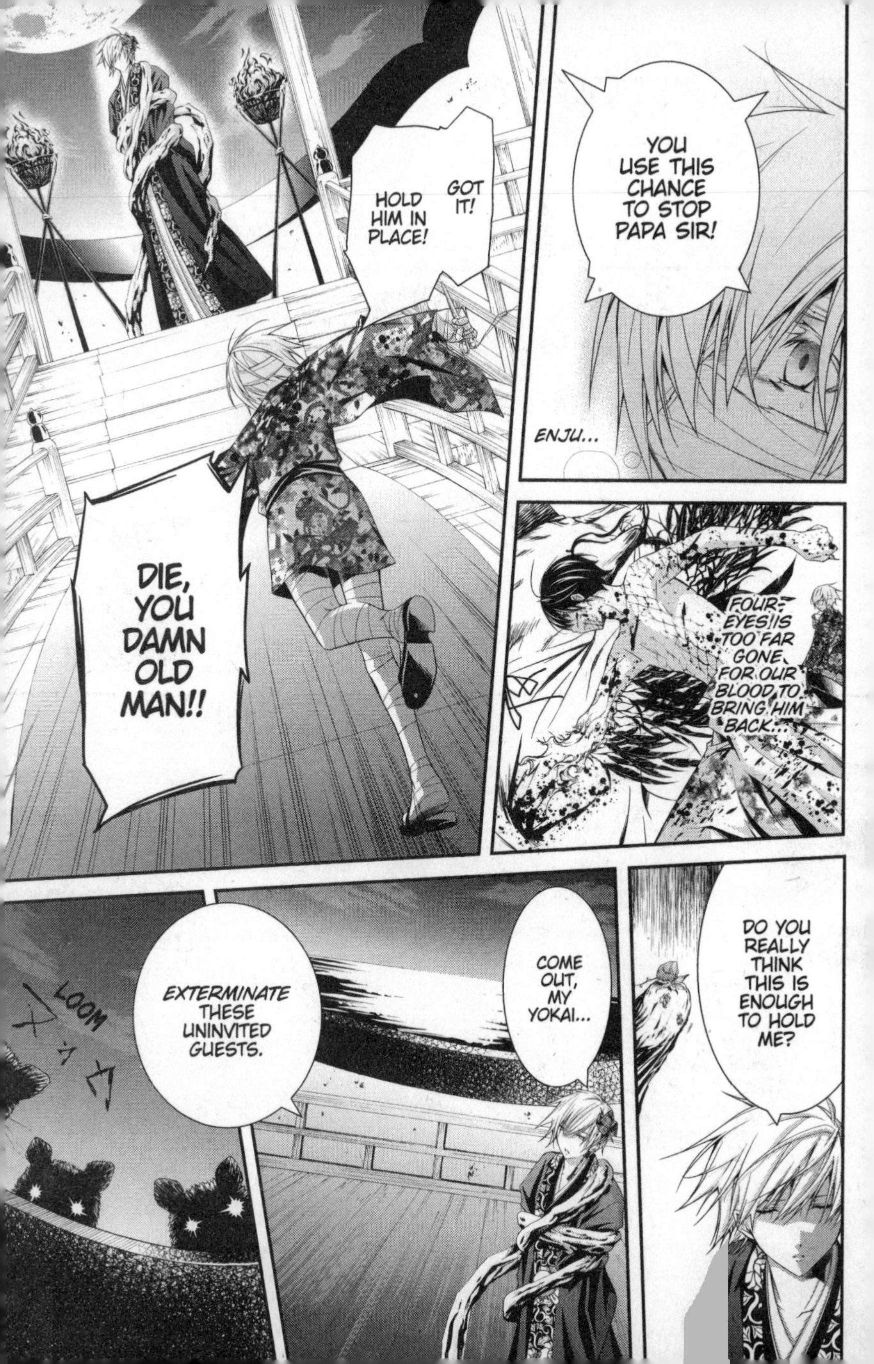
YOU USE THIS CHANCE TO STOP PAPA SIR!
ENJU...
FOUR-EYES IS TOO FAR GONE FOR OUR BLOOD TO BRING HIM BACK...
GOT IT!
HOLD HIM IN PLACE!
DIE, YOU DAMN OLD MAN!!
DO YOU REALLY THINK THIS IS ENOUGH TO HOLD ME?
COME OUT, MY YOKAI...
EXTERMINATE THESE UNINVITED GUESTS.
LOOM

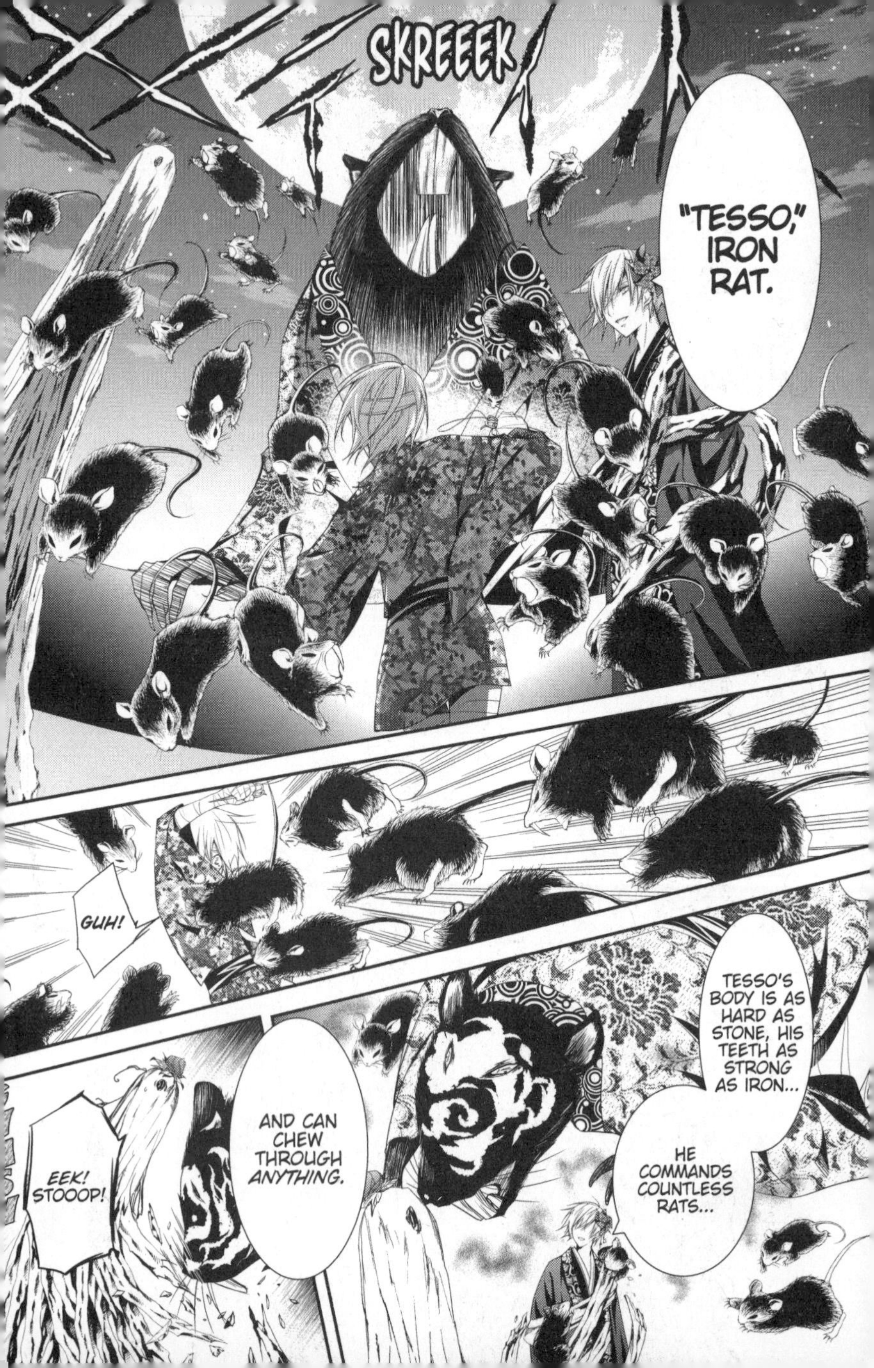
SKREEEK
"TESSO," IRON RAT.
GUH!
TESSO'S BODY IS AS HARD AS STONE, HIS TEETH AS STRONG AS IRON...
HE COMMANDS COUNTLESS RATS...
AND CAN CHEW THROUGH *ANYTHING.*
EEK! STOOOP!

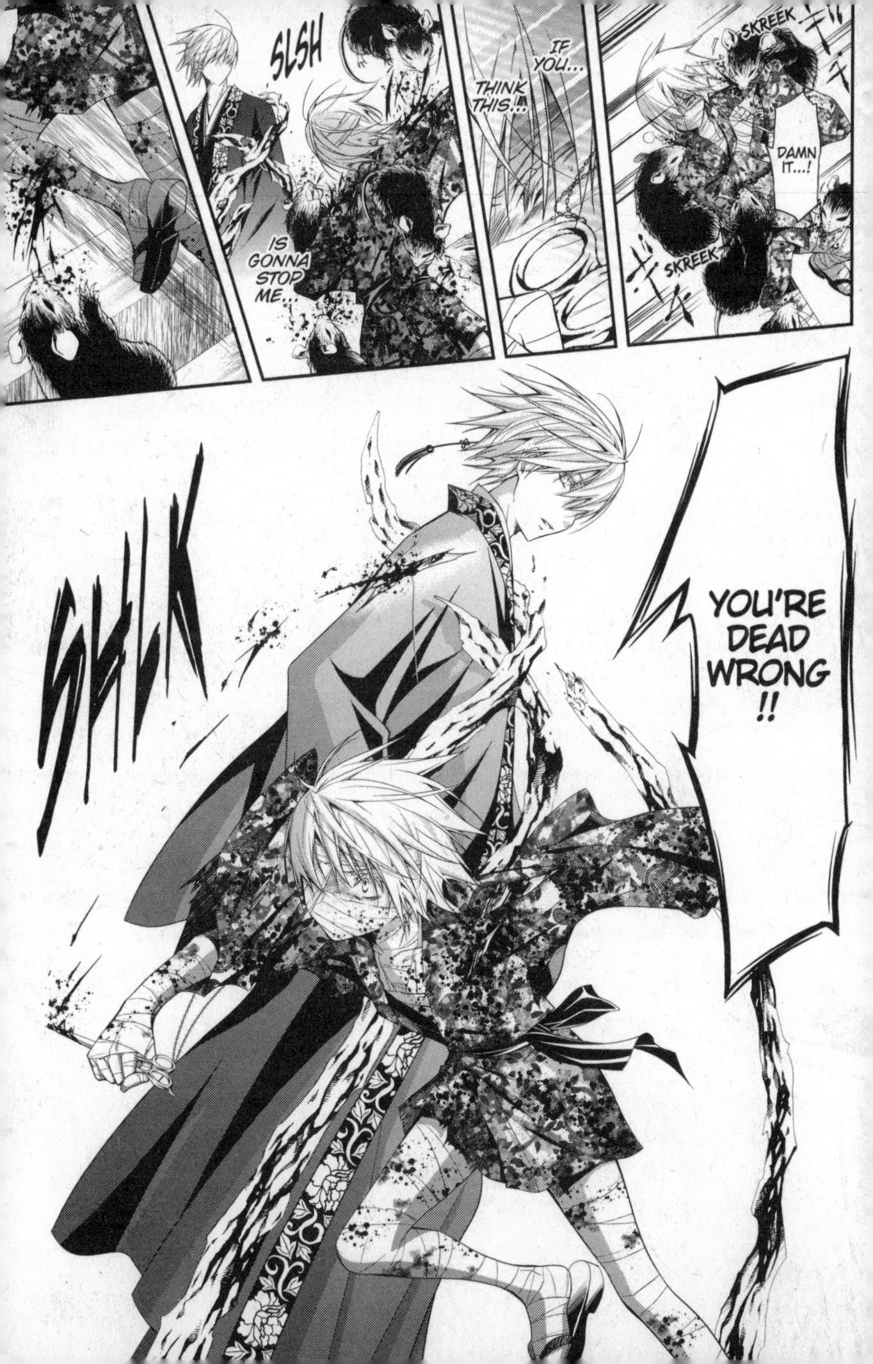
SKREEK
DAMN IT...!
SKREEK
IF YOU...
THINK THIS...
SLSH
IS GONNA STOP ME...
YOU'RE DEAD WRONG!!
SHK

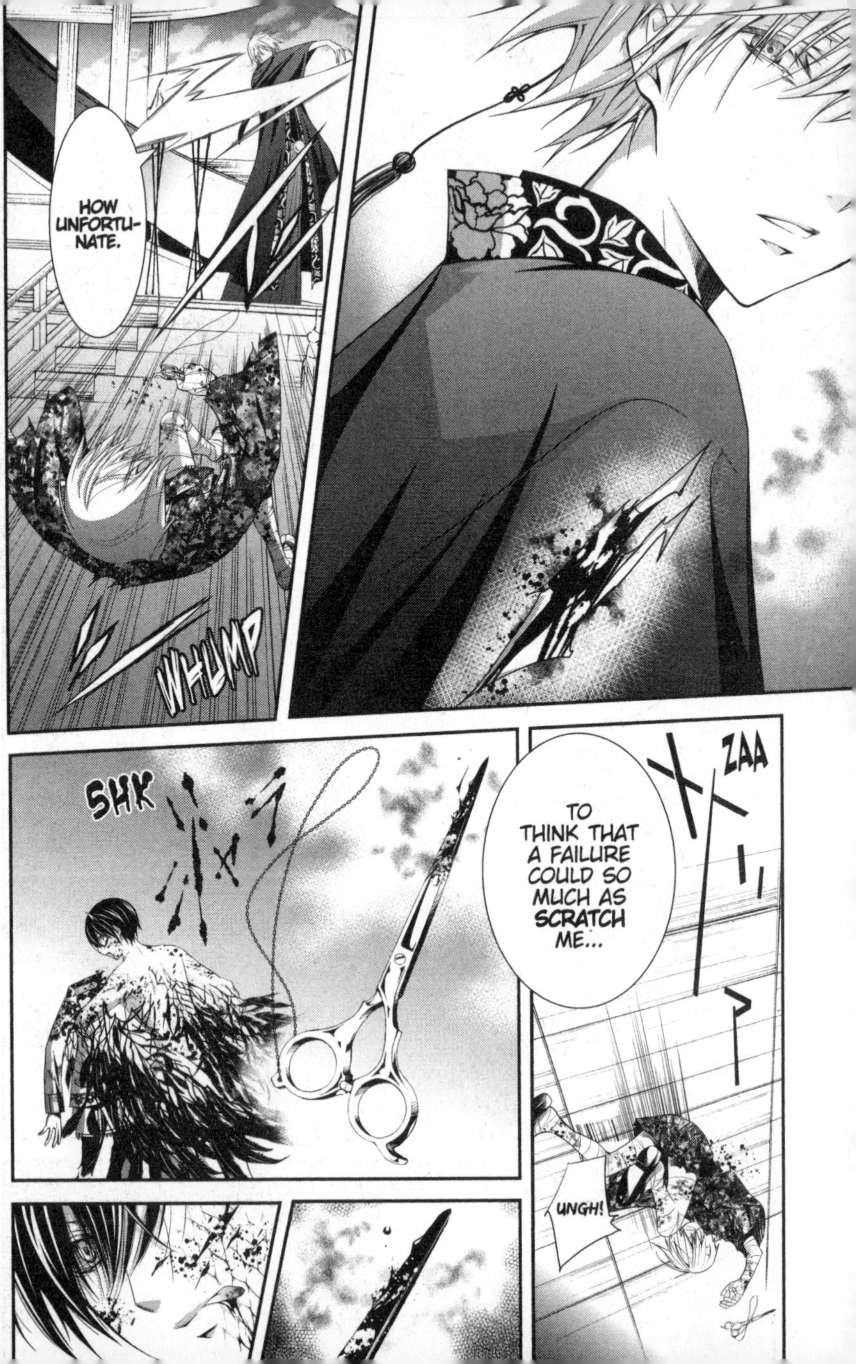
HOW UNFORTU-NATE.
WHUMP
ZAA
TO THINK THAT A FAILURE COULD SO MUCH AS SCRATCH ME...
UNGH!
SHK

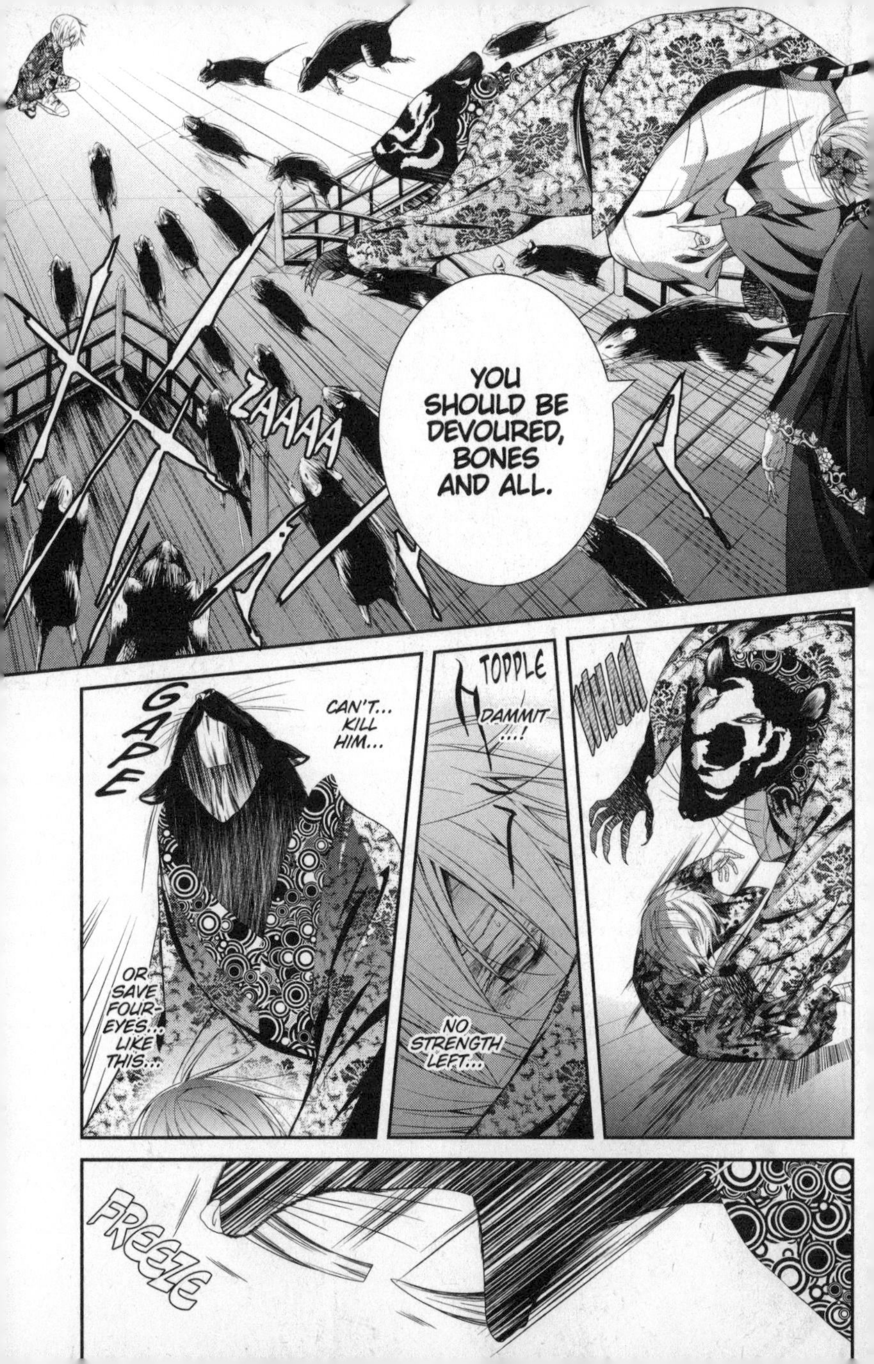
ZAAAAA
YOU SHOULD BE DEVOURED, BONES AND ALL.
WHAM
TOPPLE
DAMMIT...!
NO STRENGTH LEFT...
GAPE
CAN'T... KILL HIM...
OR SAVE FOUR-EYES... LIKE THIS...
FREEZE

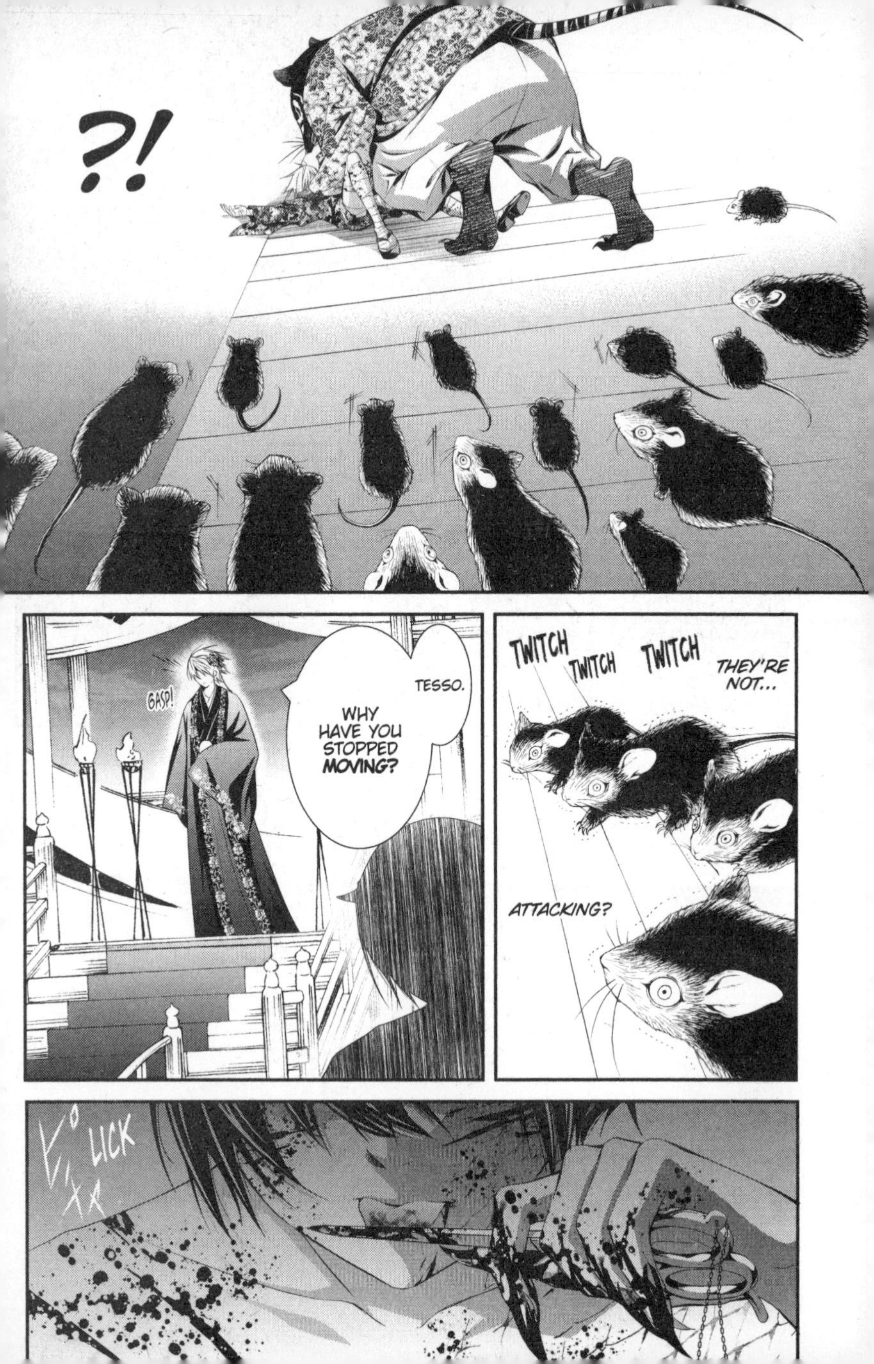
?!
TWITCH TWITCH TWITCH
THEY'RE NOT...
ATTACKING?
TESSO.
WHY HAVE YOU STOPPED MOVING?
GASP!
LICK

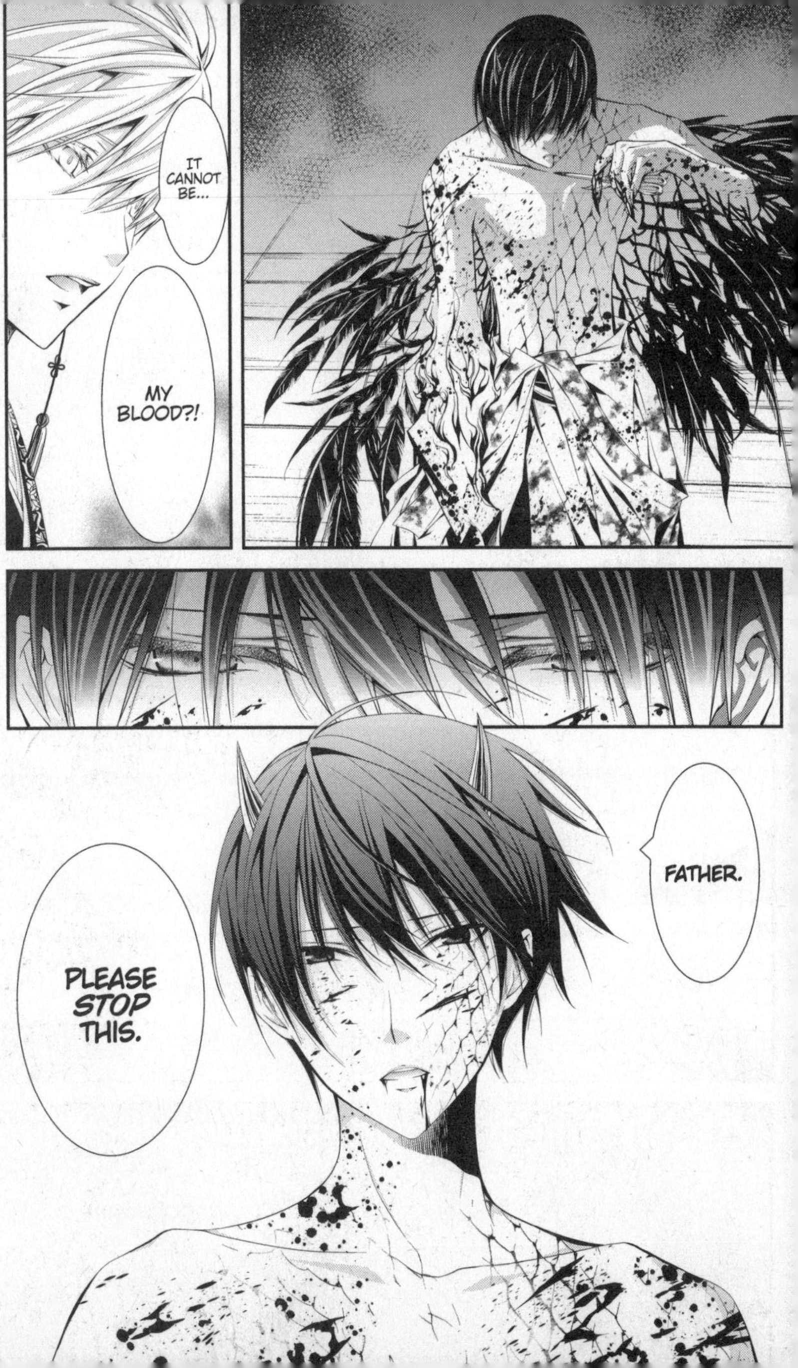
IT CANNOT BE...
MY BLOOD?!
FATHER.
PLEASE STOP THIS.

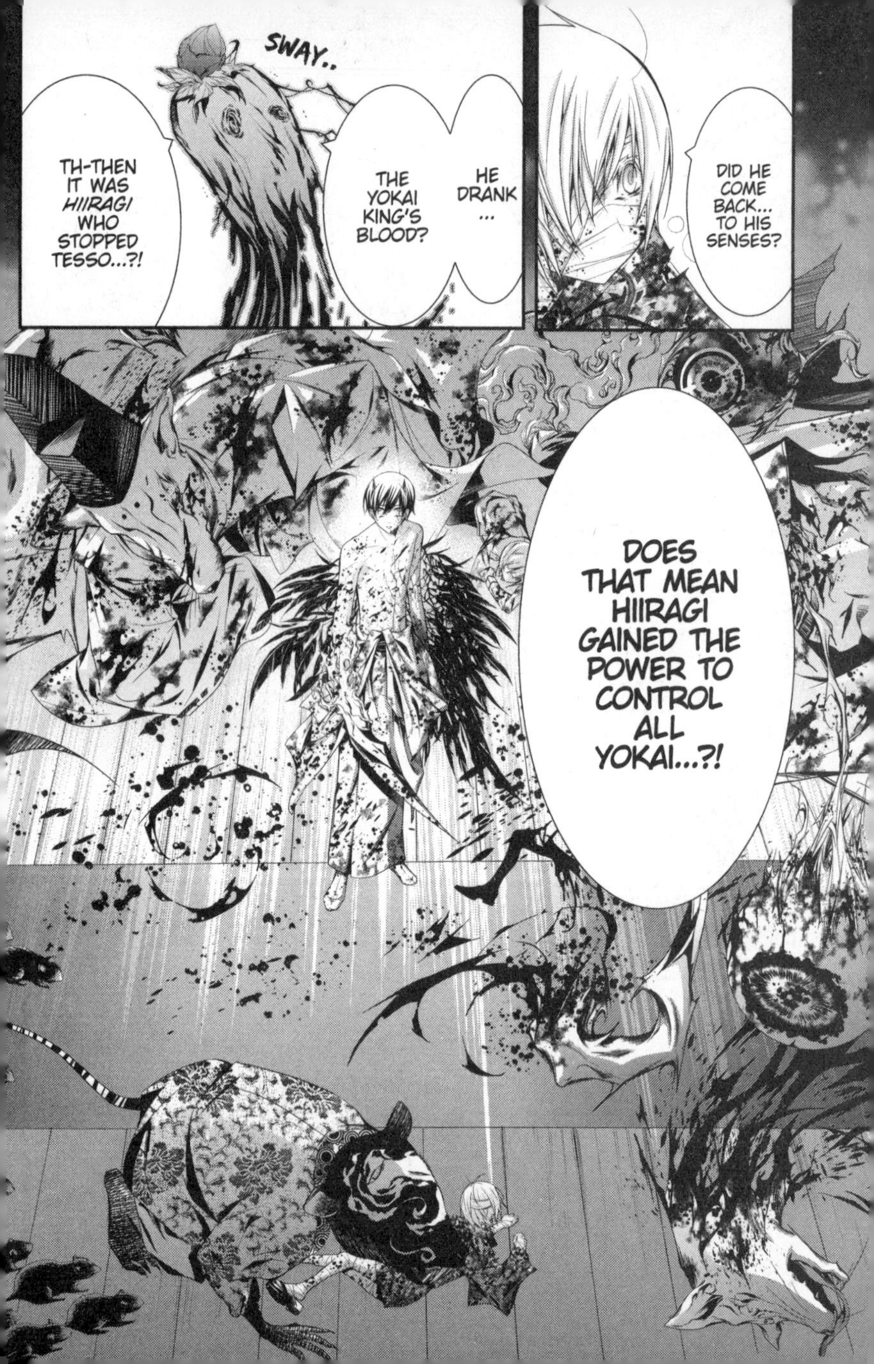
DID HE COME BACK... TO HIS SENSES?
HE DRANK ...
THE YOKAI KING'S BLOOD?
SWAY..
TH-THEN IT WAS *HIIRAGI* WHO STOPPED TESSO...?!
DOES THAT MEAN HIIRAGI GAINED THE POWER TO CONTROL ALL YOKAI...?!

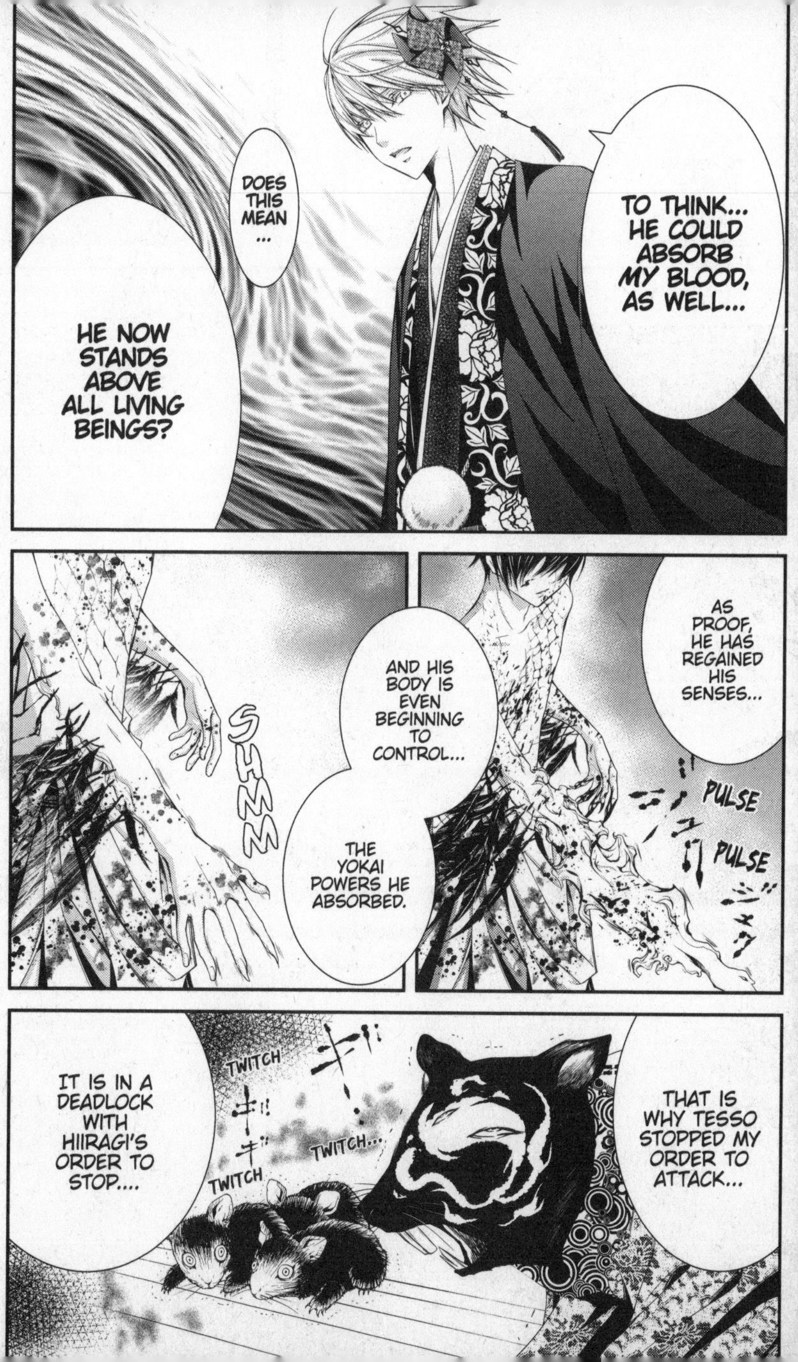
TO THINK... HE COULD ABSORB MY BLOOD, AS WELL...
DOES THIS MEAN ...
HE NOW STANDS ABOVE ALL LIVING BEINGS?
AS PROOF, HE HAS REGAINED HIS SENSES...
PULSE
PULSE
AND HIS BODY IS EVEN BEGINNING TO CONTROL...
THE YOKAI POWERS HE ABSORBED.
SHMM
THAT IS WHY TESSO STOPPED MY ORDER TO ATTACK...
TWITCH
TWITCH...
TWITCH
IT IS IN A DEADLOCK WITH HIIRAGI'S ORDER TO STOP....

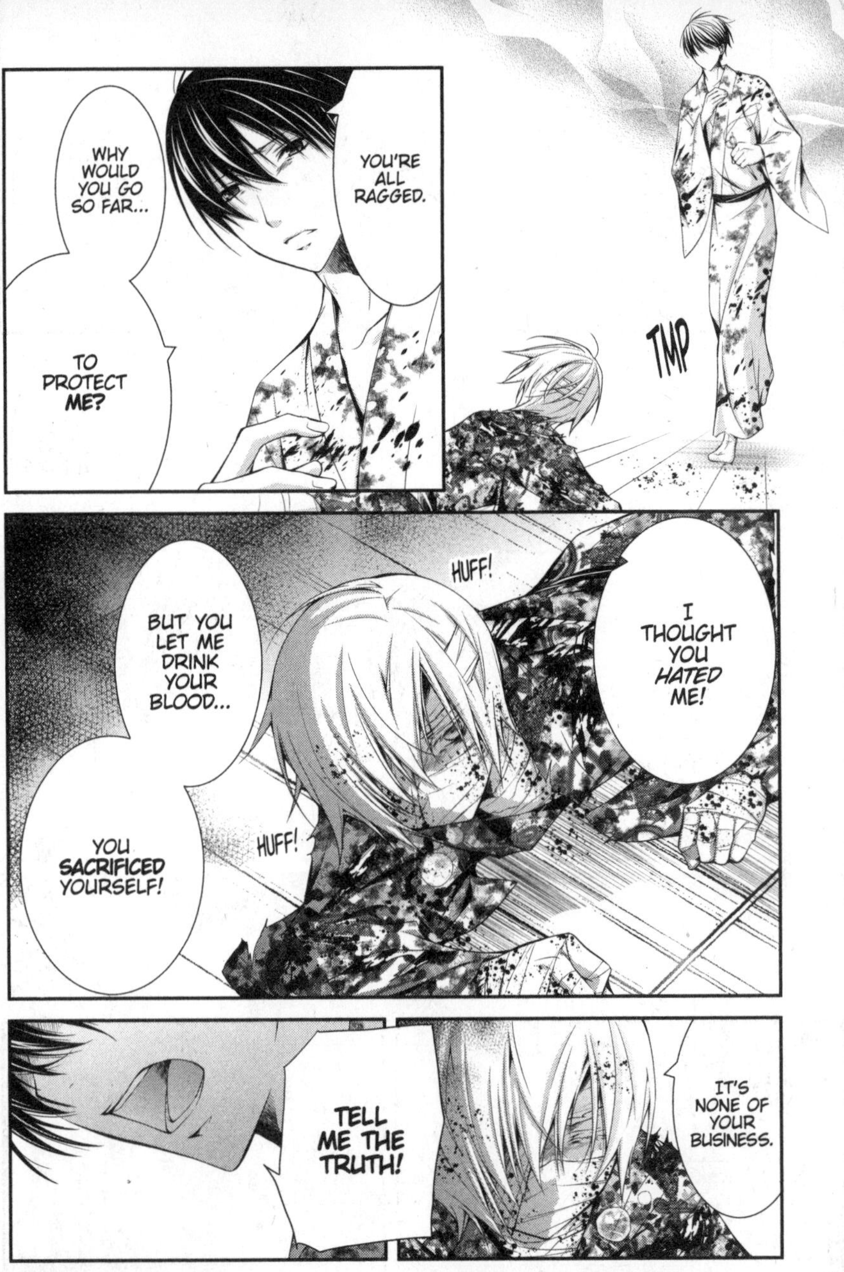
TMP
YOU'RE ALL RAGGED.
WHY WOULD YOU GO SO FAR...
TO PROTECT ME?
HUFF!
I THOUGHT YOU HATED ME!
BUT YOU LET ME DRINK YOUR BLOOD...
HUFF!
YOU SACRIFICED YOURSELF!
IT'S NONE OF YOUR BUSINESS.
TELL ME THE TRUTH!

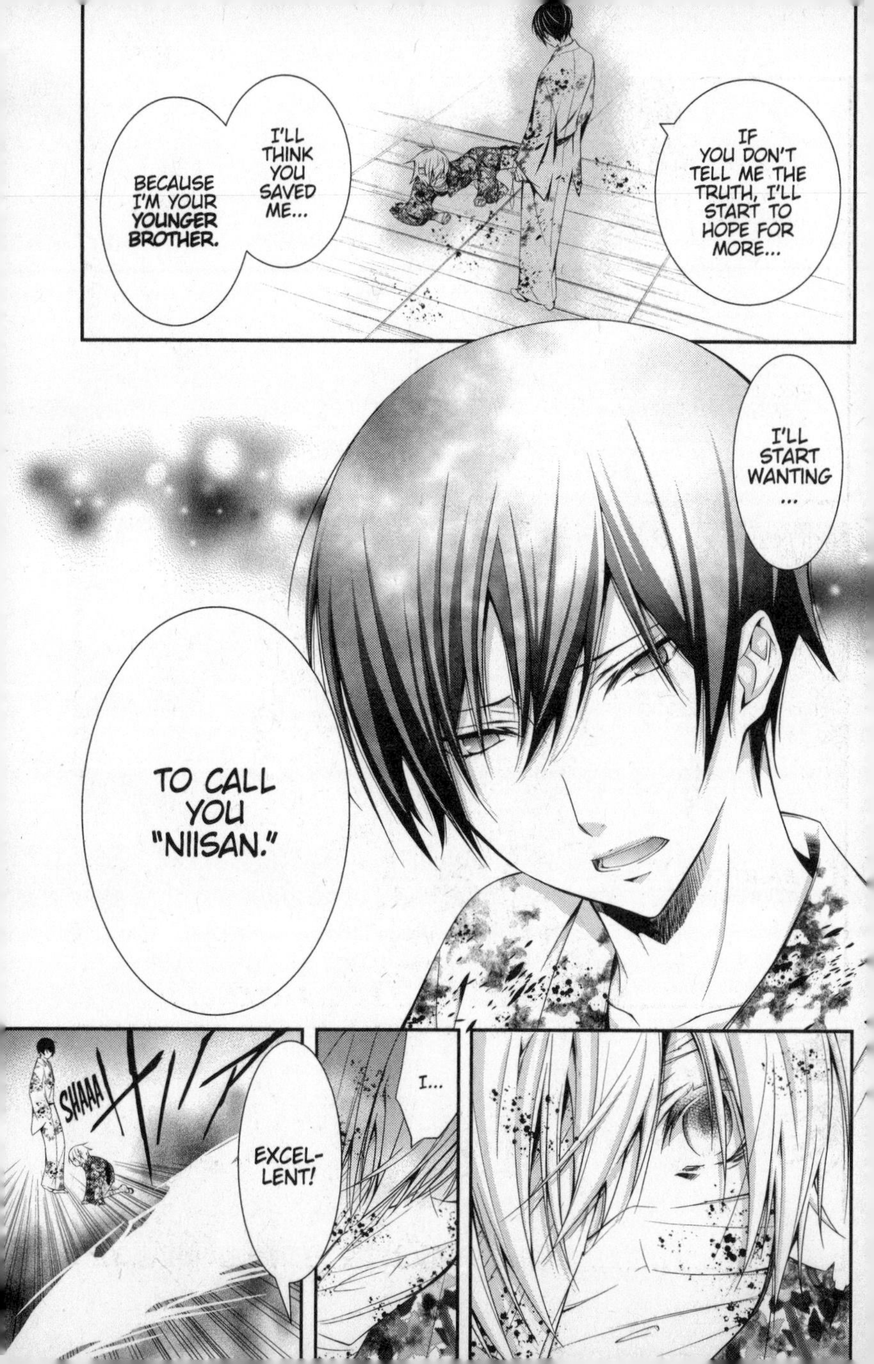
IF YOU DON'T TELL ME THE TRUTH, I'LL START TO HOPE FOR MORE...
I'LL THINK YOU SAVED ME...
BECAUSE I'M YOUR YOUNGER BROTHER.
I'LL START WANTING...
TO CALL YOU "NIISAN."
I...
EXCEL-LENT!
SHAAA

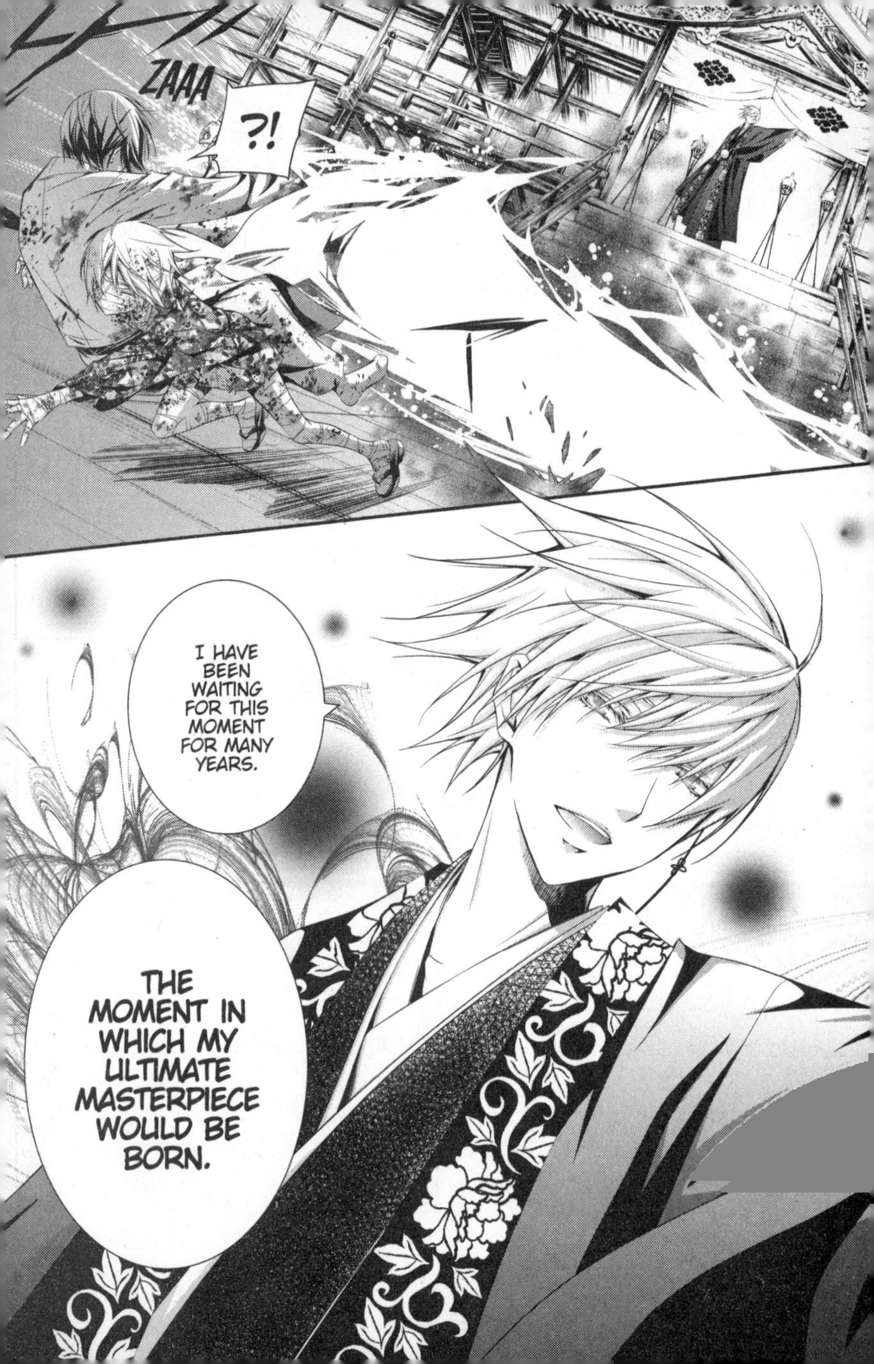
ZAAA
?!
I HAVE BEEN WAITING FOR THIS MOMENT FOR MANY YEARS.
THE MOMENT IN WHICH MY ULTIMATE MASTERPIECE WOULD BE BORN.

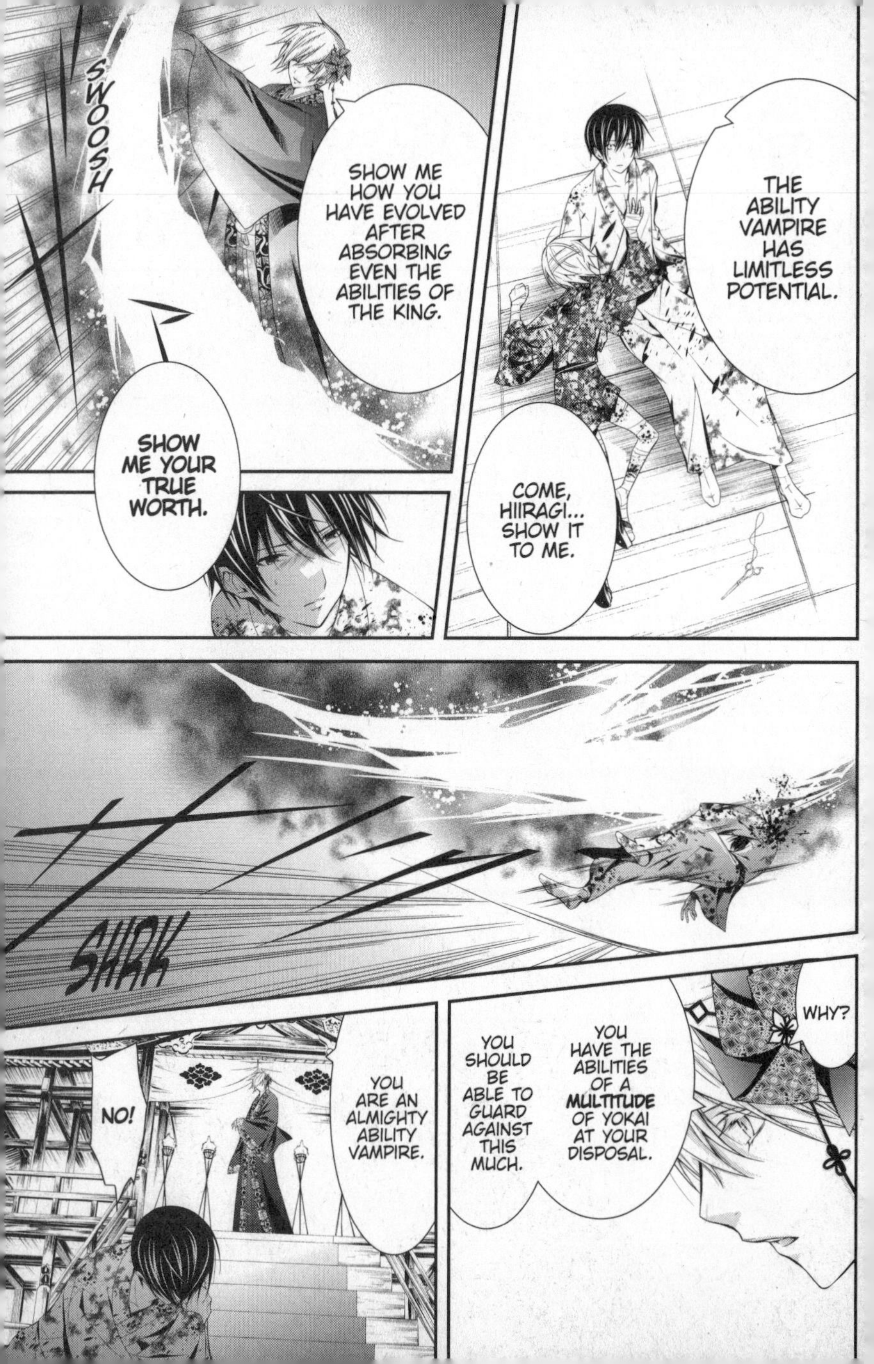
THE ABILITY VAMPIRE HAS LIMITLESS POTENTIAL.
COME, HIIRAGI... SHOW IT TO ME.
SWOOSH
SHOW ME HOW YOU HAVE EVOLVED AFTER ABSORBING EVEN THE ABILITIES OF THE KING.
SHOW ME YOUR TRUE WORTH.
SHRK
WHY?
YOU HAVE THE ABILITIES OF A **MULTITUDE** OF YOKAI AT YOUR DISPOSAL.
YOU SHOULD BE ABLE TO GUARD AGAINST THIS MUCH.
YOU ARE AN ALMIGHTY ABILITY VAMPIRE.
NO!

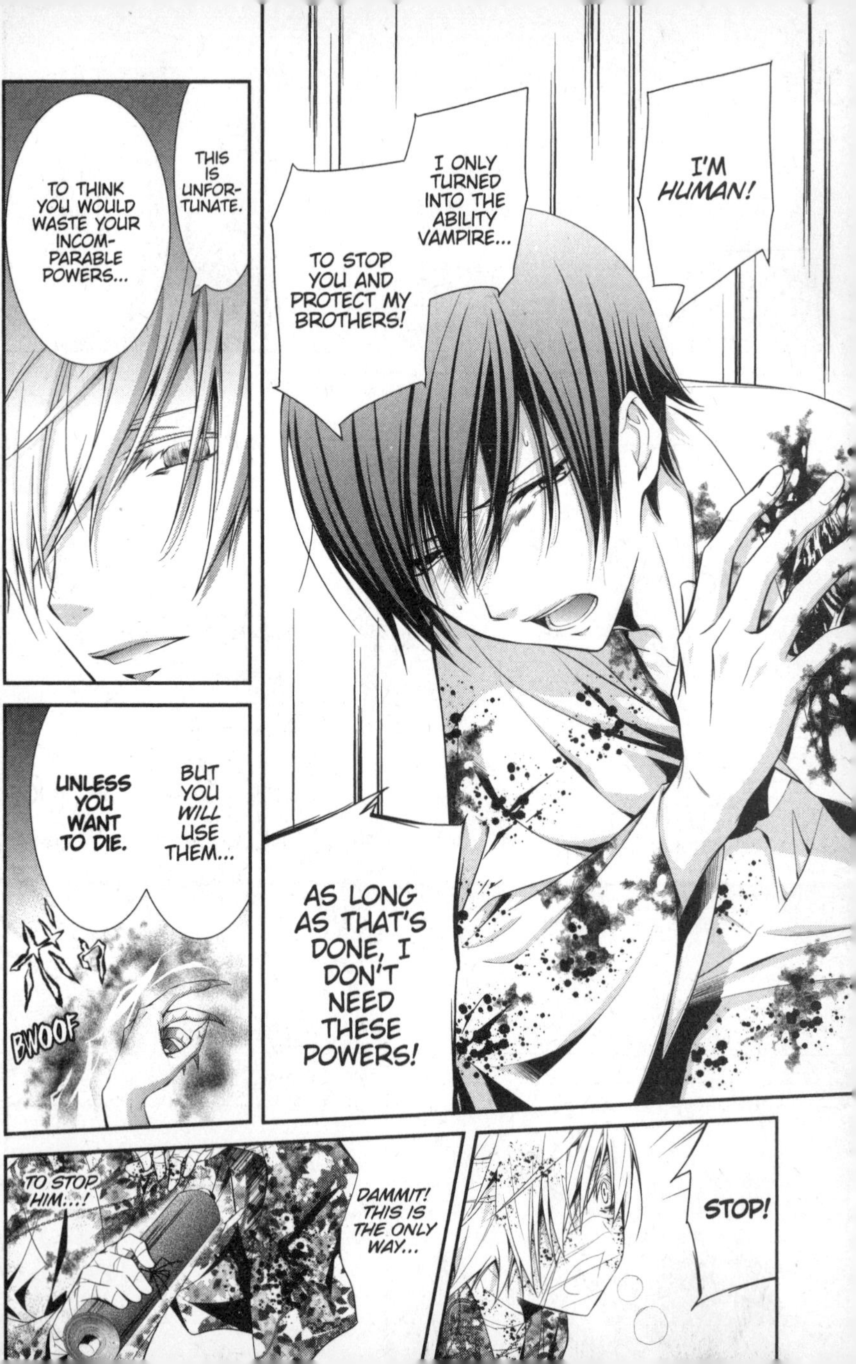
I'M *HUMAN!*
I ONLY TURNED INTO THE ABILITY VAMPIRE...
TO STOP YOU AND PROTECT MY BROTHERS!
AS LONG AS THAT'S DONE, I DON'T NEED THESE POWERS!
THIS IS UNFORTUNATE.
TO THINK YOU WOULD WASTE YOUR INCOMPARABLE POWERS...
BUT YOU *WILL* USE THEM...
UNLESS YOU WANT TO DIE.
BWOOF
STOP!
DAMMIT! THIS IS THE ONLY WAY...
TO STOP HIM...!

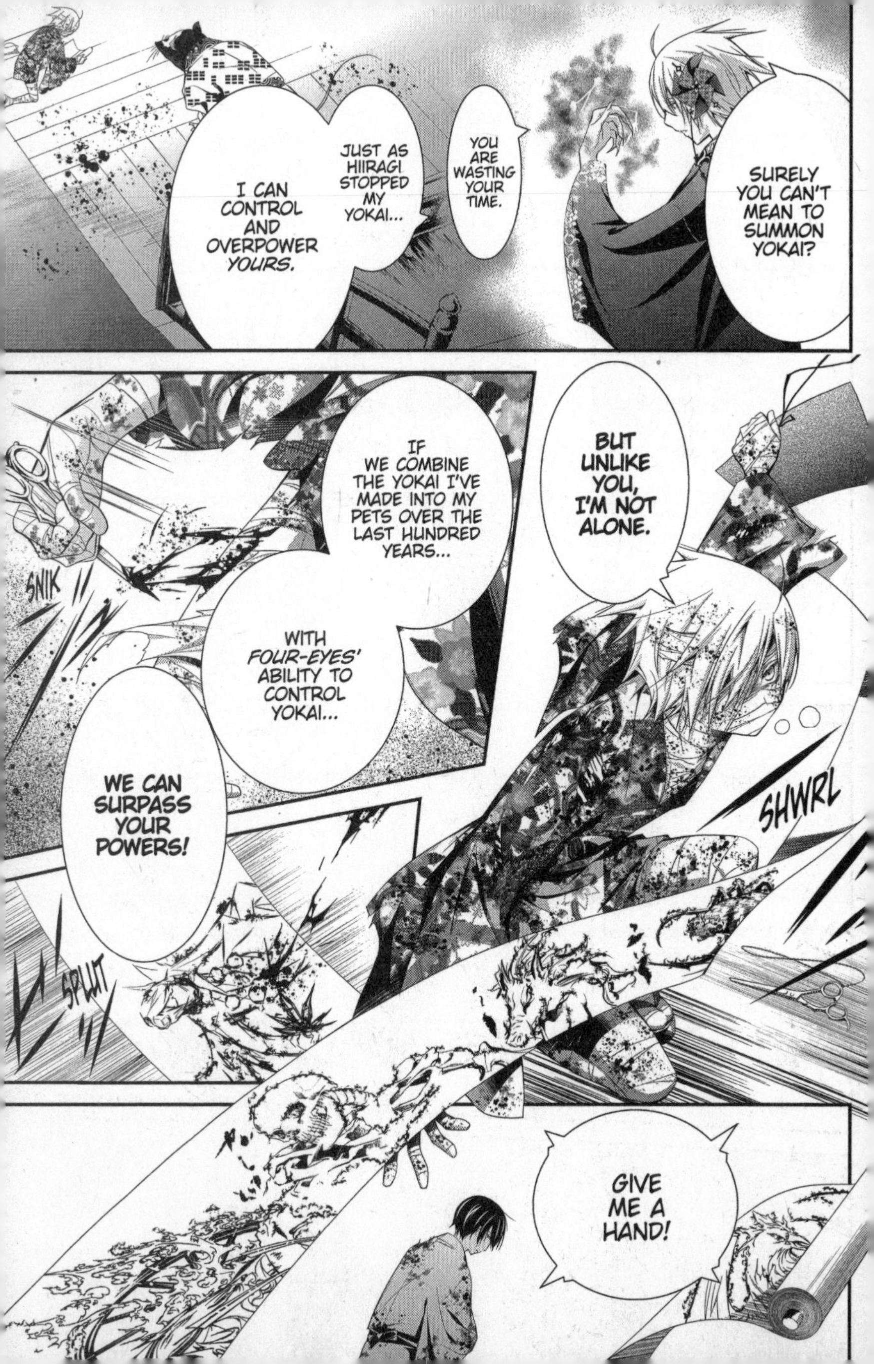
SURELY YOU CAN'T MEAN TO SUMMON YOKAI?
YOU ARE WASTING YOUR TIME.
JUST AS HIIRAGI STOPPED MY YOKAI...
I CAN CONTROL AND OVERPOWER YOURS.
BUT UNLIKE YOU, I'M NOT ALONE.
IF WE COMBINE THE YOKAI I'VE MADE INTO MY PETS OVER THE LAST HUNDRED YEARS...
WITH FOUR-EYES' ABILITY TO CONTROL YOKAI...
WE CAN SURPASS YOUR POWERS!
SHWRL
SNIK
SPLUT
GIVE ME A HAND!

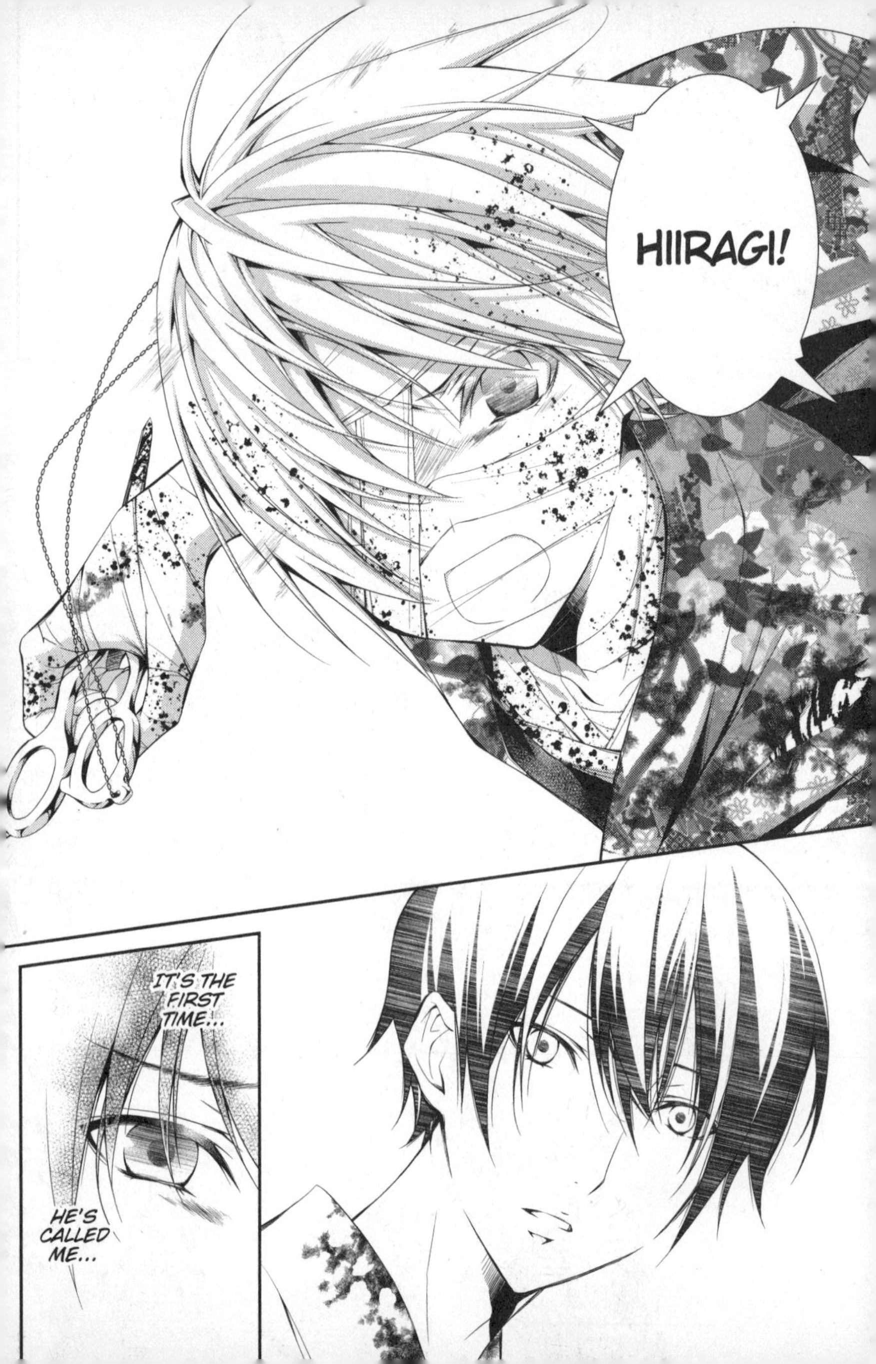
HIIRAGI!
IT'S THE FIRST TIME...
HE'S CALLED ME...

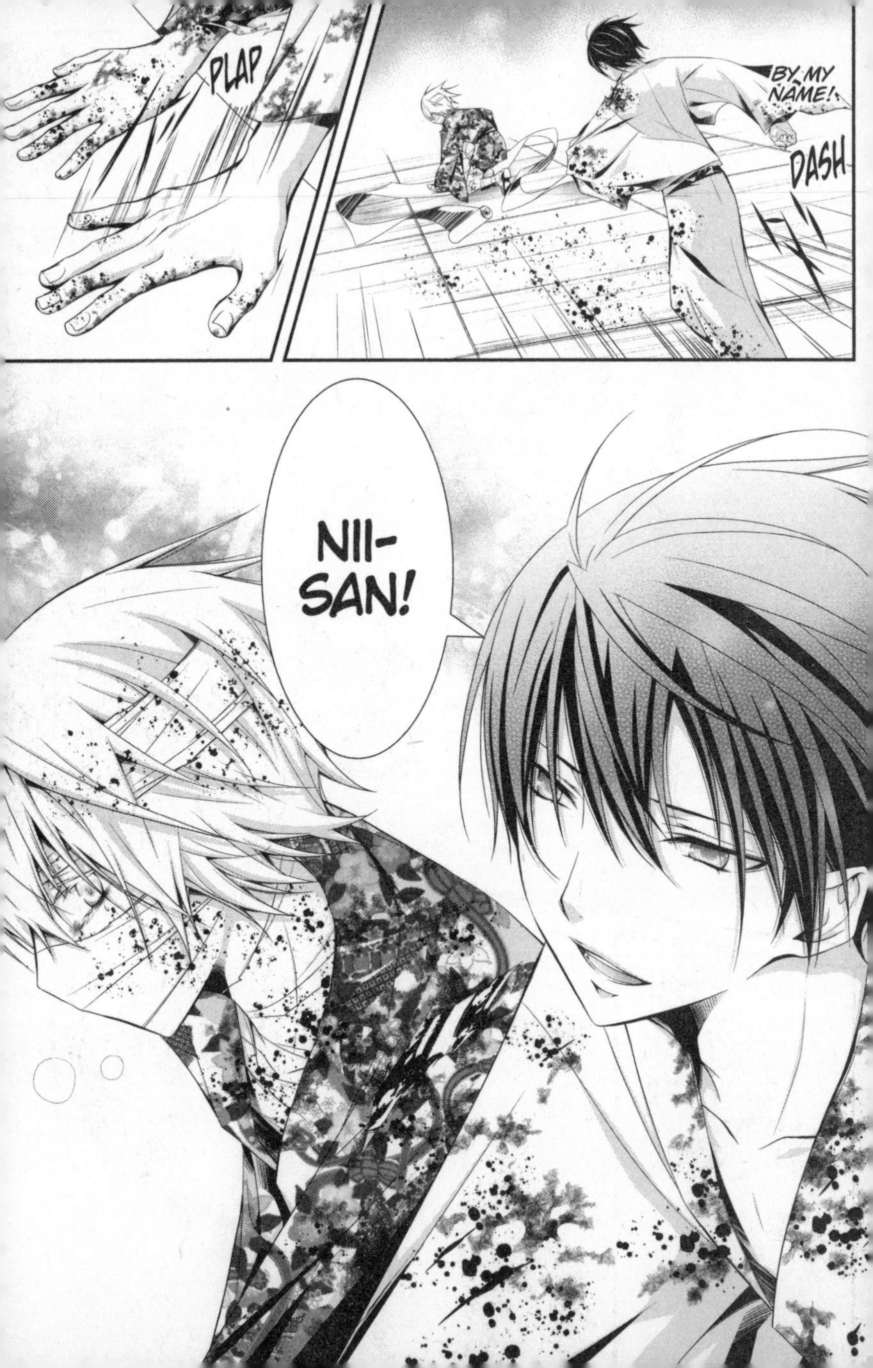
BY MY NAME!
DASH
PLAP
NII-SAN!

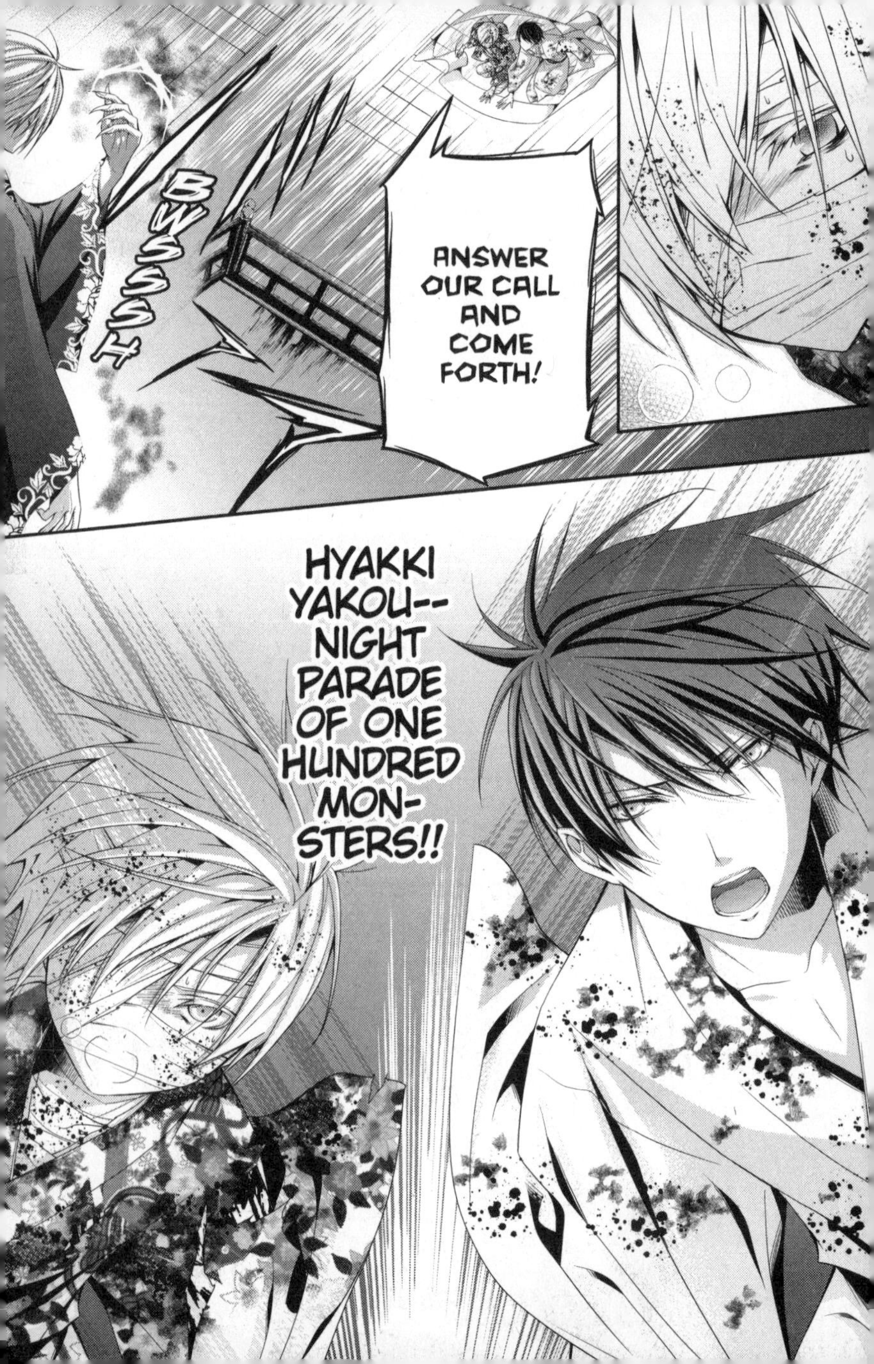
ANSWER OUR CALL AND COME FORTH!
BWSSSH
HYAKKI YAKOU-- NIGHT PARADE OF ONE HUNDRED MON-STERS!!

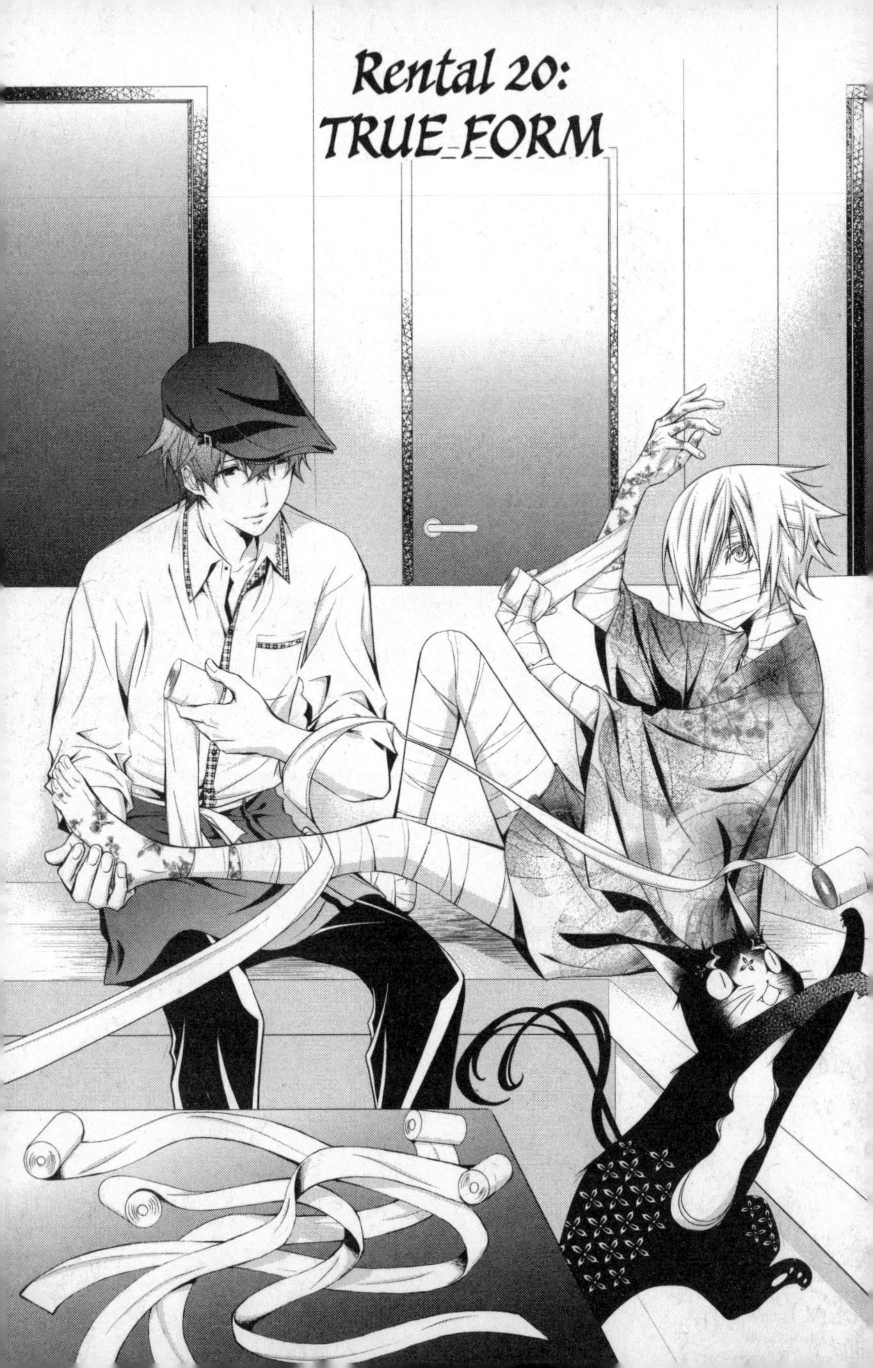
Rental 20:
TRUE_FORM

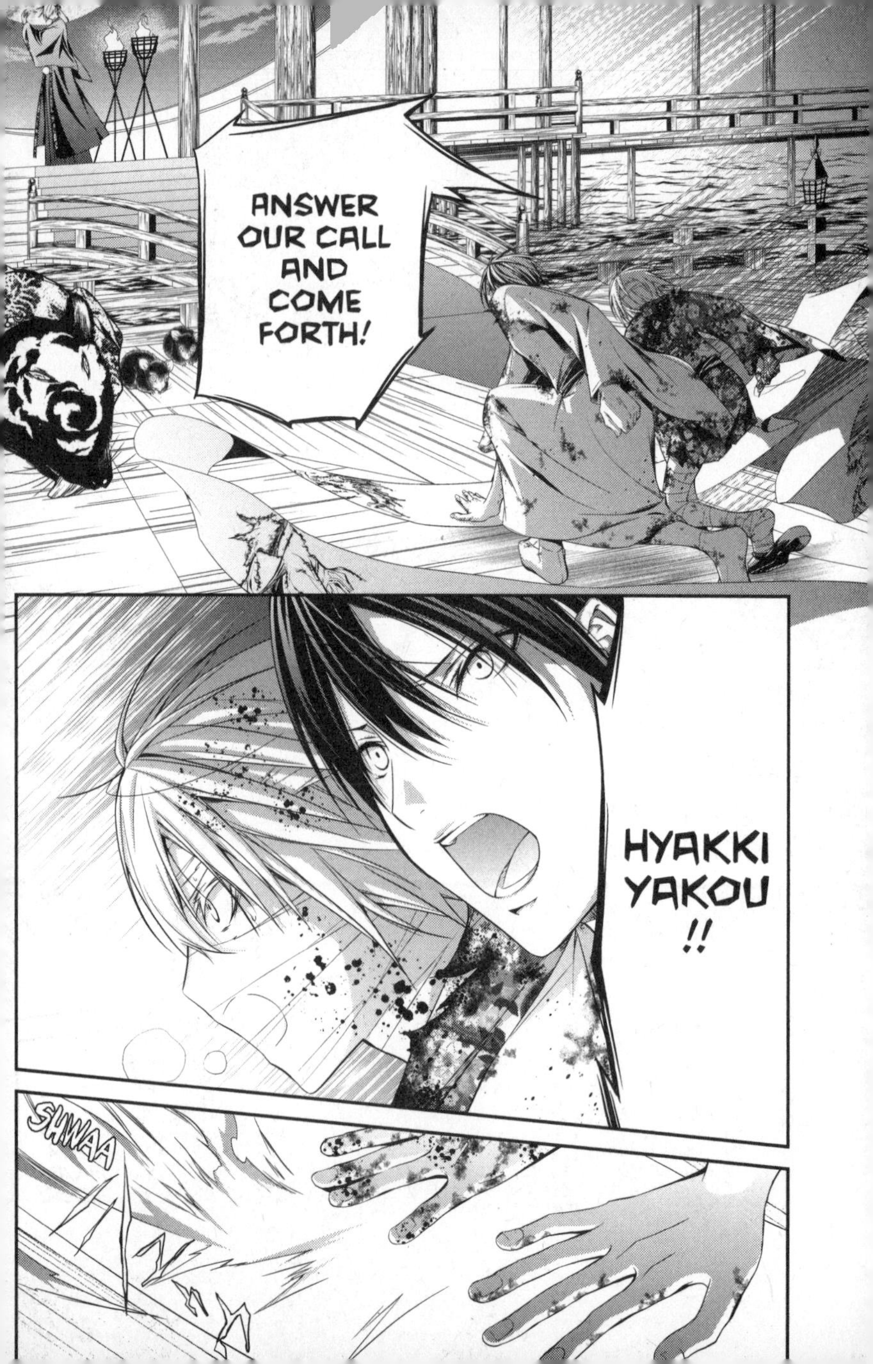
ANSWER OUR CALL AND COME FORTH!
HYAKKI YAKOU !!
SHWAA

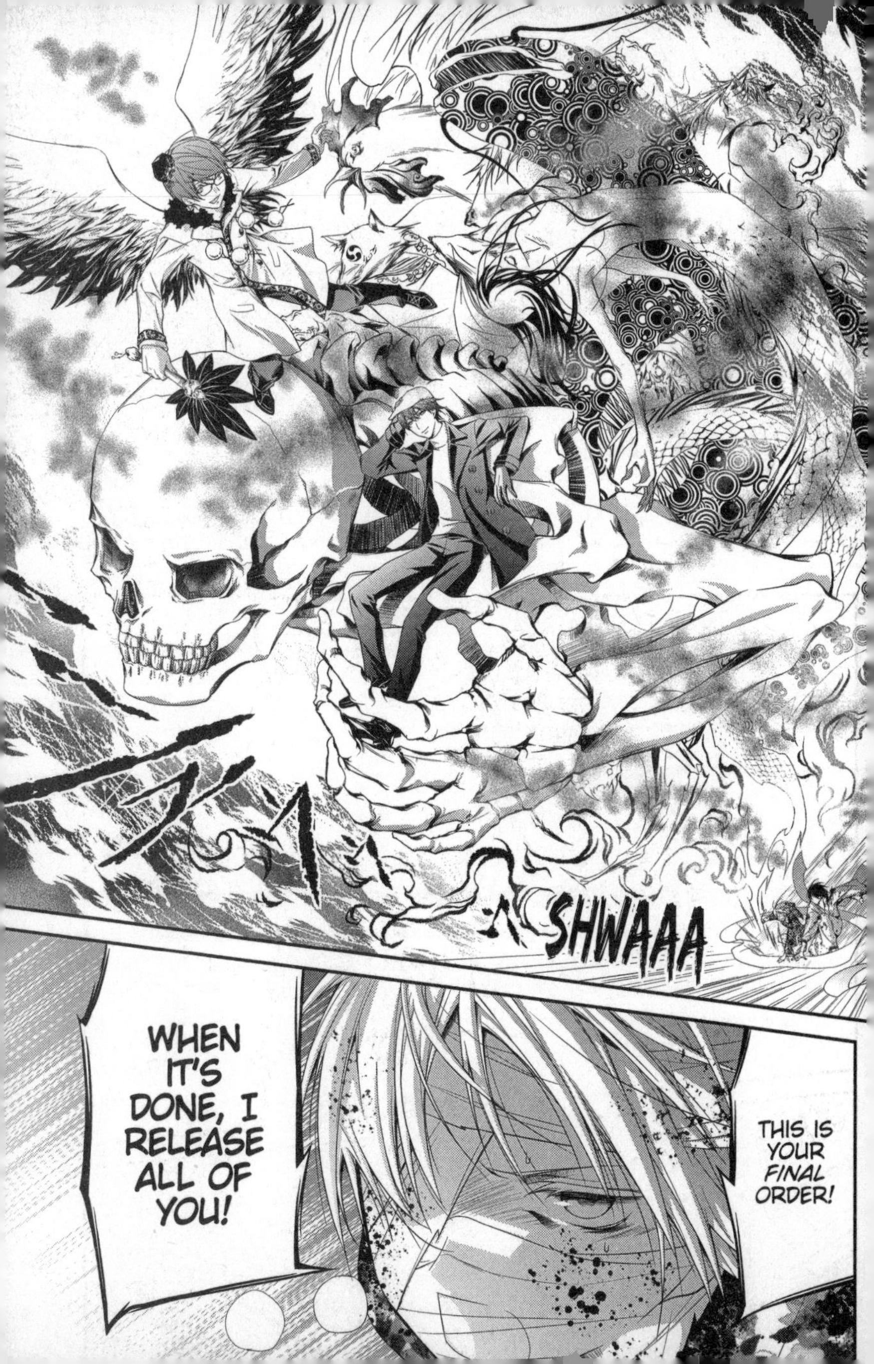

SHWAAA
THIS IS YOUR FINAL ORDER!
WHEN IT'S DONE, I RELEASE ALL OF YOU!

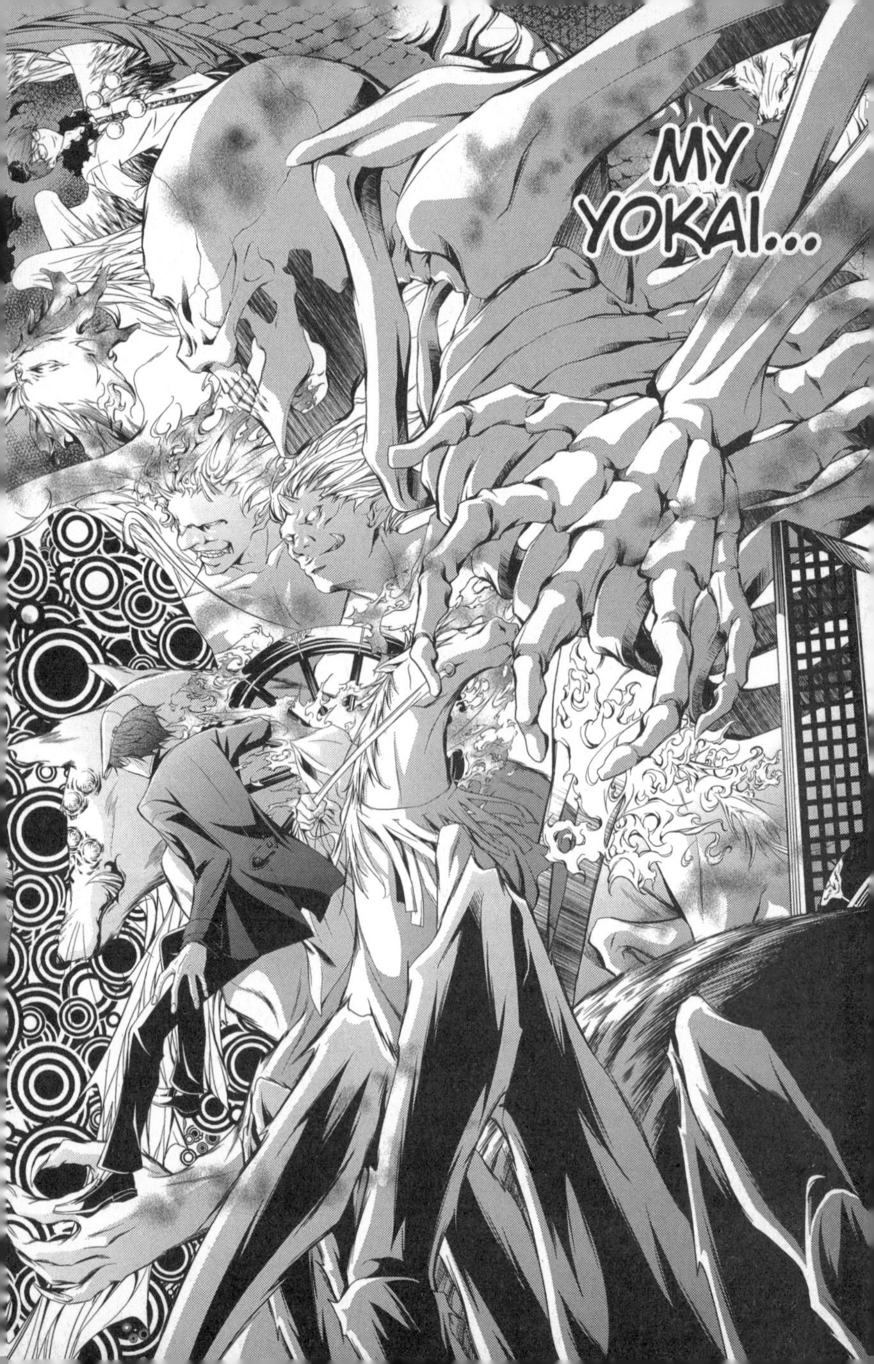
MY YOKAI...

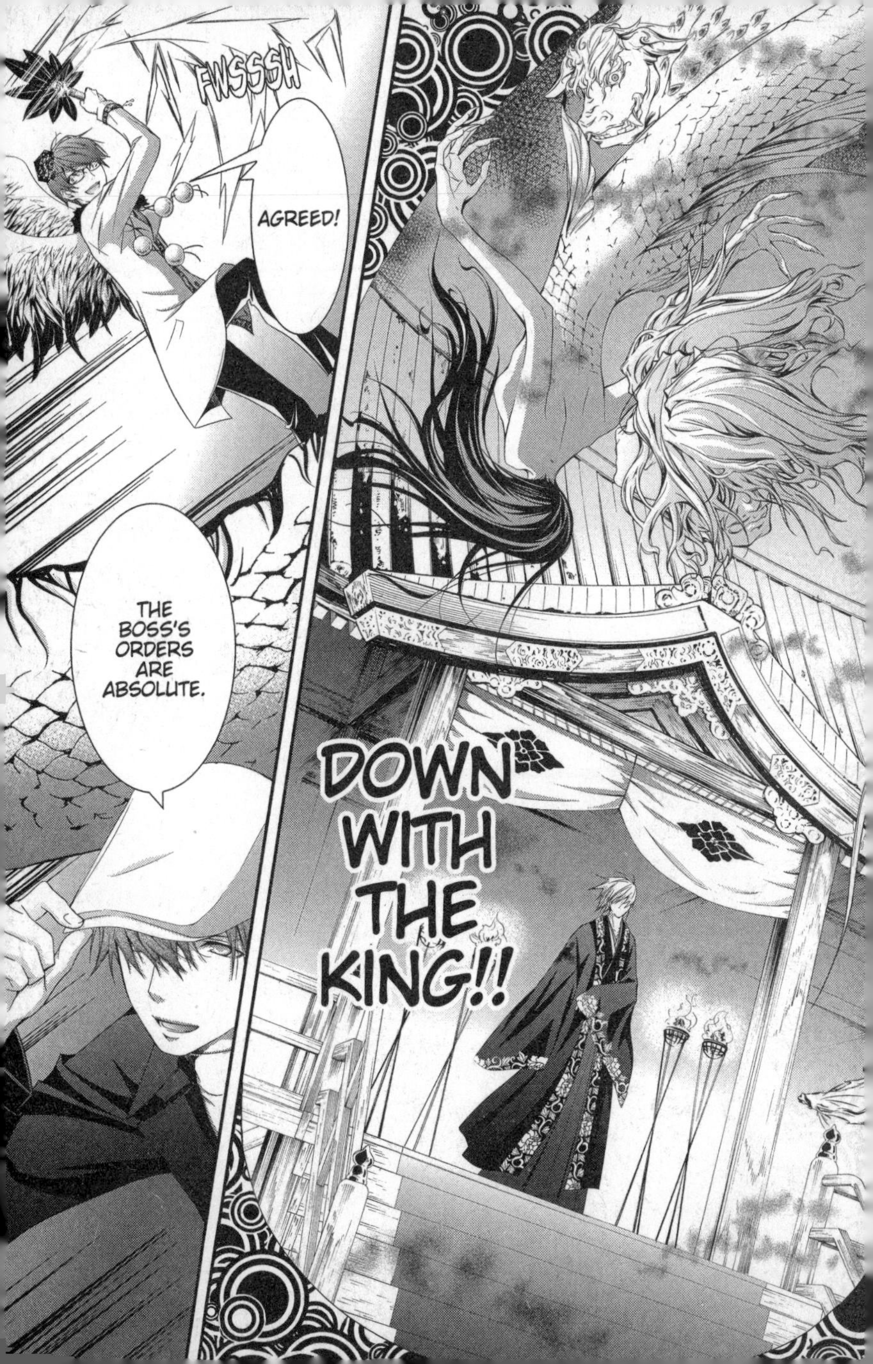
DOWN WITH THE KING!!
FWSSSH
AGREED!
THE BOSS'S ORDERS ARE ABSOLUTE.

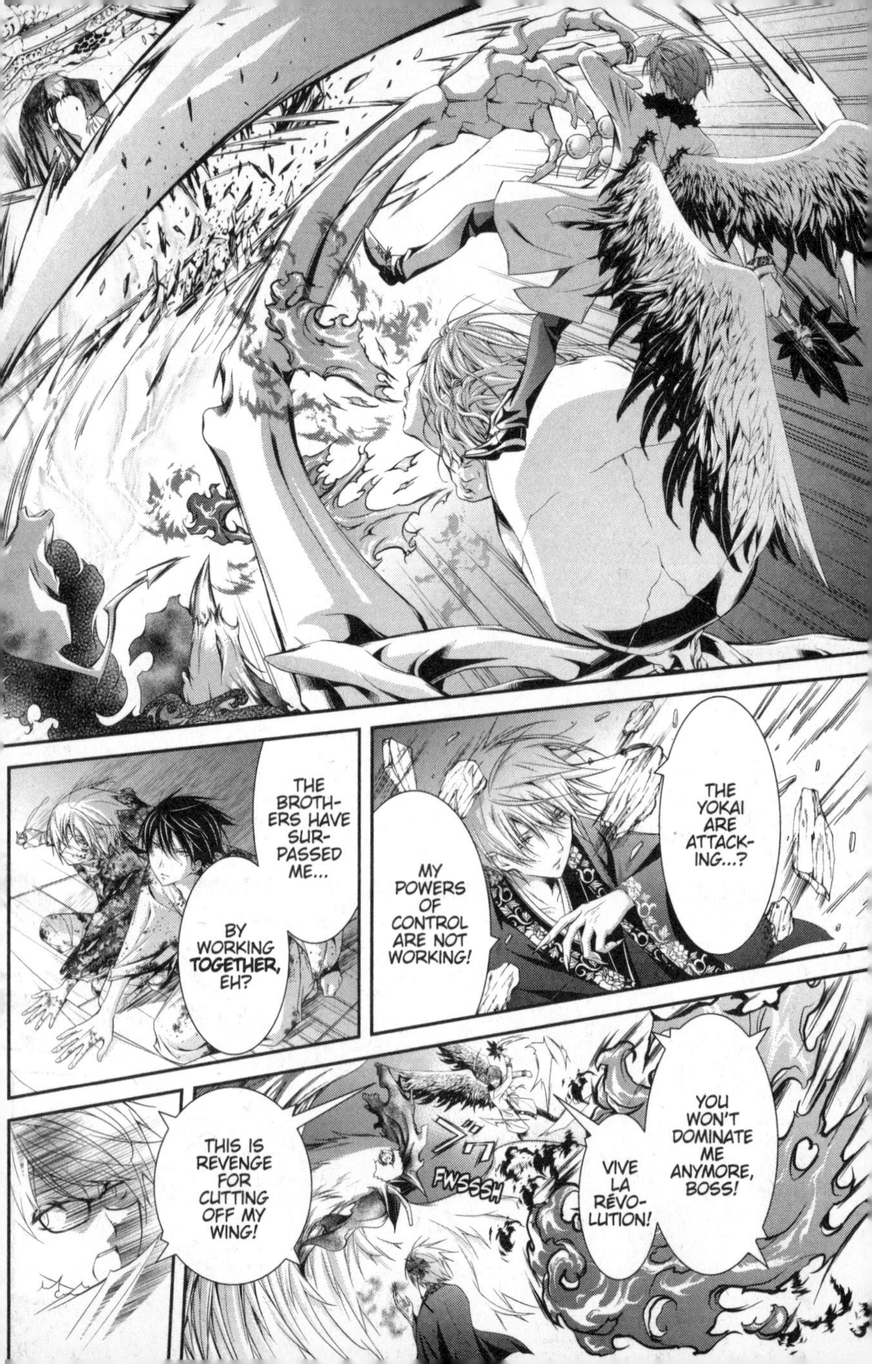
THE YOKAI ARE ATTACKING...?
MY POWERS OF CONTROL ARE NOT WORKING!
THE BROTHERS HAVE SURPASSED ME...
BY WORKING TOGETHER, EH?
YOU WON'T DOMINATE ME ANYMORE, BOSS!
VIVE LA RÉVOLUTION!
FWSSSH
THIS IS REVENGE FOR CUTTING OFF MY WING!

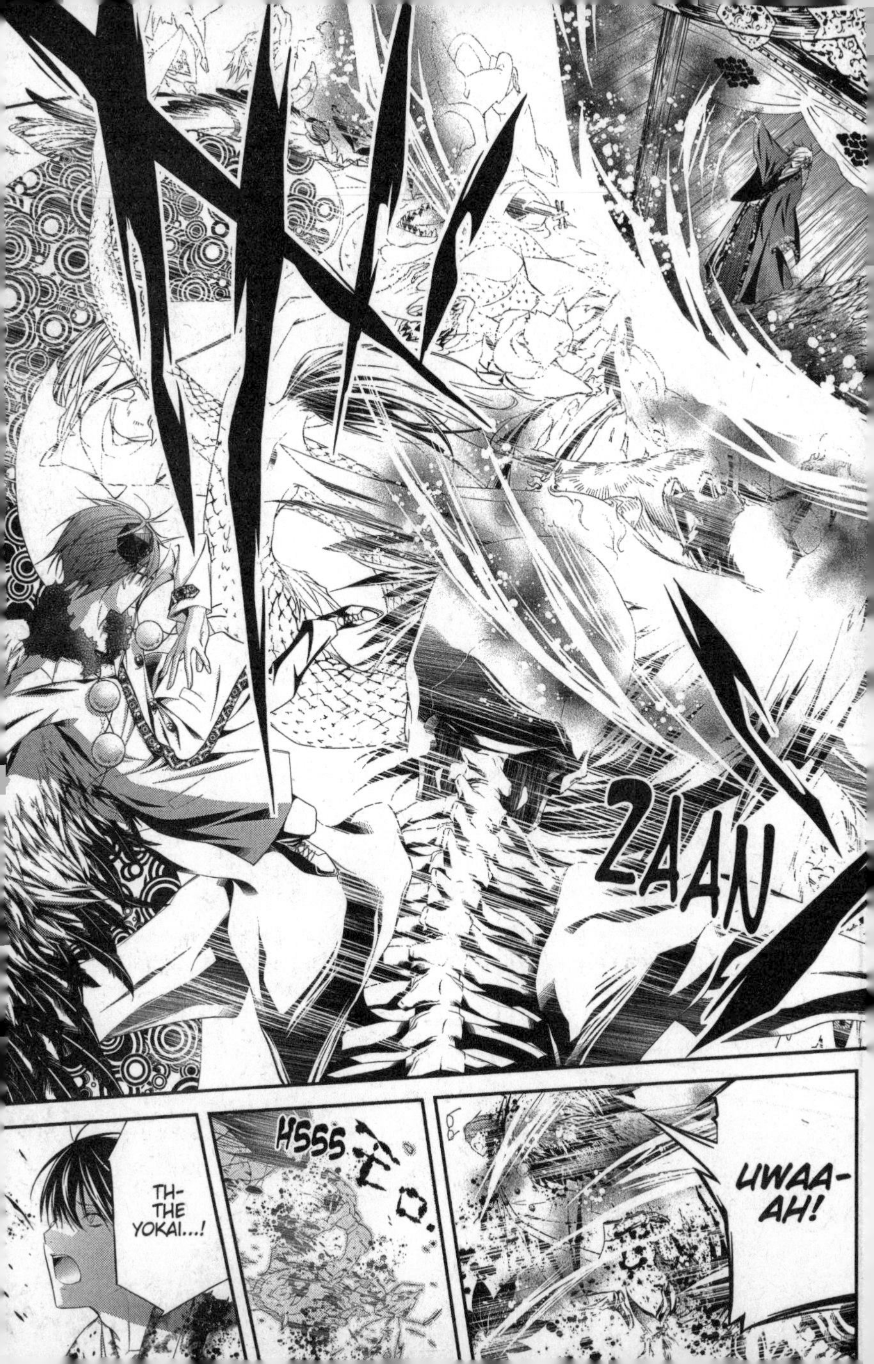
ZAAN
UWAAA-AH!
HSSS
TH-THE YOKAI...!

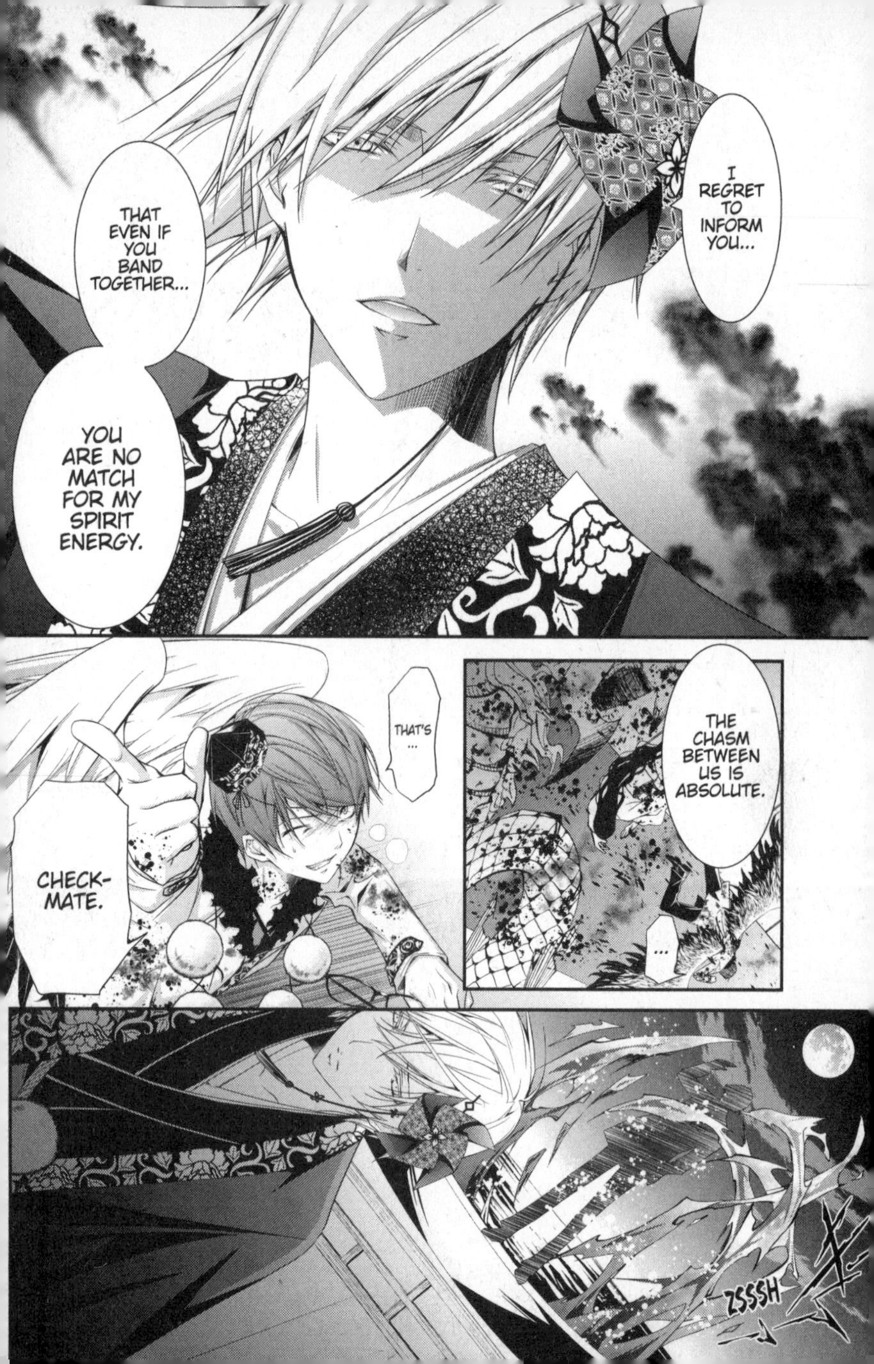
I REGRET TO INFORM YOU...
THAT EVEN IF YOU BAND TOGETHER...
YOU ARE NO MATCH FOR MY SPIRIT ENERGY.
THE CHASM BETWEEN US IS ABSOLUTE.
...
THAT'S ...
CHECK-MATE.
ZSSSH

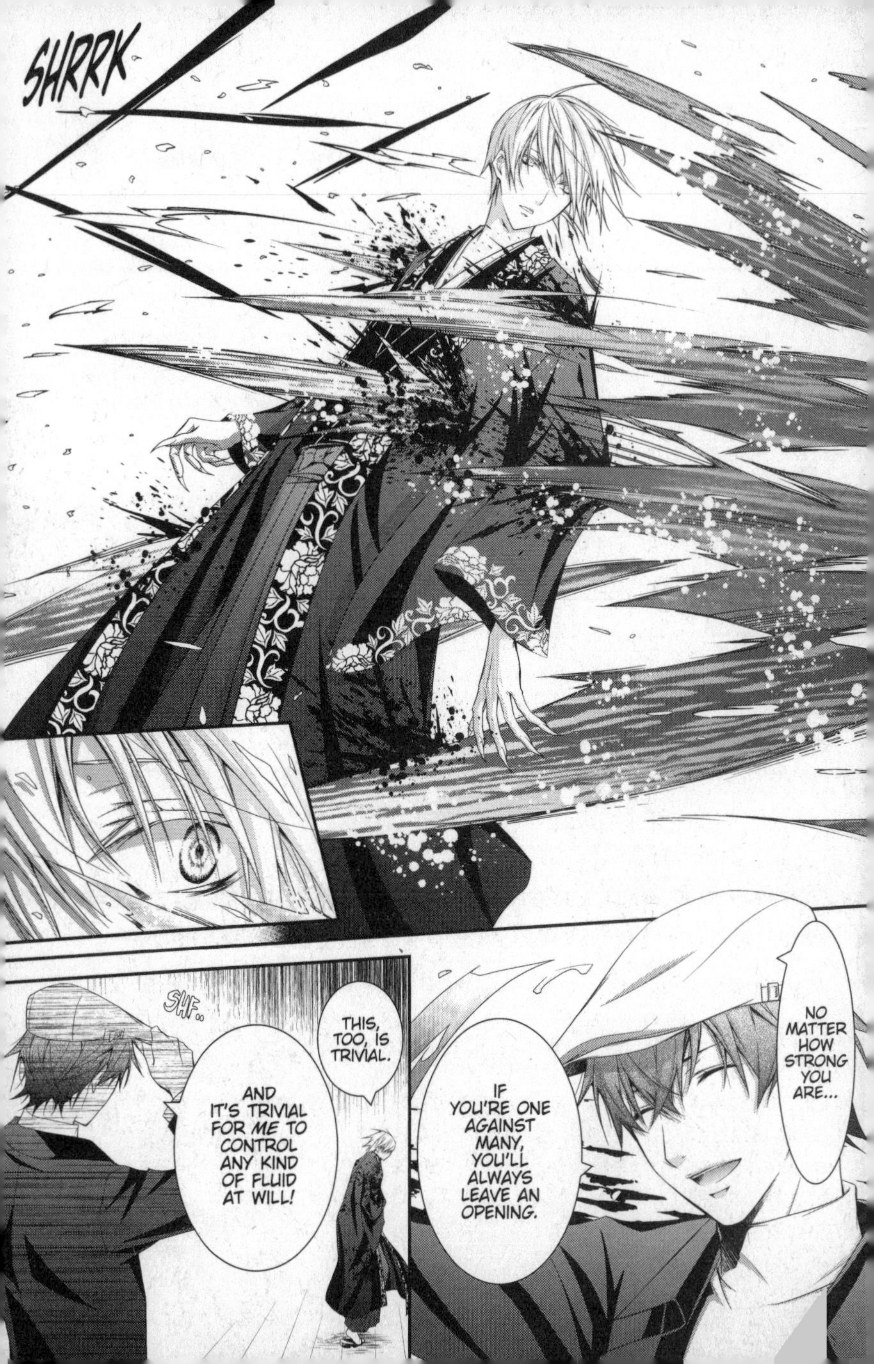
SHRRK
NO MATTER HOW STRONG YOU ARE...
IF YOU'RE ONE AGAINST MANY, YOU'LL ALWAYS LEAVE AN OPENING.
SHF..
THIS, TOO, IS TRIVIAL.
AND IT'S TRIVIAL FOR *ME* TO CONTROL ANY KIND OF FLUID AT WILL!

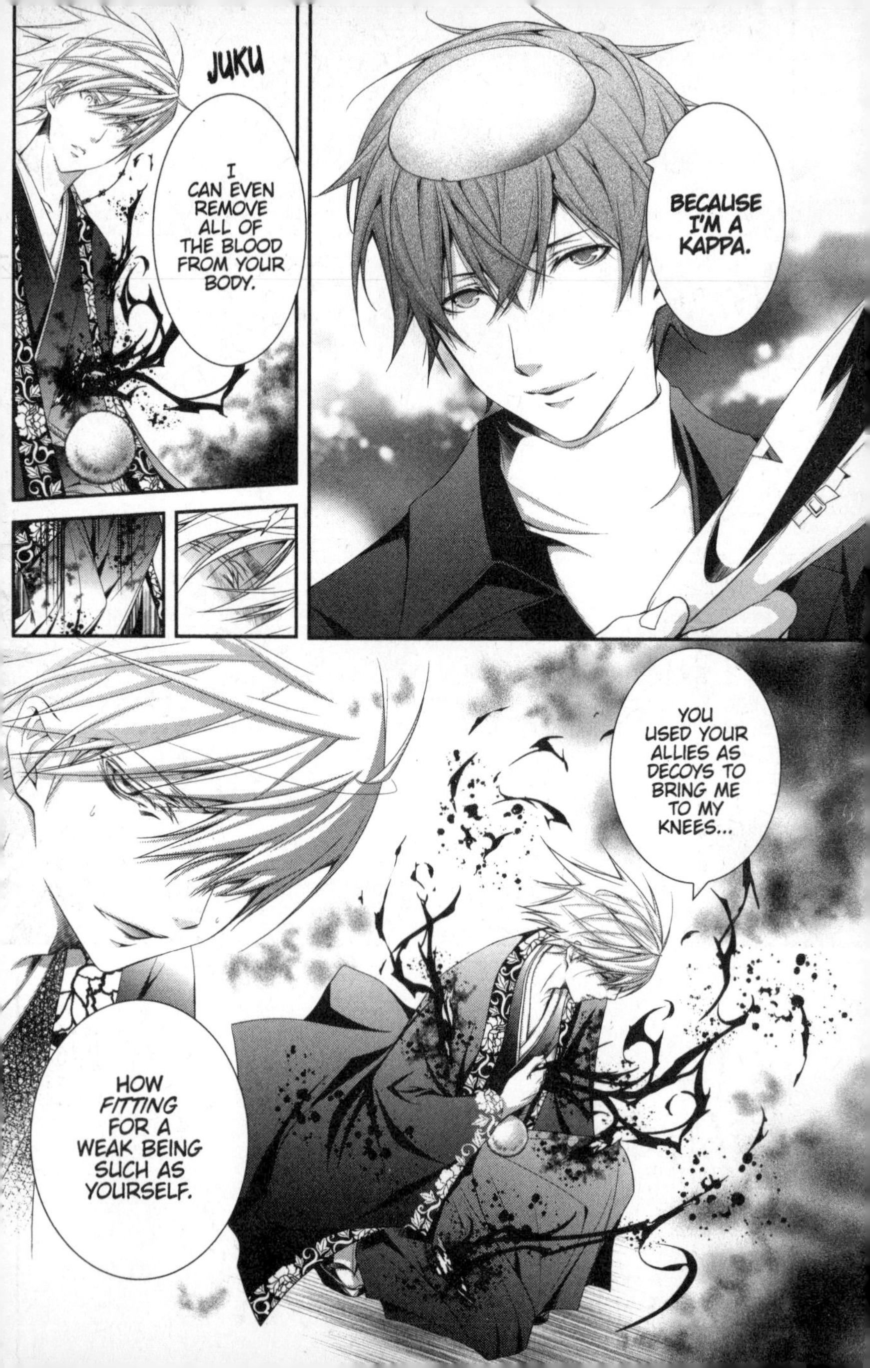
BECAUSE I'M A KAPPA.
JUKU
I CAN EVEN REMOVE ALL OF THE BLOOD FROM YOUR BODY.
YOU USED YOUR ALLIES AS DECOYS TO BRING ME TO MY KNEES...
HOW *FITTING* FOR A WEAK BEING SUCH AS YOURSELF.

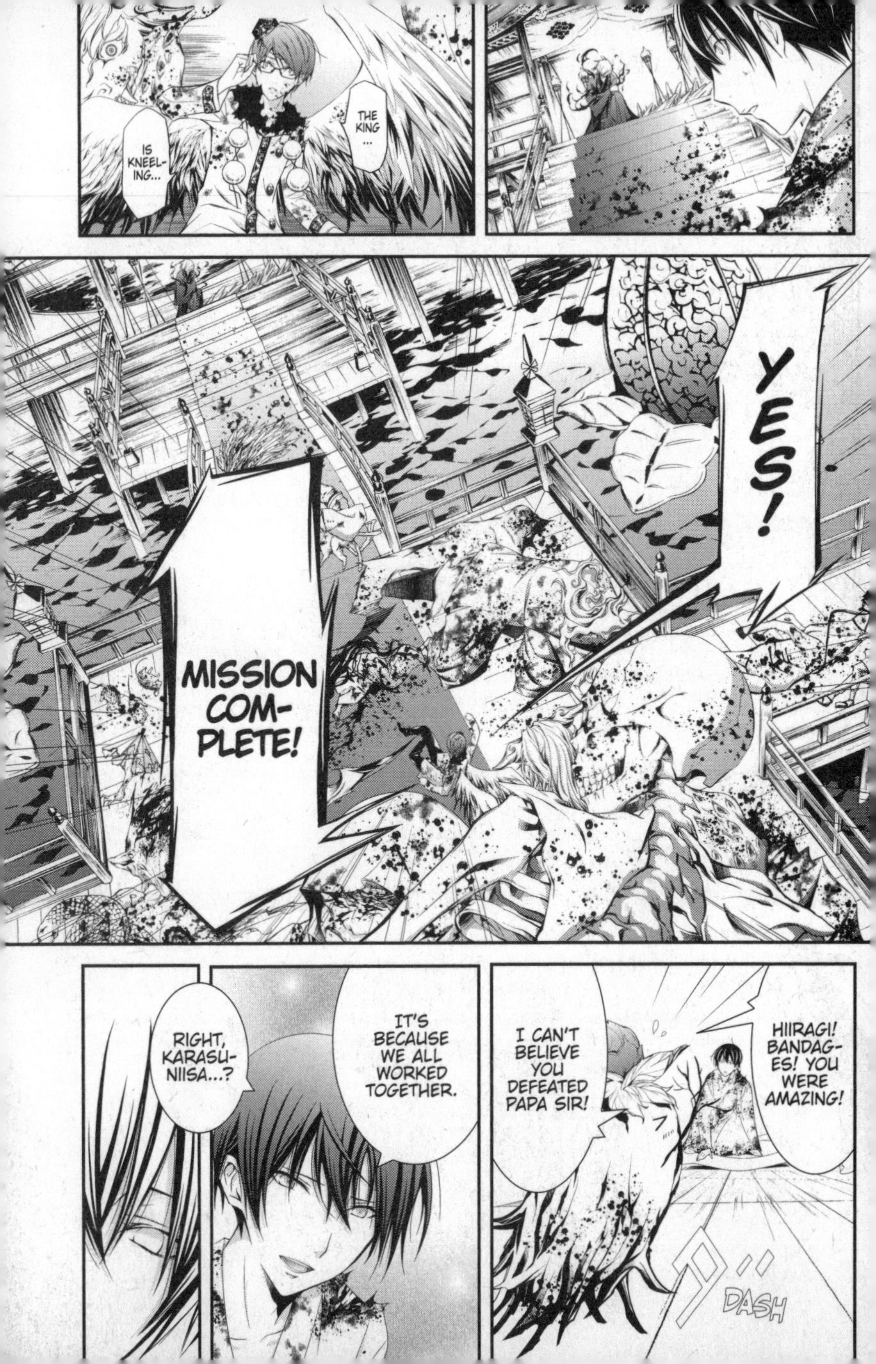

THE KING ...
IS KNEELING...
YES!
MISSION COMPLETE!
HIIRAGI! BANDAGES! YOU WERE AMAZING!
I CAN'T BELIEVE YOU DEFEATED PAPA SIR!
DASH
IT'S BECAUSE WE ALL WORKED TOGETHER.
RIGHT, KARASU-NIISA...?

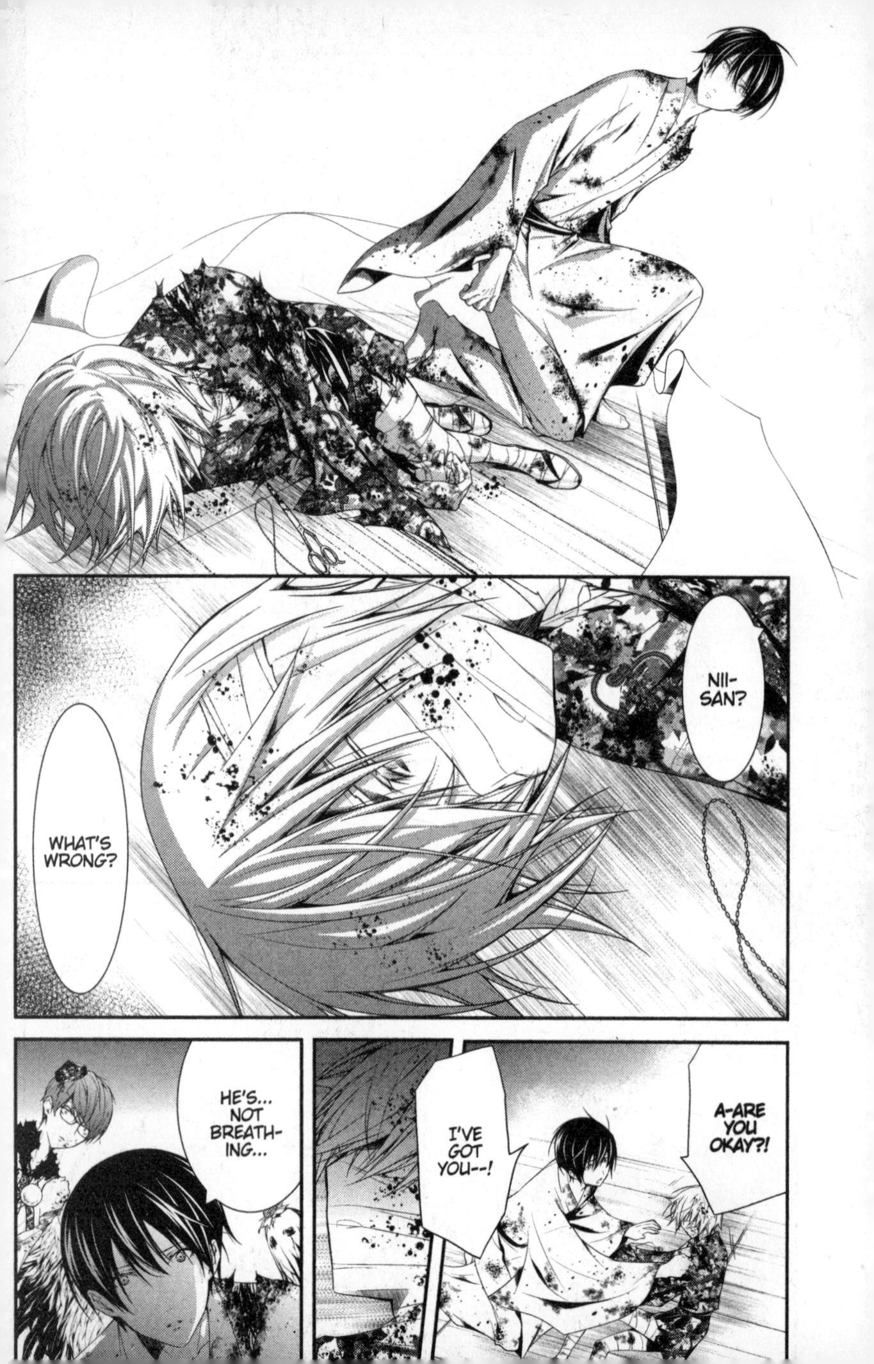
NII-SAN?
WHAT'S WRONG?
A-ARE YOU OKAY?!
I'VE GOT YOU--!
HE'S... NOT BREATH-ING...

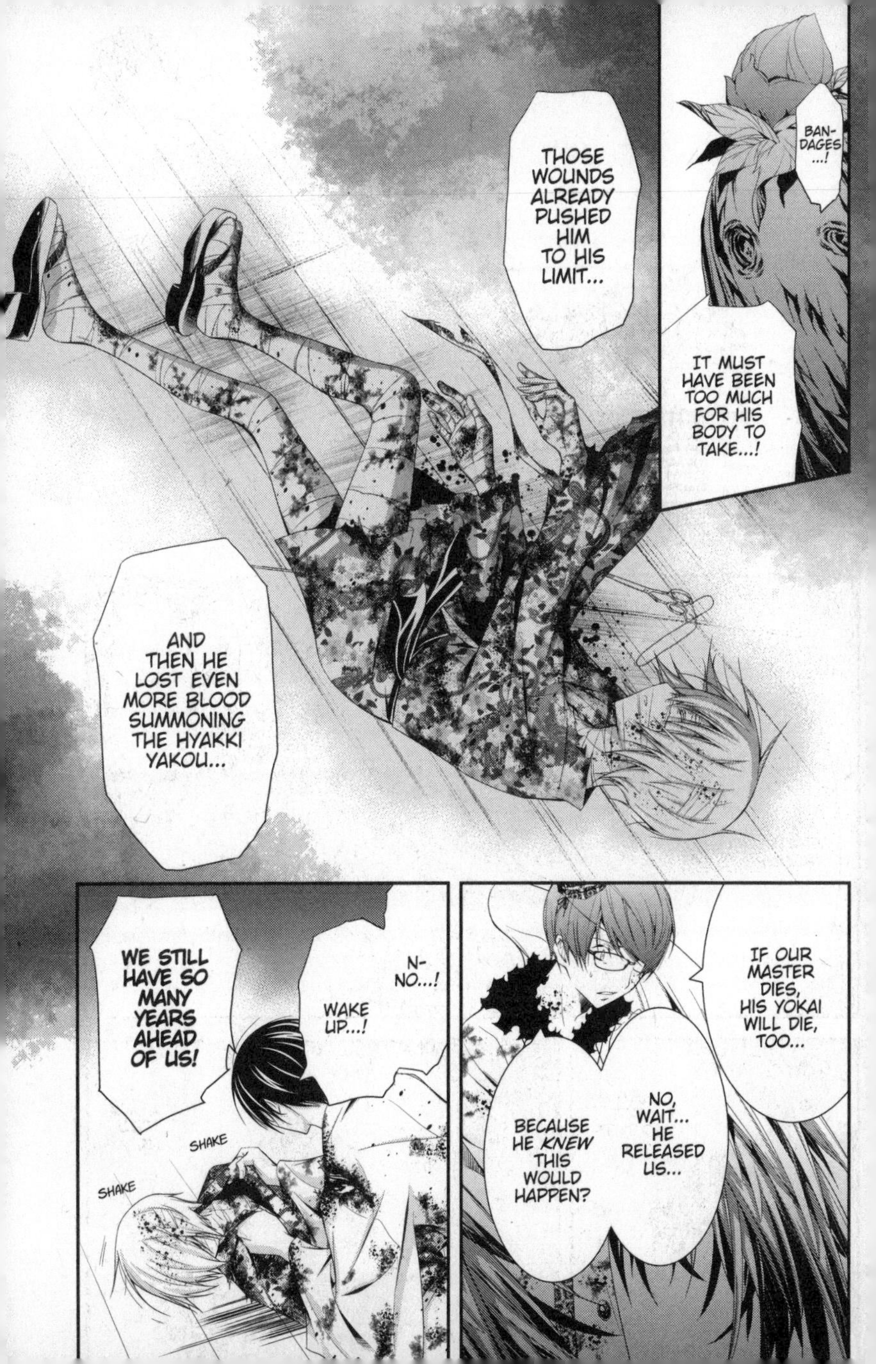
BAN-DAGES...!
IT MUST HAVE BEEN TOO MUCH FOR HIS BODY TO TAKE...!
THOSE WOUNDS ALREADY PUSHED HIM TO HIS LIMIT...
AND THEN HE LOST EVEN MORE BLOOD SUMMONING THE HYAKKI YAKOU...
IF OUR MASTER DIES, HIS YOKAI WILL DIE, TOO...
NO, WAIT... HE RELEASED US...
BECAUSE HE *KNEW* THIS WOULD HAPPEN?
N-NO...!
WAKE UP...!
WE STILL HAVE SO MANY YEARS AHEAD OF US!
SHAKE
SHAKE

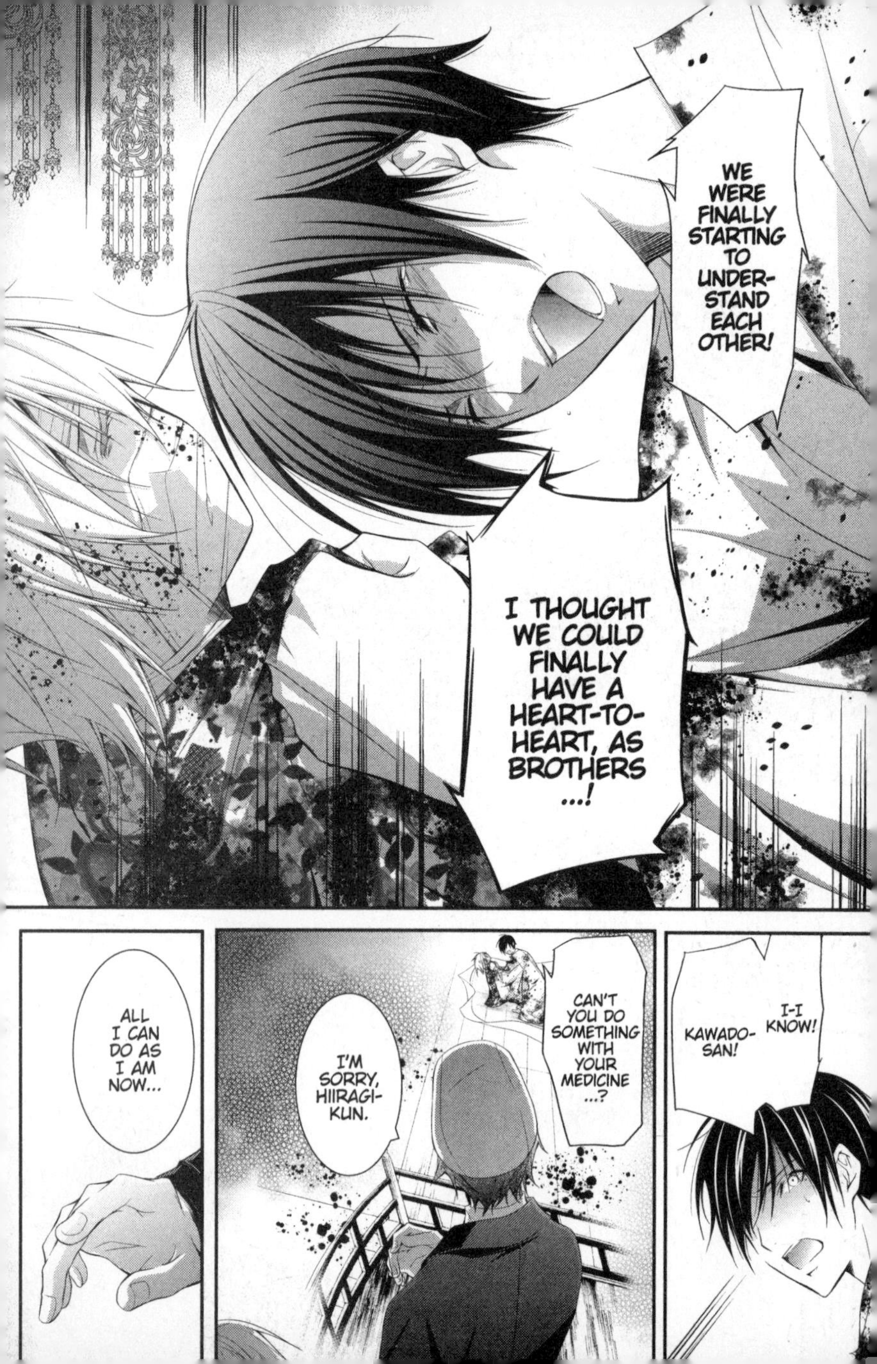
WE WERE FINALLY STARTING TO UNDER-STAND EACH OTHER!
I THOUGHT WE COULD FINALLY HAVE A HEART-TO-HEART, AS BROTHERS ...!
I-I KNOW!
KAWADO-SAN!
CAN'T YOU DO SOMETHING WITH YOUR MEDICINE ...?
I'M SORRY, HIIRAGI-KUN.
ALL I CAN DO AS I AM NOW...

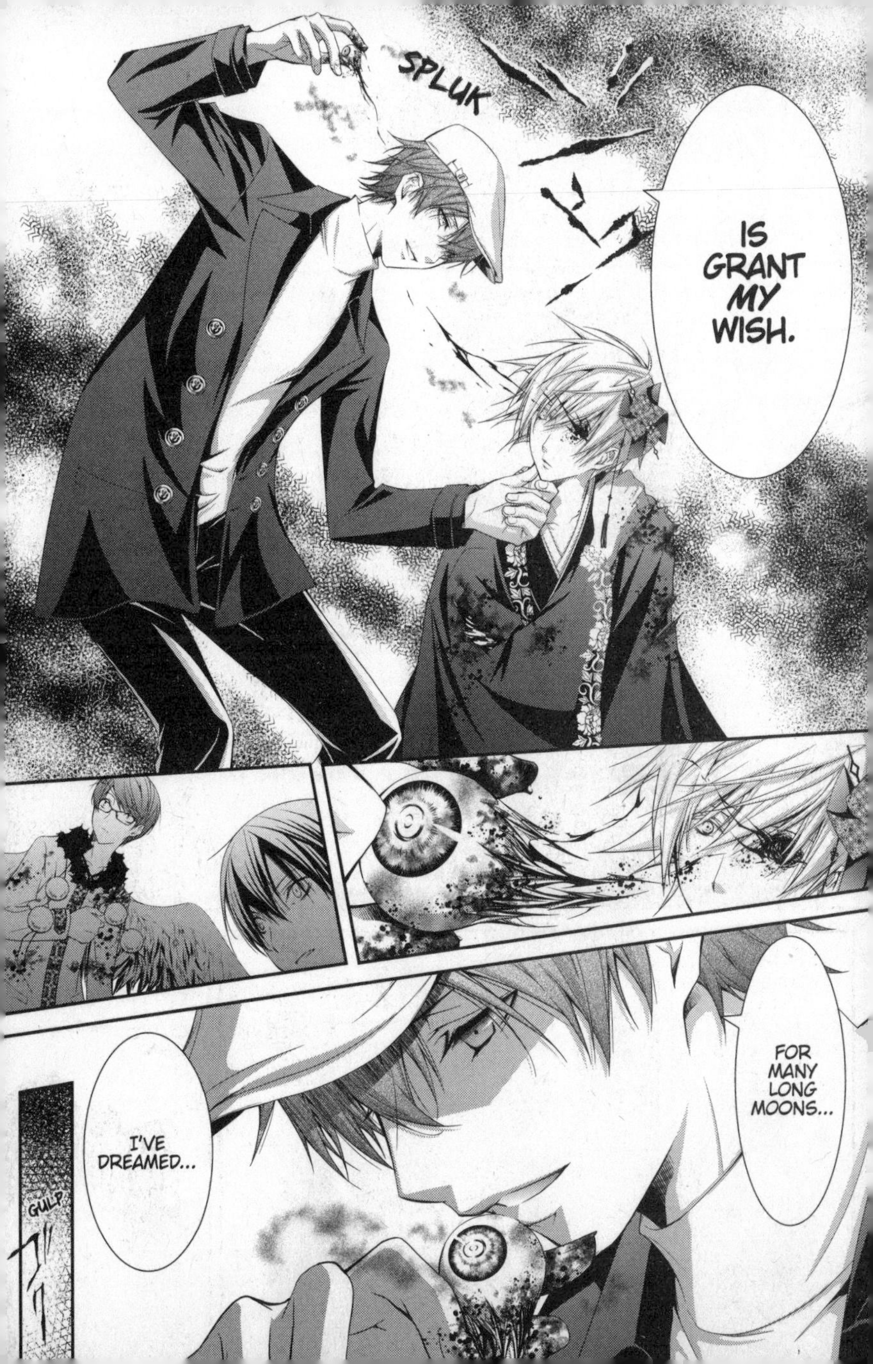
IS GRANT MY WISH.
SPLUK
FOR MANY LONG MOONS...
I'VE DREAMED...
GULP

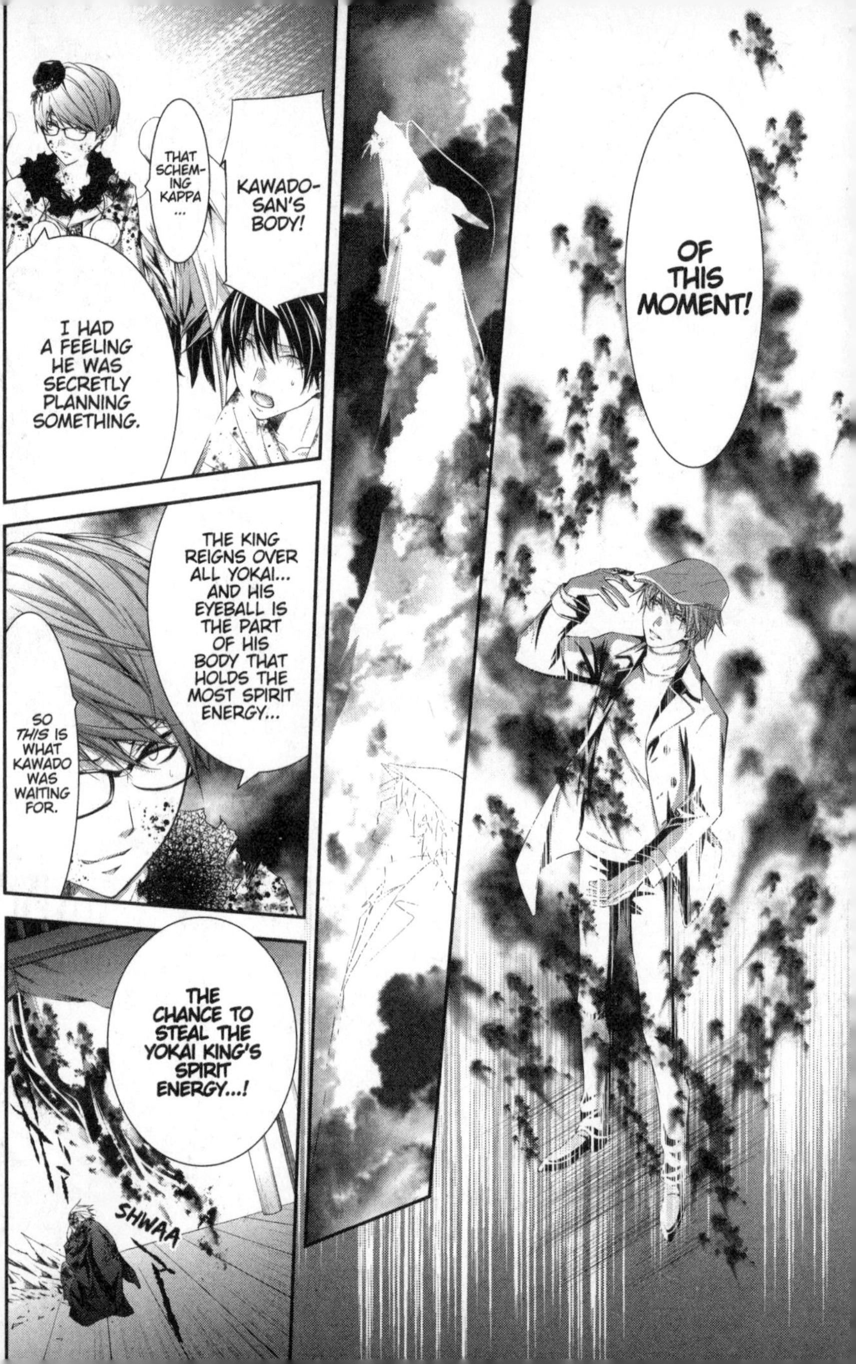
OF THIS MOMENT!
KAWADO-SAN'S BODY!
THAT SCHEMING KAPPA ...
I HAD A FEELING HE WAS SECRETLY PLANNING SOMETHING.
THE KING REIGNS OVER ALL YOKAI... AND HIS EYEBALL IS THE PART OF HIS BODY THAT HOLDS THE MOST SPIRIT ENERGY...
SO *THIS* IS WHAT KAWADO WAS WAITING FOR.
THE CHANCE TO STEAL THE YOKAI KING'S SPIRIT ENERGY...!
SHWAA

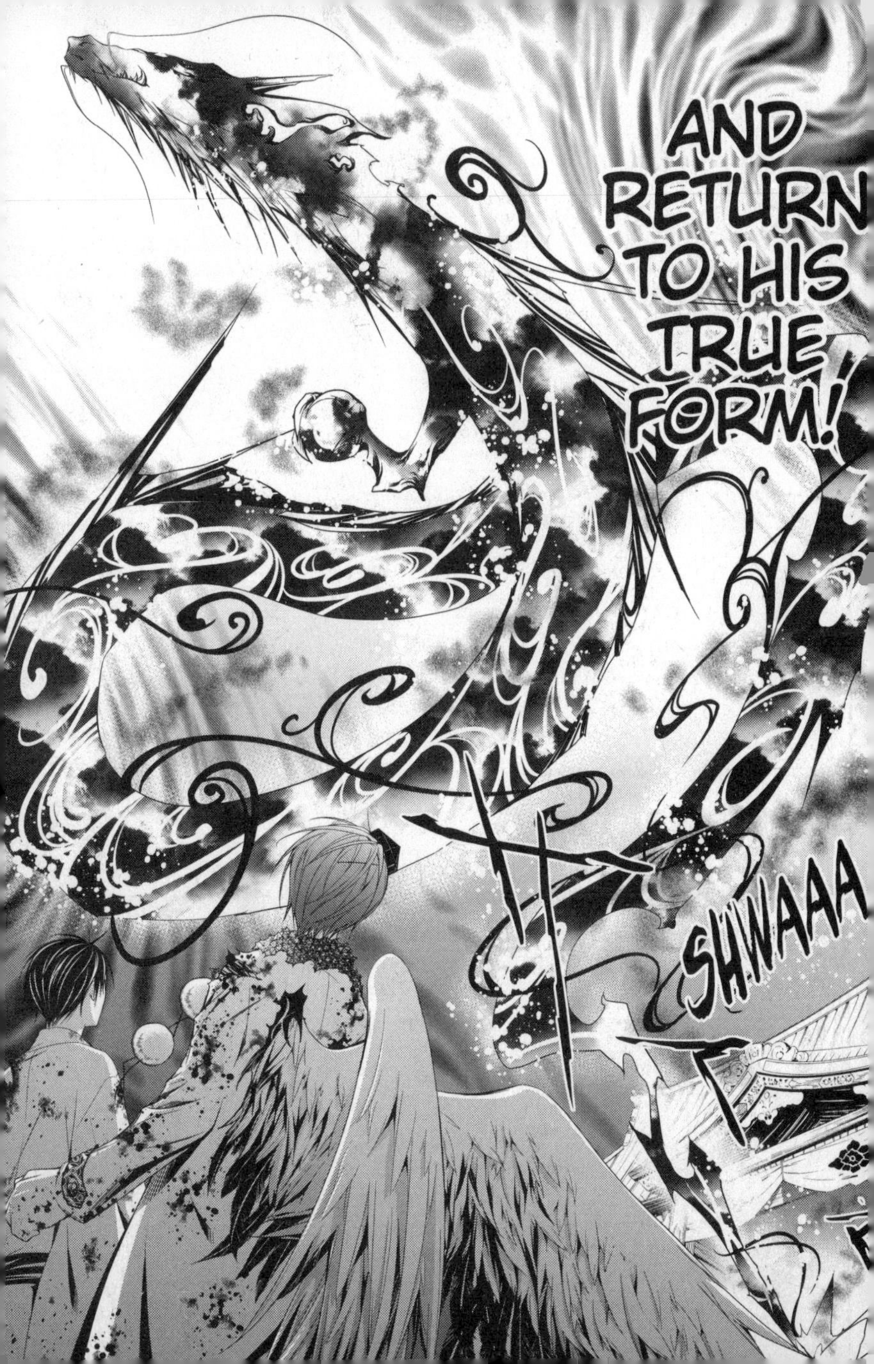
AND RETURN TO HIS TRUE FORM!
SHWAAA

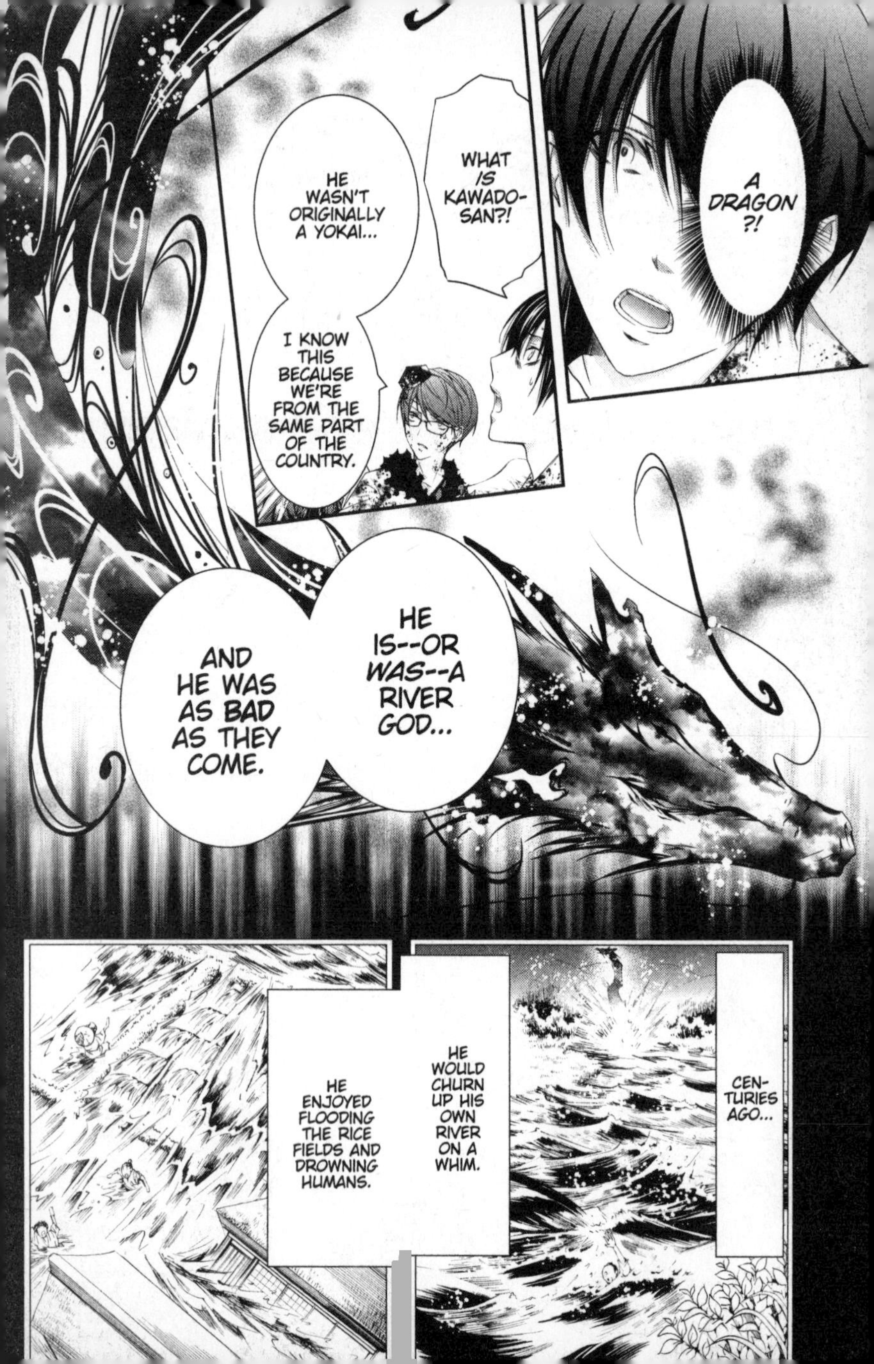
A DRAGON ?!
WHAT IS KAWADO-SAN?!
HE WASN'T ORIGINALLY A YOKAI...
I KNOW THIS BECAUSE WE'RE FROM THE SAME PART OF THE COUNTRY.
HE IS--OR WAS--A RIVER GOD...
AND HE WAS AS BAD AS THEY COME.
CEN-TURIES AGO...
HE WOULD CHURN UP HIS OWN RIVER ON A WHIM.
HE ENJOYED FLOODING THE RICE FIELDS AND DROWNING HUMANS.

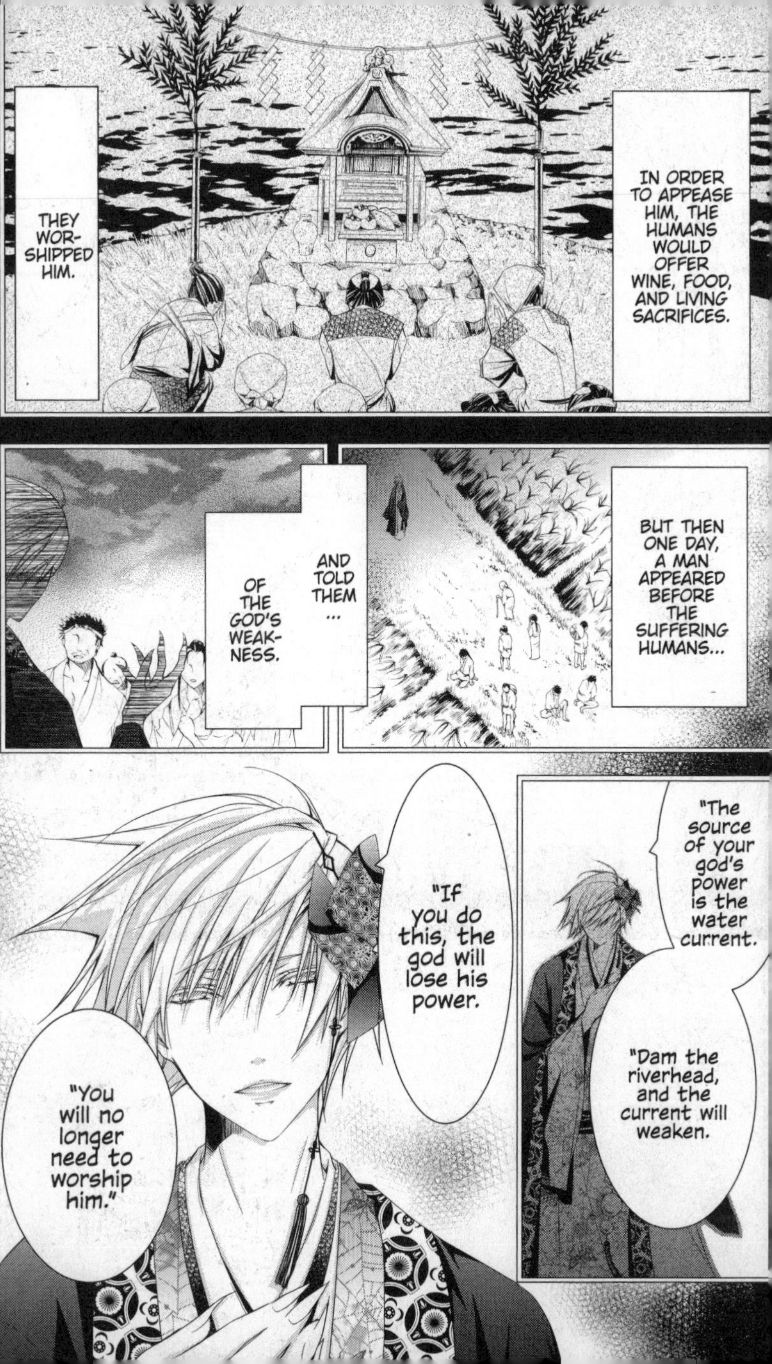
IN ORDER TO APPEASE HIM, THE HUMANS WOULD OFFER WINE, FOOD, AND LIVING SACRIFICES.
THEY WOR-SHIPPED HIM.
BUT THEN ONE DAY, A MAN APPEARED BEFORE THE SUFFERING HUMANS...
AND TOLD THEM...
OF THE GOD'S WEAK-NESS.
"The source of your god's power is the water current.
"Dam the riverhead, and the current will weaken.
"If you do this, the god will lose his power.
"You will no longer need to worship him."

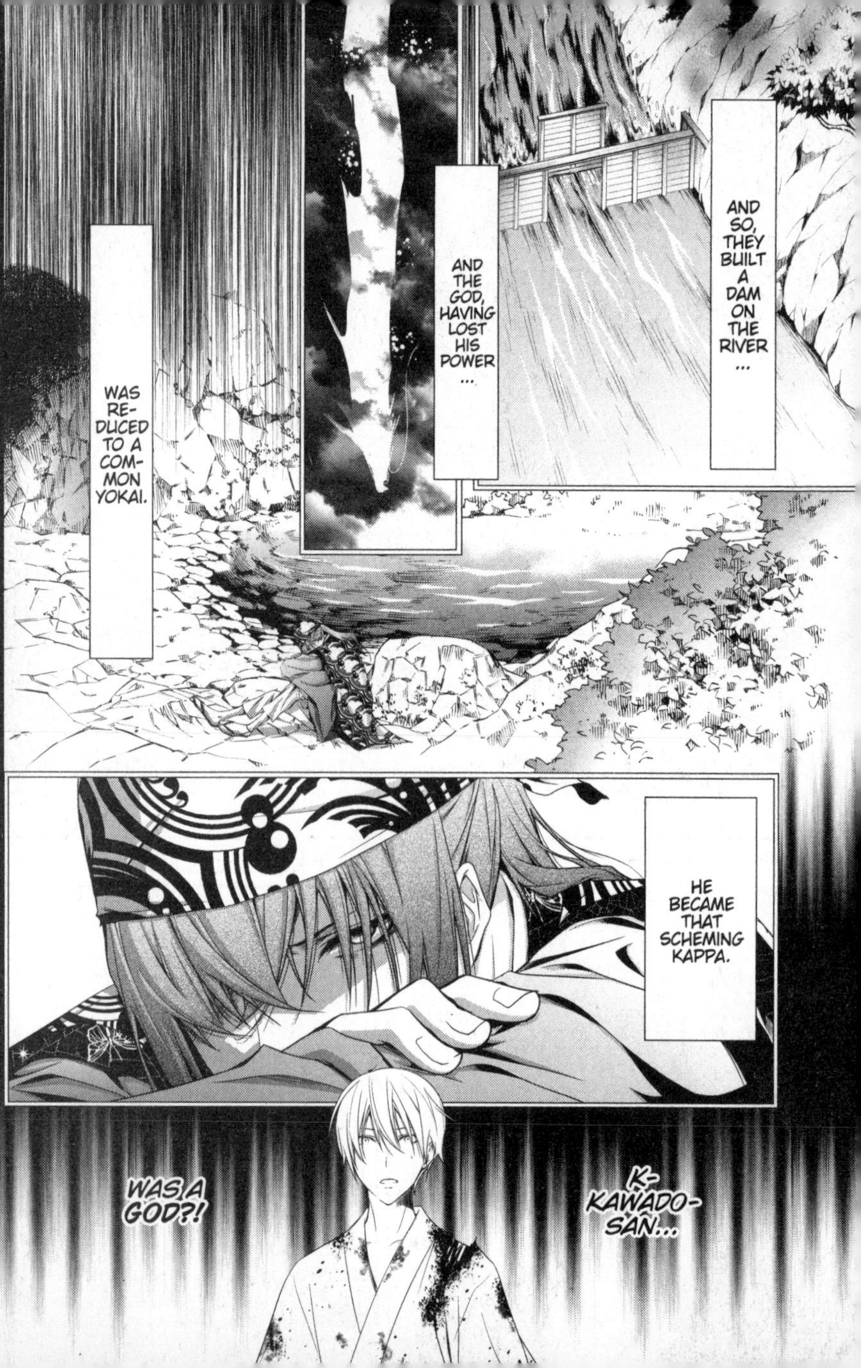
AND SO, THEY BUILT A DAM ON THE RIVER...
AND THE GOD, HAVING LOST HIS POWER...
WAS RE-DUCED TO A COM-MON YOKAI.
HE BECAME THAT SCHEMING KAPPA.
K-KAWADO-SAN...
WAS A GOD?!

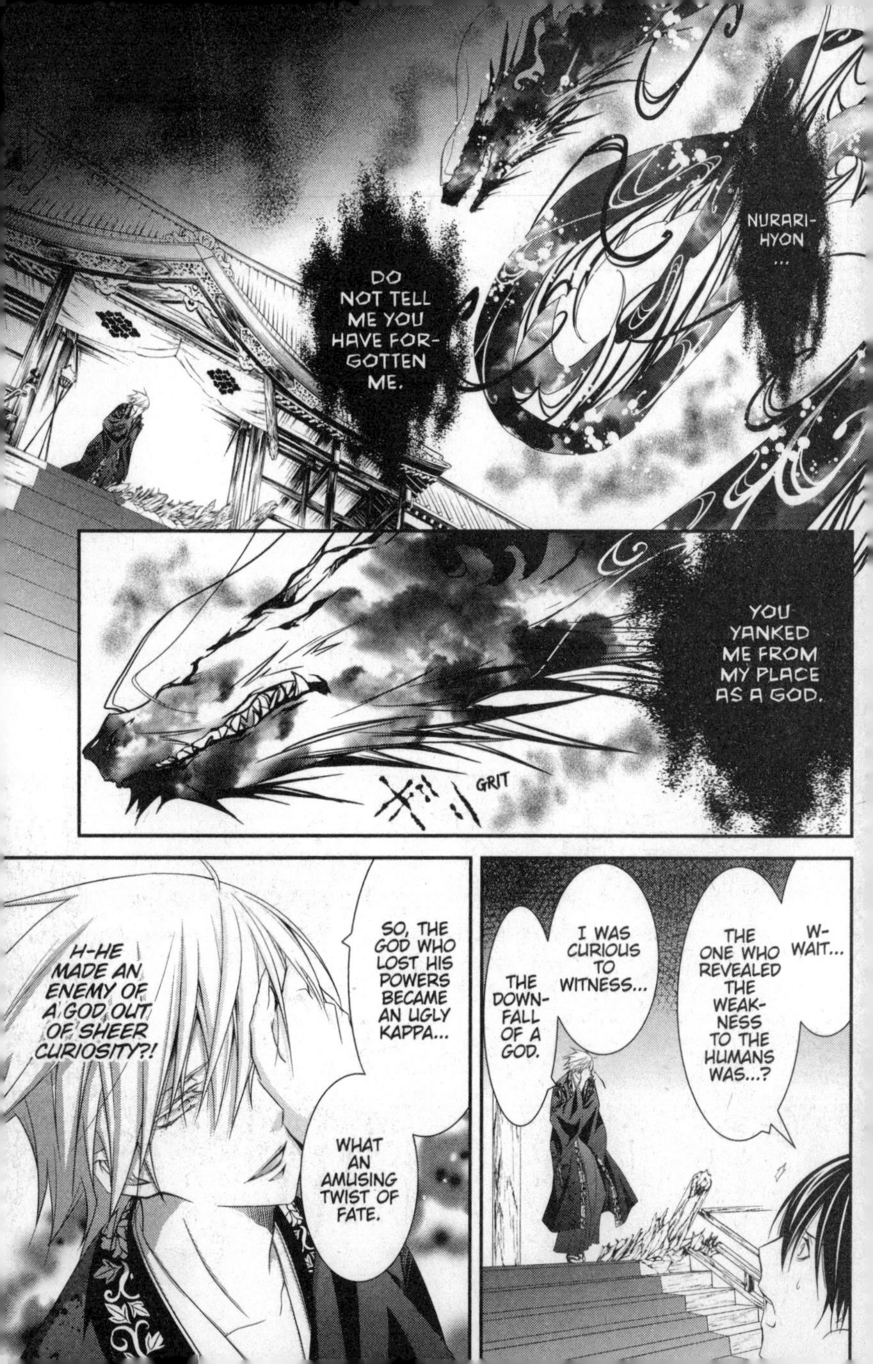
NURARI-HYON ...
DO NOT TELL ME YOU HAVE FOR-GOTTEN ME.
YOU YANKED ME FROM MY PLACE AS A GOD.
GRIT
W-WAIT...
THE ONE WHO REVEALED THE WEAK-NESS TO THE HUMANS WAS...?
I WAS CURIOUS TO WITNESS...
THE DOWN-FALL OF A GOD.
SO, THE GOD WHO LOST HIS POWERS BECAME AN UGLY KAPPA...
WHAT AN AMUSING TWIST OF FATE.
H-HE MADE AN ENEMY OF A GOD OUT OF SHEER CURIOSITY?!

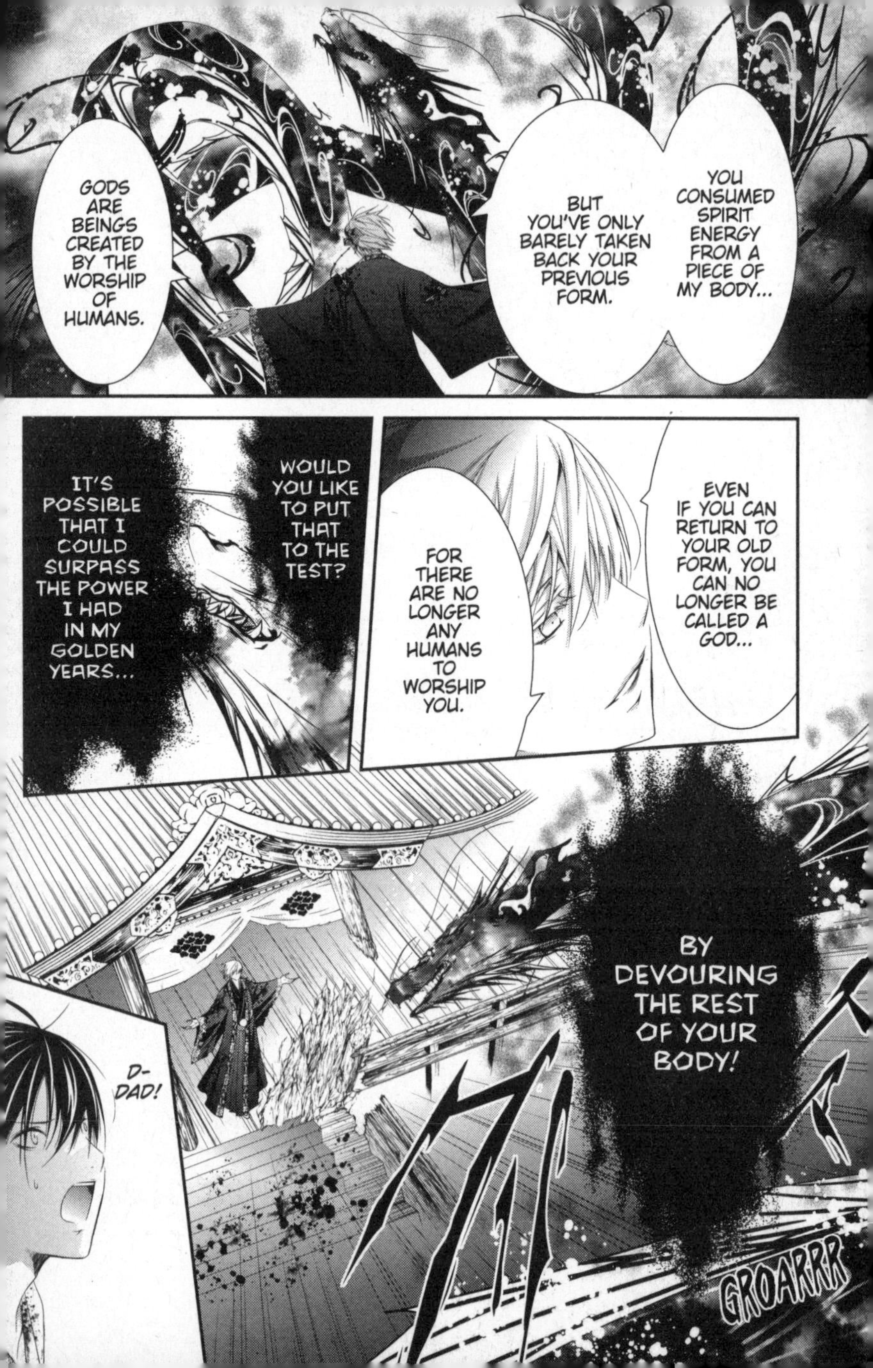
YOU CONSUMED SPIRIT ENERGY FROM A PIECE OF MY BODY...
BUT YOU'VE ONLY BARELY TAKEN BACK YOUR PREVIOUS FORM.
GODS ARE BEINGS CREATED BY THE WORSHIP OF HUMANS.
EVEN IF YOU CAN RETURN TO YOUR OLD FORM, YOU CAN NO LONGER BE CALLED A GOD...
FOR THERE ARE NO LONGER ANY HUMANS TO WORSHIP YOU.
WOULD YOU LIKE TO PUT THAT TO THE TEST?
IT'S POSSIBLE THAT I COULD SURPASS THE POWER I HAD IN MY GOLDEN YEARS...
BY DEVOURING THE REST OF YOUR BODY!
GROARRR
D-DAD!

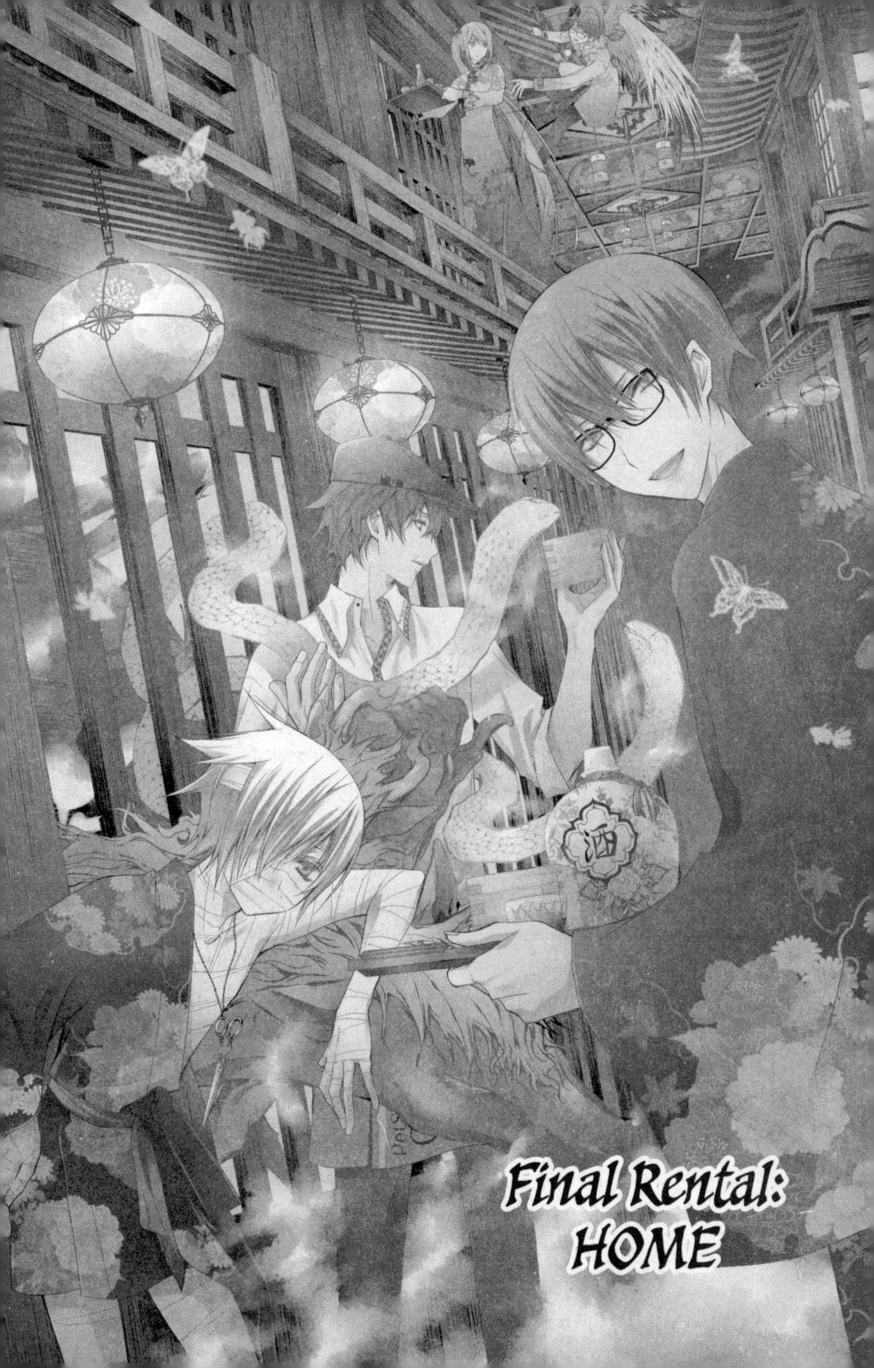
Final Rental:
HOME
酒

Yōkai Rental Shop

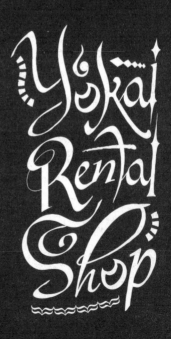

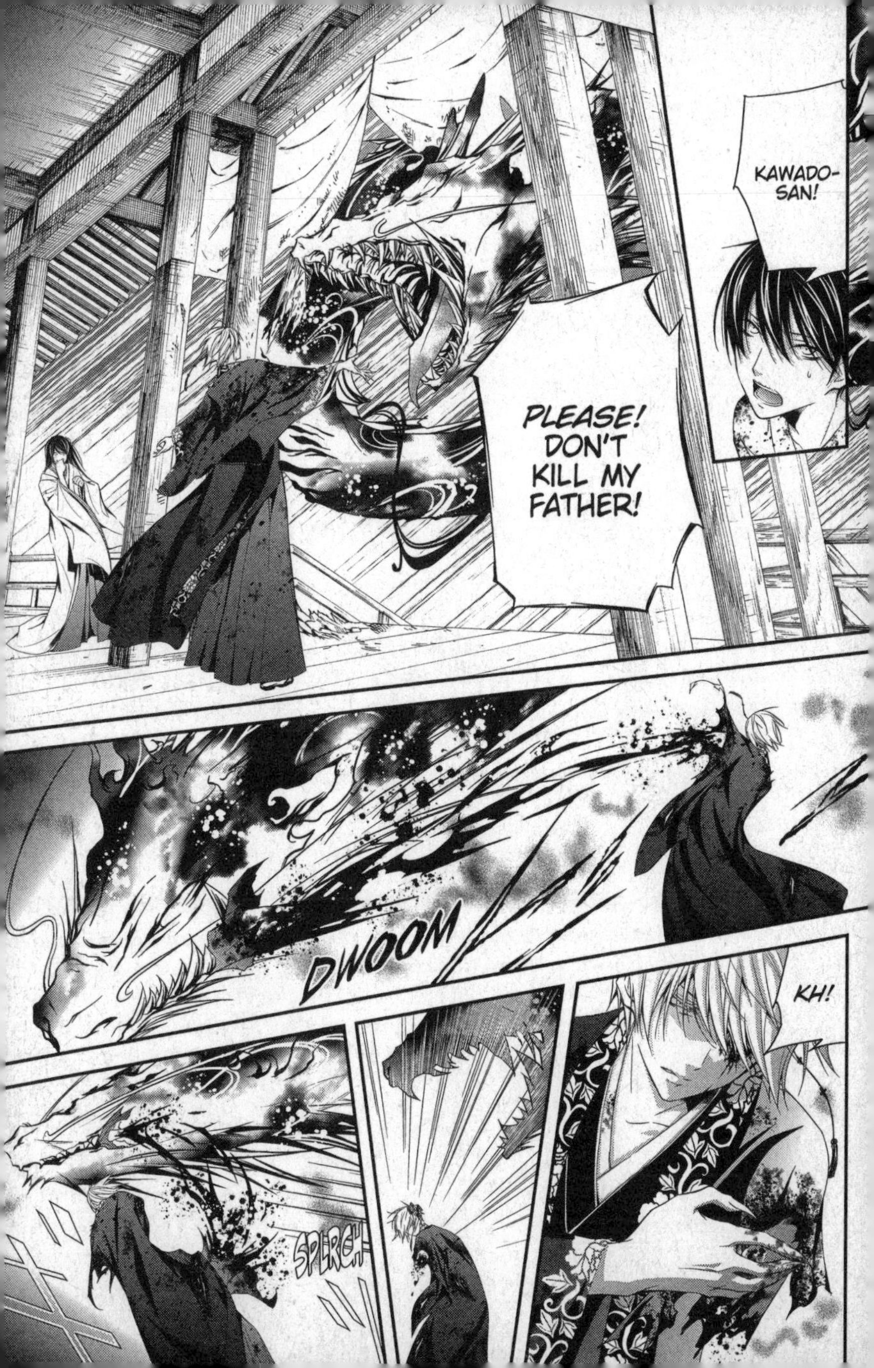
KAWADO-SAN!
PLEASE! DON'T KILL MY FATHER!
DWOOM
KH!
SPLRCH

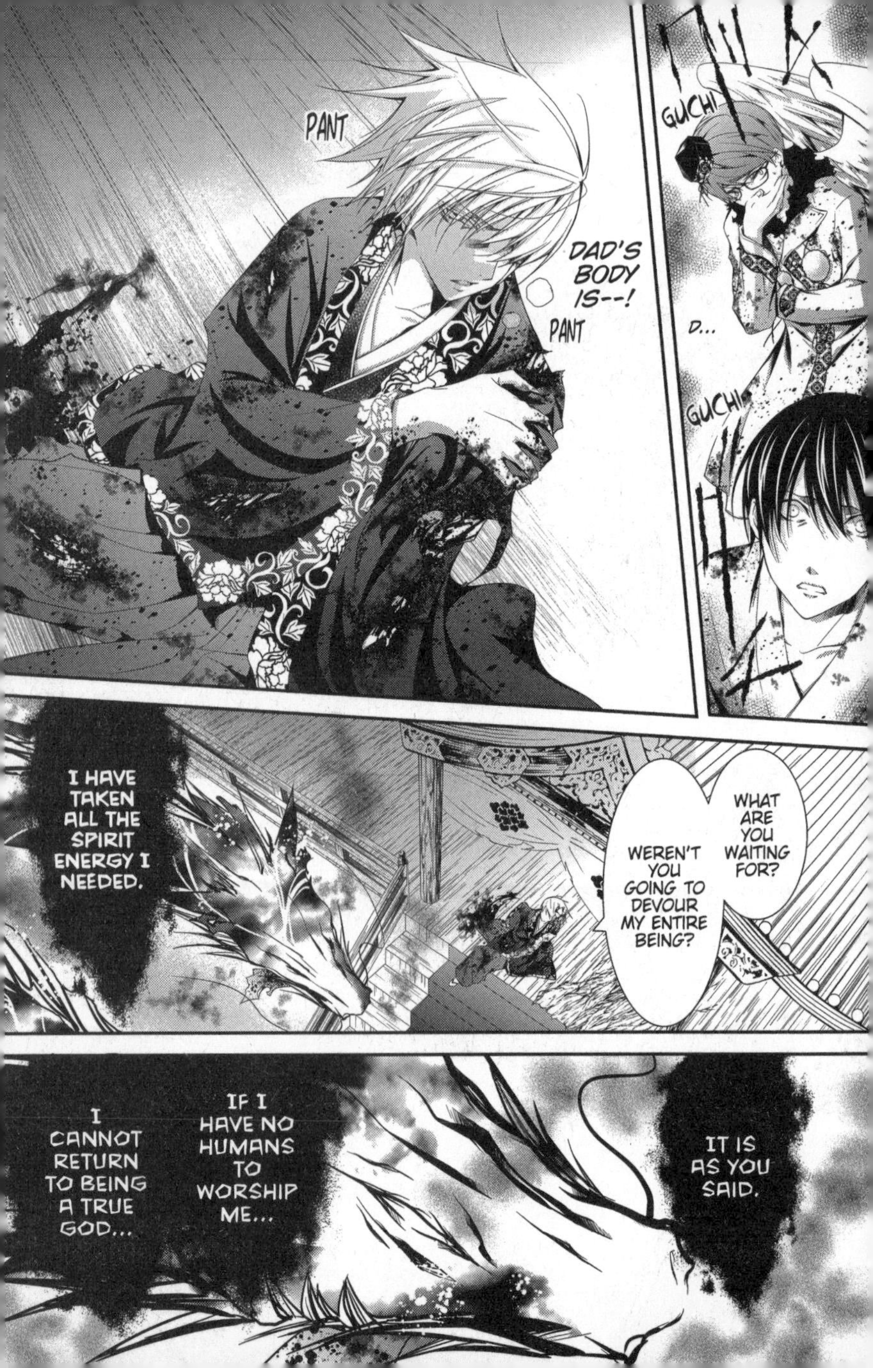
GUCHI
D...
GUCHI
PANT
DAD'S BODY IS--!
PANT
WHAT ARE YOU WAITING FOR?
WEREN'T YOU GOING TO DEVOUR MY ENTIRE BEING?
I HAVE TAKEN ALL THE SPIRIT ENERGY I NEEDED.
IT IS AS YOU SAID.
IF I HAVE NO HUMANS TO WORSHIP ME...
I CANNOT RETURN TO BEING A TRUE GOD...

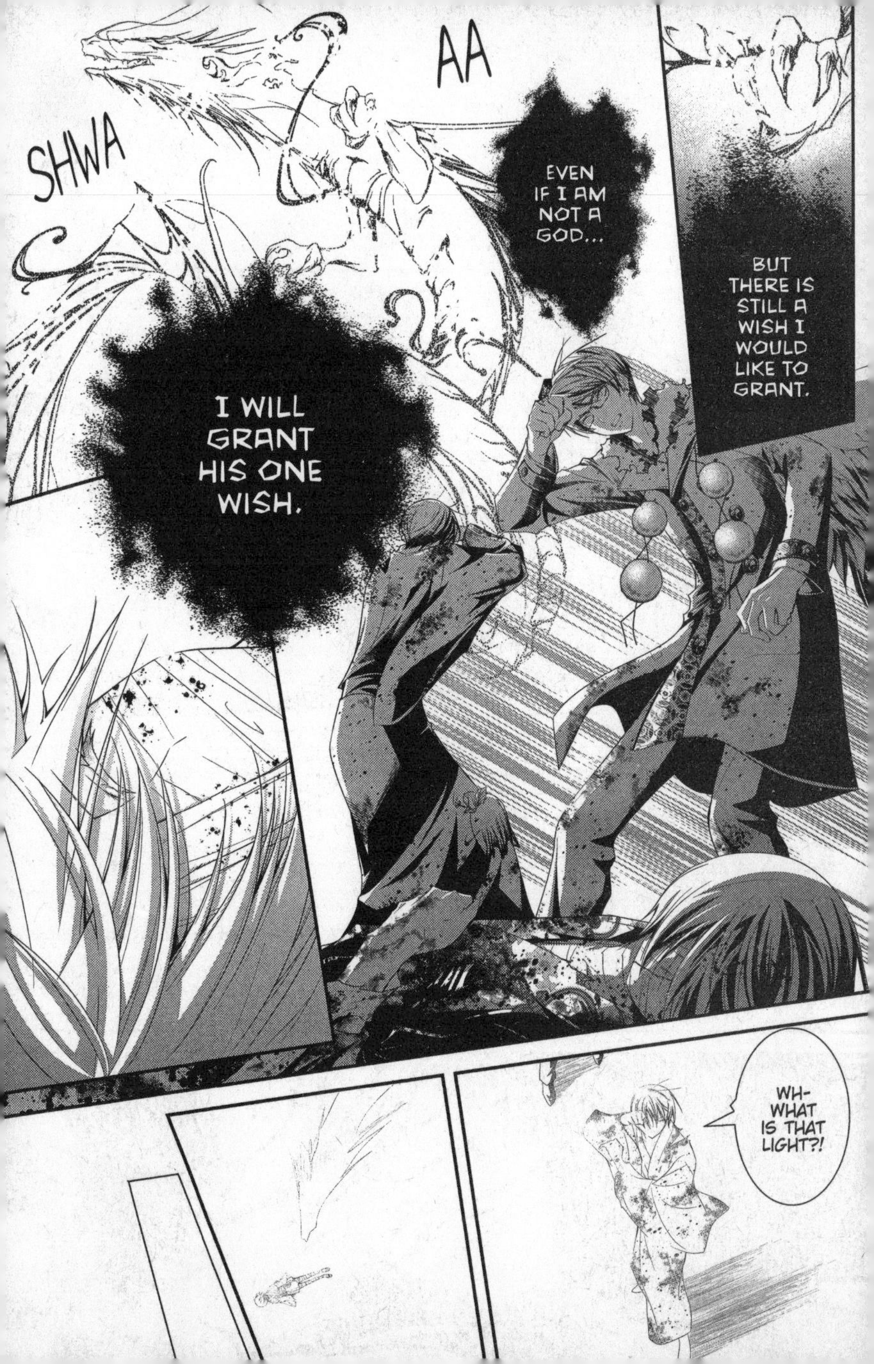
AA
EVEN IF I AM NOT A GOD...
BUT THERE IS STILL A WISH I WOULD LIKE TO GRANT.
SHWA
I WILL GRANT HIS ONE WISH.
WH- WHAT IS THAT LIGHT?!

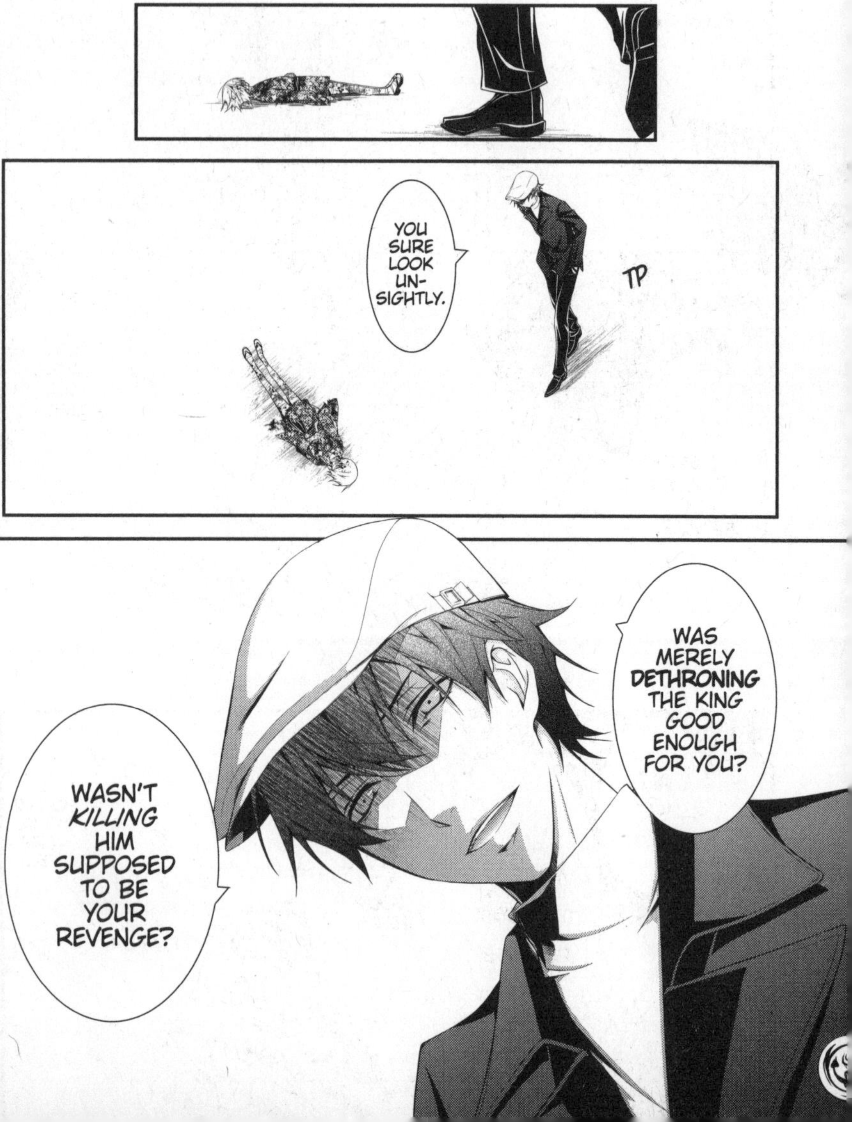
YOU SURE LOOK UN-SIGHTLY.
TP
WAS MERELY DETHRONING THE KING GOOD ENOUGH FOR YOU?
WASN'T *KILLING* HIM SUPPOSED TO BE YOUR REVENGE?

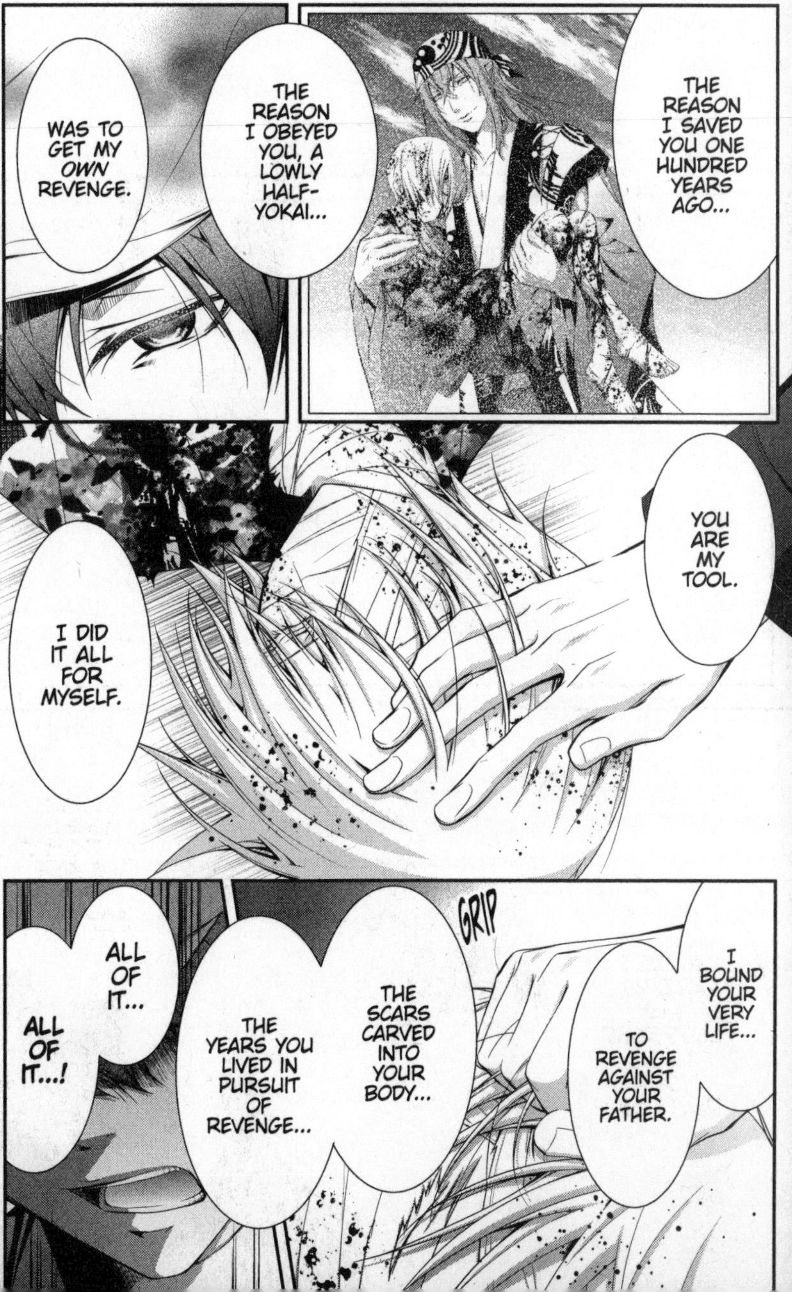
THE REASON I SAVED YOU ONE HUNDRED YEARS AGO...
THE REASON I OBEYED YOU, A LOWLY HALF-YOKAI...
WAS TO GET MY OWN REVENGE.
YOU ARE MY TOOL.
I DID IT ALL FOR MYSELF.
I BOUND YOUR VERY LIFE...
TO REVENGE AGAINST YOUR FATHER.
GRIP
THE SCARS CARVED INTO YOUR BODY...
THE YEARS YOU LIVED IN PURSUIT OF REVENGE...
ALL OF IT...
ALL OF IT...!

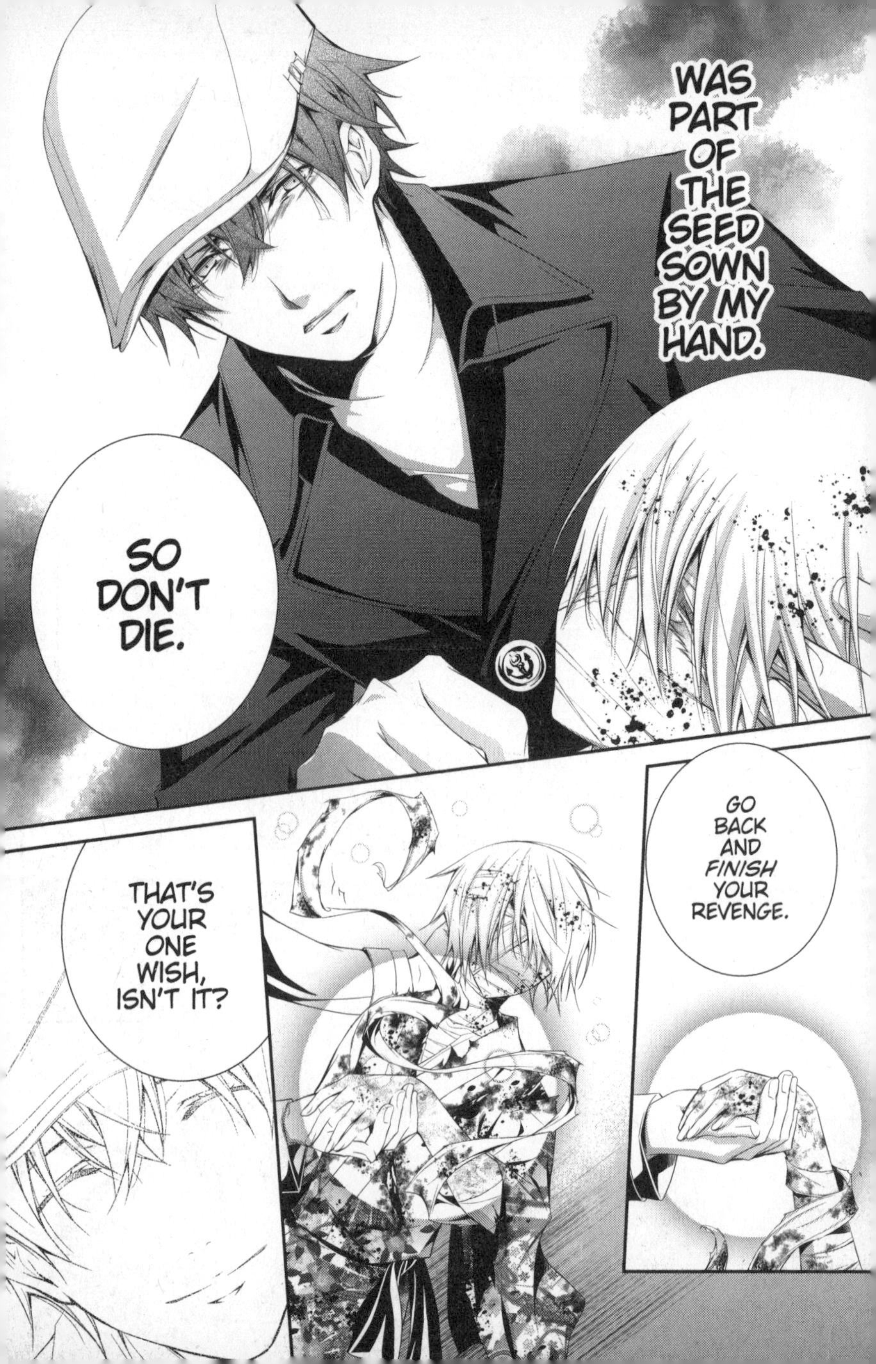
WAS PART OF THE SEED SOWN BY MY HAND.
SO DON'T DIE.
GO BACK AND *FINISH* YOUR REVENGE.
THAT'S YOUR ONE WISH, ISN'T IT?

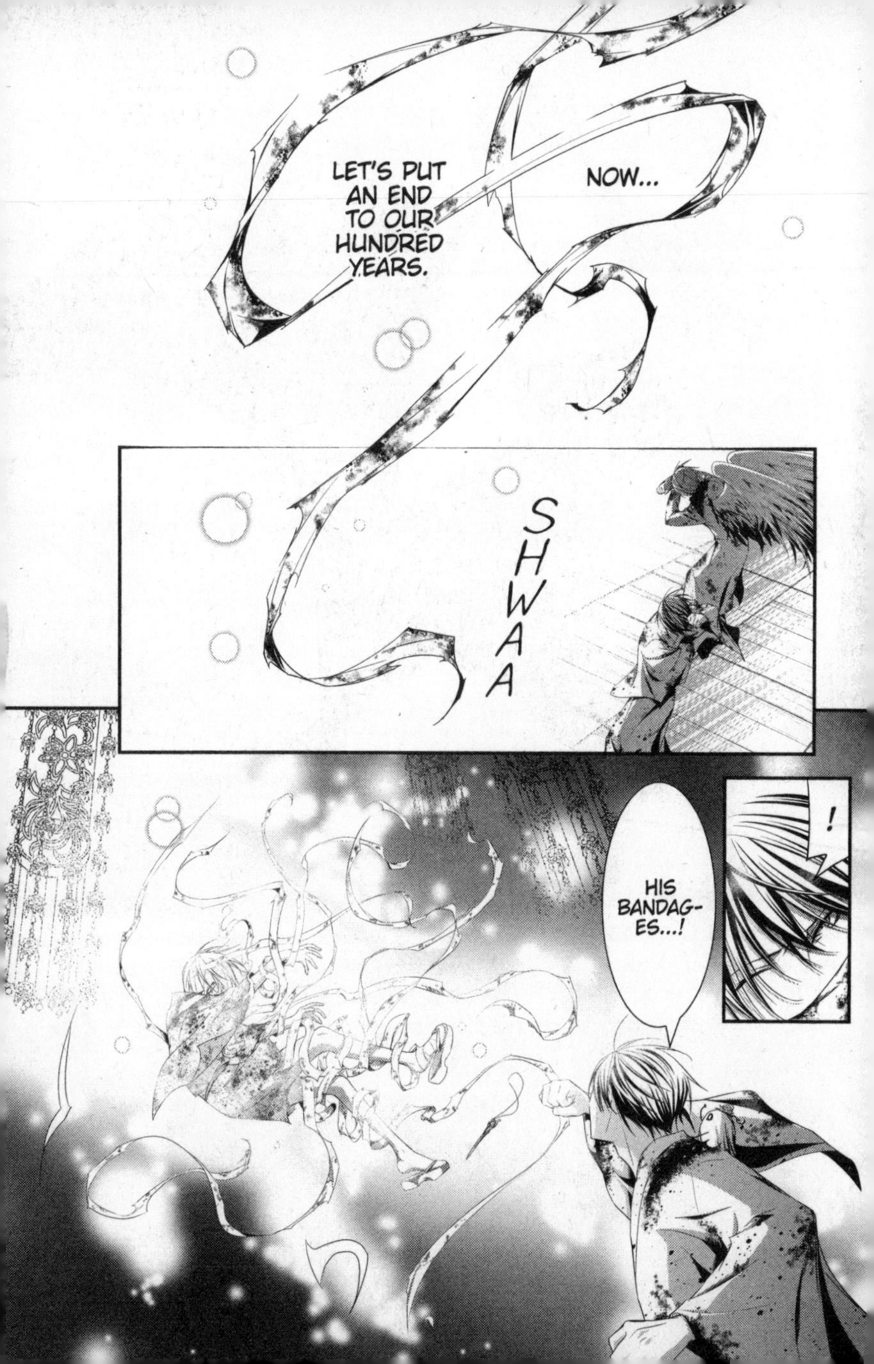
NOW...
LET'S PUT AN END TO OUR HUNDRED YEARS.
SHWAA
!
HIS BANDAG-ES...!

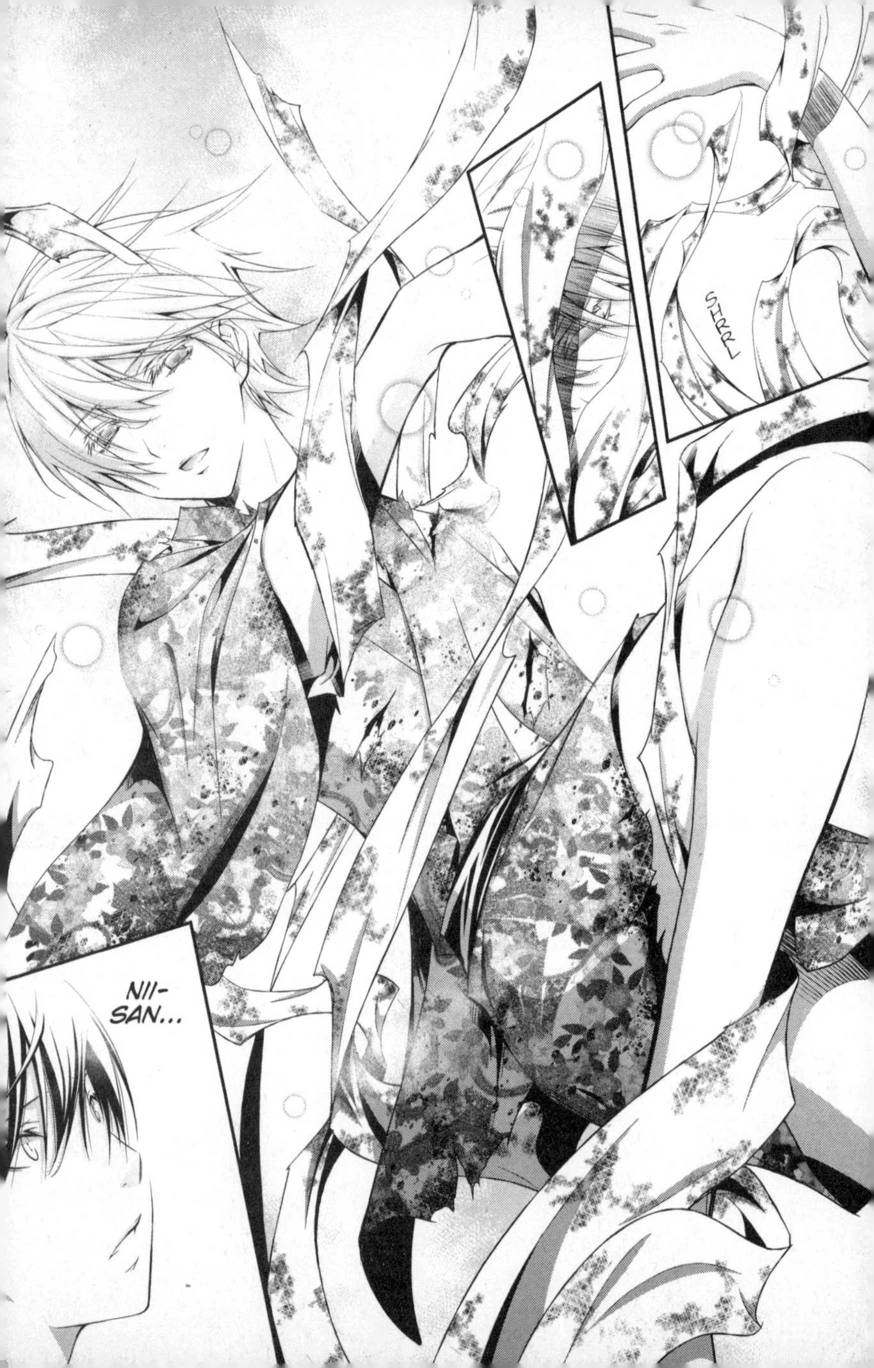
SHRRL
NII-SAN...

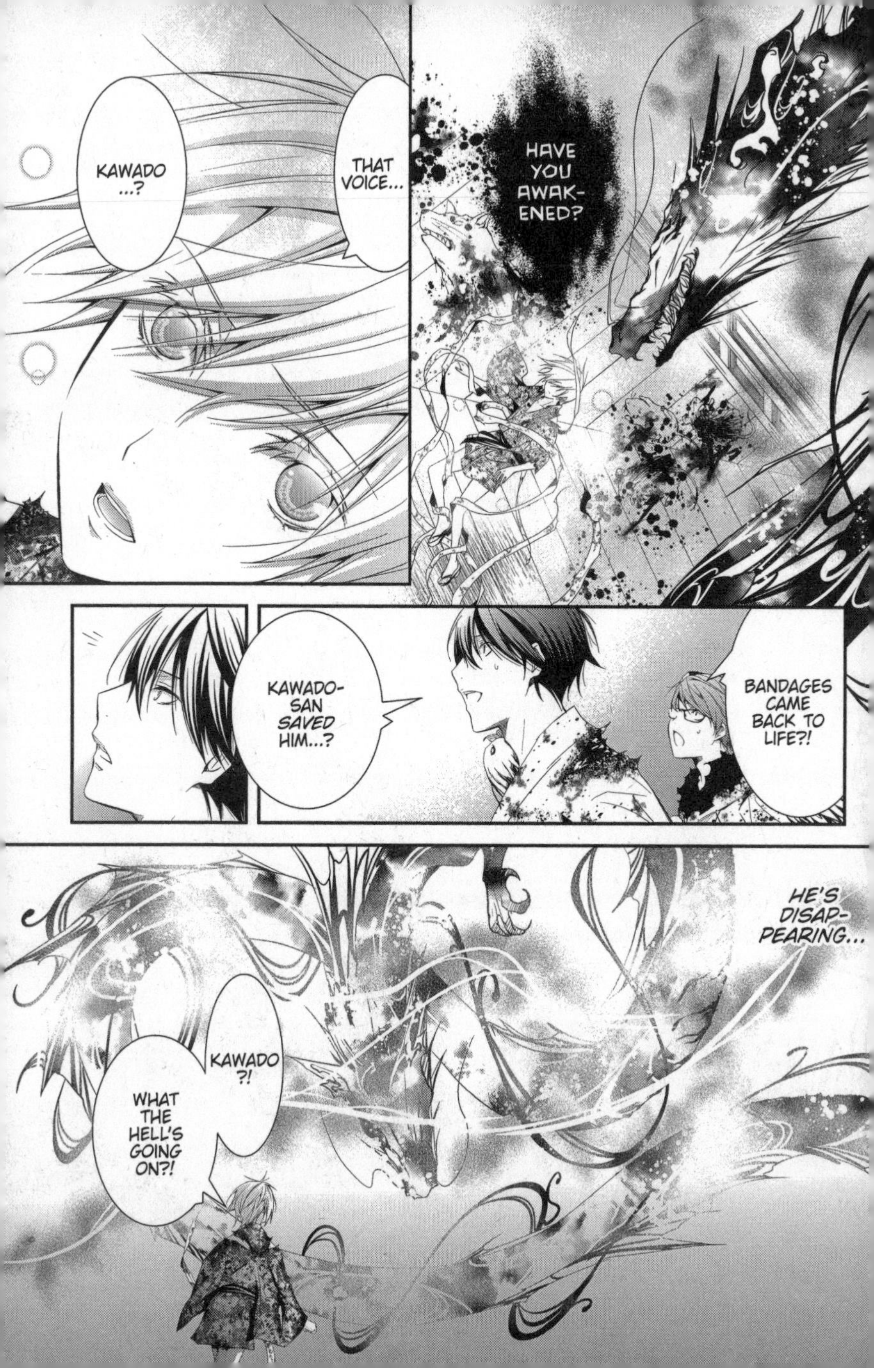
HAVE YOU AWAK-ENED?
THAT VOICE...
KAWADO ...?
BANDAGES CAME BACK TO LIFE?!
KAWADO-SAN SAVED HIM...?
HE'S DISAP-PEARING...
KAWADO ?!
WHAT THE HELL'S GOING ON?!

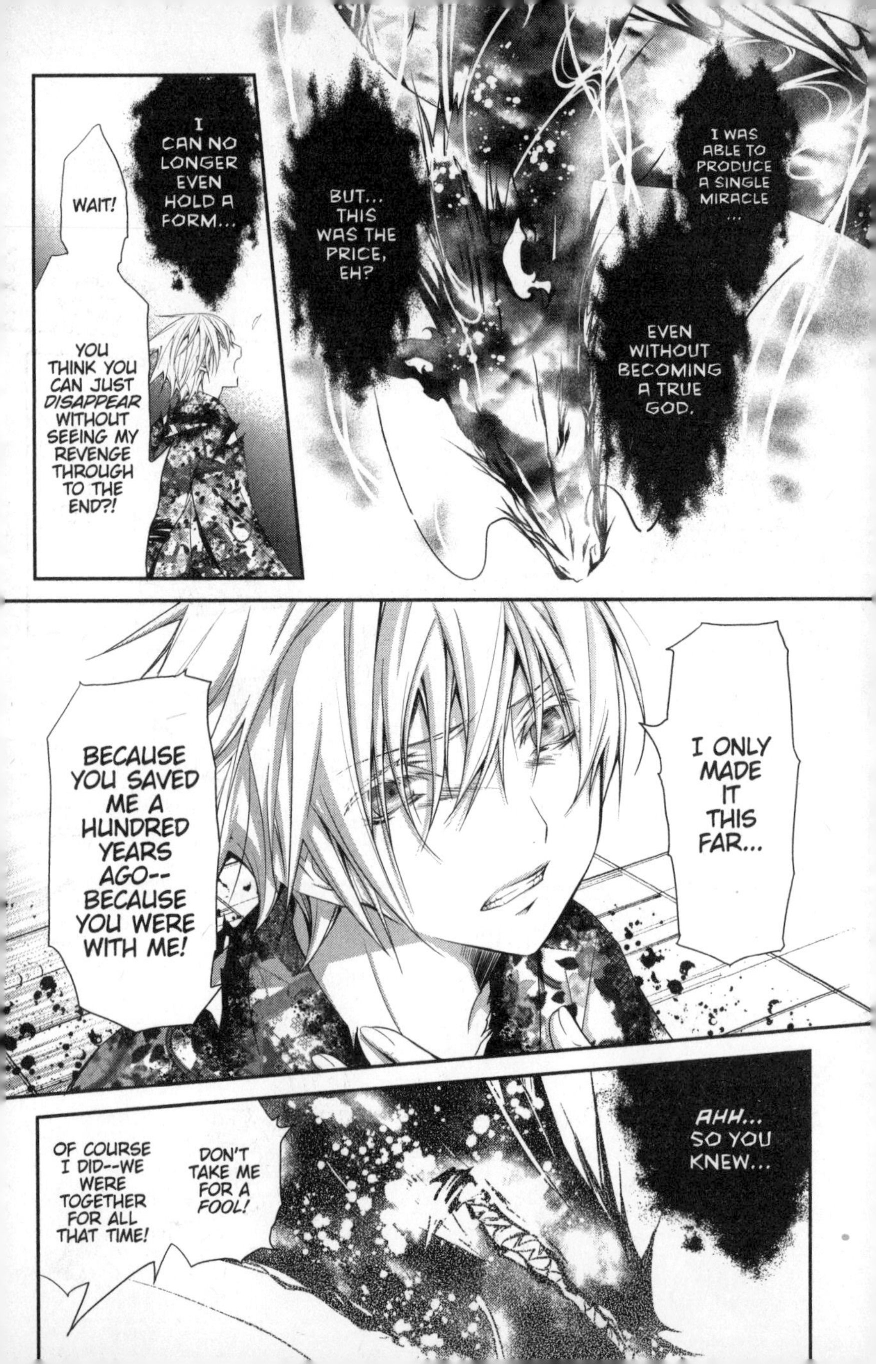
I WAS ABLE TO PRODUCE A SINGLE MIRACLE ...
EVEN WITHOUT BECOMING A TRUE GOD.
BUT... THIS WAS THE PRICE, EH?
I CAN NO LONGER EVEN HOLD A FORM...
WAIT!
YOU THINK YOU CAN JUST *DISAPPEAR* WITHOUT SEEING MY REVENGE THROUGH TO THE END?!
I ONLY MADE IT THIS FAR...
BECAUSE YOU SAVED ME A HUNDRED YEARS AGO--BECAUSE YOU WERE WITH ME!
AHH... SO YOU KNEW...
DON'T TAKE ME FOR A *FOOL!*
OF COURSE I DID--WE WERE TOGETHER FOR ALL THAT TIME!

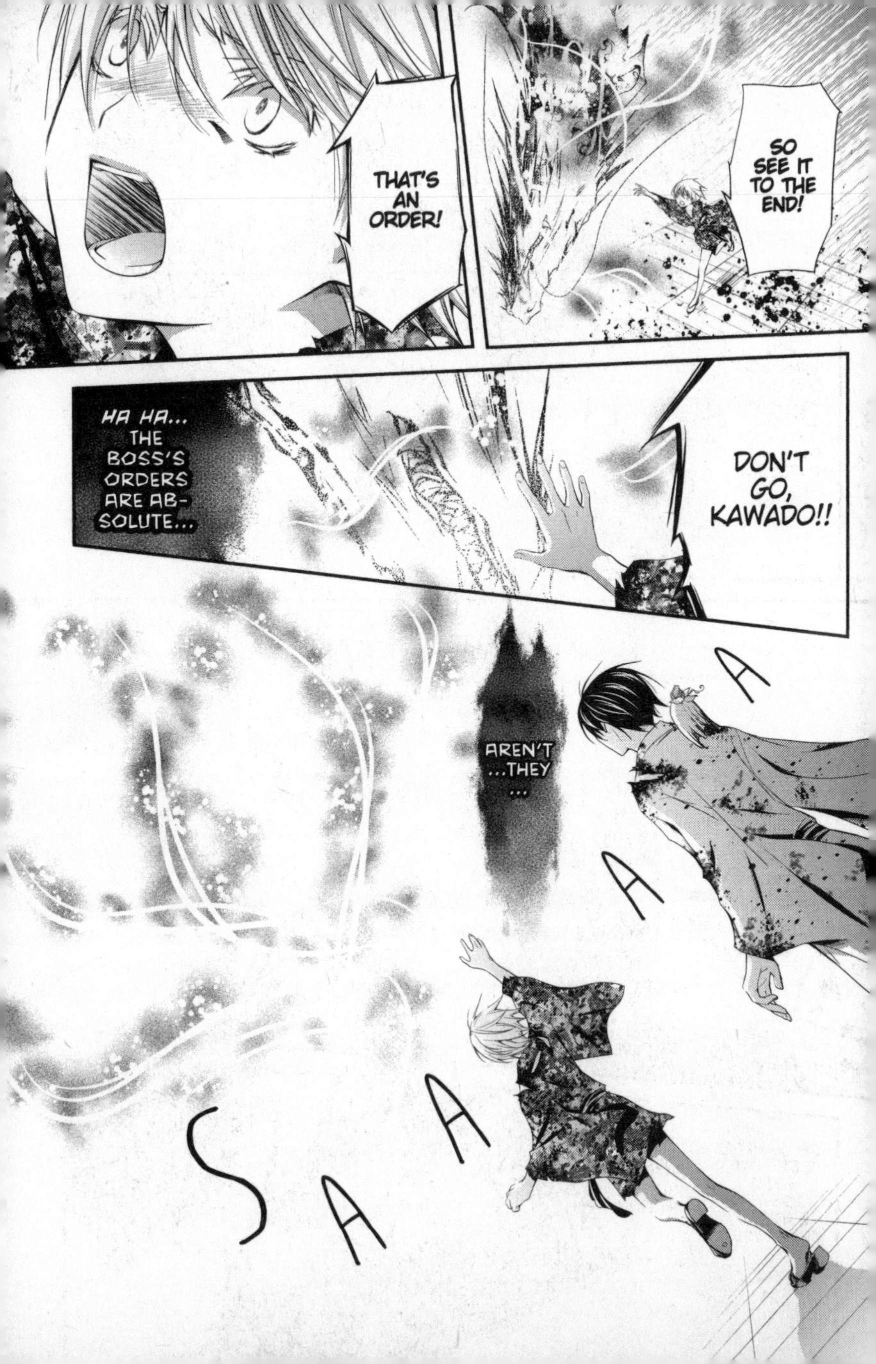
SO SEE IT TO THE END!
THAT'S AN ORDER!
DON'T GO, KAWADO!!
HA HA... THE BOSS'S ORDERS ARE AB-SOLUTE...
AREN'T ...THEY ...
SAAAAAA

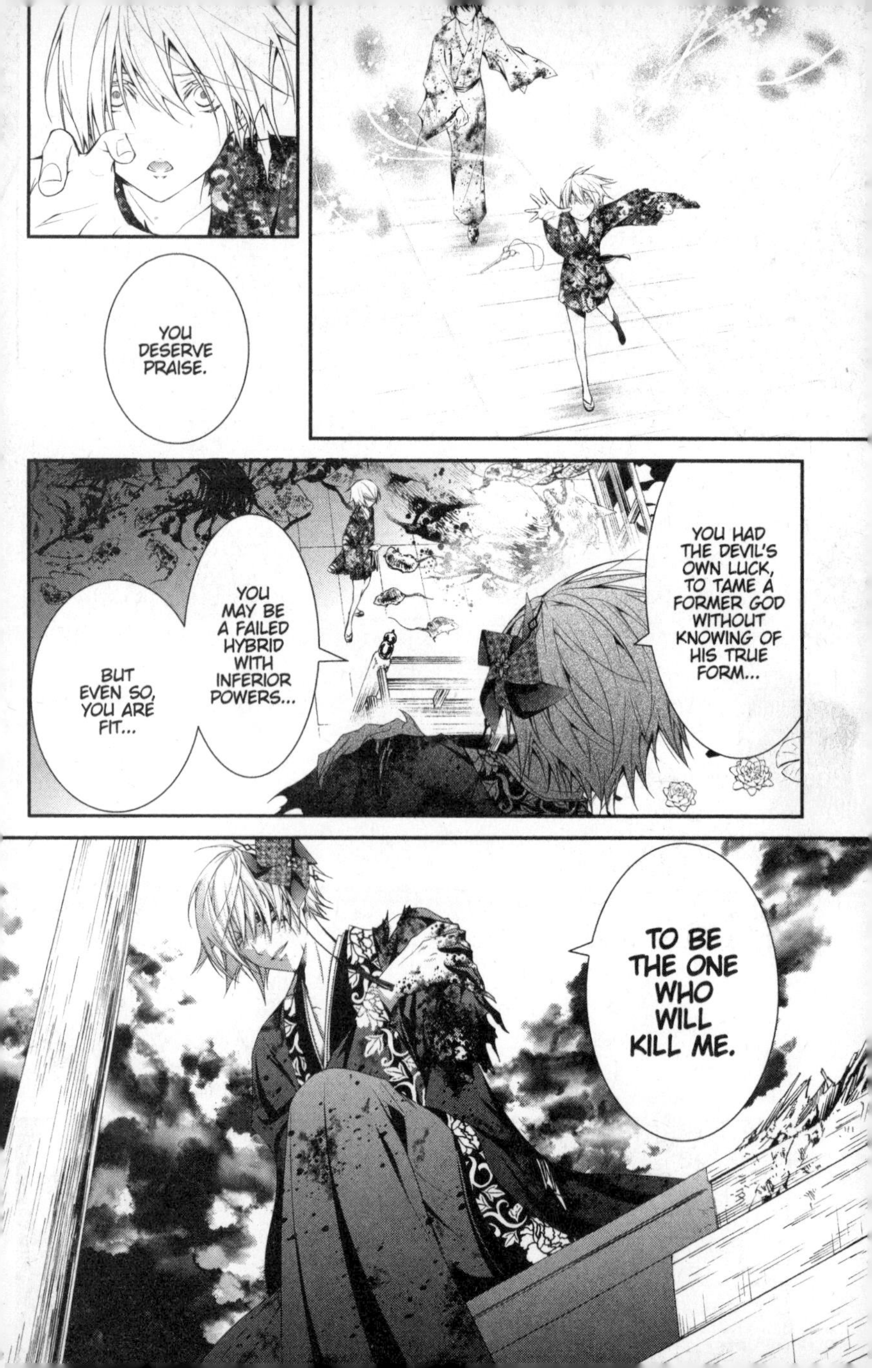
YOU DESERVE PRAISE.
YOU HAD THE DEVIL'S OWN LUCK, TO TAME A FORMER GOD WITHOUT KNOWING OF HIS TRUE FORM...
YOU MAY BE A FAILED HYBRID WITH INFERIOR POWERS...
BUT EVEN SO, YOU ARE FIT...
TO BE THE ONE WHO WILL KILL ME.

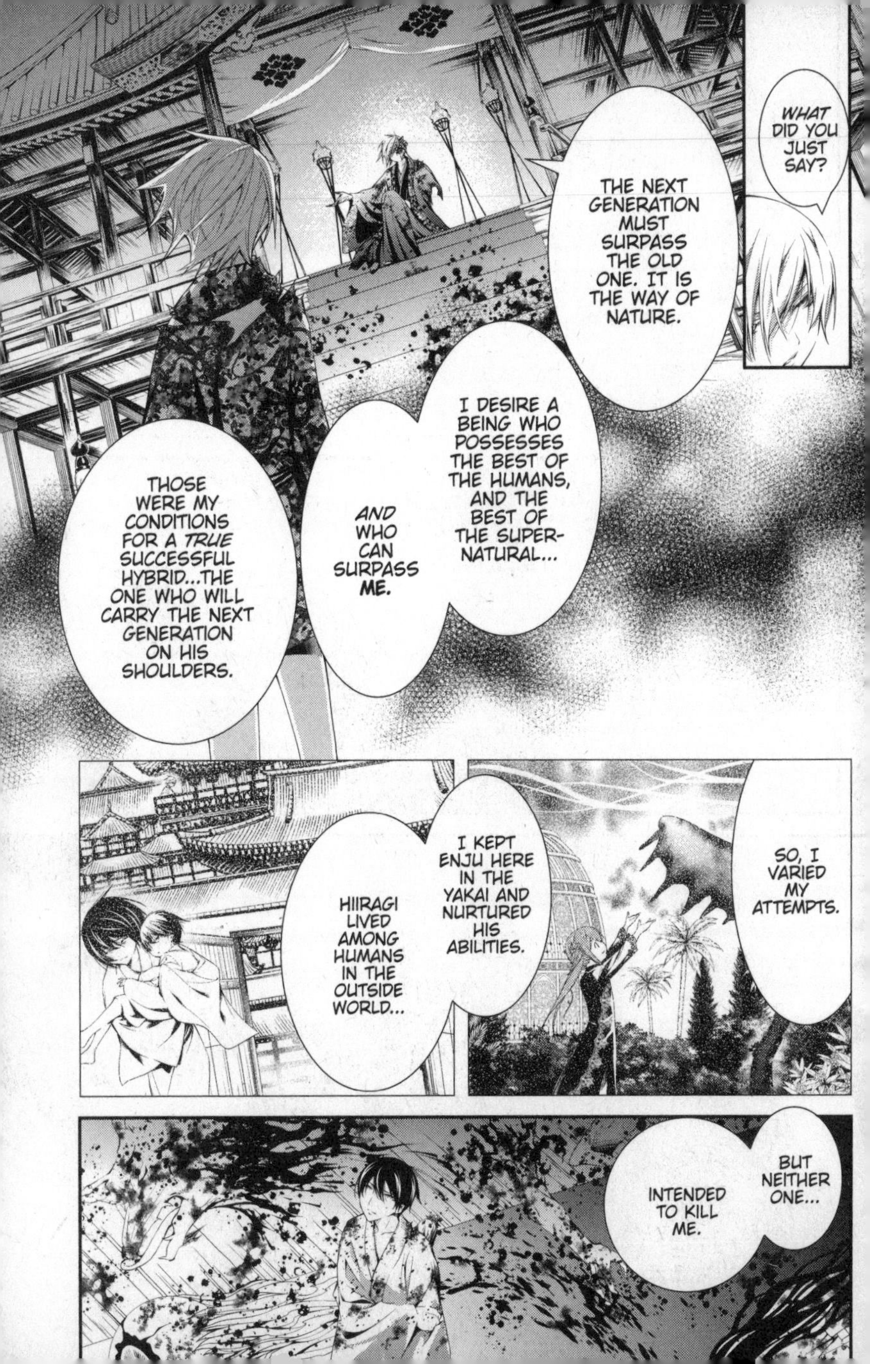
WHAT DID YOU JUST SAY?
THE NEXT GENERATION MUST SURPASS THE OLD ONE. IT IS THE WAY OF NATURE.
I DESIRE A BEING WHO POSSESSES THE BEST OF THE HUMANS, AND THE BEST OF THE SUPER-NATURAL...
AND WHO CAN SURPASS ME.
THOSE WERE MY CONDITIONS FOR A TRUE SUCCESSFUL HYBRID...THE ONE WHO WILL CARRY THE NEXT GENERATION ON HIS SHOULDERS.
SO, I VARIED MY ATTEMPTS.
I KEPT ENJU HERE IN THE YAKAI AND NURTURED HIS ABILITIES.
HIIRAGI LIVED AMONG HUMANS IN THE OUTSIDE WORLD...
BUT NEITHER ONE...
INTENDED TO KILL ME.

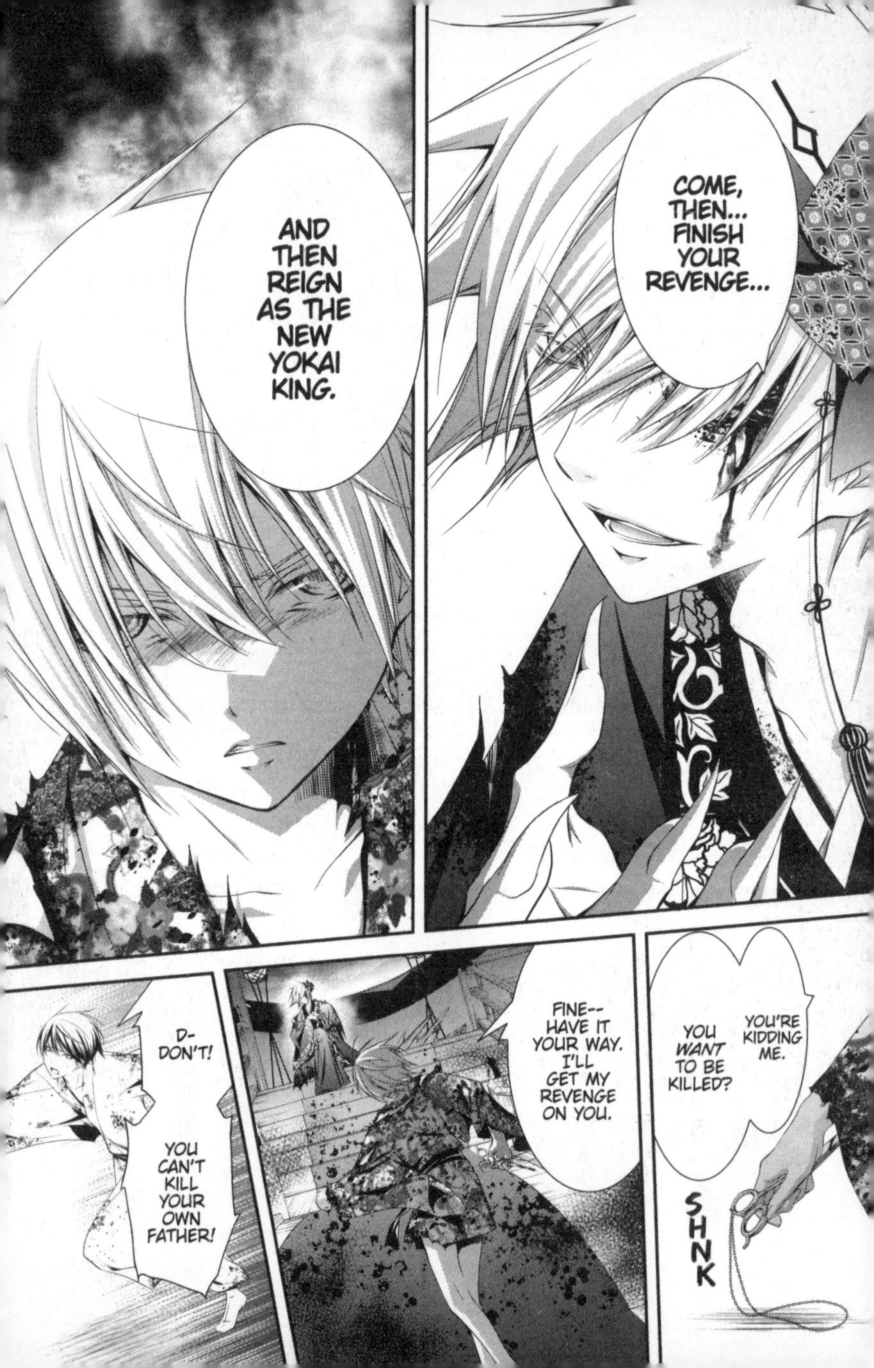
COME, THEN... FINISH YOUR REVENGE...
AND THEN REIGN AS THE NEW YOKAI KING.
YOU'RE KIDDING ME.
YOU *WANT* TO BE KILLED?
SHNK
FINE-- HAVE IT YOUR WAY. I'LL GET MY REVENGE ON YOU.
D-DON'T!
YOU CAN'T KILL YOUR OWN FATHER!

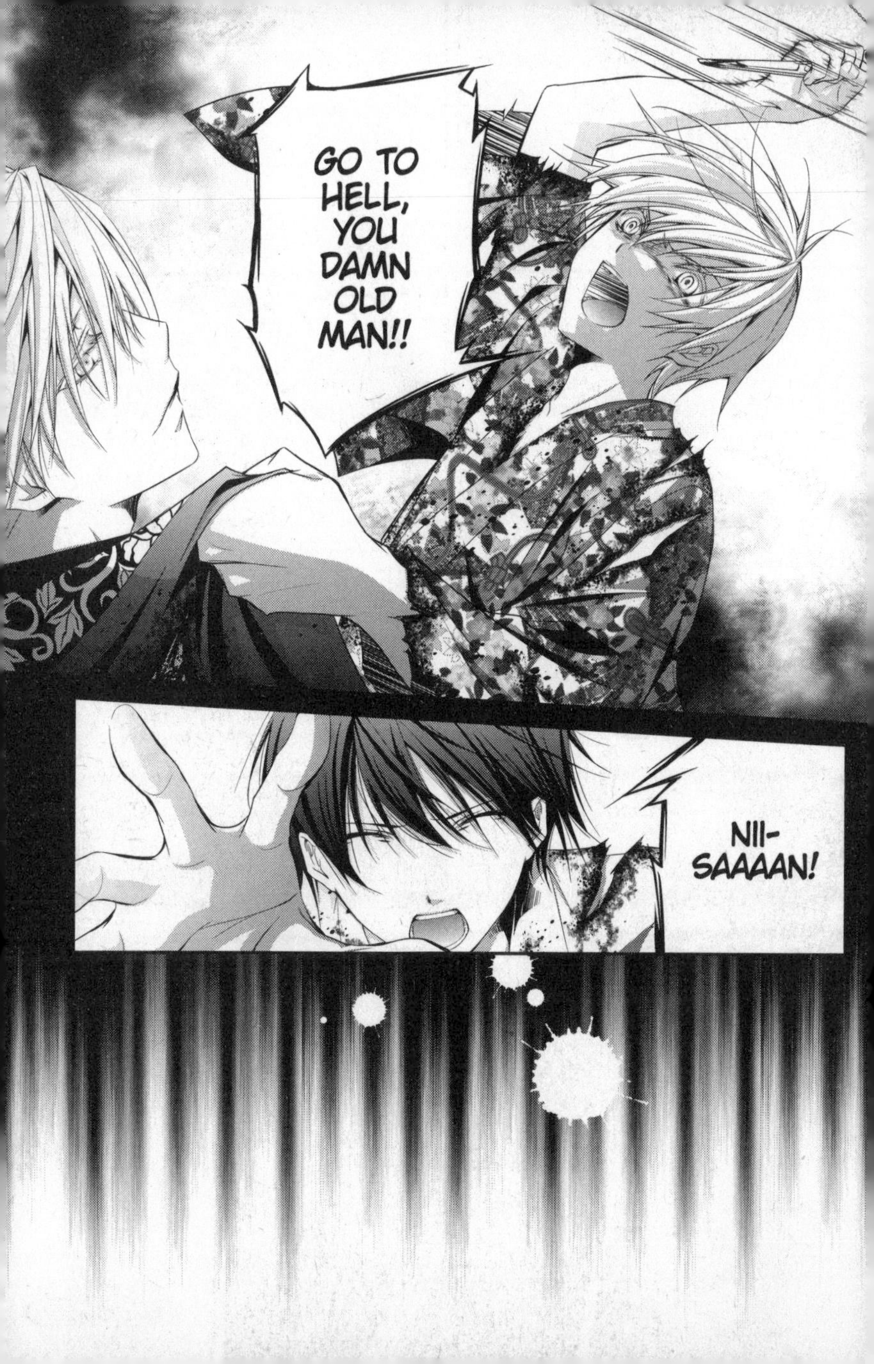
GO TO HELL, YOU DAMN OLD MAN!!
NII-SAAAAN!

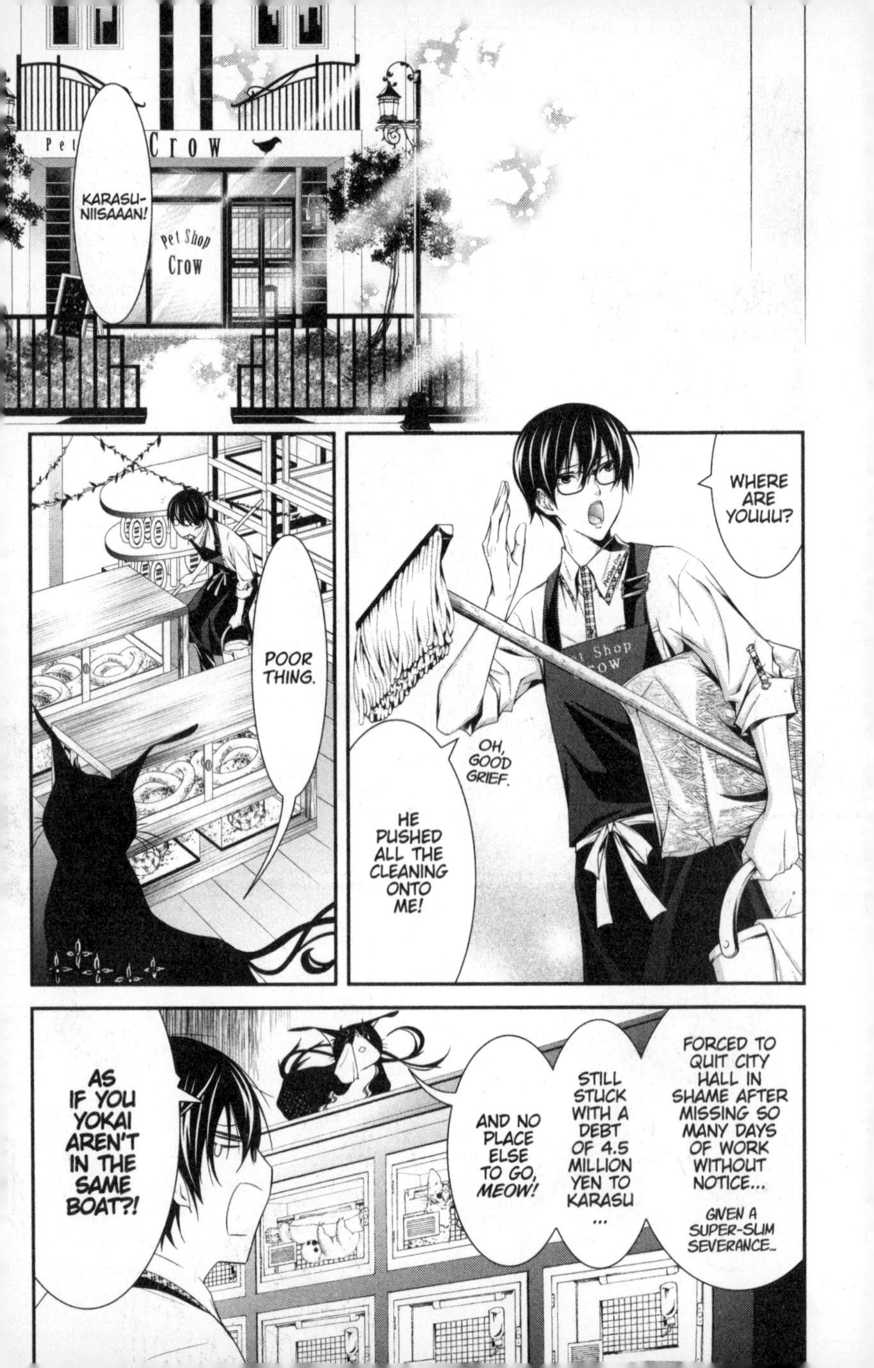
KARASU-NIISAAAN!
Pet Shop Crow
WHERE ARE YOUUU?
OH, GOOD GRIEF.
HE PUSHED ALL THE CLEANING ONTO ME!
POOR THING.
FORCED TO QUIT CITY HALL IN SHAME AFTER MISSING SO MANY DAYS OF WORK WITHOUT NOTICE...
GIVEN A SUPER-SLIM SEVERANCE...
STILL STUCK WITH A DEBT OF 4.5 MILLION YEN TO KARASU...
AND NO PLACE ELSE TO GO, MEOW!
AS IF YOU YOKAI AREN'T IN THE SAME BOAT?!

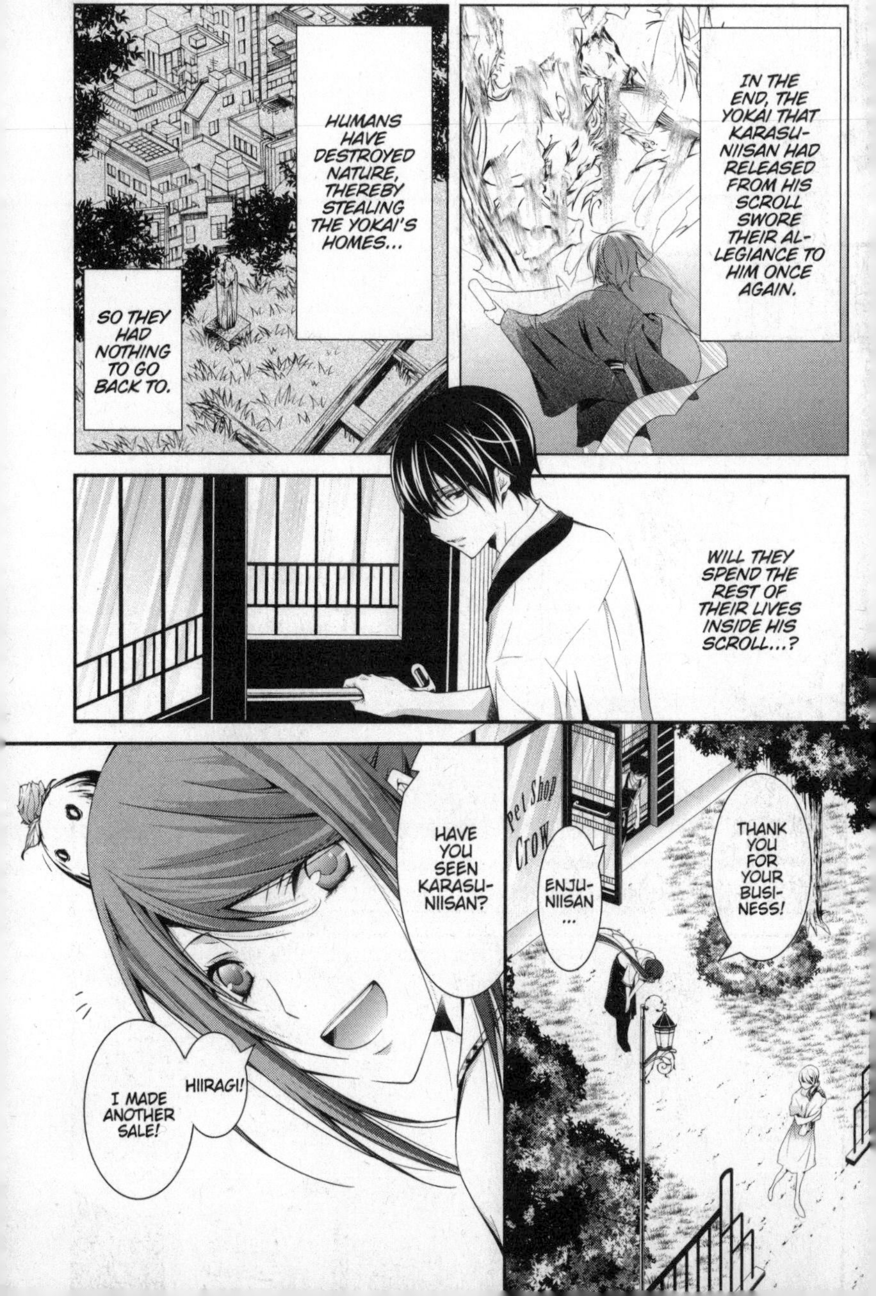
IN THE END, THE YOKAI THAT KARASU-NIISAN HAD RELEASED FROM HIS SCROLL SWORE THEIR AL-LEGIANCE TO HIM ONCE AGAIN.
HUMANS HAVE DESTROYED NATURE, THEREBY STEALING THE YOKAI'S HOMES...
SO THEY HAD NOTHING TO GO BACK TO.
WILL THEY SPEND THE REST OF THEIR LIVES INSIDE HIS SCROLL...?
THANK YOU FOR YOUR BUSI-NESS!
ENJU-NIISAN...
Pet Shop Crow
HAVE YOU SEEN KARASU-NIISAN?
HIIRAGI!
I MADE ANOTHER SALE!

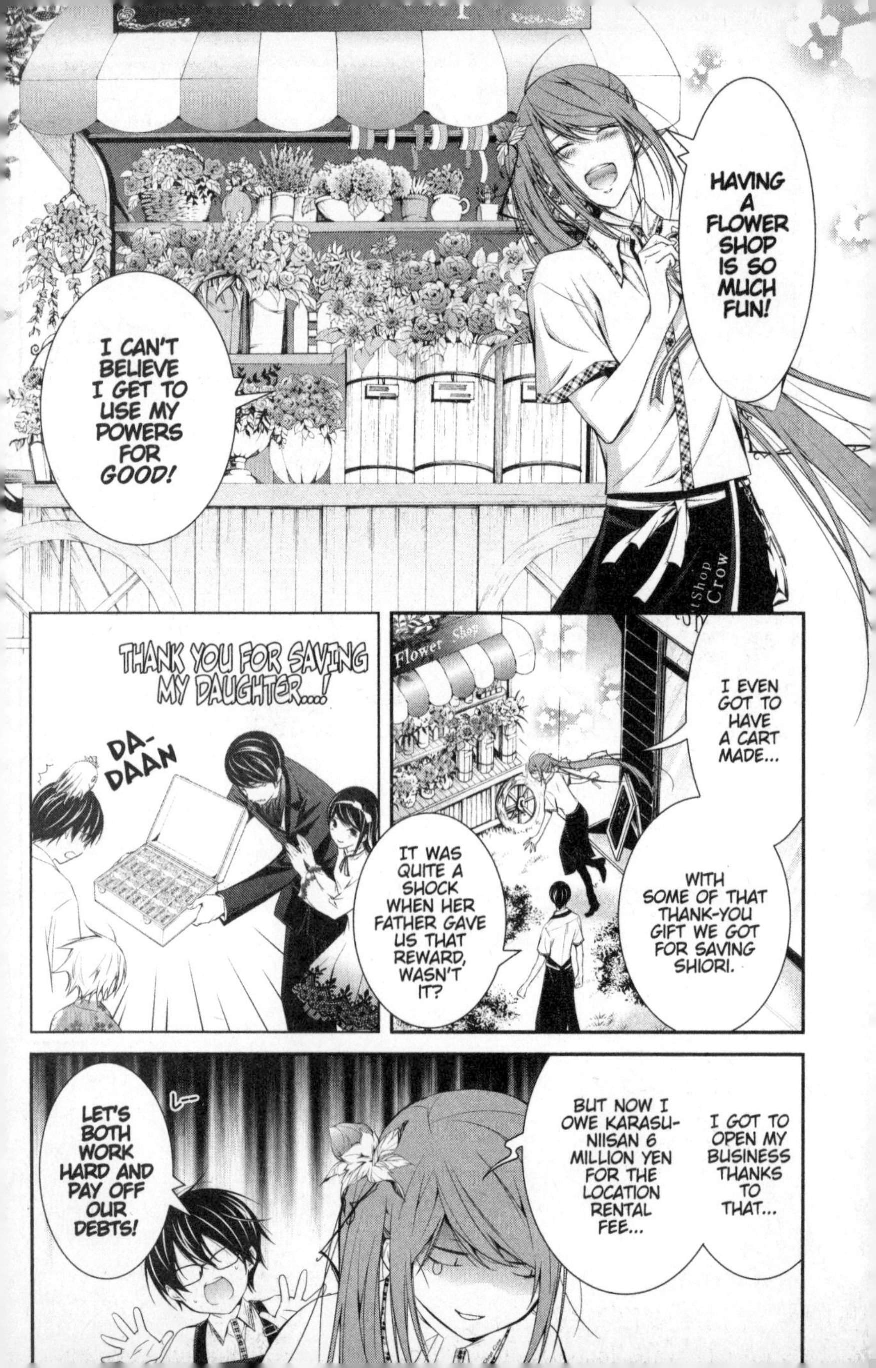
HAVING A FLOWER SHOP IS SO MUCH FUN!
I CAN'T BELIEVE I GET TO USE MY POWERS FOR GOOD!
Flower Shop
I EVEN GOT TO HAVE A CART MADE...
WITH SOME OF THAT THANK-YOU GIFT WE GOT FOR SAVING SHIORI.
THANK YOU FOR SAVING MY DAUGHTER...!
DA-DAAN
IT WAS QUITE A SHOCK WHEN HER FATHER GAVE US THAT REWARD, WASN'T IT?
I GOT TO OPEN MY BUSINESS THANKS TO THAT...
BUT NOW I OWE KARASU-NIISAN 6 MILLION YEN FOR THE LOCATION RENTAL FEE...
LET'S BOTH WORK HARD AND PAY OFF OUR DEBTS!

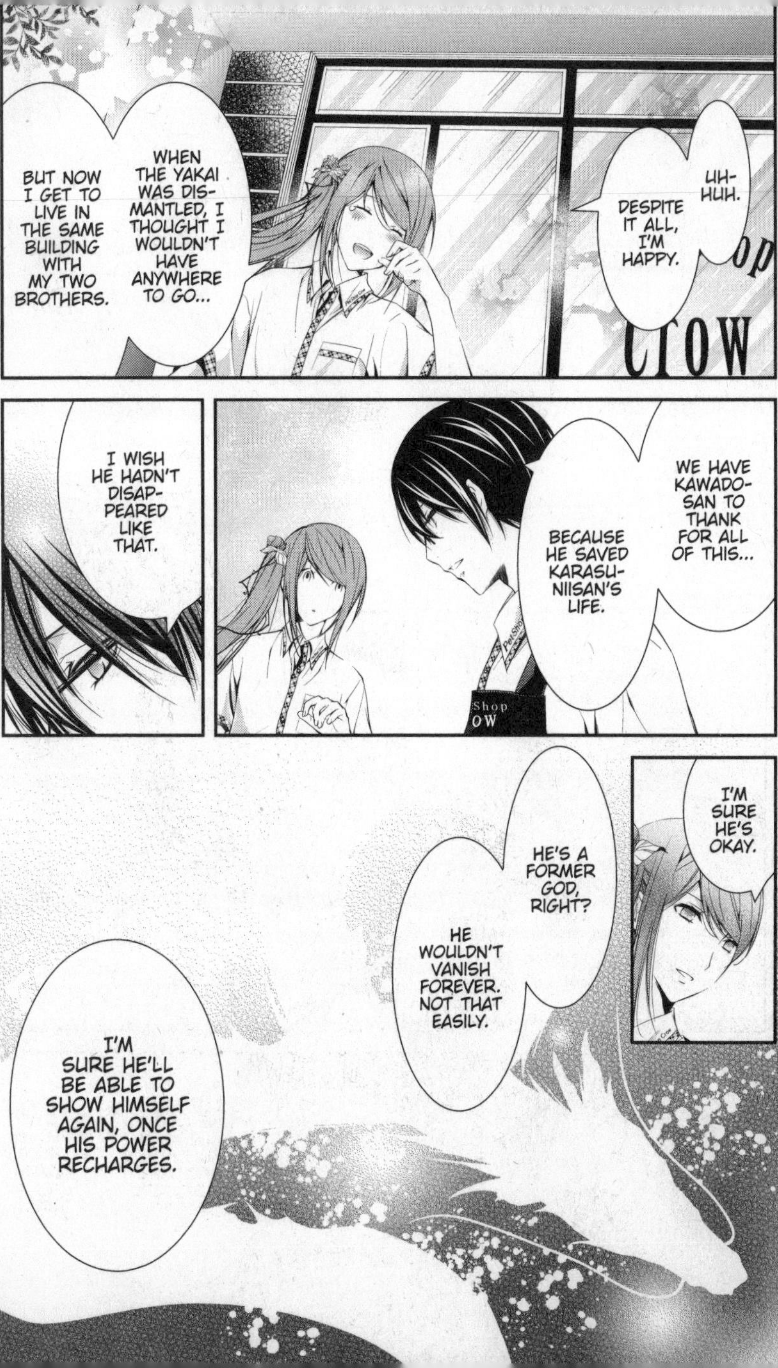
UH-HUH.
DESPITE IT ALL, I'M HAPPY.
WHEN THE YAKAI WAS DIS-MANTLED, I THOUGHT I WOULDN'T HAVE ANYWHERE TO GO...
BUT NOW I GET TO LIVE IN THE SAME BUILDING WITH MY TWO BROTHERS.
WE HAVE KAWADO-SAN TO THANK FOR ALL OF THIS...
BECAUSE HE SAVED KARASU-NIISAN'S LIFE.
I WISH HE HADN'T DISAP-PEARED LIKE THAT.
I'M SURE HE'S OKAY.
HE'S A FORMER GOD, RIGHT?
HE WOULDN'T VANISH FOREVER. NOT THAT EASILY.
I'M SURE HE'LL BE ABLE TO SHOW HIMSELF AGAIN, ONCE HIS POWER RECHARGES.

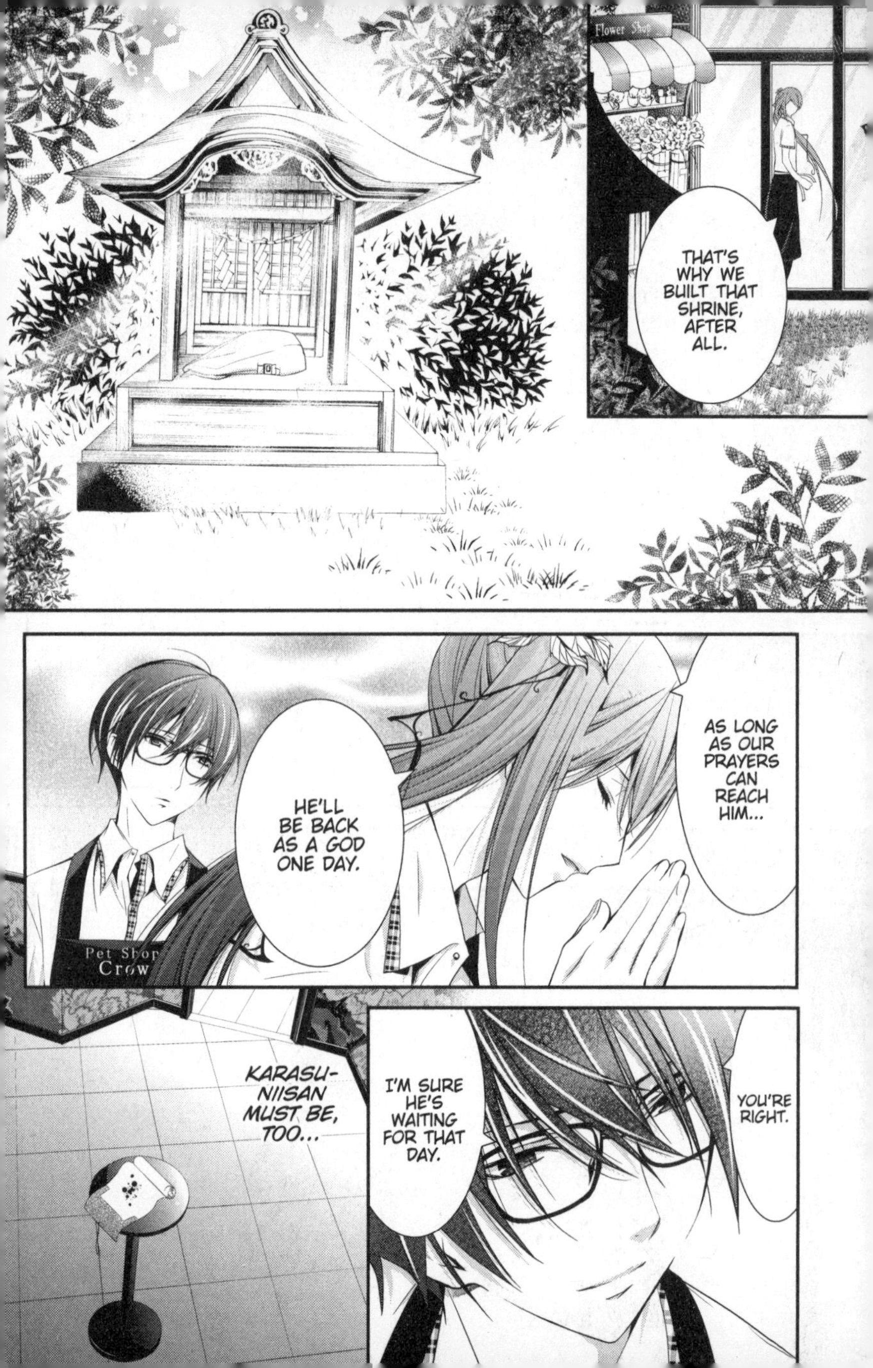
Flower Shop
THAT'S WHY WE BUILT THAT SHRINE, AFTER ALL.
AS LONG AS OUR PRAYERS CAN REACH HIM...
HE'LL BE BACK AS A GOD ONE DAY.
Pet Shop Crow
YOU'RE RIGHT.
I'M SURE HE'S WAITING FOR THAT DAY.
KARASU-NIISAN MUST BE, TOO...

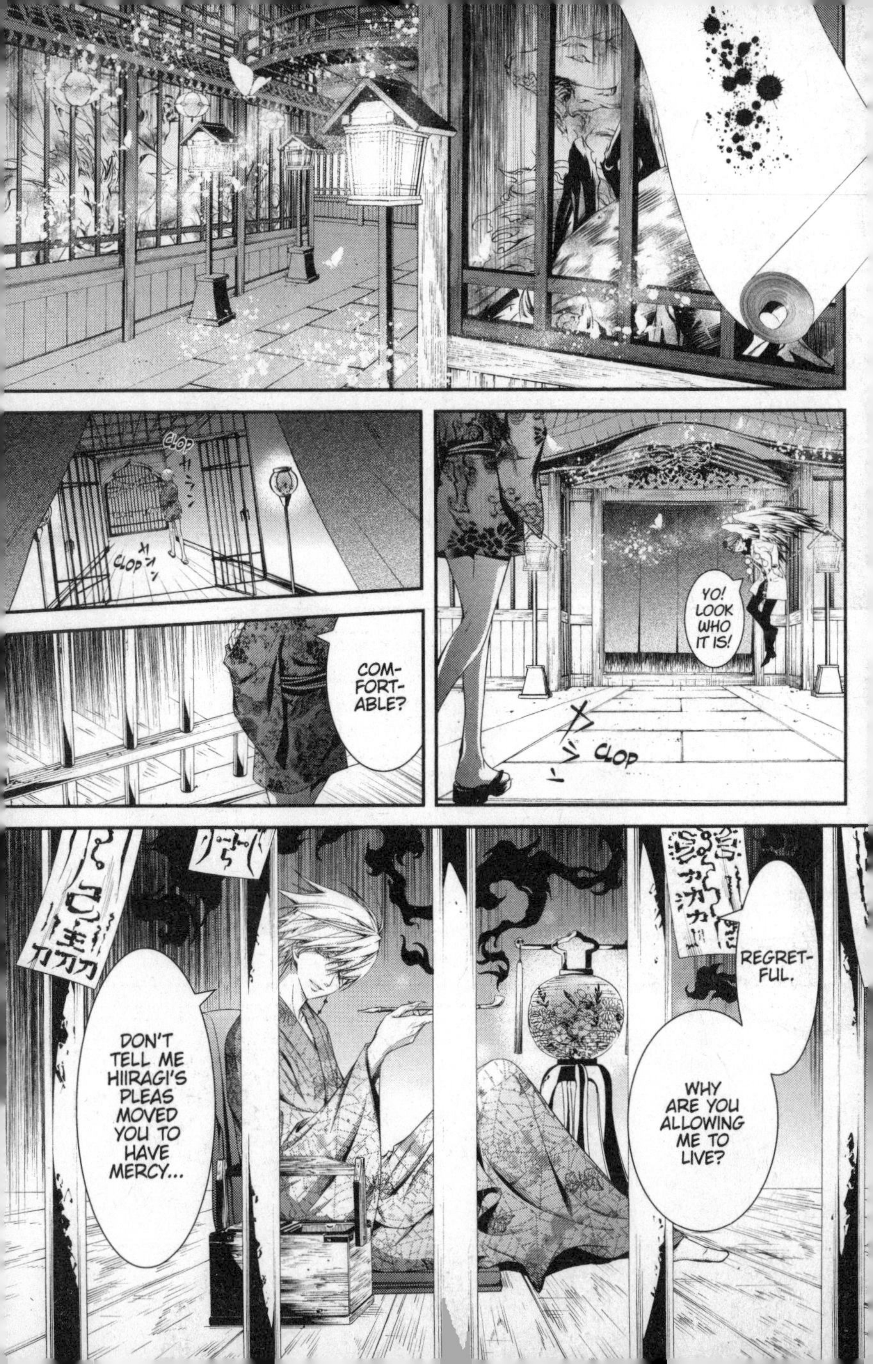
YO! LOOK WHO IT IS!
CLOP
CLOP
CLOP
COMFORTABLE?
REGRETFUL.
WHY ARE YOU ALLOWING ME TO LIVE?
DON'T TELL ME HIIRAGI'S PLEAS MOVED YOU TO HAVE MERCY...

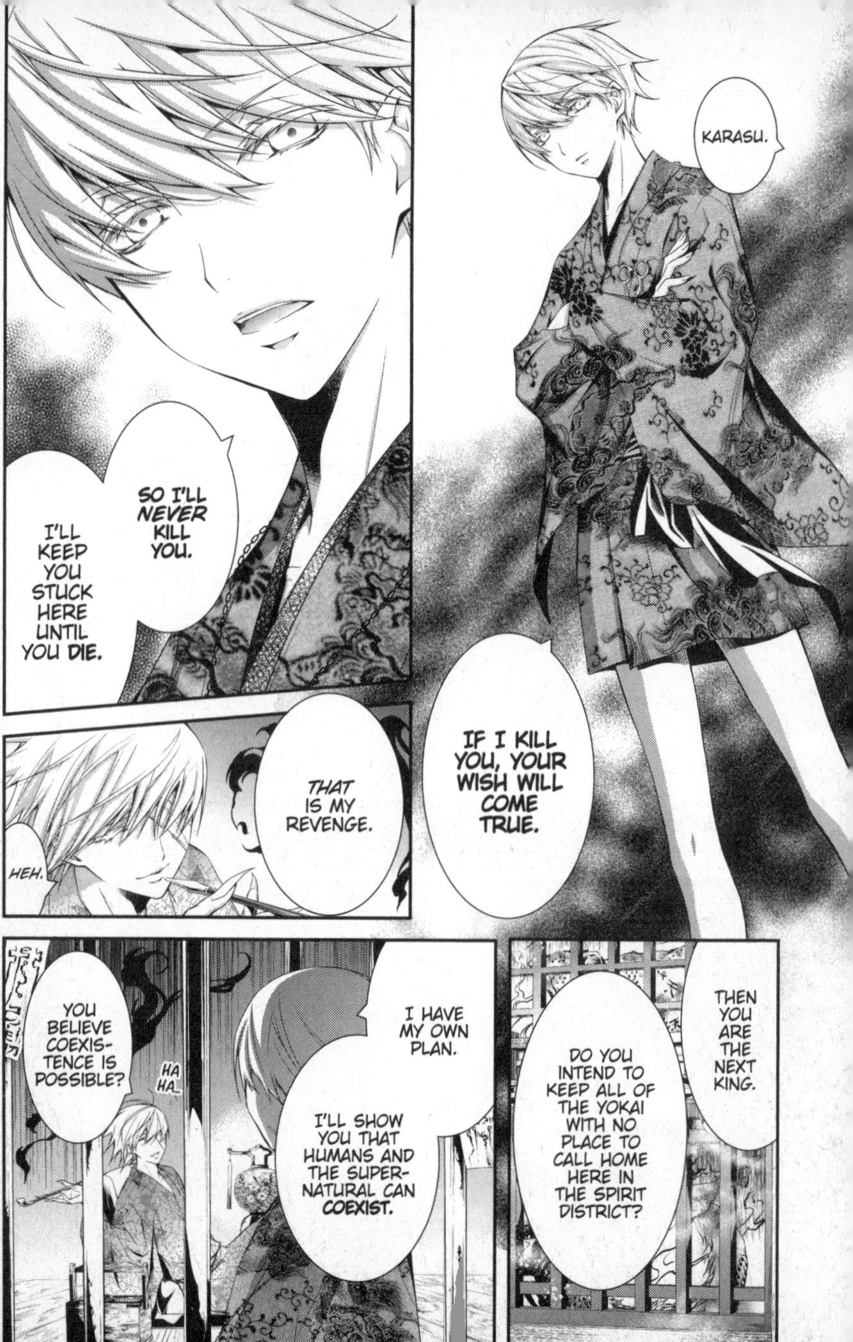
KARASU.
IF I KILL YOU, YOUR WISH WILL COME TRUE.
SO I'LL *NEVER* KILL YOU.
I'LL KEEP YOU STUCK HERE UNTIL YOU **DIE**.
THAT IS MY REVENGE.
HEH.
THEN YOU ARE THE NEXT KING.
DO YOU INTEND TO KEEP ALL OF THE YOKAI WITH NO PLACE TO CALL HOME HERE IN THE SPIRIT DISTRICT?
I HAVE MY OWN PLAN.
I'LL SHOW YOU THAT HUMANS AND THE SUPER-NATURAL CAN **COEXIST**.
YOU BELIEVE COEXIS-TENCE IS POSSIBLE?
HA HA...

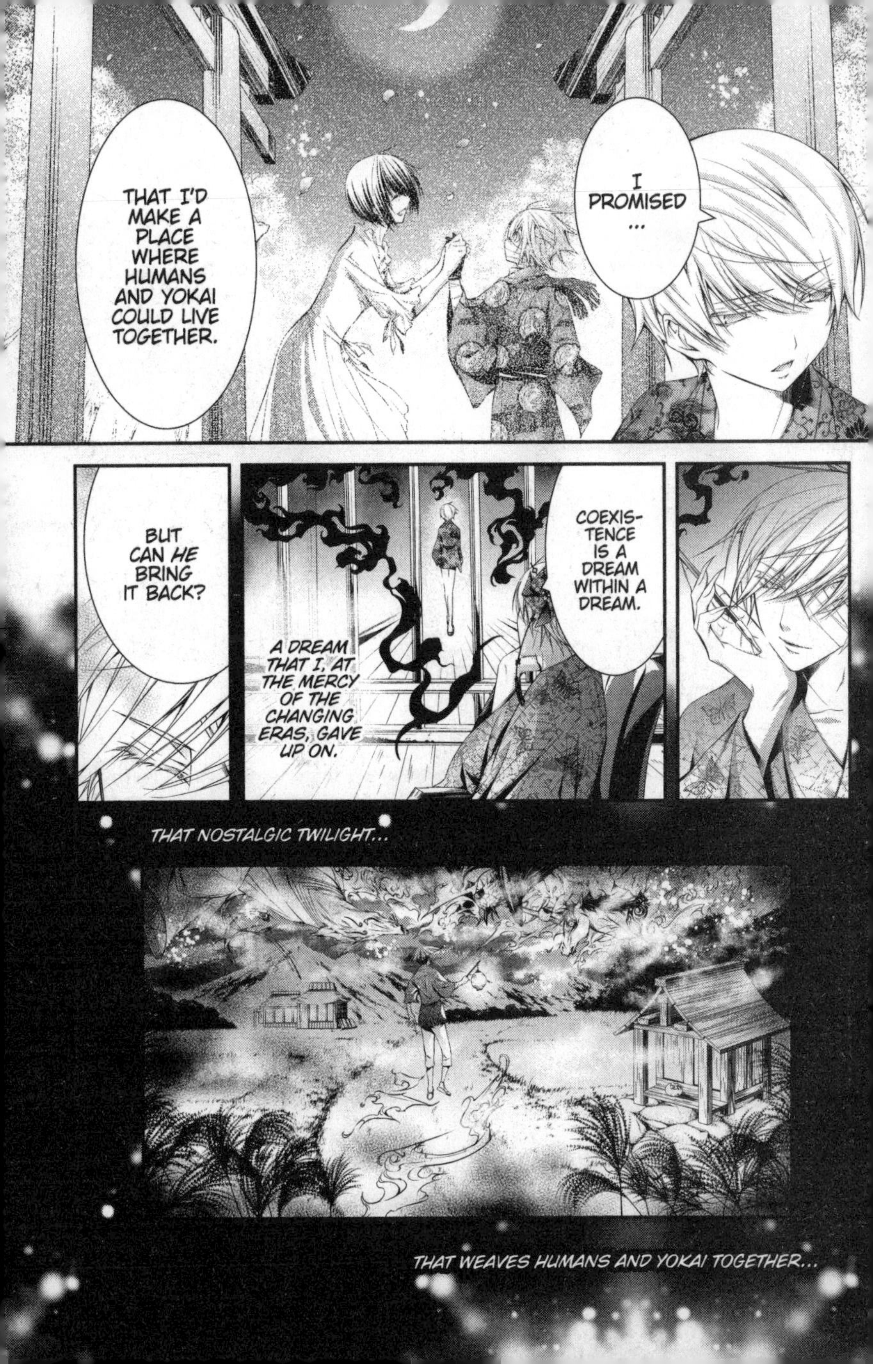
I PROMISED ...
THAT I'D MAKE A PLACE WHERE HUMANS AND YOKAI COULD LIVE TOGETHER.
COEXIS-TENCE IS A DREAM WITHIN A DREAM.
A DREAM THAT I, AT THE MERCY OF THE CHANGING ERAS, GAVE UP ON.
BUT CAN *HE* BRING IT BACK?
THAT NOSTALGIC TWILIGHT...
THAT WEAVES HUMANS AND YOKAI TOGETHER...

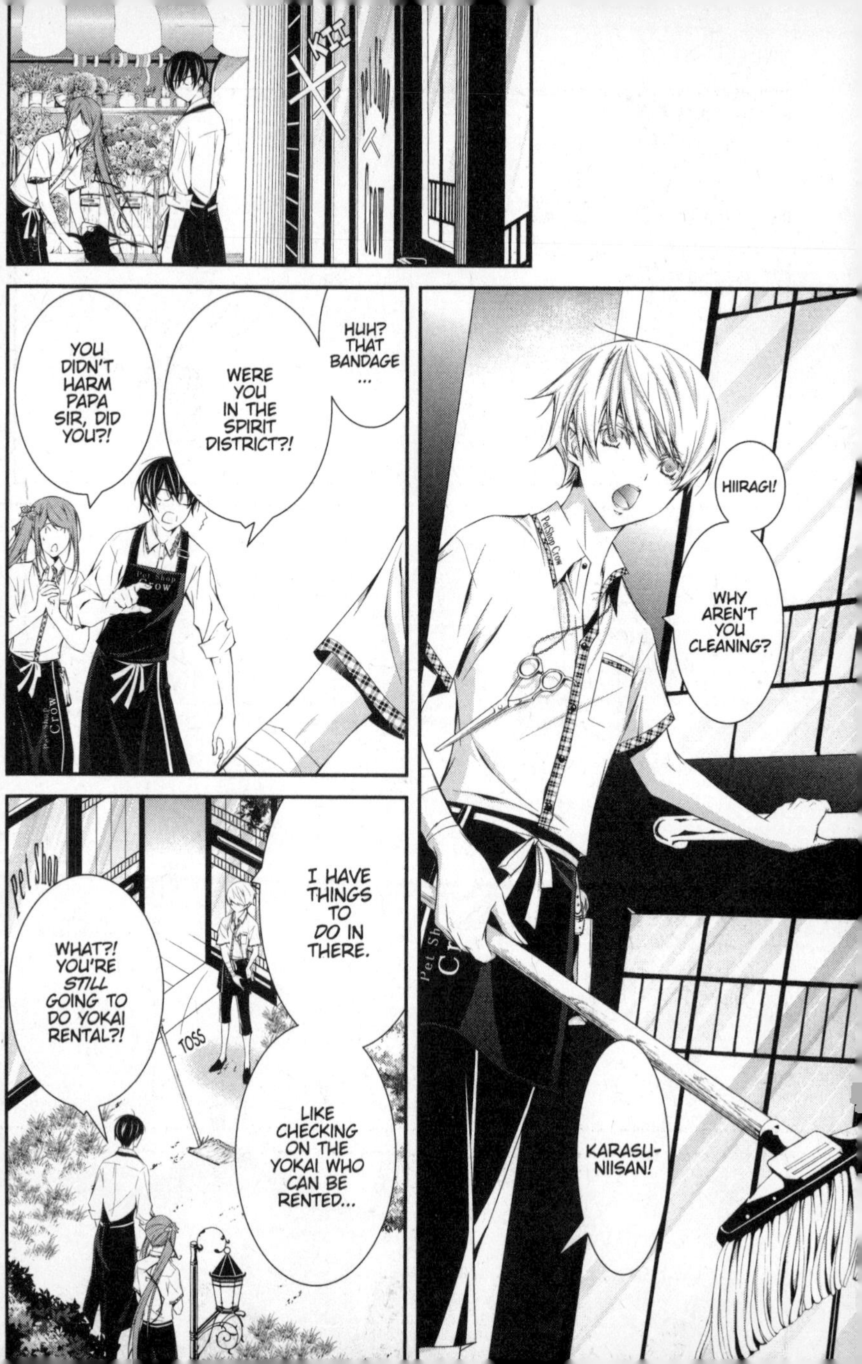
KII
HIIRAGI!
WHY AREN'T YOU CLEANING?
KARASU-NIISAN!
HUH? THAT BANDAGE...
WERE YOU IN THE SPIRIT DISTRICT?!
YOU DIDN'T HARM PAPA SIR, DID YOU?!
I HAVE THINGS TO DO IN THERE.
LIKE CHECKING ON THE YOKAI WHO CAN BE RENTED...
WHAT?! YOU'RE STILL GOING TO DO YOKAI RENTAL?!
TOSS

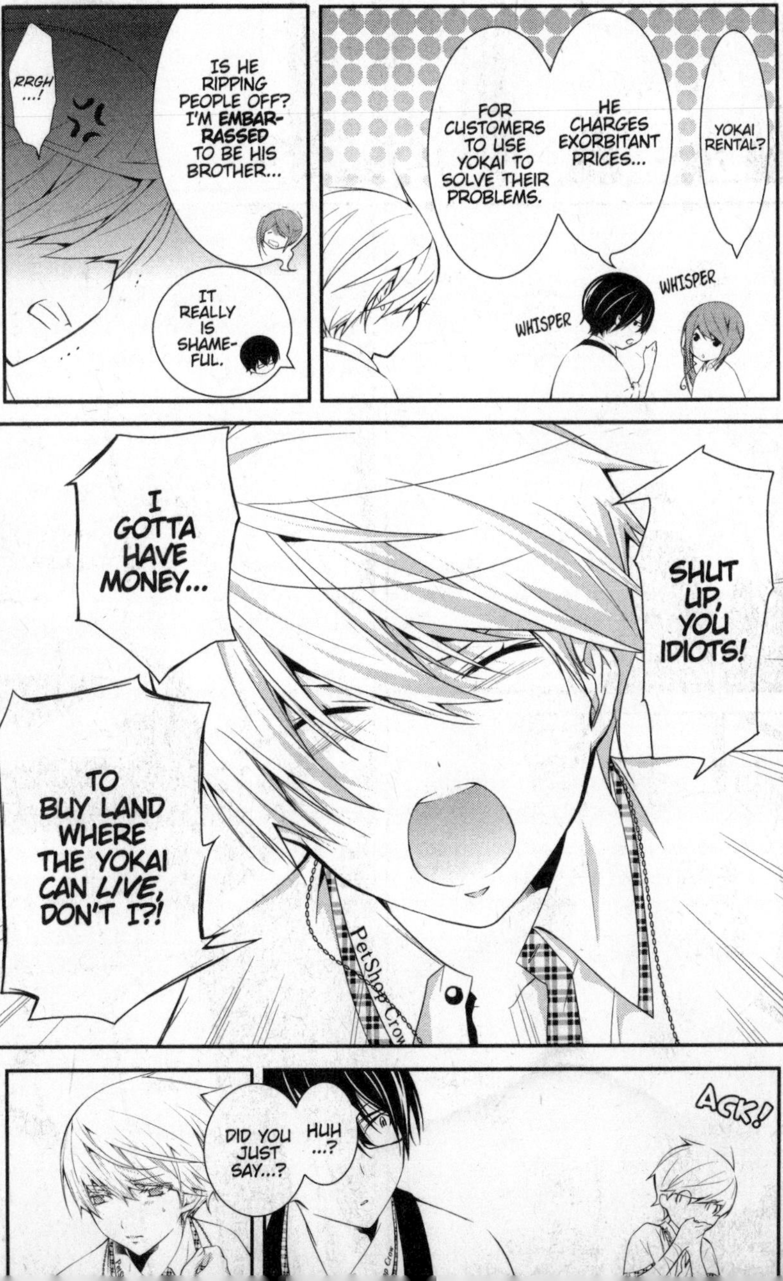
YOKAI RENTAL?
HE CHARGES EXORBITANT PRICES...
FOR CUSTOMERS TO USE YOKAI TO SOLVE THEIR PROBLEMS.
WHISPER
WHISPER
IS HE RIPPING PEOPLE OFF? I'M EMBARRASSED TO BE HIS BROTHER...
IT REALLY IS SHAME-FUL.
RRGH ...!
SHUT UP, YOU IDIOTS!
I GOTTA HAVE MONEY...
TO BUY LAND WHERE THE YOKAI CAN LIVE, DON'T I?!
PetShop Crow
ACK!
HUH ...?
DID YOU JUST SAY...?

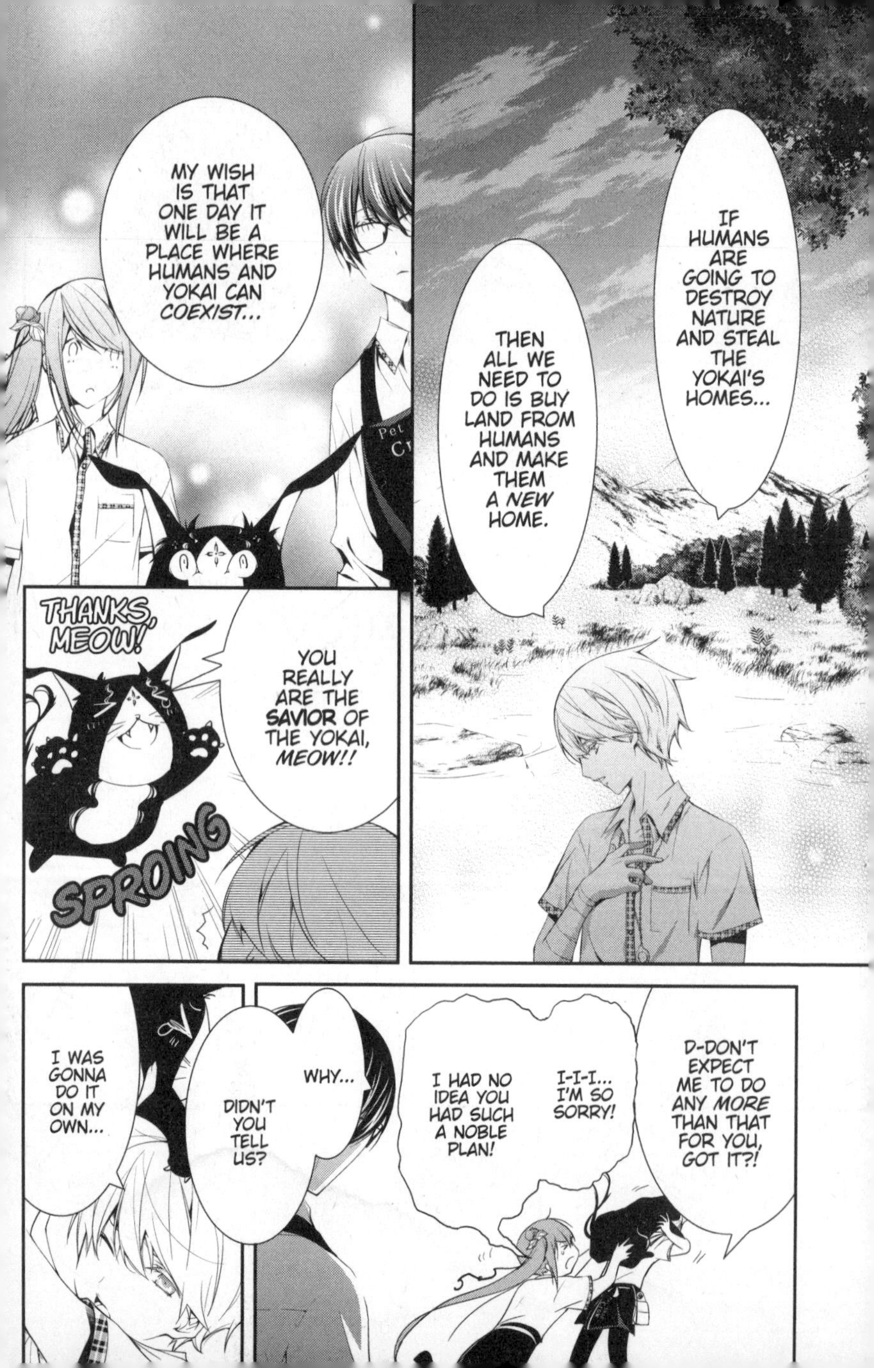
IF HUMANS ARE GOING TO DESTROY NATURE AND STEAL THE YOKAI'S HOMES...
THEN ALL WE NEED TO DO IS BUY LAND FROM HUMANS AND MAKE THEM A *NEW* HOME.
MY WISH IS THAT ONE DAY IT WILL BE A PLACE WHERE HUMANS AND YOKAI CAN *COEXIST*...
THANKS, MEOW!
YOU REALLY ARE THE **SAVIOR** OF THE YOKAI, *MEOW!!*
SPROING
D-DON'T EXPECT ME TO DO ANY *MORE* THAN THAT FOR YOU, GOT IT?!
I-I-I... I'M SO SORRY!
I HAD NO IDEA YOU HAD SUCH A NOBLE PLAN!
WHY...
DIDN'T YOU TELL US?
I WAS GONNA DO IT ON MY OWN...

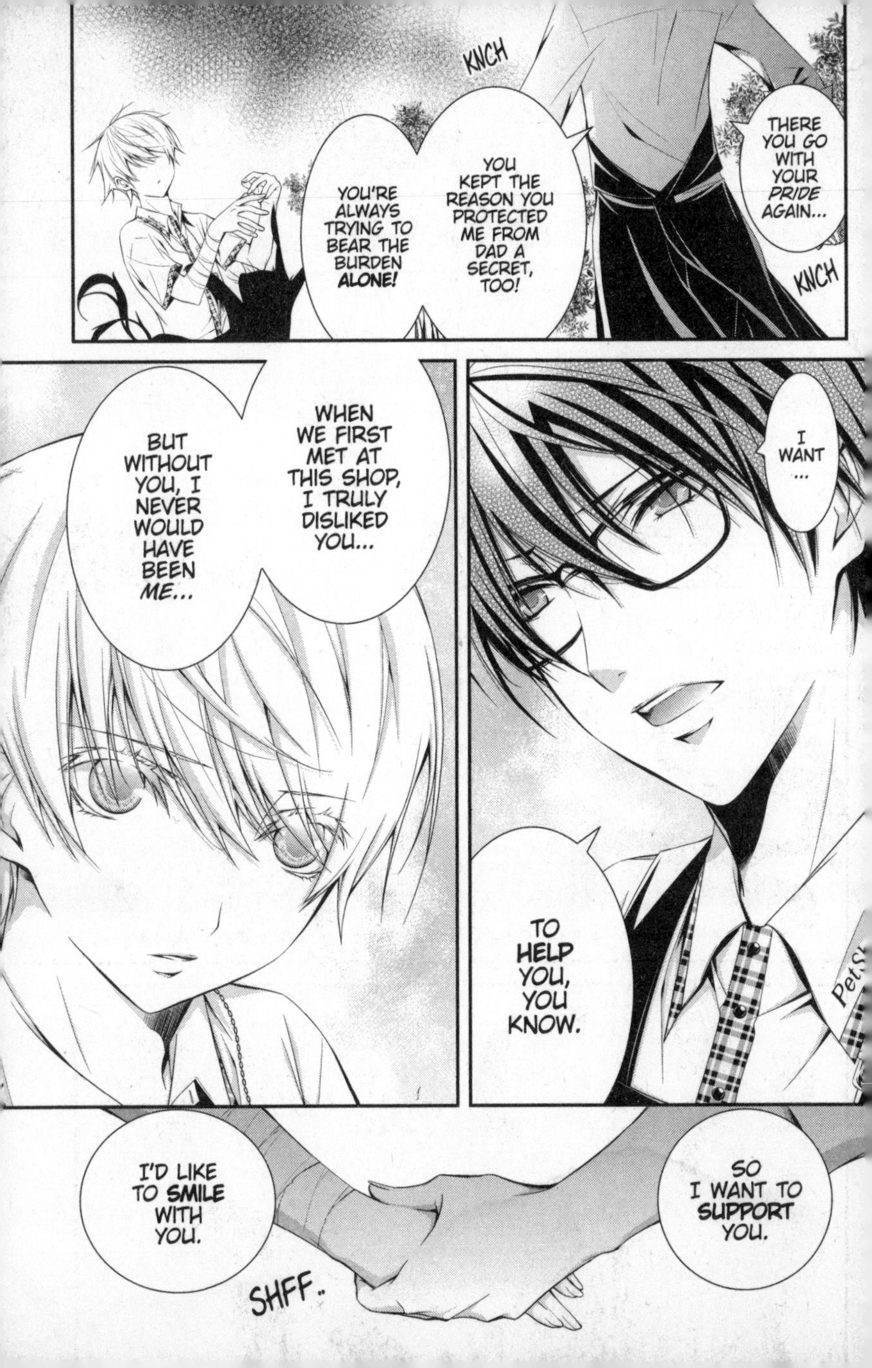
KNCH
THERE YOU GO WITH YOUR *PRIDE* AGAIN...
KNCH
YOU KEPT THE REASON YOU PROTECTED ME FROM DAD A SECRET, TOO!
YOU'RE ALWAYS TRYING TO BEAR THE BURDEN **ALONE!**
I WANT ...
TO **HELP** YOU, YOU KNOW.
WHEN WE FIRST MET AT THIS SHOP, I TRULY DISLIKED YOU...
BUT WITHOUT YOU, I NEVER WOULD HAVE BEEN *ME*...
SO I WANT TO **SUPPORT** YOU.
I'D LIKE TO **SMILE** WITH YOU.
SHFF..

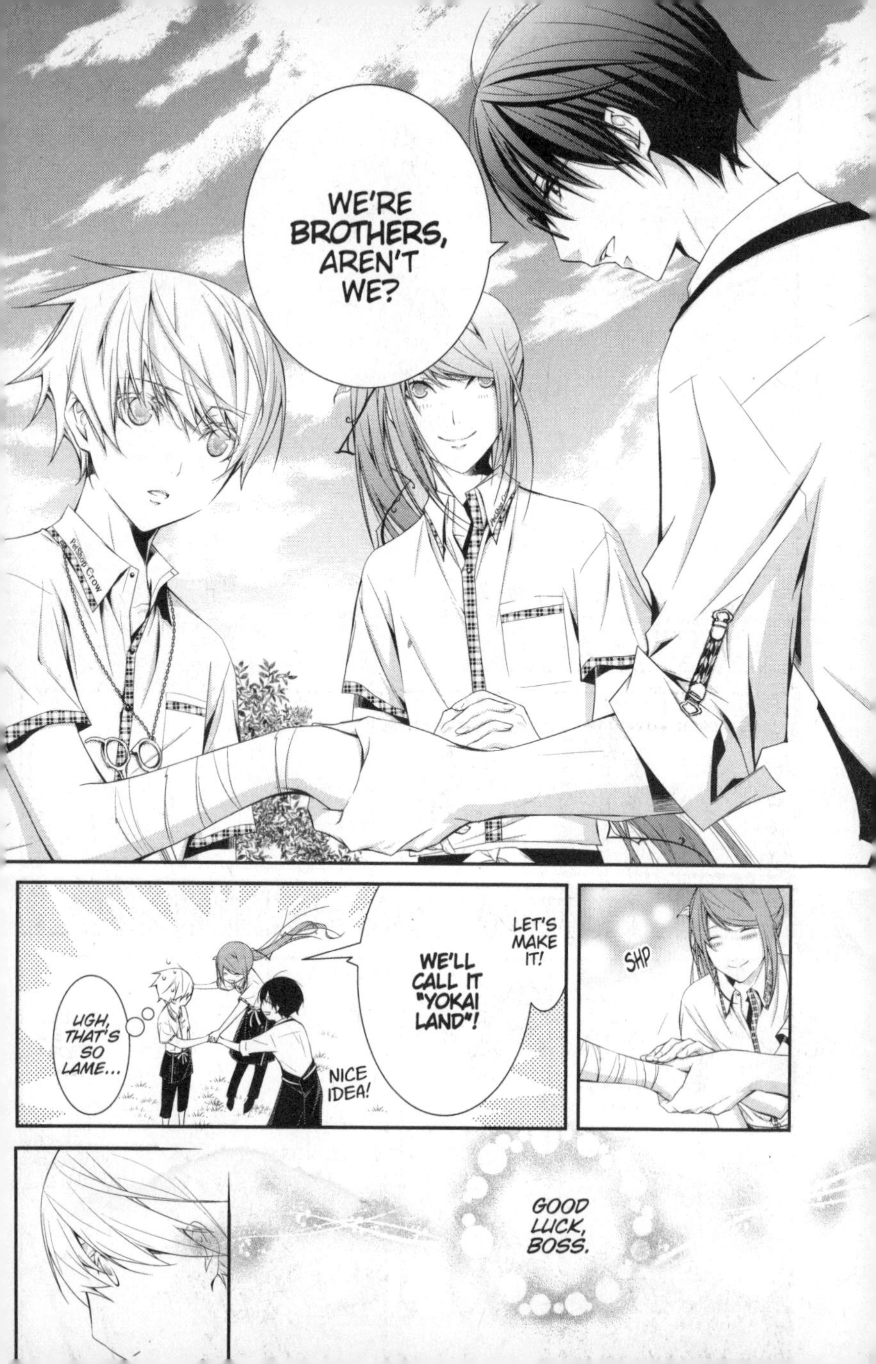
WE'RE BROTHERS, AREN'T WE?
PetShop Crow
SHP
LET'S MAKE IT!
WE'LL CALL IT "YOKAI LAND"!
NICE IDEA!
UGH, THAT'S SO LAME...
GOOD LUCK, BOSS.

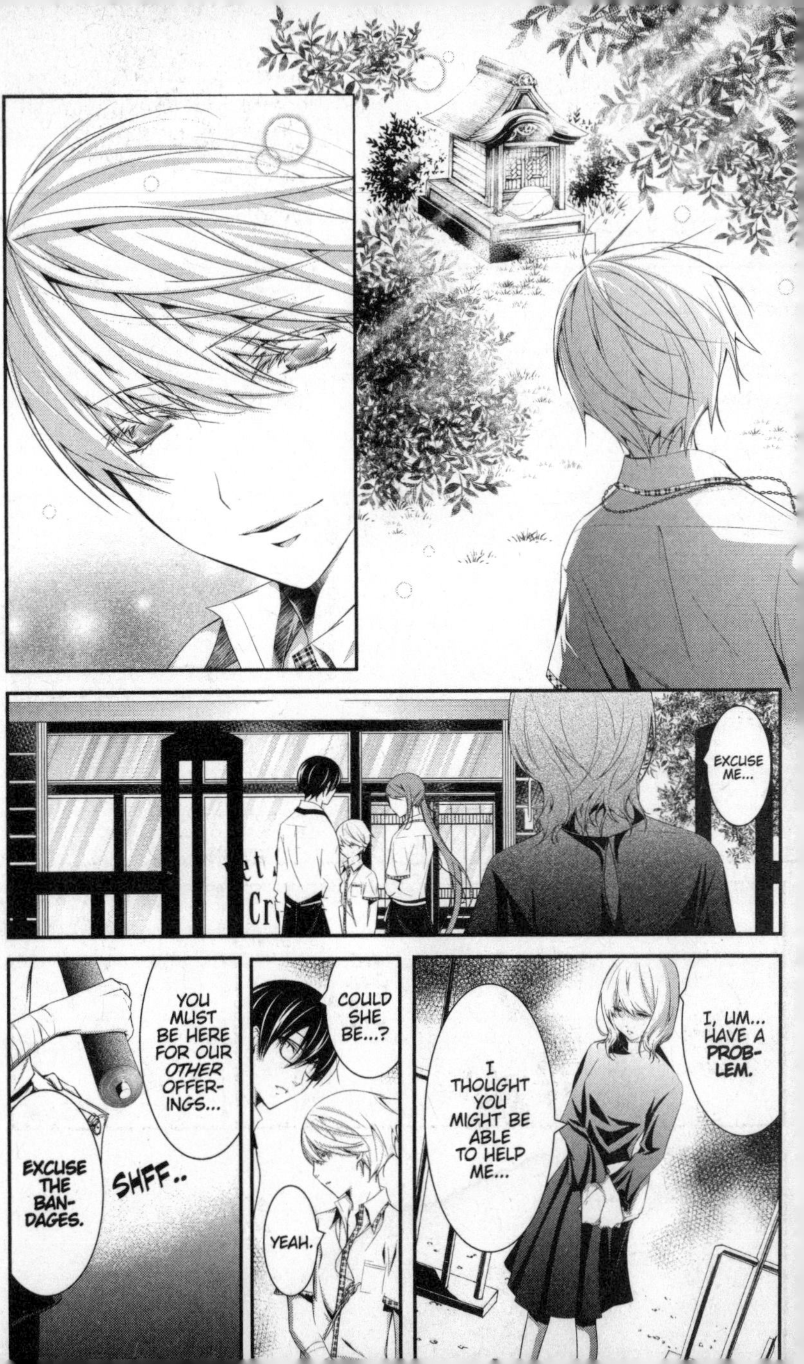
EXCUSE ME...
I, UM... HAVE A PROB-LEM.
I THOUGHT YOU MIGHT BE ABLE TO HELP ME...
COULD SHE BE...?
YEAH.
YOU MUST BE HERE FOR OUR *OTHER* OFFER-INGS...
SHFF..
EXCUSE THE BAN-DAGES.

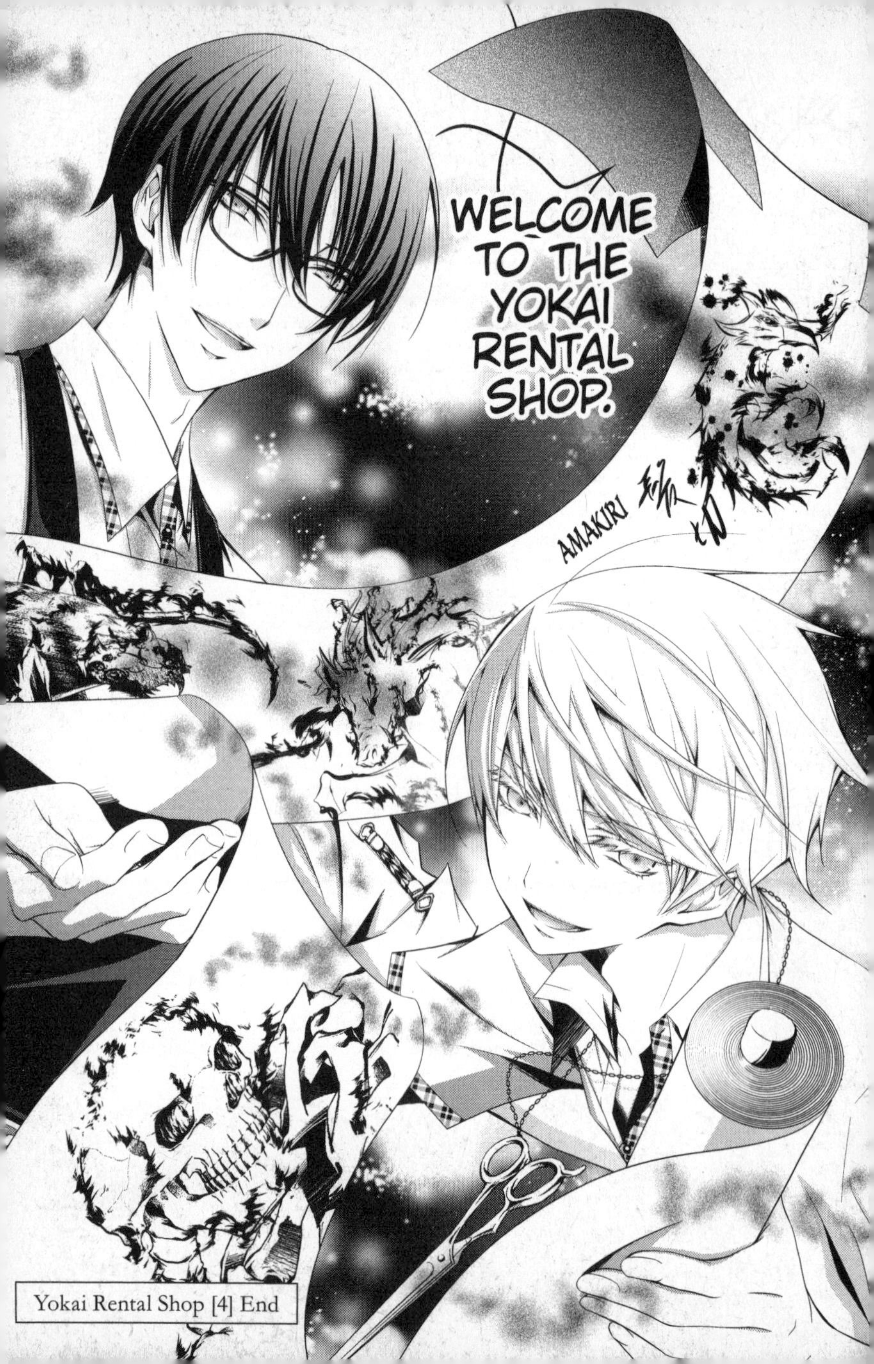
WELCOME TO THE YOKAI RENTAL SHOP.
AMAKIRI

Yokai Rental Shop [4] End

[AFTERWORD]

Hello, Shin Mashiba here. Thank you so much for picking up Volume 4. I'd decided that for this series, I would make the final chapter an actual "happily ever after" sort of ending. How did you like it? I'm so very, very grateful to everyone who stuck with this series to the end.

[Assistants]

◇ Wan Wan Shiroi-sama <black inks, screen tones>
◇ Riru Shirayukii-sama <shadow tones>
◇ MOAI-sama <information>
◇ Maru-sama <backgrounds>
◇ Mori-sama <backgrounds>
◇ Katou-sama <backgrounds>

Thanks to your incredible assistance, I managed to safely reach the final chapter in another manga series. You helped me so, so, so much.

[Square Enix]

◇ My editor, Kumaoka-sama
◇ The editor-in-chief
◇ Everyone who was involved

From the steps before serialization to the backstories and more, you put so much careful thought into this series that you allowed me to draw a final product that surpassed my own imagination. Thank you so much.

[Main Reference Books]

Nihon youkai daijiten (Japanese Yokai Dictionary) / Illustrations: Mizuki Shigeru / Compilation: Murakami Kenji (Kadokawa Shoten)
Zusetsu Nihon youkai taizen (Illustrated Compendium of Japanese Yokai) / Author: Mizuki Shigeru (Kodansha)
Youkai zukan (Yokai Picture Scroll)/ Writing: Kyogoku Natsuhiko / Editing and commentary: Tada Katsumi (Kokusho Kankokai)

SEVEN SEAS ENTERTAINMENT PRESENTS

Yokai Rental Shop

story and art by SHIN MASHIBA

VOLUME 4

TRANSLATION
Amanda Haley

ADAPTATION
Julia Kinsman

LETTERING AND RETOUCH
Rina Mapa

COVER DESIGN
KC Fabellon

PROOFREADER
Danielle King
B. Lana Guggenheim

EDITOR
Jenn Grunigen

PRODUCTION ASSISTANT
CK Russell

PRODUCTION MANAGER
Lissa Pattillo

EDITOR-IN-CHIEF
Adam Arnold

PUBLISHER
Jason DeAngelis

YOKAI NIISAN VOL. 4
©2017 Shin Mashiba / SQUARE ENIX CO., LTD.
First published in Japan in 2017 by SQUARE ENIX CO., LTD.
English translation rights arranged with SQUARE ENIX CO., LTD. and
SEVEN SEAS ENTERTAINMENT, LLC. through Tuttle-Mori Agency, Inc.
Translation © 2017 by SQUARE ENIX CO., LTD.

No portion of this book may be reproduced or transmitted in any form without
written permission from the copyright holders. This is a work of fiction. Names,
characters, places, and incidents are the products of the author's imagination or
are used fictitiously. Any resemblance to actual events, locales, or persons, living
or dead, is entirely coincidental.

Seven Seas books may be purchased in bulk for promotional, educational, or
business use. Please contact your local bookseller or the Macmillan Corporate
and Premium Sales Department at 1-800-221-7945, extension 5442, or by e-mail
at MacmillanSpecialMarkets@macmillan.com.

Seven Seas and the Seven Seas logo are trademarks of
Seven Seas Entertainment, LLC. All rights reserved.

ISBN: 978-1-626929-30-2

Printed in Canada

First Printing: October 2018

10 9 8 7 6 5 4 3 2 1

FOLLOW US ONLINE: *www.sevenseasentertainment.com*

READING DIRECTIONS

This book reads from *right to left*, Japanese style.
If this is your first time reading manga, you start
reading from the top right panel on each page and
take it from there. If you get lost, just follow the
numbered diagram here. It may seem backwards at
first, but you'll get the hang of it! Have fun!!

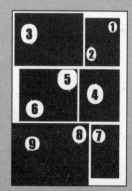